Politics, Theology and History is a major new book by a prominent academic and an active politician. It ranges widely across the disciplines of theology, political theory and philosophy and poses acute questions about the basic moral foundations of liberal societies.

Lord Plant focuses on the role that religious belief can and ought to play in argument about public policy in a pluralistic society. He examines the potential political implications of Christian belief and the ways in which it may be deployed in political debate. The book is a contribution to the modern debate about the moral pluralism of western liberal societies, discussing the place of religious belief in the formation of policy and asking what sorts of issues in modern society might be the legitimate objects of a Christian social and political concern.

Raymond Plant has written an important study of the relationship between religion and politics which will be of value to students, academics, politicians, church professionals, policy makers and all concerned with the moral fabric of contemporary life.

RAYMOND PLANT is Professor of European Political Thought at the University of Southampton and a Member of the House of Lords. He was a Home affairs spokesperson for the Labour Party from 1992 to 1996, and Master of St Catherine's College, Oxford, from 1994 to 2000. Lord Plant's main publications are *Social and Moral Theory in Casework* (1970), *Community and Ideology: An Essay in Applied Moral Philosophy* (1974), *Hegel* (1974), *Political Philosophy and Social Welfare* (with H. Lesser and P. Taylor-Gooby, 1979), *Philosophy, Politics and Citizenship* (with A. Vincent, 1983), *Hegel: Second Edition* (1983) and *Modern Political Thought* (1994).

POLITICS, THEOLOGY AND HISTORY

Religion increasingly is seen as a renewed force, and is recognized as an important factor in the modern world in all aspects of life – cultural, economic, and political. It is no longer a matter of surprise to find religious factors at work in areas and situations of political tension. However, our information about these situations has tended to come from two main sources. The news-gathering agencies are well placed to convey information, but are hampered by the fact that their representatives are not equipped to provide analysis of the religious forces involved. Alternatively, the movements generate their own accounts, which understandably seem less than objective to outside observers. There is no lack of information of factual material, but a real need for sound academic analysis. Cambridge Studies in Ideology and Religion meets this need. It attempts to give an objective, balanced and programmed coverage to issues which – while of wide potential interest – have been largely neglected by analytical investigation, apart from the appearance of sporadic individual studies. Intended to enable debate to proceed at a higher level, the series should lead to a new phase in our understanding of the relationship between ideology and religion.

A list of titles already published in the series is given at the end of the book.

POLITICS, THEOLOGY AND HISTORY

RAYMOND PLANT

University of Southampton
Honorary Fellow of St Catherine's College, Oxford

CAMBRIDGE
UNIVERSITY PRESS

PUBLISHED BY THE PRESS SYNDICATE OF THE UNIVERSITY OF CAMBRIDGE
The Pitt Building, Trumpington Street, Cambridge, United Kingdom

CAMBRIDGE UNIVERSITY PRESS
The Edinburgh Building, Cambridge CB2 2RU, UK
40 West 20th Street, New York, NY 10011–4211, USA
10 Stamford Road, Oakleigh, VIC 3166, Australia
Ruiz de Alarcón 13, 28014 Madrid, Spain
Dock House, The Waterfront, Cape Town 8001, South Africa

http://www.cambridge.org

First published 2001

Printed in the United Kingdom at the University Press, Cambridge

Typeface 11/12.5pt Baskerville   *System* 3b2   [CE]

A catalogue record for this book is available from the British Library

ISBN 0 521 43320 7 hardback
ISBN 0 521 43881 0 paperback

To
The Master and Fellows
St Catherine's College
Oxford

We do not know what to do, but our eyes are upon you.
2 Chronicles 20.12.

World remains World. But God is God
Karl Barth, *Kriegszeit und Gottesreich*

Contents

Preface

A good deal of modern political theory in recent years has been dominated by issues to do with liberalism, pluralism and the claims of community. The present book aims to be a contribution to that debate. It does, however, come to the issues in an indirect way. Most of the current literature is written in a rather abstract way and leads to conclusions of a rather general sort about the place of moral communities, such as those of religious believers, within a liberal society. This book starts in the opposite direction. It looks at the idea that religious belief, in this case Christian belief, has clear implications for the nature and organisation of society and politics, and goes on to look at how all of these ideas relate to the politics of a liberal society. It therefore tries to answer three questions:

What, if any, are the social and political implications of Christian belief?

If there are such implications, to which aspects of modern society do they relate?

What role, if any, should such beliefs play in the policies of a liberal society?

The book aims, therefore, to be part of a modern debate about the relationship between liberalism and moral and religious pluralism.

The book has had a very long period of gestation and has been through many drafts written for different audiences. I first thought about the project in the late 1980s and since then I have been fortunate enough to be asked to give various series of lectures which have allowed me to focus more clearly upon my concerns. So the present book brings together the following:

The Stanton Lectures in the Philosophy of Religion at Cambridge University 1989–1991; The Sarum Lectures at Oxford University in Hilary Term 1991; the Samuel Ferguson Lectures at the University of Manchester in 1993; the Scott Holland Lectures at Manchester Cathedral in 1994; the Gore Lecture at Westminster Abbey and Birmingham Cathedral in 1996; the R. H. Tawney Lecture in London in 1999; the Eleanor Rathbone Memorial Lecture at the University of Bristol in 1997; the St George's House, Windsor Castle Lecture in 1997 and the John Baillie Lecture at Edinburgh University in 1996. I am pleased to thank the various electoral boards and trustees of these lectures and institutions for inviting me to give them and for the incentive they provided to reflect upon my rather zigzagging approach to these problems.

I should also like to thank St John's College and Jesus College, Cambridge for hospitality during my tenure of the Stanton Lectureship, and Christchurch, Oxford for hospitality during my tenure of the Sarum Lectureship. I am also indebted to Harris Manchester College, Oxford, of which I am pleased to be an Honorary Fellow, for the use of its library. Thanks are also due to Sally Collins, Librarian of St Catherine's College, Oxford, for help in tracking down arcane materials.

As a non-theologian, whose reading in theology has been sporadic and ill disciplined, I owe a number of people great debts for intellectual help: Professor Nicholas Lash, Bishop Steven Sykes and Professor Nicholas Sagovsky in Cambridge; Professor O. and Dr J. O'Donovan, Professor M. Wiles, the Rt. Revd Rowan Williams and the Very Revd John Drury at Christchurch; John Lucas at Merton College and Dr Ernest Nicholson Provost of Oriel in Oxford; members of the DASH group and in particular the late David Nicholls; Professor John Haldane of St Andrew's University who gave me some of his writings; and Brendan McLaughlin at St Catherine's College who put me right about Prudentius. Special thanks are also due to Professor Duncan Forrester and Professor David Pailin who invited me to lecture at Edinburgh and Manchester Universities respectively and who have been friends and intellectual guides of many years standing. I would also like to thank Professor

Ronald Preston and Canon John Atherton who have taken an interest in this book during its evolution.

I also acknowledge a debt to the late Fr. J. Westmoreland and to the late Fr. K. Richardson of St Augustine's Anglican church in Grimsby, who taught me most of what I know about Christian belief and whose own faith was uncluttered by the doubts and complexities which form the substance of this book. Fr. Westmoreland gave me a book on Goethe when I was about thirteen and created an interest in continental thought during the *Goethezeit* which has stayed with me ever since and which makes intermittent appearances in the book.

During the main period of writing this book I was Master of St Catherine's College, Oxford and I have been pleased that I have been able to finish it before demitting office at the end of 1999. I owe an enormous debt to my two secretaries Margaret Lavercombe and Judith Arneil who not only typed the book but also balanced the frantic pressures of a life divided between academic work, administration and politics. Without them the book would never have been completed. I would also like to thank Jane Parker, my secretary in Southampton, for her enormous help in the final stages. I have also been much helped by Gillian Maude who copy-edited the manuscript for Cambridge University Press.

I have to thank my family, and particularly my wife Katherine for her support during an exceptionally busy period in my life: *Wir leben durch die Lieb' allein*. The book is dedicated to all our friends and colleagues at St Catherine's College.

CHAPTER I

Liberal society and political theology

A Christian Sociology recognises that there are objective social relationships which can be judged better or worse from a doctrinal Christian standpoint. The Church historically and actually has something to say about the nature of government, the liberty of the person, economic justice and the right distribution of property. The key word of this sociological question for the Christian is *justitia*, which transcends questions of personal attitudes and connotes a 'rightness' in political economic and other social relationships themselves for the Christian faith to proclaim. (V. A. Demant, *Christian Polity*)

> And the world which seems
> To lie before us like a land of dreams,
> So various, so beautiful, so new
> Hath really neither joy, nor love nor light,
> Nor certitude, nor peace, no help for pain;
> And we are here as on a darkling plain
> Swept with confused alarms of struggle and flight,
> Where ignorant armies clash by night.
> (M. Arnold, *Dover Beach*)

My aim in this book is to consider two themes which can be kept separate, but which I shall interrelate. The first theme is the nature, scope and, more radically, the possibility of political theology, by which I mean the possibility of relating Christian beliefs in a coherent and rigorous way to the problems of social, economic and political organisation. The second set of issues has to do with the moral foundations, if any, on which modern democratic liberal societies in the West rest. I relate the two themes in the following way: if we assume that liberal societies need to have some kind of moral foundation and be based upon a substantial set of moral beliefs, then how far can or should Christian beliefs contribute to that set of beliefs which would be foundational for liberalism? Indeed, even if it was thought that Christian beliefs were relevant and important in this context, should beliefs on which a liberal society rests owe anything at all to a comprehensive and metaphysical belief system which is not at all universally shared in a liberal and pluralistic society? It is often argued that in some sense a liberal democratic state has to be neutral between conceptions of the good[1] and, if it is, in what sense, if any, could it draw from the Christian traditions of social and political thought for its own moral justification? So the problem on which I wish to focus is the moral basis of a liberal society and the role, if any, that Christian belief can or ought to play in the justification of that set of beliefs. I shall say more about the problem of the moral foundations of liberalism shortly.

Before moving to that discussion, however, it might be that any way of posing the problem is question-begging – not just in terms of the assumption that liberal society needs a moral basis, but whether it is, in fact, possible to develop a Christian political theology. Is it possible to draw out of Christian beliefs anything very determinate in terms of social, economic or political insights, or is it better to see Christianity as more concerned with issues of private and personal morality and personal salvation? Only if it is possible to claim that Christian beliefs could produce a reasonably determinate set of social and political insights would it make sense to link, as I want to do in this book, questions relating to Christian beliefs about politics with issues to do with the moral foundations for liberal democratic societies. If social and political theology is impossible, then it is rather redundant to go on to ask what could or should be the role of Christian beliefs about politics in justifying the moral framework of a liberal democratic and pluralistic society.

---

[1] See, for example, R. Dworkin, *A Matter of Principle* Harvard University Press, Cambridge, Mass., 1985, pp. 181–213, 335–72; *Taking Rights Seriously* Duckworth, London, 1977, pp. 240–78.

Hence, these are my two themes and, as we shall see, their explication leads into very many extremely complex questions.

The book falls into three parts. The five chapters in Part I will look in some detail at the complexities involved in the idea of a political theology: to examine whether and how Christian beliefs can be regarded as entailing political principles. Part II will look at a number of inescapable moral problems relating to the organisation of a liberal society. These have to do with issues to do with freedom, social justice, human rights and the market order. Part III seeks to unite the two themes of Christian beliefs and the moral basis of liberalism in ways which, I hope, draw from the depths of the argument dealt with in the previous two sections and to focus on the question about the relationship between religious beliefs and the moral bases of a liberal society.

Before embarking further, I want to go back briefly to the issue of the moral basis of liberalism. It seems clear that, after a brief period of intense optimism following the end of the Cold War, an optimism perhaps best exemplified by Francis Fukuyama's *The End of History and the Last Man* in which he argued that in a sense we know the final form of human history: namely, a liberal democratic society and a market economy, we are now, only a short time later, much less certain about the place of liberal societies in the history of humankind. Liberal societies face many challenges: two of the most obvious of which come from a resurgent political nationalism and militant and fundamentalist forms of religion. Both of the movements embody considerable moral force and fervour and, as such, they might be thought of as moral as much as any other kind of challenge to a liberal political order. They are particularly acute challenges precisely because there is a degree of confusion about the sort of moral foundations on which liberal societies are based and, indeed, whether the idea of moral foundations has any sort of place in thinking about modern politics.[2] The reason for

---

[2] For this view see R. Rorty, *Contingency Irony and Solidarity* Cambridge University Press, 1989, *passim* and *Objectivism Relativism and Truth* Cambridge University Press, 1991, p. 197.

the challenges are numerous, and in these introductory remarks, I shall note them rather than discuss them in detail, since this will come later in the book. I shall sketch out some of the often quoted challenges to a liberal social and political order to illustrate where many critics of liberalism see its moral weaknesses lie.

There are, first of all, the cultural critics of liberalism who argue that, because liberal societies place such value on individualism and individual choice, such societies do not offer very much by way of an endorsement of a public and collective realm in which collective values can be pursued and given legitimacy. On the contrary, it is argued that liberal societies seek only to sustain a framework of rules for the private pursuit of goods through individual effort and mainly through the market. The formulation and maintenance of these rules which are to do with maintaining the framework of individual choice is about as far as a liberal society goes in terms of a public and collective common good. This conception is well explained by Charles Larmore:

To avoid the oppressive use of state power, the liberal goal has therefore been to define the common good of political association by means of a minimal moral conception . . . the terms of political association must now be less comprehensive than the views of the good life about which reasonable people disagree . . . fundamental political principles must express a moral conception that citizens can affirm together, despite their inevitable differences about the worth of specific ways of life.[3]

It is argued by critics that, as such, liberalism has a very attenuated idea of a common life and does not meet the needs of human beings – particularly the needs for a sense of belonging, for solidarity with others, and for a sense of 'being at home' in the world.

At the same time, it is argued, the liberal looks to neutrality from the state. It is not the job of the state to favour one conception of the good over another. We have no rational way to arbitrate in an objective way between different conceptions

---

[3] C. Larmore, *The Morals of Modernity* Cambridge University Press, 1996, p. 123.

of the good held by individuals and groups in society and, if the state is to treat individuals with equal concern and respect, it cannot institutionally favour one conception of the good over another. Neutrality and impartiality are among the chief virtues of public institutions for the liberal. This view is some-times, although not necessarily, associated with an attitude of moral subjectivism. That is to say with the idea that morality is a matter of individual choice and that clashes between such values mean that, since there is no sense in which one person's moral view can outweigh that of another, then politics is turned into bargaining between different moral positions and is nothing more elevated than that. Even if one does not take the view that values are subjective, it is still possible to argue, as many liberals such as Isaiah Berlin do, that not all values are compatible or commensurable and that there will be endemic clashes and disputes about the order of priority in which values are put. These can only be reconciled by human choice – choices which are frequently tragic or agonistic. Thus, to favour one conception of the good over another in the constitutional arrangements of a liberal society would be to reflect one way of reconciling values over others. There is no way a political perspective can track a comprehensive and coherent moral reality – choice has to be at the heart of the ordering of values. Thus Berlin argues: 'Some among the Great Goods cannot live together. That is a conceptual truth. We are doomed to choose and every choice may entail an irreparable loss'.[4] It is sometimes claimed to follow from all of this that a liberal society is more concerned with *rights* rather than with views of the *good;* more concerned with a theory of citizenship focussed on the needs of human beings whose essence is understood in terms of agency and autonomy, as centres of choice rather than a more substantial sense of common identity and common purpose. The politics are *nomo-cratic*, concerned with rules and rights, rather than *telocratic*, which would be concerned with a set of common goods and

---

[4] I. Berlin, 'The Pursuit of the Ideal' in *The Proper Study of Mankind* ed. H. Hardy and R. Hausheer, Chatto and Windus, London, 1997.

purposes.[5] It is argued that telocratic politics requires a comprehensive doctrine which will embody an overall conception of human purposes and human flourishing. Lacking such agreed comprehensive doctrines in Western societies, we should affirm a minimal political good based upon rights to equal freedom and autonomy, not a specific conception of both the good and virtue.

Critics of liberalism argue that these sorts of features put liberalism at a very sharp disadvantage compared with those rival movements, whether animated by religion or by nationalism, that pose part of the global challenge for a liberal society just because they do have a strong sense of their own moral basis and embody a robust sense of common identity.[6] Even cultural critics of liberalism from within the Western tradition have seen a kind of void at the heart of what it takes to be an individualistic liberalism.

T. S. Eliot, a sympathiser with the Christendom position in political theology, in *Choruses from the Rock*, for example, evokes the lack of a sense of community in modern liberal society:

> What life have you if you have not life together?
> There is no life that is not in community,
> And no community not lived in praise of God.
> . . .
> And now you live dispersed on ribbon roads,
> And no man knows or cares who is his neighbour
> Unless his neighbour makes too much disturbance
> But all dash to and fro in motor cars,
> Familiar with the roads but settled nowhere.
> Nor does the family even move about together,
> But every one would have his motorcycle,
> And daughters ride away on casual pillions.

He also evokes the loss of public meaning to life and the link between this loss of public meaning and a sense of the transcendent:

---

[5] For the strategy of putting the right before the good see J. Rawls, *A Theory of Justice* Clarendon Press, Oxford, 1972.

[6] See M. Sandel, 'Introduction' to *Liberalism and Its Critics* New York University Press, 1984. N. Rosenblum, *Another Liberalism* Harvard University Press, Cambridge, Mass., 1987.

Much is your reading, but not the word of God.
Much is your building, but not the House of God.
Will you build me a house of plaster, with corrugated roofing,
To be filled with the litter of Sunday newspapers.

. . .

And the wind shall say: 'Here were decent godless people:
Their only monument the asphalt road
And a thousand lost golf balls.'[7]

On this view there is a void at the heart of liberal society which ultimately can only be remedied by a rediscovery of the transcendent: 'Can you keep the city that the Lord keeps not with you?'

Liberal society, in contrast, has been compared by one of its defenders to a hotel.[8] In an hotel people come together under a set of rules which govern their interactions during their stay. The rules are meant to facilitate their private ends whatever they may be. Individuals are anonymous. If they wish to enter into group activities this is a matter of choice. The hotel does not itself, as a condition of being there, offer a sense of common purpose or common identity. The guests at the hotel have no positive duties to one another unless they choose to assume such obligations. The hotel is focussed on anonymity, privacy, contract and rules, not on a common purpose or a common notion of human fulfilment. Eliot points to a similar analogy in his poem:

When the Stranger says: 'What is the meaning of this city?
Do you huddle close together because you love each other?'
What will you answer? 'We all dwell together
to make money from each other?' or 'This is a community.'

It is, however, instructive to compare this view with that of Barth in his influential essay 'The Christian Community and

---

[7] T. S. Eliot, *Collected Poems 1909–1962* Faber and Faber, London, 1963. It has to be said, however, that the basis of this view is rather ambiguous for Eliot. He once argued that it would be better to worship a golden calf than nothing at all, whereas in *The Idea of a Christian Society* (2nd edition, Faber and Faber, London, 1982) he argues: 'What is worse of all is to advocate Christianity not because it is true, but because it might be beneficial.'

[8] By N. Barry in an unpublished presentation to the Speaker's Commission on Citizenship.

the Civil Community' in which he emphasises that, in the modern liberal state, ideas about the transcendent cannot be incorporated into the constitutional structure or for that matter public deliberation. He argues as follows:

The civil community embraces everyone living within its area. Its members share no common awareness of their relationship to God, and such an awareness cannot be an element in the legal system established by the civil community. No appeal can be made to the Word or Spirit of God in the running of its affairs. The civil comunity as such is spiritually blind and ignorant. It nas neither faith, nor love, nor hope. It has no creed and no gospel. Prayer is not part of its life, and its members are not brothers and sisters.[9]

In the critics' view, such a conception of society is too attenuated because the duties of the citizens of a liberal society are reduced to the negative duties of mutual non-interference. Nomocratic or purposeless liberalism (purposeless, that is, in terms of its public dimension) stands in marked contrast to those more teleological forms of politics, whether nationalist or religious. Critics of liberalism have argued that all that liberalism offers is a cold politics of individual choice and rights that protect autonomous human beings who are the sources of such choices. On this view, we have to recapture ideas about community and common good as a basis for a new kind of politics that will go beyond individualist liberalism. Hence, the current popularity of 'communitarianism' both as an active response to the perceived deficiencies in liberal political theory and as a political movement which seeks to restore a sense of common value and purpose to Western societies. Under the influence of such pressure, theorists have sought to counter the idea of a fragmented, anonymous society, captured well in the 'hotel' image by comparing society with a family embodying mutual concern and a school for duty and obligation as well as rights. This view has popularity on both the communitarian right and left in politics[10] which do have a strong sense both of collective purpose and collective identity.

---

[9] K. Barth, 'The Christian Community and the Civil Community' in K. Barth, *Selected Writings* ed. C. Green, Collins, Glasgow, 1989 p. 267.

[10] See S. Kautz, *Liberalism and Community* Cornell University Press, Ithaca, 1995, ch. 1.

Compared with politics with a religious dimension, commentators on liberalism have often argued that liberalism offers a politics devoid of any consolation, of having nothing to offer the individual outside the circle of his/her own desires and choice. In this sense, it might be thought that liberalism perhaps holds up a rather optimistic view of the person. Eric Fromm[11] famously argued the case that, in fact, individuals will find it very difficult to cope with not only the anonymity of liberal society, which has been lauded by some theologians such as Harvey Cox,[12] but also the burden of personal judgement and choice in morality and politics, and that they are likely to fall prey to movements such as fascism and other totalitarian movements which offer a wider framework of meaning and significance to the individual than is available in liberalism.

We need to pause at this point to attempt to refine some of these issues. A nomocratic view of politics – one which puts rights and rules before the good and a sense of virtue can be seen to be the result of tendencies in modern thought and modern society which are sometimes mixed together but are conceptually distinct. Each of these different conceptualities poses questions about the relationship between liberal society and religious belief. We can distinguish at least the following strands of thought.

First might be the recognition of moral diversity – that is to say, the recognition that reasonable people can disagree about conceptions of the good. Indeed, it is possible for individuals and groups, while affirming their own comprehensive religions and metaphysical doctrines which yield the specific conceptions of the good that they hold, to accept that reasonable people can disagree with these doctrines. The political challenge here, then, is to provide a constitutional framework for dealing with reasonable disagreement. Such a political order, if it is to be secure, would then have to be seen as legitimate by people such as religious believers who accept that it is reasonable to disagree about such matters.

---

[11] E. Fromm, *The Fear of Freedom* Routledge and Kegan Paul, London, 1962, *passim*.
[12] H. Cox, *The Secular City* Penguin, Harmondsworth, 1968, *passim*.

The second alternative might, following Charles Larmore,[13] be called pluralism – that is to say a positive view that there may be many forms of human good and forms of human flourishing and that these are not necessarily compatible one with another. Again, on this view, the political problem is how to justify political principles to those who hold specific conceptions of the good while accepting that there may be many ways in which we could indeed flourish as human beings.

A third possibility, which is rather different from the other two, is scepticism. This would embody the claim that not only do human purposes and values diverge, but also there are no wholly compelling objective or intersubjective reasons which could be advanced for any particular conception of the good. In this sense a liberal political order is a response to doubt about, and ungrounded subjective preference for the different conceptions of the good held in a liberal society.[14]

A fourth alternative is rather different, namely, that a liberal society does embody its own specific and rich conception of the good – human autonomy and moral agency. That is to say that a liberal society is not just or even primarily a matter of devising principles to deal with moral diversity or moral scepticism but, in fact, is about procuring an institutional framework for the achievement of the overarching good of human autonomy. In this sense, liberalism would be perfectionist; it would be about the framework for achieving a specific conception of human good, namely an autonomous and self-directing life.[15] The issue that this would pose for the religious believer invited to endorse such a conception of liberalism would be how far a religious believer could see as legitimate a political order which placed human autonomy at the centre of the value system animating a liberal society. If these are possible but not mutually compatible ways in which liberalism might be justified, they nevertheless embody different conceptions of the moral basis of a liberal society and, as I have suggested, pose rather different questions about the relationship between religious belief and political justification in a liberal society. These issues will be more fully

---

[13] Larmore, *Morals* p. 122.   [14] Ibid.
[15] See J. Raz, *The Morality of Freedom* Clarendon Press, Oxford, 1986.

explained in Part III. For the moment, however, I want to draw a contrast and to explain further one side of the contrast. We could perhaps distinguish between the idea that liberalism can be given a moral justification because it is a principled position whether based upon pluralism, reasonable disagreement or the more perfectionist idea of autonomy and seeing liberalism as a coping mechanism. On the former view, the task will be to establish a substantive moral basis for liberal principles which could be accepted by individuals or religious communities without these communities losing a sense of their own identity, or individuals losing their sense of their own moral priorities. The point is, though, that liberalism on this view has its own reasoned foundation.

The alternative, however, is to see liberalism as, so to speak, a coping mechanism which will enable society to get along in the context of pluralism. This is what John Rawls calls a *modus vivendi*.[16] A *modus vivendi* is typically a bargain between individuals and groups with roughly equal power who have prudential reasons for entering into the bargain. In this sense, a *modus vivendi* is a coping mechanism and is closely linked to the idea of scepticism – that is to say, if we accept moral scepticism, then there can be no compelling reason to accept any moral or political principle and, thus, if liberalism is linked to scepticism, then it seems as though it has to be seen as a *modus vivendi* rather than as a political position which could be founded on rationally justified principles. As Larmore argues:

Individuals who have different ideas of the good life, but are of roughly equal power, may strike a bargain according to which the political principles to be established will not favour any of these moral ideals. The approach is basically a Hobbesian one, since it aims to ground a moral principle (neutrality) on a non-moral, purely prudential basis.[17]

That is to say, liberal thinkers might accept that in a morally subjectivist world their own value basis cannot be sustained, but

[16] J. Rawls, *Political Liberalism* Columbia University Press, New York, 1993, p. 146 and J. Rawls, 'The Idea of An Overlapping Consensus' in *Philosophical Papers* ed. J. Freeman, Harvard University Press, Cambridge, Mass., 1999, sect. 3, p. 430.

[17] Larmore, *Morals* p. 133.

nevertheless a liberal political order is the best way we have of coping with subjectivism. But this is emphatically *not* the only way of coping. The extreme alternative is a Nietzschean politics of the *will*: to stand in the way of, and face down, alternative moral views. It may seem rather melodramatic to take Hitler as an example of someone taking this view, but in *Mein Kampf* he does talk about 'granite principles' and a brazen cliff to be erected in the face of what he calls the 'free world of ideas'.[18] Moral scepticism can be *overcome* as much as *coped with*, and, if there is no substantial moral basis for moral and political judgement, then it is difficult to have a rational basis for choosing one way rather than another and for endorsing liberalism as the best way of dealing with moral scepticism. Rawls, for example, argues that many will not want a liberal society because it means abandoning the idea of political community. He argues then as follows:

the hope of political community must indeed be abandoned, if by such a community we mean a political society united in offering a general and comprehensive doctrine. This possibility is excluded by the fact of pluralism together with the rejection of the oppressive use of state power to overcome it.[19]

However, these will not be powerful arguments against someone who embraces politics of the will – they already reject the main tenets of liberalism, such as the point about state power. Many liberal thinkers, including Rawls, accordingly have argued that liberalism has to have a substantive moral basis, and cannot just be a strategic coping mechanism.[20]

In addition, it can be argued that an endorsement of moral scepticism as a basis for liberalism can put liberalism at a disadvantage in terms of defending itself against forms of politics which claim moral certainty. Why stand up for liberalism if its moral basis is wholly subjective (if indeed it has a moral foundation at all) and has no objective or intrinsic value? This is a point made vigorously by Michael Sandel, a contemporary critic of liberalism: 'If one's convictions are only

---

[18] J. P. Stern, *Hitler: the Führer and the People* Fontana, London, 1975.
[19] Rawls *Collected Papers* p. 431.
[20] See R. Dworkin, 'What Liberalism Isn't' *New York Review of Books* 20 Jan. 1983.

relatively valid, why stand for them unflinchingly? . . . if
freedom has no morally privileged status, if it is just one value
among many, then what becomes of liberalism?'[21] Adherents of
other sorts of moral principles will sacrifice themselves for such
principles. Why should anyone seek sacrificially to defend
liberalism if it does not embody a set of substantive moral
ideals?

The idea that liberalism is a response to moral scepticism
poses major problems for liberal politics in morally diverse
societies in which there are religious groups who feel very
strongly that society should respond to other political demands,
that arise out of their own religious beliefs and which they take
to be true. On one liberal view, a religion should, in fact, limit
its public demands, but, if this requirement is rooted in a
political philosophy which endorses a kind of scepticism about
morality, including its own morality, then such a requirement
will not cut much ice with a religious viewpoint which takes its
own claims to be *true*. Liberalism from this prospective will be
seen as a kind of fundamentalism – a fundamentalism of doubt
or scepticism in relation to morality and, as such, will be weak
in the face of claims to the truth. It is perhaps worth quoting a
short passage from Gibreel's dream in Salman Rushdie's *Satanic
Verses* when the following occurs:

Question: what is the opposite of faith? Not disbelief, too certain, too
closed, itself a kind of belief.
Doubt is the opposite of belief.[22]

A politics of *doubt*, if that is, indeed, at the heart of liberalism,
will be an unsure ground in responding to political demands
which are regarded by their adherents as *true*.

Indeed, one does not have to be quite so apocalyptic about
the problems with a *modus vivendi* approach to the justification of
liberalism for, as Charles Larmore has pointed out, such a form
of liberalism is inherently unstable:

It [*modus vivendi*] seems inherently unstable, since it is hostage to the
shifting distribution of power: individuals will lose their reason to

---

[21] Sandel, *Liberalism and its Critics*, p. 8.
[22] S. Rushdie, *The Satanic Verses* Viking, London, 1988, p. 92.

uphold the agreement if their relative power or bargaining strength increases significantly. Also, the attempt to explain the special authority of moral principles in terms of prudence (maximisation of individual preference satisfaction) has never yet succeeded, and there seems little reason to suppose it ever will.[23]

If, however, liberalism is defective when seen as a coping mechanism rather than being rooted in principle, then the problem for conceiving of how religious beliefs might relate to the justification of liberalism shifts. It turns into questions about what are the principles that are foundational for liberalism and how can these principles be justified to members of religious communities with their own comprehensive doctrines and conceptions of the good?

All of these issues in liberalism are complex and subtle, and some of these complexities and subtleties, including the postmodernist insistence, most strongly associated with Richard Rorty, that liberalism does not need philosophical foundations, will be considered in the course of subsequent chapters. If, however, the critics of liberal democratic societies are correct in their belief that liberal societies do need something more substantial by way of a moral defence and, indeed, depend upon the maintenance of certain moral virtues, then the question arises about how such a moral defence of liberalism is to be mounted given the recognition of what Rawls calls the fact of moral pluralism within liberal societies. This has particular salience to those citizens who are Christians. Does the moral defence of a liberal democratic order have to depend upon invoking moral resources which are, in some sense, neutral between the different moral and religious traditions such as Christianity represented in a liberal society, and, if so, what is the relationship between such resources and those found within particular moral traditions? Or is it rather that if there is a moral defence to be mounted it has to be rooted in and drawn from the different moral traditions that make up the pluralist range of beliefs in a liberal society? So my concerns in this book partly emerge from an understanding of the moral dilemmas of a liberal society, but they also relate directly to the nature of

---

[23] Larmore, *Morals* p. 133.

Christian belief and the role, if any, which such beliefs can and should have in thinking about the moral foundations of a liberal society. Western Christians are involved in liberal society in a number of ways: they are citizens of liberal societies; they are inheritors of belief systems clashes between which historically played a significant role in the formation of liberal societies. So my basic question is this: if Christian belief does necessarily entail consequences about social, economic and political modes of organisation, what part, if any, should these beliefs play in a citizen's deliberations about not just specific public policies, but also some of these more profound dilemmas concerning the nature of a liberal political order that I have tried to set out in a very schematic way in these remarks.

As I have said, the book will concentrate on two interrelated themes: the question of the relationship between a liberal democratic political order and its moral life and the issue of what, if anything, Christian belief could or should be able to contribute to the development of an appropriate moral context and form of justification for a liberal democratic society. A logically prior question, however, in the light of the second focus of the argument is the possibility of political theology. If the Christian religion is either misunderstood if it is assumed to have implications for the ordering of politics and society, or, if it is argued that, while it may embody political and social impera-tives, these are opaque and indeterminate, then the question on which I want to focus does not really arise. So Part I will concentrate on how, if at all, theological insights can be brought to bear upon issues of basic political organisation and morality.

Political theology is concerned with an account of the nature of the state, the community and the various forms of voluntary organisation which characterise modern civil society, and the economy which, in the modern world, means primarily the nature and the role of the market economy. Of course, the churches have been far from reticent in making judgements about modern politics and economics in recent years, but there is, I think, some point in trying to stand back from these specific pronouncements to look in a more focussed way upon the assumptions that have to be made in order for there to be a political theology. In a sense, the book attempts to answer the quasi-Kantian question of how is political theology possible?

Any answer to this question has, I believe, to address two further issues. The first has to do with the nature of theology itself, namely, how can theological insights be brought to bear upon the complexities of modern society; the second has to show that in its crucial aspects modern society raises absolutely basic moral questions which cannot be evaded despite the great strength of those intellectual movements which encourage us to evade them. It has been argued, for example, by A. MacIntyre,[24] that the deep problems involved in the justification of moral principles in modern societies have led to enormous pressures for those societies to be *demoralised* in a literal sense. Instead of institutions and practices of society being seen as embodying moral principles, they are seen primarily in terms of problems of management and of technical expertise. Technique has come to displace virtue in the governance of society. So the economy is regarded as a morally free zone to which moral principles do not apply, and politics becomes more and more concerned with bureaucratic management rather than with an attempt to embody some conception of the common good or the good life. If, however, this demoralisation of politics and economics does not make sense, as is argued in chapters 7, 8, 9 and 10, then moral questions, however difficult, still lie at the heart of modern politics and economics. They cannot be displaced by technique and bureaucracy. Thus, if there are theological insights that are salient for politics, economics and society, they must be salient at the points at which these basic moral questions are raised by the organisation of society itself. In a sense then, my approach is dialectical. In Part I, I try to identify different approaches which have been taken by theologians in an attempt to address the world of politics and economics, and to evaluate the strengths and weaknesses of these different approaches. In Part II, I try to

---

[24] A. MacIntyre, *After Virtue* 2nd edition, Duckworth, London, 1985. See also J. Habermas 'The Entwinement of Myth and Enlightenment: Max Horkheimer and Theodor Adorno' in *The Philosophical Discourse of Modernity* Polity Press, Cambridge, 1985.

explain the nature of the ineliminable moral problems raised by modern society as the appropriate site for theological concern. In the final part, I try to develop an approach to the understanding of these problems which attempts to answer two questions: the first is how might such moral issues be handled theologically; the second is in some ways more intractable, namely, what is the role of the theological insights arising from a faith community in the public deliberation and politics of a liberal democratic society? Is it appropriate that moral beliefs about politics and economics which are rooted in metaphysical beliefs should form part of the political and deliberative forum of a liberal democratic society in which such beliefs are not widely shared, or not as widely shared as they once used to be?

Before beginning the analysis of political theology, I want to put some flesh on the bare bones of my argument outlined above, and the best way to do that is for the moment to emphasise, in what, as we shall see as the argument progresses, is rather too crude a way, the tension between the universal and the particular which lies at the heart of political theology. Theology might be thought of as a discipline which seeks to arrive at some general truths about the nature of God and God's action in the world. On the other hand, political communities, their beliefs and values are highly specific and particular. The nature of God might be thought (at least in classical theism) to be timeless and unchanging,[25] whereas politics is always about the ways of life of particular communities at particular times and in particular places. The initial dilemma of political theology might be thought to be this: how can theology, which seeks to make coherent and cogent claims about the nature of God who is universal and in whose mind there is no distinction to be made between male and female, Greek or Roman, Jew or Gentile, be relevant to the realm of politics? Politics constitutes precisely the realm of difference where to be a member of a nation, or a race, or a gender, or a community is to have interests and purposes which are not in harmony with one another and which are interpreted differently and priori-

---

[25] Process Theology with dim echoes of Hegel avoids some of the problems discussed in this section.

tised differently according to time, place and circumstance. This is a particular problem for liberalism. As we have seen, some defenders of liberalism, Isaiah Berlin for example,[26] have seen liberalism as embodying the recognition that all things of value are not compatible. There is no way of procuring a coherent account of the relationship between things that we value – for example liberty and equality. All political action involves tragic choices between values. Liberalism is, in John Gray's words, 'agonistic'.[27] If this is so, how would a Christian approach to liberalism cope with this agonistic feature, given that it is a feature of classical theism that value comes from God, that God's mind is coherent and that values relate to one another in structured ways. On such a universalist and coherentist position the *true* relationship between values is there to be tracked. It does not issue in agonistic choices.

Some critics of Christianity, Rousseau for example, have made the critique of universalism very trenchantly, namely, that since Christianity is based on the ideas of a universal transcendent God it cannot, unlike pagan religions, which have their roots in particular societies and culture, provide a way of addressing and securing a firm moral basis for social and political unity and citizenship. Rousseau argues that in a pagan world where each state worshipped its own gods:

each state, having its own cult just as it had its own government, made no distinction between its Gods and its laws . . . The gods of the pagans were in no sense jealous gods; they divided the governance of the world between them. Even Moses and the Hebrew people sometimes lent themselves to the idea by speaking of the God of Israel.[28]

Christianity, however, particularly after the Council of Jerusalem, made a shift to the idea of a universal God; but how can such a universal God's nature be linked to the particularities of politics and social organisation of specific societies? Given

[26] See I. Berlin, *Four Essays on Liberty* Oxford University Press, 1969; I. Berlin 'Does Political Theory Still Exist?' in *Philosophy, Politics and Society Series II* ed. P. Laslett and W. G. Runciman, Blackwell, Oxford, 1962.

[27] J. Gray, *Isaiah Berlin* HarperCollins, London, 1995, particularly ch. 6 and, within that, p. 168.

[28] J. J. Rousseau, *The Social Contract* Book IV ch. 8, ed. and trans. by F. Watkins, Nelson, London, 1953, p. 143.

Rousseau's view that religion was a central unifying force in society which gave greater moral sanctions to the law, such a universal religion must be inimical to the unity of a particular society and 'thus' he argues 'one of the great bonds unifying particular societies remains without effect . . . I know of nothing more contrary to the social spirit'.[29] Whatever the cogency of these specific strictures, they do illustrate one dimension of the problem of the relationship between the nature of a universal transcendent God as made articulate in theology and the specificity of a particular society.

If the universal is stressed, then we are likely to end up with a form of political theology which is, as it were, deduced from some basic doctrine of God, creation and the human person which, in turn, is held to underpin rather generalised assertions about the nature of political values such as freedom, social justice, the common good and rights. These might be too vague and indeterminate to link into anything like the ways of life of particular societies, and will not provide rich enough moral ground for Christian political commitments. On the other hand, if the emphasis is placed upon particular communities and their ways of life, it will not be at all clear how these more fragmentary judgements about particular societies will relate to more general beliefs about the nature of God and, in particular, the coherence of God's will in terms of values and the implications of such beliefs for a more general theistic account of the nature of human politics, economics and community life. Professor Duncan Forrester puts the points sharply:

Political theology is contextual theology. It addresses itself to a particular situation at a specific time. This is one reason for the diversity of political theologies: since each is rooted in a particular context, they have different agendas and emphases. And despite its concern with the context, political theology is theology i.e. it endeavours to relate the classical Christian theological tradition to a modern situation. Both the classical and contextual are necessary. The local needs to be related to the universal, the particular to the unchanging.[30]

---

[29] Ibid. p. 149.
[30] D. Forrester, *Theology and Politics* Blackwell, Oxford, 1988 p. 150.

This poses the problem with which I want to grapple from the side of theology, but it does not solve it. Forrester is surely right to emphasise that political theology has to be contextual and that the local has to be related to the universal – the problem, though, is how this is to be done. There is no uncontroversial answer to this question, and the next five chapters will look at the diverse answers that have been offered. We shall look at the idea that a theology of history is necessary to link the particular to the universal. This approach will be considered both in terms of illustrative examples drawn from the history of theology as in Augustine, Calvin and Hegel, and in contemporary approaches, as in John Cobb and Wolfhart Pannenberg. We shall consider the approach of systematic theology, the idea that any political judgements that can be derived from Christian belief have to be derived inferentially from more basic doctrines about the nature of God and creation. In this context, ideas about natural law and a natural order within which politics takes place will also be examined. There is, however, the view that both the approach which rests on a theology of history and that which relies on systematic theology are fundamentally flawed. This view derives particularly from the narrative approach to theology as exemplified in the work of Hauerwas and McClendon and post-liberal theologians such as Lindbeck, and these arguments will be assessed. Finally, we shall look at natural law approaches to these issues in both their classical and modern forms.

If there can be a theology of politics and society, then there have to be themes and circumstances towards which it is directed, and Part II of the book will attempt to clarify what might be thought of as both the potential site and scope for a theology of politics. This is a very important issue because theologians *qua* theologians do not possess expertise in political economy, political science or sociology, so quite what insights can we expect from theology and what should their scope be? At this stage the obvious answer is: wherever modern society throws up issues of collective moral concern and collective moral responsibility. That is fine so far as it goes. It does, however, neglect the fact that there are different pressures being exerted which would have the effect of demoralising a good deal of economic and social life in the sense of seeing them as being immune to moral appraisal – as with the outcomes of the economy; or as not implying any kind of collective responsibility – as with poverty; or as not implying any particular moral input into basic political concepts such as liberty; or, as in the case of social justice – arguing that this indisputably moral notion is illusory. So the second task of a general account of political theology is to attempt to show that the world of politics and economics cannot be reduced to technique, or managerial control and adjustment that raise no great moral dilemmas. This attempt will be made in chapters 7, 8 and 9. In addition, we need to consider another important aspect of modern society for the possibility of political theology. Earlier in this chapter, I stressed the extent to which the basic dilemma of political theology is to link the universal and the particular, with politics and economics being part of the world of the particular. However, contemporary emphasis on globalisation and associated ideas of 'the end of history'[31] has led to the suggestion that some central aspects of modern society, such as the market economy and liberal democracy, although originating in particular places against a background of specific cultures and institutions, they are now part of the universal, and that liberal democracy and the market economy will, in some sense, mark the final form of human social, political and economic evolution. A political theology, however it is rooted in the different approaches described earlier, needs to be able to take some kind of account of these claims. So, just for example, a form of political theology which regarded a theology of history as central to the mediation of universal and particular cannot in seriousness neglect the claims that the liberal market order stands at the end of history in some sense, and that the global economy is the ineluctable form within which humankind has to live.

These are all deep and complicated issues, many of which will undoubtedly evade my attempt to focus on them fully.

---

[31] As, for example, F. Fukuyama *The End of History and the Last Man* Penguin, Harmondsworth, 1992.

Whether we are Christians or not, we need a clear account of what might be taken to be the reasonable political implications of religious belief, and, if my arguments make that seem to be a touch more complicated than it looks at first sight, then that, too, is a gain, it seems to me. When church leaders pronounce upon politics and economics, they are, to an extent, both invoking a kind of authority, and they need to be clear about how they can have authority in this field. Equally, they are putting their authority 'on the line', and, if that authority is to carry conviction, those who invoke it must be aware of its site and scope if it is not to be undermined. Finally, however, Christians in Britain, Western Europe, the USA and many other parts of the world are also citizens of liberal democratic societies that have to have constitutional structures or conventions which secure the allegiance of people of many faiths and none. What, then, is the role of Christian beliefs about politics in the context of a liberal pluralistic society, and how far, if at all, should political and economic doctrines that are underpinned by metaphysical beliefs, which are not shared by all in that society, become part of legitimate political debate and pressure?

PART I

The possibility of political theology

All thoughts, all creeds, all dreams are true,
All visions wild and strange;
Man is the measure of all truth
Unto himself. All truth is change:

All men do walk in sleep, and all
Have faith in that they dream:
For all things are as they seem to all,
And all things flow like a stream.

There is no rest, no calm, no pause,
Nor good nor ill, nor light nor shade,
Nor essence nor eternal laws:
For nothing is but all is made.   (Tennyson οἱ ῥέοντες)

Theology and politics: context community and prophecy

You only have I known of all the families of the earth: therefore I will punish you for all your iniquities.   (Amos)

Then the Lord put forth his hand, and touched my mouth. And the Lord said unto me. Behold I have put my words into thy mouth. See I have this day set thee over the nations and over the kingdoms, to root out and to pull down, and to destroy, and to throw down, to build and to plant.   (Jeremiah)

The aim of this part as a whole is to explore the possibility of political theology, and in this chapter I shall focus on the nature, role and purpose of prophecy in the Judaeo-Christian tradition.

There are three reasons for doing this. The first is that the prophetic role has been invoked in recent years, for example by the authors of *Faith in the City*, as a basis for the argument that the church has a legitimate prophetic role in relation to modern society and politics. The prophets of the Old Testament were involved in judging, admonishing and cursing those who held political power in Israel and other nations surrounding it, and so, it might be argued, there is nothing at all unscriptural in the modern church adopting a critical attitude towards the policies and principles which underpin modern politics. In addition, those who have advocated the development of an explicitly political theology have also appealed to the prophetic tradition to provide legitimacy for this endeavour. Finally, it might be argued, for reasons which I hope will become clear as this chapter progresses, that Old Testament prophecy leads quite

25

naturally into the question of a theology of history or theodicy, which is going to be the main focus of the next chapter. One way of putting the point is to say that the prophets had solved the problem of the mediating link between universal and particular in relation to the link between Yahweh and Israel and its history. Any sort of political theology has to face this question because, while we may possess universal principles, these have to be applied in particular cases by the use of judgement. This judgement has to be guided if it is not to be wholly arbitrary, and the link between universal and particular via judgement is crucial.

There is no doubt that the prophets were involved in judging and admonishing both political authorities and political policies, so what was it that made the prophetic office possible? Or, to put the matter another way, what was it that gave the prophets authority to judge and admonish in this way? Such authority would have to have two strands: the nature of the authority that they claimed from God, and the way that those who received such prophecy and took it to their hearts regarded it as authoritative. The prophets judged both the public and private culture of Israel, but what institutional and cultural setting made this possible?

It is at least arguable that two things had to be in place to make these prophetic utterances both legitimate and intelligible. These are *tradition* and *covenant*. Israel had a sense of common purpose rooted in the emerging idea of Israel being the chosen people of Yahweh and that the relationship between Yahweh and Israel was defined in terms of the covenant. These traditions obviously grew over time, and they were susceptible to different interpretations and emphases which made the proper understanding of them controversial. Indeed, not only were interpretations of the society's relationship to Yahweh susceptible to different interpretations of what the relationship demanded, but also these demands were not lived up to and, of course, prophecy is partly about this matter. That is to say that the prophets used their understanding of the relationship between Yahweh and Israel as the basis for an internal critique of Israel's moral and political performance. It can be argued that there was a bedrock of common understanding, common assumptions and a common purpose for Israel, and prophecy was about the interpretation and definition of this. Similarly, too, there was the conception of a covenant between Israel and Yahweh and of Israel's special role within the nations which allowed the prophetic office to be confined not only to the judging of Israel. Prophets were not, therefore, purely charismatic figures, deriving their prophetic authority from their own extraordinary powers and personalities which enabled them to claim Yahweh's sanction for what they said and for their judgements, but rather their authority was rooted in the relationship in which they stood to their interpretations of theodicy, a shared history and the understanding of the demands of the covenant which was assumed to be authoritative for the society.

There is, first of all, a general point to be made here about the nature of authority. It is not possible, I think, to have purely charismatic authority as a prophet – an authority to be explained in terms of the charismatic rather than in terms of the background set of tradition and practices of the society within which the supposed charismatic authority operates. This is a crucial point and is directly counter to Weber's own work on prophecy which he set out in *The Sociology of Religion*. Weber argues as follows:

We shall understand 'prophet' to mean a purely individual bearer of charisma, who by virtue of his mission proclaims a religious doctrine or divine commandment. . .For our purposes here, the personal call is the decisive element distinguishing the prophet from the priest. The latter lays claim to authority by virtue of his service in a sacred tradition, while the prophet's claim is based on personal revelation and charisma . . . the prophet, like the magician, exerts his power simply by virtue of his personal gifts.[1]

This is surely a mistake. To be authoritative both in terms of the roots of the legitimacy of the prophecy and the effect that it has on its hearers, the prophet has to relate what he has to say back to the common understandings held by those in the society within which he articulates his prophecy. This point has been very well made by Peter Winch in his essay on 'Authority':

[1] M. Weber, *The Sociology of Religion* Beacon Press, Boston, pp. 46–59.

Weber says quite explicitly that charismatic authority is not at all tied to tradition. In the same strain he remarks that the characteristic attitude of the charismatic leader is: 'It is written that . . . But I say unto you' . . . Charismatic authority is conceived as a *revolutionary* force, as one of the main agencies by which new ways of living and thinking are introduced into society. Granted that this is so, it is still very misleading to oppose charisma to tradition. The point about it is not that it stands apart from established ways of doing things, but that it stands to them in a very special relation. Apart from the tradition to which it stands in such relation, it is quite unintelligible and inconceivable.[2]

The intelligibility of prophecy which is a necessary condition of its authority and effectiveness requires these background conditions, and the authority of prophecy cannot be explained primarily in terms of charisma. Having said this, however, the specification of the context against the background of which authority is intelligible is complex and controversial but, at the same time, of prime importance for thinking about political theology. Is the intelligibility of the prophet's message linked to a context which is local and particular to a specific religious way of life and practice, or can it be made intelligible against a broader background of norms and practices not rooted in the particularities of a specific form of religious practice – a background such as natural law? The issue of universal and particular is therefore central to the characterisation of the nature of prophecy.

These considerations have led Michael Walzer to advance a general account of the nature of prophecy and these background conditions. The link between the universal and the particular, between Yahweh and Israel, in his view, is not to be found in the personality of the prophet but in the way in which the prophet is able to show the people 'their own hearts since the law is not in heaven; it is a social possession', as Walzer says. He argues that the prophet seeks to get Israel to remember, to turn back and to repent:

the knowledge is easily renewed for the Torah is not an esoteric teaching. It is not hidden, obscure, difficult. . .The teaching is avail-

---

[2] P. Winch, 'Authority' in *Political Philosophy* ed. A. Quinton, Oxford University Press, 1967.

able, common, popular – so much so that everyone is commanded to speak about it:

> And these words which I command thee this day shall be in thine heart: And thou shalt teach them diligently unto thy children, and thou shalt talk of them when thou sittest in thine house, and when thou walkest by thy way and when thou liest down and when thou risest up (Deuteronomy 6.6–7).

Prophecy aims to arouse remembrance, recognition, indignation, repentance. In Hebrew the last of these words derives from a root meaning 'to turn, to turn back, to return' and so implies that repentance is parasitic upon a previously understood morality. The same implication is apparent in prophecy itself. The prophet foretells doom, but what motivates his listeners is not only fear of coming disasters, but also a knowledge of the law, a sense of their own history, and a feeling for religious tradition.[3]

Prophecy is for Walzer an internal and dialogical critique which is strictly dependent upon this common background of common history, law and covenant. In support of this view he cites Greenberg in *Prose Prayer* in which he argues that 'prophecy presupposes common ground on which the prophet and the audience stand'.[4] The same point can be substantiated by looking at other biblical scholars too. As Professor Gene Tucker argues:

> Studies of the prophets . . . shows that they constantly appeal to and reiterate ancient traditions. This appeal and reiteration occurs in two ways. First, as already indicated, with regard to the laws and obligations of the people, they always take it for granted that Israel has long known what is expected in the covenant with Yahweh. They rarely cite the laws themselves, but their accusations and indictments are based on old legal traditions. The problem is not that Israel did not know, but that Israel did not do. So the prophets introduce no new and higher morality, and do not even appear to radicalise old laws which were sufficiently demanding to begin with. Second, all of the prophets stand in certain theological traditions which had been important for centuries before them.[5]

---

[3] M. Walzer, *Interpretation and Social Criticism* Harvard University Press, Cambridge Mass., 1987. p. 74–5.

[4] M. Greenberg, *Biblical Prose Prayer as a Window to the Popular Religion of Ancient Israel* University of California Press, Berkeley, Calif., 1983.

[5] G. M. Tucker, 'The Role of the Prophets and the Role of the Church' in *Prophecy in Israel* ed. D. L. Petersen, SPCK, London, 1987, p. 167.

J. Muilenberg makes much the same point too in 'The Office of the Prophet in Ancient Israel'[6] when he argues that the prophets were to be understood as 'covenant mediators'. This is not in any sense to deny that they were Yahweh's messengers, but rather that they represented to the people of Israel what were the demands of the covenant within which Israel already stood.

These background conditions made prophecy possible and its judgement and admonishment to be intelligible to those who heard. This has to take place against these shared understandings. So, for Walzer, and implicitly for these other biblical commentators, prophecy produces a dialogical form of social criticism. So for Walzer the prophet is not to be understood as a missionary speaking to an alien culture, but as a severe kind of interpreter of the common moral inheritance of Israel. Sometimes, as Walzer argues, the prophet does prophesy to another society as Jonah did in Nineveh but there can be no internal dialogue with an alien society and so Jonah condemns from a kind of moral distance:

He [Jonah] is a detached critic of Ninevan society, and his prophecy is a single sentence: 'Yet forty days and Nineveh shall be overthrown' . . . this is prophecy without poetry, without romance, allusion, or concrete detail. The prophet comes and goes, an alien voice, a mere messenger, unconnected to the people and the city.[7]

These common understandings which Jonah and Nineveh do not share are crucial to prophecy and they are, as I have said, rooted in covenant, law and tradition with the prophet as internal mediator, as Muilenberg argues. The nature of their authority is rooted in these common understandings.

One element of understanding prophecy in this way is to argue that Israel had what might anachronistically be called a *theology of history*, by which I mean two things in this context. First of all there is the emerging idea of Israel as a nation with a special relationship to Yahweh who looks over it and protects its interests and guides its history as in the Exodus. Secondly, there

---

[6] J. Muilenberg, 'The Office of the Prophet in Ancient Israel' in *The Bible and Modern Scholarship* ed. J. Hyatt, The Abingdon Press, Nashville, 1967, pp. 74–97.
[7] Walzer, *Interpretation and Social Criticism* p. 77.

is a view about the role of Israel amongst the generality of
nations. The argument for this first point is implicit in the
points made thus far, but the second also seems clear enough
amongst biblical scholars. Walter Eichrodt has argued this case
in some detail in his 'Faith in Providence and Theodicy in The
Old Testament' in *Festschrift Otto Procksch:*

All statements which have to do with Yahweh's rule over the nations
are given shape by their own experience of his historical guidance:
because Canaan is promised to Israel as a home, the Canaanites must
experience Yahweh's supremacy over them and endure punishment
for their godlessness. Because Pharaoh opposes Israel's exodus from
Egypt, he is humbled by Yahweh. Now and again the view gains
prominence that a universal moral law is binding for all peoples in
relation to God and places them within the domain of God's action.
So it is when the sins of the Canaanites are said to be responsible for
their expulsion from the land or when the repute of the wanton and
outrageous deeds of the Sodomites reaches Yahweh and induces him
to intervene. In this consciousness of moral obligation of all peoples
an important element is no doubt present which effectively paved the
way for a comprehensive view of the destiny of the nations.[8]

This point is related particularly to Israel's destiny among the
nations not only as the result of Yahweh's role in the deliverance
from Egypt, but also for example when:

in the circles of Elijah and Elisha the Aramaean came to be recognised as no longer merely national enemies but as a rod prepared by
Yahweh for chastening this degenerate people. Thereafter Amos went
on to place Israel's history in the midst of the history of other peoples,
and he pointed out emphatically that they were guided by the will of
Yahweh in the same fashion as Israel. Here Israel is placed on the
same level as the pagans, not only with respect to divine judgement,
which hands both over to punishment (Amos 1 and 2) but also as an
object of divine care. Israel and the heathen are valued alike: 'Art you
not like the Ethiopians to me O people of Israel?' says the Lord. 'Did I
not bring up Israel from the Land of Egypt and the Philistines from
Captor and the Syrians from Kir?'[9]

Eichrodt goes on to point out that the same point can be
made about Isaiah in the destruction that the Assyrians

---

[8] Translated as 'Faith in Providence and Theodicy in the Old Testament' in *Theodicy in
the Old Testament* ed. J. L. Crenshaw, SPCK, London, 1983, p. 22.
[9] Ibid. p. 23.

wrought on the states of the Near East: Isaiah was able to see divine providence at work (Isaiah 10.5ff).[10] A similar point he argues is also to be found in Isaiah 41.25, 43.14, 44.28, 45.1–7, and 46.10. Eichrodt's conclusion is that:

the Israelite faith in providence is filled with universal content, and a positive evaluation of history is made possible, by means of which even terrible catastrophes can be endured, and even valued, as constructive elements in world events.[11]

This argument about theodicy, universal history or a theology of history is also supported by von Rad when he argues:

Isaiah sets this saving act of Yahweh in the widest possible historical context, namely that of universal history. Nothing is improvised here: Isaiah says very clearly that Yahweh 'predetermined' his work long ago (Isaiah 22.11; cf. Isaiah 37.26). This work of Yahweh thus enfolds the whole realm of world history as it was understood at the time; and the way in which the world empires who were proudly strutting about on this very stage of history came into collision with God's plan is one of the great themes to which Isaiah returned again and again:

> Yahweh of hosts has sworn:
> As I have planned it, so shall it stand,
> to break Assyria in my land;
> upon my mountains will I trample him under foot . . .
> This is my purpose, resolved concerning the whole earth,
> this is the hand, stretched over all the nations.[12]

These points, it has to be said, stand in some degree of contrast with Walzer's view of prophecy as internal dialogical critique and interpretation, since this incipient theology of history which Eichrodt and von Rad point to implies a degree of *universality* which Walzer's interpretation seems to undermine. I shall return to this point shortly, but for the moment I want to continue a little further on the theme of a theology of history. The emphasis on a theology of history as a background condition of prophetic interpretation has been insisted upon by von Rad when he argues that: 'in principle Israel's faith is grounded in a theology of history. It regards itself as based upon historical

---

[10] Ibid. p. 24.   [11] Ibid.
[12] G. von Rad, *The Message of the Prophets* SCM Press, London, 1968, pp. 132–3.

facts, and as shaped and reshaped by facts in which it saw the hand of God at work'.[13]

If the interpretation of Israel's own nature, existence and faith is based upon a theology of its own history, together, as we have seen, with an interpretation of the role of other nations in respect of such a history, then it is not implausible to make two further claims. First of all, that Yahweh as the universal God is related to the specificity, not only to the nature and evolution of Israel as a political unit, but also to *surrounding nations* such as the Canaanites, the Philistines, the Egyptians, the Assyrians and others. Von Rad makes the very important point that in both Amos and Isaiah this theology of history as it applies to nations other than Israel is not confined to the effect of those nations upon the fortunes of Israel but to those nations themselves and their own national destinies. So he argues that, in relation to *Amos*: 'The stanza against Gaza is of particular interest, since its subject is injuries done by the Philistines to the Edomites, that is to say injuries which do not affect Israel at all (Amos 1.6–8).'[14]

This leads von Rad to make a point of quite fundamental importance both in relation to scholarly interpretation of the nature of prophecy and in relation to the possible link between an understanding of the nature of prophecy and political theology. Von Rad's claim is that this idea of history, in which God guides and punishes other nations not just because of their relation to the future and flourishing of Israel, implies also some conception of a universal law or universal morality. Thus he says of Amos:

The poem against the foreign nations revealed the strength of Amos' reaction to breaches of the unwritten law of international relations – and not simply to those breaches which brought suffering to Israel . . . Amos' Yahweh watches over the established order of international law not only in Israel but also among the other nations, and whenever they are broken he imposes a historical punishment on the culprits.[15]

I shall return to this point shortly, but for the moment it is worth pointing out that this would lead to a rather different

---

[13] G. von Rad, *Old Testament Theology*, Oliver and Boyd, Edinburgh, 1962, vol 1, p. 106.
[14] Von Rad *The Message* p. 166.
[15] Ibid.

account of the nature of prophecy than that provided by Walzer. Walzer's main point is that prophecy is best understood in an internal dialogical manner related to and made authoritative by its link to the covenant and the religious traditions of Israel. Von Rad's point, however, is that there is also a conception of a general moral law and a universal history against the background of which the prophet is able to utter his prophecies. This is potentially important for an understanding of any analogy between a modern political theology and the nature of prophecy. If the modern church is held to have a prophetic office on the analogy with the prophets of the Old Testament, this could mean that the church has to follow either the dialogical or the universalist view of prophecy (assuming for the moment that they are exclusive). On the dialogical view, an appeal would have to be made to shared beliefs and understandings about politics and society within which a particular church operates, and to work with these resources in a way that seeks to procure some kind of prophetic message for society. Alternatively, if the universalist view is taken, the assumption is that there are general moral values which are God given and which apply to all people everywhere whatever the history and circumstances of that society. The first approach, the communitarian one, is rooted in context, community, the politics of difference and the narrative and ethos which holds a society together, with consequential problems for a cogent account of the nature of the scope of the moral values held by a Christian. The second attempt to solve this problem, but perhaps at the cost of indeterminate generality, is the nature of the values espoused, just because of their very universality. A good deal of the argument in this book will move between these two poles.

The second important point here is that the task of prophecy in its public and collective role in relation to both Israel and other nations depends upon this understanding of God's action in history. In so far as political theology and the prophetic function of the church in politics derive their inspiration from the prophets of ancient Israel and from their theology of history, how far is a theology of history still necessary to fulfil this function today? This will be the theme of my next two chapters.

I want, however, to return to Walzer and discuss further this question of the nature of the theology of history, and the associated idea of a universal morality in relation to his account of prophecy as an internal and dialogical exercise. It would seem that what might be called an internal theology of history, that is to say one which interprets history in relation to the flourishing or the chastisement of Israel, should cause no great problem for Walzer, since he could well argue that a sense of Israel's own history under the providence of Yahweh could be regarded as part of the set of common localised understandings which make prophecy possible. This would also apply to that aspect of a theology of history in relation to the fate of other nations which had contributed to Israel's self-understanding, as, for example, the Exodus and the role of Egypt in the formation of Israel's national destiny. The difficulty for Walzer's position comes, for example, with Eichrodt's and von Rad's account of Amos and Isaiah where it would seem that Yahweh is regarded by these prophets as having an interest in other nations not merely in so far as they contributed to the fortunes and flourishing of Israel but, as it were, for their own sake. When this point is coupled with the idea in Amos and Isaiah (and indeed Jonah in relation to Nineveh) that there is a basic and universal moral law, then a clear problem is posed for Walzer and those biblical critics who agree with him, that the prophets are covenant mediators, interpreters and critics of an ongoing, particularistic moral and religious tradition and ethos. That is to say, that on Walzer's view, prophecy has to make sense against the background of the specific morality of Israel as defined by its sense of its own history, its traditions and the covenant. As we have already seen, there is one way of interpreting all of this, particularly in relation to Amos and Isaiah, which runs rather strongly against the Walzer interpretation of the nature of prophecy, and this difference of interpretation is to the highest degree significant in relation to the nature of political theology. The alternative interpretation would stress the more universal aspects of the theology of history and the moral law of all nations. This point is made particularly clearly by J. Moltmann, and he links together universal moral law and the judgement of Yahweh in relation to this with a theology of history with an eschatological dimension:

the extension to all peoples of the threat of judgement and of the promise of salvation in itself already involves what T. C. Vriezen calls the 'missionary task of Israel' – the task of being a light to the Gentiles and a witness for Yahweh in his controversy with the gods of the nations. But the more the new saving action of God that is to come outstrips all analogies from the history of Israel's dealings with its God in past experience and tradition, and the more that the judgement that begins with Israel moves on through the history of the nation, the more clearly there appear the first signs of a *Universal Eschatology of Mankind.*[16]

He goes on to make the important point, however, that this history does not imply a predetermined cause for events. 'It is not a history surveyed apocalyptically from the standpoint of the end at which all things stand still, but is a future announced from the midst of the process of history. . . They see judgement and history in the light of the freedom of Yahweh not as an immutable fate.'[17]

What he has in mind here is twofold. First of all, the prophets see their prophetic utterances as having the potential to change the course of history. 'They know that they themselves and their message are a factor in the movement of the history of God.'[18] Secondly, they accept that the judgement of Yahweh on Israel and on the nations can be repented of by Yahweh. What they have in view, according to Moltmann, is a theology of history which is not predetermined, but rather Yahweh's constancy and faithfulness in history and thus 'distinct from any fatalistic apocalyptic view of history'. The mobility of history as the prophets see it, and as they stand in it with their own witness can therefore be called a 'purposeful conversation of the Lord of the future with Israel'. These points are important for the next chapter which will focus more fully on the nature of a theology of history in the Christian tradition. The Old Testament does imply a universal theology of history, that is to say one which transcends a concern with the nature of Israel and

---

[16] J. Moltmann, *Theology of Hope* SCM Press, London, 1967, p. 130.
[17] Ibid. p. 133.   [18] Ibid. p. 132.

that along with such a theology of history goes a conception of universal morality, or common morality, or even natural law. On this view, Walzer is perhaps mistaken to interpret prophecy as internal to common understandings of history and covenant; the prophets saw themselves on this view as speaking for a more universalist conception of morality. This point has been strongly defended recently by J. R. Porter and John Barton as well as by the earlier authorities Eichrodt and von Rad whom I have already mentioned. Porter argues as follows:

At one time it was thought that the prophets were appealing to the Covenant and the law but it is curious that they hardly ever mention the Covenant and scholars are now more inclined to believe that they challenge those they condemn to act in accordance with what we might call 'natural law' or 'natural morality', that is, with generally accepted standards of humane and decent behaviour which human conscience could recognise.[19]

One scholar whom Porter has in mind is John Barton, whose *Amos' Oracles Against the Nations* argues for example that: 'Social morality understood both as impartiality in justice and care for the rights of the helpless, is not merely a human convention, but almost a part of the order of nature, self evident to any right thinking man.'[20] In Barton's view it is also essential that the universality here is *not* seen as deriving from the universalisation of the covenant as part of the specific experience of Israel.

As he says:

The moral obligation owed by foreign nations must be not less but more evident than those imposed on Israel, if these chapters are to serve their purpose. And so we must reject any interpretation that sees such universal morality as deriving from rather than as presupposed by, the special moral response demanded of the covenant people.[21]

This is more or less an exact reversal of Walzer's position and one which Barton supports with the following quotation from H. W. Wolff in his *Joel and Amos* page 101: 'that Yahweh is the

---

[19] J. R. Porter, 'Wealth and Poverty in the Bible' in *Christianity and Conservatism* ed. M. Alison and D. C. Edwards, Hodder and Stoughton, London, 1990, p. 110.

[20] J. Barton, *Amos's Oracles Against the Nations* Cambridge University Press, 1980, p. 43.

[21] Ibid.

only God of Israel and of the world of nations is not a theme of his message but its very evident presupposition'.

This point is defended even more explicitly by Barton when he argues that:

the prophet Isaiah, working in Jerusalem in the eighth century BC, already had a developed understanding of the basis of morality which has more affinities with western theories of natural law than has usually been thought, and less in common with the notion of moral imperatives as 'revealed' or positive law given by God as the terms of a 'covenant' or contract with the people of Israel, than is supposed by many Old Testament specialists.[22]

This exact claim is also reinforced by James Barr[23] and H. H. Schmid in *Wesen und Geschichte der Weisheit: Eine Untersuchung zur Altorientalischen und Israelitischen Weisheit Literatur*. In respect of Schmid, Barton makes the following important point:

For Schmid the primary horizon of the Old Testament is not God's choice of Israel and the giving to them of the law, but the creation of the world and the moral order derives from its created character . . . This neatly inverts the usual assumption that the Bible is all about God uttering imperatives to his chosen people, and reinstates instead a concern with the natural moral order of the created world.[24]

Let us assume that the prophets did speak for a universal morality, not one just entrenched within Israel's historical common understanding, this would be of the greatest significance in relation to the relationship between prophecy and modern political theology. The issue at stake here, which will occupy the next four chapters, is this: if we adopt the Walzer view of the nature of prophecy, then this would imply that a modern Christian political theology formulated on the basis of the analogy with ancient prophecy would be addressed to those within the common understanding of the Christian faith community. If, however, we take the view that the prophets were speaking about a natural morality, a natural law or a natural

---

[22] J. Barton, 'Ethics in Isaiah of Jerusalem' in the *Journal of Theological Studies*, 32:1 (1981). The point is made again in *Ethics and the Old Testament* SCM Press, London, 1998, chs. 4 and 5.

[23] J. Barr, *Biblical Faith and Natural Theology* Clarendon Press, Oxford, 1993, p. 101.

[24] Barton, *Ethics and the Old Testament* pp. 67–8.

moral order which is God given, then by analogy a political prophetic office for the modern church would allow it to speak for what might be taken as an assumed natural moral order which all persons of good will might come to accept. This distinction in relation to modern Christian social and political thought is not at all fanciful. There are those such as Stanley Hauerwas who would very much endorse the Walzerian approach to these issues and insist that Christian approach to political theology is internal to the narrative which defines the Christian community and binds it together. Hauerwas, as we shall see in later chapters, is severely critical of what he calls a morality based on the 'social generalities' of natural law. The alternative approach is to be found in liberal political theologians like Wogaman and, from a very different natural-law perspective, the British Catholic Bishops in their recent report *Common Good*. This philosophical and theological difference is not only academic, but also leads to a very different strategy for the churches' involvement with social and political issues. If one came to believe that Scripture authorised the idea of a natural order or a common morality then this would sanction an approach to politics which could also involve non-Christians, since such general standards of morality could be accepted by all right-thinking people whether Christian or not.

It is certainly true that Walzer recognises the universalist aspects of prophecy, but he makes two points against the impact of this kind of universalism. The first is that the content of this universalist approach is very minimal indeed, and is usually invoked only in relation to acts of extreme violence, and that apart from this the universalism is virtually non-existent. The second is that such universalism is inert as a form of moral constraint and motivation until it is linked to, or fleshed out, by the social meanings which these prohibitions have within a particular society with common values and a common history, as in the case of Israel:

Prophecy would have little life, and little effect, if it could not evoke memories of this sort. We might think of prophecy, [in the alternative universalist sense] then, as an academic exercise. In a strange country, Amos would resemble Samson in Gaza. Not eyeless but tongueless: he might indeed see the oppression, but he would not be able to give it a name or speak about it in the hearts of the people.[25]

It is prophecy 'without poetry, without resonance, allusion or concrete detail. The prophet comes and goes, an alien voice, a mere messenger unconnected to the people of the city.' Since the aim of prophecy, for Walzer, is to arouse remembrance, recognition, indignation and repentance, it has to make use of the rich and thick moral and religious notions of a specific people, not the abstract generalities of a natural moral order which can only be minimalist. Their focus, Walzer argues, is on the fate of the covenanted community.[26] In support of this view, he quotes Linblom who argues that prophetic teaching: 'is characterised by the principle of solidarity. Behind the demand for charity and justice . . . lies the idea of the people, the people as an organic whole, united by election and covenant.'[27] There is a clear analogy here with the approach of narrative theologians to political theology in the modern world; namely, that an approach to political theology has to be seen as internal to the Christian narrative and the life of Christian discipleship, not as based on a set of social generalities which seeks to embody an inert set of universalist and, for that reason, minimalist, moral values. The natural law approach, on the other hand, can claim support from within the Old Testament, as Barton and others have made clear. As Barton argues, Protestant tradition, whether in its Barthian or its narrative form, has taken the view that moral teaching has 'often concerned itself with the right way of life for those who have made a decision for God in Christ and therefore live within the fellowship of the church'.[28] Catholicism, on the other hand, has had what he argues is the strength of its universalist position based upon natural law and a natural moral order. It has been argued by critics of the natural order/law approach that this subordinates the narrative of the Bible to exemplars or reminders of general moral principles which can be understood and justified on other

[25] Walzer *Interpretation and Social Criticism* pp. 91–2.
[26] Ibid. p. 80.
[27] J. Lindblom, *Prophecy in Ancient Israel* Fortress Press, Philadelphia, 1962, p. 344.
[28] Barton, *Ethics and the Old Testament* p. 60.

grounds.[29] It is part of Barton's purpose to argue, as we have seen, that natural law and natural moral-order thinking is implicit in the Bible itself, whereas the Walzerian view favours the narrative approach. These different views lead, as we shall see in subsequent chapters, to quite different approaches to the nature of political theology. What is clear enough at this stage is that the nature of prophecy in the Old Testament is controversial and ambiguous enough for the modern church not to be able to appeal to the prophetic tradition in a straightforward manner to legitimise its political theology and political praxis, since the tradition to which it appeals is very unclear and disputed in precisely its most important respect for political theology, namely, the relationship between the universal and particular.

It is also worth pointing out at this juncture that some of these issues relating to prophecy and context have a direct parallel in political theory, a point which is partly explained by the fact that Walzer is a distinguished analyst of the prophetic tradition, as well as being a notable political theorist. We shall see the emergence of these parallels in more detailed form as the argument proceeds, but for the moment it is worthwhile pointing out the following similarities.

The first, and perhaps the most general, is between universalism and particularism. That is to say, whether the task of social and political thought is to develop universal, rational, general theories based upon an account of human nature and purposes situated in the context of an interpretation of the role of human beings in nature and the cosmos, or is political thought best situated within a specific social and political context concerned with the interpretation and the critique of social and political arrangements using the moral and intellectual resources available in that context, as Walzer argues.

Closely allied to this theme is that of abstraction versus a more situated form of social and political understanding. A universalist approach, rooting an account of social and political institutions in a universalist account of human nature and

---

[29] See W. C. Spohn, *What are They Saying about Scripture and Ethics?* Paulist Press, New York, 1984.

human purposes, has to develop such a conception by abstracting from the particular circumstances in which human beings 'live, move and have their being' in which they develop a specific identity and inherit a particular moral tradition. Or should social and political thought eschew such abstraction and focus primarily upon the resources embodied in specific moral traditions?

A further dimension of this theme is that of foundationalism and anti-foundationalism, that is to say should we be engaged in the intellectual pursuit of some general, universalist, abstract foundations for understanding politics and social institutions, or should social and political understanding exclude the search for foundations and rather accept what is given, as Wittgenstein said: 'ways of life'. Such ways of life cannot be given general foundations but are accepted as ongoing practices.

Finally, there is the contrast between reason and narrative. A universalist approach based upon the search for rational foundations for politics has to downplay the role of narrative and ethos in the foundation and maintenance of society in favour of general theories.

All of these contrasts are explicit in the different accounts of prophecy we have considered. The covenantal stress within prophecy embodies many of the assumptions of the particularist, narrative, anti-abstractionist view. The argument that the prophets had developed a conception of a universal natural-law or natural-morality approach parallels in important ways the view of more foundationalist political theories. As we shall see, these themes are central to contemporary approaches to political theology. Indeed, they have important consequences for thinking about the relationship between political theology and the legitimacy of liberal society. Many liberals, and indeed their narrative and communitarian critics, have argued that the justification of a liberal political order depends crucially on the idea that it is possible to identify a rational set of general principles by abstracting precisely from the different local, particularistic, narratively formed and community-based forms of identity which people have. For liberals, this abstraction is a central virtue of liberal society when faced by a plurality of groups with different identities and narratives supporting different conceptions of the good. For the narrative thinker, whether a narrative theologian or a political philosopher, such abstraction is a denial of some of the basic aspects of human identity and sense of being in the world.

These issues will be explained in more detail later, but before doing so I want in the next two chapters to consider more fully the idea of a theology of history which, as we have seen, has also arisen out of the prophetic tradition. It might be thought that the detailed contrasts I have just drawn between the universal and the particular in political theology would be overcome by a theology of history which, of necessity, combines both general principles with the narratives of particular societies.

CHAPTER 3

God, history and political theology

Glorious things of thee are spoken
  Zion city of our God.   (Psalmist)

It belongs to the very nature of the state that it is not and
cannot become the Kingdom of God.   (Barth)

Nihil Solidum. Nihil Stabile.   (Augustine)

In the previous chapter I looked at the way in which the
prophetic tradition of the Old Testament could be taken as
uniting the universal and the particular: the nature of God and
the world of politics with all its particularity. As we have seen,
scholars are engaged in controversy about exactly those aspects
of prophecy which bear most closely on this issue. I have now to
turn to the idea of a theology of history as a way of seeking a
mediation between religious belief and politics. Obviously
states, political communities and political societies are historical
products and achievements. They have a history, and an understanding of this history is vital to the understanding of the
present structure and nature of these institutions. This also
means that states and political communities, and the values and
principles, beliefs and attitudes which play a role in holding
them together, are highly specific and particular historical
creations and, therefore, one aspect of the dilemma of relating
the universal and the particular in theology is the relationship
between God and history. One way in which what Professor
Forrester[1] calls the classical tradition in theology has sought to

---

[1] D. Forrester, *Theology and Politics.*

44

link these is through a theology of history: an account of God's relationship to the historical process, a relationship which gives that process a general meaning and rationality. Against this background, political theology can take place both at the general level of an account of the nature of political society from a theological perspective and at a more specific level of talking about particular political values such as freedom and justice and struggling against particular forms of human oppression, or, perhaps equally typically within the Christian theological tradition, of providing some kind of theological justification for inequality or endorsement of the social structure and the beliefs and values underpinning such structure within particular societies. In this sense, a theology of history which has to say something about actual historical events and processes is one attempt at providing a mediating link between the particular and the universal. Such a 'meta-history' as Hayden White[2] calls it or 'meta-narrative' as Lyotard[3] calls it provides a link between the universal and the particular, a link which seems to be indispensable if political theology is going to both be an academic discipline within theology and, equally importantly, provide a link between theistic belief and actual political praxis.

Writers as diverse as Augustine, Calvin and Hegel and, closer to our own day, idealist thinkers such as T. H. Green have all situated their views about the nature of politics and Christian political responsibility within a general conception of history, and it is against this background that they were able to reason about the nature of the state, the role of political institutions and their scope and general place in human life as this is lived under God and his judgement. This is natural enough and possibly necessary once we understand the state and political societies as having a history and, therefore, being steeped in particularity. Two contemporary theologians who share this perspective, although operating from rather different theo-

---

[2] H. White, *Metahistory: The Historical Imagination in Nineteenth Century Europe*, Johns Hopkins University Press, Baltimore, 1973.

[3] F. Lyotard, *The Postmodern Condition* trans. G. Bennington and B. Massumi, Manchester University Press, 1984.

logical presuppositions, are John Cobb and Wolfhart Pannenberg. They see the need for a theology of history which will
undergird a political theology to be a basis for Christian
political practice although discussion will be reserved for the
next chapter. John Cobb argues as follows:

Concrete judgements responsibly directive of political practice cannot
derive from the memory of Jesus' passion even when one is informed
by the social sciences. The meaning of what is occurring in the world
can be derived only from an overview of what has happened in the
past and its significance for the present. From Augustine to Hegel and
Marx such overviews played a crucial role in shaping western thought
and specifically Christian theology. But in recent times they have
fallen into disrepute . . . But if we cannot engage in responsible
political practice without an historically informed view of what is
taking place, and if the views offered by others are not satisfactory,
then Christians, for the sake of political practice, should enter the field
recognising that they do so from their own perspective shaped by the
memory of Jesus. What we would then develop would be a theology of
history.[4]

Pannenberg makes a rather similar claim, having argued
that, for some of the reasons that were discussed in the previous
chapter, the Old Testament prophets were able to have an
engagement in the public world because the whole of Israel
shared a theology of history which gave a unity to life, particularly between religion and the public realm. However, this is
no longer the case. Nevertheless, Pannenberg seems to be
convinced that political praxis by Christians needs both a
political theology and a theology of history:

If we recognise the close association of revelation and history and try
to seek the Christ revelation in terms of its actual connexion with
world history, then we can live and act as Christians in our particular
historical situation without any break. We do not have to switch to
another system when we are concerned with the actual demands of
our historical circumstances and the decisions to be made within
them. The difficulty of Christian ethics today is that apparently we
have to act on two quite distinct levels, and must jump from that of
the Christian faith on to that appropriate to the factual situation, in
order to act at all . . . The reason for that kind of transition disappears

[4] J. Cobb, *Process Theology as Political Theology* Manchester University Press, 1982.

once we have understood the inner association of revelation and history. Even modern history, from which the situations of our present activity are derived is then encompassed by divine revelation.[5]

In the next chapter I shall say more about Pannenberg's conception of the nature of this process, but before doing that I want to give something of a thumbnail sketch of how history, politics and theology are related in the writings of some of the thinkers I have mentioned, namely Augustine, Calvin, and Hegel, partly to illustrate the general point that I am making, namely, the historical link that has existed between political theologies and theologies of history in the West, before going on to try to identify a series of questions which their thought provokes in relation to any contemporary understanding of a theological approach which will link together an understanding of history, politics and the Christian faith. In his book, John Cobb argues for the centrality of a theology of history for a theological approach to politics. However, I want to argue that it is very difficult to see how this could be achieved in the modern world. If it is both central to political theology and yet cannot be achieved, then obviously this poses a series of questions about the viability of political theology.

AUGUSTINE OF HIPPO

Augustine of Hippo (AD 354–430) is a vitally important figure in the development of political theology which he pursues largely through *De Civitate Dei*. Augustine developed to maturity within the Roman Empire following the acceptance of Christianity as the official religion of Rome by Constantine. The acceptance of Christianity by Constantine and carried forward by Theodosius was seen by some Christian thinkers as providential and, in a sense, the end and consummation of history. As Eusebius argues in *Tricennelia* xiv.4, the Empire accepted as its sacralising ideology the one true religion and this was providential: 'Together, as from one starting point, two great powers came forth

---

[5] W. Pannenberg, *Faith and Reality* Search Press, London, 1975, p. 89.

to civilise and unite the whole world, the monarchy of the
Roman Empire and the teaching of Christ.'[6]

Given that the Empire had a mission to unite the whole
human race under one form of authority which had Christian
sanction, the role of the Empire thus had a pivotal place in
converting the world to Christ.[7] Prudentius' 'Contra Orationem Symmachi' were directed at showing that the glories of
Rome could not be credited to the ancient Gods of Rome and
that the Christian God whom Rome had officially espoused
played his part in the success and peace of Rome:

> en ades, Omnipotens, concordibus influe terris:
> iam mundus te, Christe, capit, quem congrege nexu
> pax et Roma tenent. capita haec et culmina rerum
> esse iubes, nec Roma tibi sine pace probatur
> et pax ut placeat facit excellentia Romae
> quae motus varios simul et dicione coercet
> et terrore premit.[8]

[Come then Almighty; here is a world of harmony! do Thou enter it.
And earth receives Thee now O Christ which peace and Rome hold
in a bond of union. These thou commands to be the heads and the
highest powers in the world. Rome without peace finds no favour with
Thee; and it is the supremacy of Rome keeping down disorders by the
awe of her sovereignty that secures the peace so that thou hast
pleasure in it.]

And further:

> hanc frenaturus rabiem Deus undique gentes
> inclinare caput docuit sub legibus isdem
> Romanosque omnes fieri, quos Rhenus et Hister
> quos Tagus aurifluus, quos magnus inundat Hiberus
> corniger Hesperidum quos interlabitur et quos
> Ganges alit tepidique lavant septem ostia Nili
> ius fecit commune pares et nomine eodem
> nexuit et domitos fraterna in vincla redegit.[9]

---

[6] Eusebius, *Triakontaeterikos (Tricennelia)* ed. I. A. Heikel, *Eusebius Werke*, J. C. Hinrichs,
xiv.4, see H. A. Drake trans., *In Praise of Constantine* University of California Press, Los
Angeles, 1967.
[7] Eusebius, ibid. xvi.6.
[8] Prudentius 'Contra Orationem Symmachi' in *Prudentius* vol. 2, Harvard University
Press, Cambridge, Mass., 199, lines 635–40.
[9] Ibid. lines 602–609.

[To curb this frenzy God taught the nations everywhere to bow their heads under the same laws and become Romans – all whom Rhine and Danube flood or Tagus with its golden sheen or great Ebro, those through whose lands glides the horned river of the western world, those who are nurtured by the Ganges or washed by the warm Nile's seven mouths. A common law made them equals and bound them by a single name, bringing them by a conquest into the bonds of brotherhood.]

Equally, the link between the function of the Empire and the role of God in history could hardly have been put more starkly by Cosmas Indicopleustes when he argued that:

While Christ was still in the womb the Roman Empire received its authority from God as the agent of the dispensation which Christ introduced, since at that very time began the never-ending line of the successors to Augustus. The Empire of the Romans thus participated in the majesty of the Kingdom of Christ, for it transcends, so far as any earthly realm can, every other power; and it will remain unconquered until the final consummation.[10]

The link between the universal and the particular – God/Christ with the Roman Empire – with a theology of history could hardly be more close. God became incarnate during the Roman Empire and that Empire (which was crucial to the achievement in Christ's atoning work in the crucifixion) then becomes, transcendentally, the instrument whereby the whole world is redeemed by the message of Christ. In this sense, as Markus argues, the *tempora Christiana* have become a distinct phase in the history not only of the Roman Empire, but of salvation.[11] In his early development, Augustine accepted a good deal of this, as Peter Brown makes clear in his biography *Augustine of Hippo* as does R. Markus in *Saeculum*. Brown argues that, at this stage of his life, Augustine

'felt that he lived at a long foretold turning point of history' . . . Reading his Bible, Augustine had come to see the events around him as part of a divinely inspired process, foretold a thousand years before, by David in the *Psalms* and by the Prophets of Israel. The Catholic

---

[10] Cosmas Indicopleustes, *Christian Topography* published as *Topographie Chrétienne* ed. Wolska, Canus, Editions du Cerf, Paris, 1968–73 vol. 2, p. 74.

[11] R. Markus, *Saeculum: History and Society in the Theology St Augustine* Cambridge University Press, 1970, p. 31.

Church had spread throughout the world 'it is written; it has come true'.[12]

This linking of Rome and its empire with salvation history central to Eusebius, Prudentius and Cosmas Indicopleustes and echoed at this earlier stage by Augustine also allowed Augustine to adopt a recognisably classical view of the role of politics and the state. Plato and Aristotle had taught, albeit in different ways, that the state was the vehicle for human fulfilment,[13] the association within which the human *telos* could be attained. The link between Rome and Christian hope was, for Augustine, a centrally important aspect of his early view of the role of politics which was heavily influenced by his still significant commitment to Neoplatonism in its Plotinian form. This classical view of the role of politics, as Markus has argued, contrasts rather sharply with the Judaeo-Christian view. On this view, the problem of political arrangement was not first to sort out the natural moral order and then track it in social arrangements. Rather, as Markus says: 'Only God's saving act could establish the right social order.'[14] The link between Rome and the flourishing of Christianity did not, at this stage, lead Augustine towards the more Judaeo-Christian view. If the Roman Empire could facilitate the Christian life, then politics could be seen still as central to human fulfilment on the classical model.

This confidence in the theology was, however, misplaced because, *contra* to Cosmas Indicopleustes' assumption, the Roman Empire did not 'remain unconquered until the final consummation'. By 406, the Western Provinces of the Roman Empire were under attack by barbarians, and Rome itself was sacked by the Goths in 410. At such a juncture, many Romans reacted against Christianity and blamed the fate of Rome on its betrayal of its religious traditions. These historical contingencies completely upset the optimistic theology of Eusebius and Cosmas, and Augustine tries to show in *De Civitate Dei* how a Christian thinker could respond to such a drastic reversal in

---

[12] P. Brown, *Augustine of Hippo: A Biography* Faber and Faber, London, 1967.
[13] See J. M. Rist, *Augustine: Ancient Thought Baptised* Cambridge University Press, 1994, p. 205.
[14] Markus *Saeculum* p. 74.

what was lately celebrated as part of God's plan in history which is the theology of Eusebius or the poetry of Prudentius. In the light of these events, Augustine struggled to articulate a new theology of history which would not be such a force for Christian triumphalism in the secular world, and which led to a greater subtlety in his account of the relationship between the role of politics and institutions in God's action in history, and a rejection of the idea that Christian belief could play a role in sacralising a particular form of political power.

In doing so, his thought moved away from a classical account of the role of the *polis* in human fulfilment to one in which the Christian attitude to the state is to be seen as much more ambiguous. In Augustine's mind, a growing awareness of political instability goes hand in hand with the development of theological and philosophical reasons for shifting his views on the relationship between the individual and society.[15]

Augustine's reading and meditating on St Paul in the mid 390s[16] played a crucial role in changing his conception of politics from a Neoplatonist and teleological one to one with the emphasis on the more tragic character of social life, the fallenness of human nature, the inability of human beings to bring harmony to their own lives except by the grace of God. The earthly city is no longer the school for virtue as it was for Plato and Aristotle, but rather virtue must 'be sought in the teeth of the works and ideas of a secular society'.[17]

The earthly city is one in which each group pursues its own interests and the gratification of its desires and in which men have conflicting aims. Political authority is necessary because of man's corrupted nature, but his nature cannot be redeemed by politics. As Markus says:

In Augustine's mature thought there is no trace of a theory of the state as concerned with man's fulfilment, perfection, the good life, felicity or with educating man towards such purposes. Its function is more restricted: it is to cancel out at least some of the effects of sin.[18]

Augustine sees the *Civitas Dei* and the *Civitas Terrena* as

---

[15] Rist, *Augustine* p. 205.   [16] See Markus *Saeculum* p. 81.
[17] See Rist *Augustine* p. 225.   [18] Markus, *Saeculum* p. 95.

characterised by orientation towards two different values.[19] The *Civitas Dei* develops by purity of heart and a love of the good which can come only by the grace of God; *Civitas Terrena* is characterised by the *libido dominandi*, the selfish love which produces both the need for and the tension within the *Civitas Terrena*. Of course, this side of the *eschaton* the two loves and the two cities are inextricably intertwined.[20] At times Augustine wavers somewhat in his assessment of the relative importance of the particular form that political authority has in the life of the Christian. He says

What does it matter under whose rule a man lives, being so soon to die, provided that the rulers do not force him to do impious and wicked acts? Did the Romans do any harm to other nations when they subdued them and imposed Roman law, apart from the vast slaughter of the wars?[21]

Having set out a broad sketch of Augustine's changing vision on the appropriate Christian approach to political theory, it is important to look now at the role of history in his theology to see how this plays a role in the development of such a theory. In this context, I want to stress the centrality of the role of a theology of history as I have defined it. As Gilkey says: 'With Augustine . . . the question of the meaning of the sequence of history's events poses itself as a central theological problem both with regard to the events of an individual's own life and with regard to the events that constitute history as a whole'.[22]

The first of these, how God relates to the life and history of the individual, is, broadly speaking, the subject-matter of *The Confessions*; the latter, about the nature of God's relationship to history as a whole, again broadly speaking, is the subject-matter of *De Civitate Dei*. Despite the great interest of the former, I shall be concerned mainly with the latter, since the aim of these few remarks is to see how Augustine linked his view of the nature of

[19] Augustine, *De Civitate Dei* trans. as *The City of God* by D. Knowles, Penguin, Harmondsworth, 1972, Book xiv, ch. 28.
[20] Ibid., Book xix, ch. 17.
[21] Ibid. Book v, chap. 17 cf Book xix, ch. 19.
[22] L. Gilkey, *Reaping the Whirlwind; A Christian Interpretation of History* Seabury Press, New York, 1976, p. 165.

God and his purposes for human beings to an account of political society within the structure of divine providence.

There are a number of general principles which inform Augustine's approach to this problem. First of all, he sees God as the sovereign of history and, specifically, that history in its detail has to be seen against the background of eschatology or God's ultimate purposes. God's sovereignty, furthermore, has to be seen not just in relation to acts like particular divine interventions such as miracles, or what some modern evangelical theologians call 'God's mighty works', but also as a sovereignty which acts in and through the normal course of historical events and the lives of individuals as historical actors. Further, this means that God does not act as a cause in history alongside other causes of historical events, but rather in and through those events themselves. This is so in regard not just to Christian history, and in particular in relation to the Roman Empire, but, as Augustine points out in Book v, chapter 21 of *De Civitate Dei*, God had done the same for the Assyrians and Persians. As Peter Hodgson says: 'God gives power to emperors both good and bad, who serve the divine purpose without knowing it, such is the cunning of divine providence.'[23]

Finally, providence works through and not against or contrary to human freedom, through human voluntary acts, even acts that are sinful. Indeed, providence is, in a sense, made necessary by human sinfulness, otherwise the eschatological aim of God would be impossible for humans to advance. It is certainly true that the sinful acts of men in history, following the passions of their fallen nature, may obscure the working of providence, so that to a degree it is hidden, but, as I have said for Augustine, the operation of divine providence means that human history as the morally ambiguous or morally dubious acts of men actually furthers the eschatological aims of God. It also follows from this, for Augustine, that human life is governed neither by fate nor by chance; rather, history, under the sovereignty of God, moves towards the realisation of human

---

[23] P. Hodgson, *God in History: Shapes of Freedom* Abingdon Press, Nashville Tenn., 1986, p. 17. I am indebted to Hodgson for many insights used in this chapter.

powers as these are understood from a Christian point of view. However, and this is very important for Augustine, the *eschaton* is beyond history; that is to say, the Kingdom of God is not to be understood as consummation or redemption in the historical process as such, and not in the world of the Roman Empire *pace* Eusebius and Prudentius. Rather, providence works so that the secular world of political institutions and their history nurtures the circumstances within which divine grace can operate within individual lives. In this sense, the historical process under providence fulfils or at least serves a trans-historical goal. This goal is served in the world within particular political societies, in the church as a community in which people can experience grace, come to serve God and achieve their goal as God has ordained it for them. So the work of providence within history is directed towards sustaining the church within which people come to experience grace. The church, so to speak, prefigures the Kingdom of God within the world, but it is not the consummation of that kingdom because, as he points out in Book xx, the church is full of wheat and tares and itself stands under the judgement of God. Human beings are free, and people cannot be coerced into salvation, but, on the other hand, human freedom, in the fallen state is too enmeshed in sin for individuals to attain their fulfilment in the terms that God defines for them. Providence, in the historical process, nurtures the church as the one institution through which people can receive the grace to prepare themselves for this fulfilment. In this sense, therefore, God's action in history is to operate through the willing of individuals and the historical circumstances in which this willing takes place so that salvation can be attained through acts which would otherwise be self-destructive and sinful. The worldly city, the basis of the historical process, is warped by sin, by self-seeking and by coercion, and as the result of this wars and revolution follow of necessity; nevertheless at both the level of the individual, as he argues in *The Confessions*, and at the level of social institutions, as he argues in *De Civitate Dei*, God uses these warped and sinful actions and motives to provide a space for an intimation of the *Civitas Dei* in the church and in the lives, through grace, which Christian people live in this intimation of the true *Civitas Dei* which is the Kingdom of God.[24] So it follows, as Gilkey argues, that:

> The highest possibility for history's communities is a relative order based on self love, one possibly softened by Christian ruler and Christian subjects, the goal of history is not a developing order of communal life that might in its own character approach the eschatological goal of real love and real order. For Augustine no earthly order stands at the end of history.[25]

What matters for Augustine about the worldly order is that it provides a framework within which the church can exist and flourish as a human space in which grace can grow as an intimation of the real *Civitas Dei*, as he says:

> it is important for us also that this people should possess this peace in this life, since, so long as the two cities are intermingled we also make use of the peace of Babylon, so that in the meantime they are only pilgrims in the midst of her. That is why the Apostle instructs the Church to pray for kings of that city and those in high positions, adding these words: 'that we may ever lead a quiet and peaceful life with all devotion and love'.[26]

This peace, he says, is both providential and 'affords a solace for our wretchedness'. Thus the sovereignty of God in history is a response to man's fallen state, enabling the historical process to provide this kind of condition which will allow the *eschaton* to be achieved. History is only instrumental in that work, and the *eschaton* is not achieved within history, but beyond it; nevertheless, history and human institutions have a rational structure through the action of providence which will allow this to be achieved. Political institutions, or the earthly city, have the providential function of providing the basis for peace and a degree of justice attained between clashing wills and interests, and within this type of civil order the church can exist as a vehicle for worship, discipline and the growth of religious discipleship. The Christian can, therefore, have a rational and instrumental attitude to such political institutions. The church is universal, in the service of a universal God, as the following

---

[24] See Markus, *Saeculum* p. 174.
[25] Gilkey, *Reaping the Whirlwind* p. 168.
[26] Augustine, *De Civitate Dei* Book XIX, ch. 17.

passage makes clear, but, given that specific societies exist to provide a framework within which good can be pursued, the church can reasonably see the point of such institutions:

While the Heavenly City, therefore, is a pilgrimage in this world, she calls out citizens from all nations and so collects a society of aliens, speaking all languages. She takes no account of any difference in customs, laws and institutions by which earthly peace is achieved and preserved – not that she annuls or abolishes any of these rather, she maintains them and follows them (for whatever divergences there are among the diverse nations, these institutions have one simple aim – earthly peace), provided that no hindrance is presented thereby to the religion which teaches that the one supreme God is to be worshipped.[27]

Hence, Augustine has a theology of history which allows him to deal sometimes in some detail with the nature of particular historical events, as I have suggested in the case of the Assyrians, and allows him to make some kind of judgements about the nature and function of political institutions and their role in human life according to his idea of the kind of flourishing which God has ordained for man. This leads him to argue that no Christian holds an absolute sense of allegiance to the *Civitas Terrena*, because human beings have a higher good to achieve than that which can be achieved in the earthly city; but he does have an allegiance in so far as the form of civil peace allows the church to fulfil its ministry and providential role. In Book XIX, Augustine defends peace as 'those things essential for mortal life'. Markus sums up Augustine's position as follows: 'Augustine thus came to see secular societies as intermediate provisions, forms of social organisation within which the "heavenly city" transcending them all, was temporarily contained while on the pilgrimage to its final goal.'[28]

The City of God, in which only true peace can be found, is a universal society which overcomes all limited forms of association. In chapter 19, Augustine defines a commonwealth as 'A gathering of a multitude of rational beings united in fellowship

---

[27] Ibid. Book XIX, ch. 19.
[28] R. Markus, 'The Latin Fathers' in *The Cambridge History of Medieval Political Thought 350–1450* ed. J. H. Burns, Cambridge University Press, 1988, p. 107.

by sharing a common love of the same things.' The Christian community is united as a *Civitas Dei* by their common love of God. Hence Augustine's theology of history enables him to provide both an account of the rational structure of history and the purposes of human society, but it also enables him to relativise all human institutions. For him, no human institution can be deified and no human institution can demand unconditional obedience. As Markus says: 'The very terms of Augustine's critique of the sacralisation of the Roman Empire implied a protest against the readiness to see within any society the ultimate eschatological conflict prematurely revealed in visible identifiable form. All we can know is that the two cities are present in any historical society.'[29] Because of the inextricable link between the two cities in any historical circumstances, it is impossible to identify finally the boundaries of either, and all Christian political orientations must be aware of the deep-seated ambiguity – the result of operating *in tenebris socialis vitae.*

So, how are we to sum up Augustine's political theology and its relationship to history and indeed to the theology of history? Perhaps the first thing to stress is the centrality of history in *De Civitate Dei* and to Augustine's mature thought generally. Rüdiger Bittner has argued for the view that, for Augustine, history is critical to the knowledge of God:

According to *De Vera Religione* 7.13 the chief part to take in the Christian religion is the 'narrative (*historia*) and prophecy of the temporal dispensations of divine providence for the salvation of mankind'. Just because the dispensations of divine providence for the salvation of mankind are temporal, it takes *historia*, a narrative of things past, and prophecy, a narrative of things to come, to represent them.[30]

This is, at least in part, at the basis of Augustine's critique of the role of philosophy in religion. Philosophical rationality is abstract and timeless, but the basic events of the Christian faith take place in time and the only way to grasp what takes place in time is by narrative and by stories (*De Civitate Dei*, Book II, ch.

---

[29] Markus, *Saeculum* p. 101.
[30] R. Bittner, 'Augustine's Philosophy of History' in *The Augustinian Tradition* ed. G. Matheus, University of California Press, Berkeley, Calif. 1999, p. 345.

7). So a full conception of the nature of Christian truth requires not just general, timeless philosophical truths, but also the historical and the contingent:[31] temporalia praeterita et futura quae pro salute hominum gessit et gestura est aeternitas divinae providentiae. (*De Agone Christiniano* 13.15). So: temporaliter gestum est et scientiam pertinet quae conditione historica continentur (*De Trinitate* XIII 1.2).

So there is this limitation on Platonism on the scope of abstract, timeless truths – a central theme of Book VIII of *De Civitate Dei* and an emphasis upon narrative and the historical in a full account of theological truth. Alongside this in his mature thought is also the rejection of the idea of a natural law or natural order in at least one central understanding of it. For Augustine, the natural law does indeed apply to the physical world of nature, but it does not apply directly to the world of human will. So it is not as if political and moral understanding could somehow track an understanding of a natural and objective reality outside itself. Human law, despite some of these views in his early thought, does not 'track' eternal law which can be known by reason and is written in the heart of man. On such a view, positive law specific to time, place and circumstance must be derived from the eternal law if human beings were to achieve the perfection of their nature (*De Libero Arbitrio*). So in these writings, to be valid, positive law has to be derived from eternal law because it embodies an order which, if we follow it in our lives, will lead to God (*De Ordine*). However, by about AD 390, his views on these themes have begun to change. Markus argues that from *De Vera Religione* there is no basis for thinking that Augustine's view was that valid human law must be derived from eternal law.[32] The role of the law becomes less a positive contributor to the perfection of humanity and much more to deal with externalities: public order, security and property. This shift is crucially important for political theology not just in Augustine, but subsequently. For Augustine, as Rist makes clear, by 'natural order' means 'only the order which we find in the physical world'.[33] Now the

---

[31] Ibid. p. 346.   [32] Markus, *Saeculum* p. 89.
[33] Rist, *Augustine* pp. 214ff.

eternal law is seen as the will of God and it does not prescribe human laws, rather, as Rist says, it is a pattern against which human legislation can be checked.[34] However, for public authorities as opposed to private individuals, this process is ambiguous and unclear because of the shadows of darkness which cloud human society. Judgement in civic life is unavoidable yet:

> In view of this darkness that attends the life of human society, will our wise man take his seat on the judges' bench, or will he not have the heart to do so? Obviously, he will sit; for the claims of human society constrain him and draw him to this duty; and it is unthinkable that he should shirk it.[35]

This is very important for, as Markus argues, it means, as Augustine argues in *Contra Faustum*, that the idea of eternal law has two dimensions: the natural world and the world of will. This change of emphasis links political theology and history in a decisive way:

> The earlier assimilation of all order, human social, political, to a single cosmic order which manifested the external law is decisively rejected. Such order as there is in human affairs, in the societies of man, their arrangements and their historical careers, is no longer part of a cosmic natural order.[36]

Hence the history, the narratives of how providence works in this realm of will, uncertainty and fragility, is essential to Augustine's political thought. Politics is no longer about tracking the cosmic order necessary for human perfection; it is about the much more contingent, but nevertheless intelligible, historical circumstances under which particular societies are able to secure a degree of social and political order *in tenebris socialis vitae*.

This means also a rejection of the classical idea of politics as providing for the fulfilment of human nature and human purposes. This requires that government to be legitimate must fulfil a particular view of the good, rooted in the character of human life and human purpose. Augustine, however, came to

---

[34] Ibid.
[35] Augustine, *De Civitate Dei* Book xx, ch. 6.
[36] Markus, *Saeculum* p. 91.

take a more modest view of what constituted the political. Obviously we need some account of what makes politics what it is. As he asks: remove justice, and what are kingdoms but gangs of criminals on a large scale? What are criminal gangs but petty kingdoms?

The crucial point, though, is to do with justice. If justice is defined in a rich sense of righteousness in a Christian context, then no state will ever be more than a band of robbers since the achievement of righteousness as part of perfection is part of the heavenly kingdom not the earthly city (*De Civitate Dei* xix, ch. 23) . If a commonwealth depends upon a common sense of righteousness in the full biblical sense, then there can be no commonwealth in the *civitas terrena*. In the next chapter of *De Civitate Dei*, however, Augustine adopts a more modest and, to speak anachronistically, more neutral conception of the political when he says: 'A people is an association of a multitude of rational beings united by common agreement on the objects of their love.'[37] So a 'state' exists where there is a coherent set of interests shared by its members and, while it is possible to judge and question the moral value of such interests, these judgements are irrelevant to the question of whether or not a state exists. However, there will be some common purposes for, as Augustine argues, earthly peace and security are common interests of all:

the earthly city, whose life is not based on faith, aims at earthly peace, and it limits the harmonious agreement of citizens concerning the giving and obeying of orders to the establishment of a kind of compromise between human wills about the things relevant to mortal life.[38]

Christians who are part of the heavenly city and have ultimate purposes that transcend earthly peace and order and the facilitation of private purposes also share in this more united common aim and do not 'hesitate to obey the laws of the earthly city by which those things which were designed for the support of this mortal life are regulated'.

---

[37] Augustine, *De Civitate Dei* Book xix, ch. 24.
[38] Ibid.

In the final chapter of his *Saeculum*, Markus points out that Augustine's version of social life, and indeed the history of human societies which is part of understanding God's providence, springs from a sense of the conflicting purposes, the uncertainties and tensions of society coupled with the fact that political judgement has to occur in a shadowy and ambiguous moral context. He describes Augustine's conception of politics as neutral and pluralist[39] excluding ultimate commitments and allegiances from the sphere of political interests. This version he links to a modern version in Karl Barth's *The Christian Community and the Civil Community* which was quoted in the first chapter. While liberal is not the most obvious word to come to mind when looking at Augustine's theology, there is a case, anachronistic to be sure, that could lead one to say that Augustine gave a theological defence of a liberal and pluralist state, and situated this within a developed account of a theology of history and one which conforms to Barth's dictum that: 'It belongs to the very nature of the state that it is not and cannot become the kingdom of God.'[40]

CALVIN

Ernst Troeltsch says the following about Calvinism:

After a period of initial success Lutheranism failed to advance. This must be attributed, in the main, to its stress on personal piety, its acceptance of the existing situation, its acquiescence in the objectivity of the means of grace, as well as its lack of capacity for ecclesiastical organisation, and its non-political outlook. It was the destiny of Calvinism to extend the Reformation of the Church throughout Western Europe, and thence out into the New World . . . The primary reason for this widespread expansion of Calvinism was the fact that it gained a footing among Western nations at a time when they were passing through a great process of political development. There is, however, a deeper reason, and one which lies within the essence of Calvinism itself, which explains why it almost or entirely crowded out the rudimentary beginnings of Lutheranism and of the

---

[39] Markus, *Saeculum* p. 178. For a vigorous critique of this view cf. J. Milbank, *Theology and Social Theory* Blackwell, Oxford, 1990, p. 400ff.

[40] Barth, 'The Christian Community and the Civil Community' p. 280.

Anabaptist movement, which were also present in those lands. This deeper reason lies in the active character of Calvinism, in its power for forming churches, in its international contacts, and its conscious impulse towards expansion, and, most of all, in its capacity to penetrate the political and economic movements of Western nations with its religious ideal, a capacity which Lutheranism lacked from the beginning.[41]

Of course, Troeltsch is capturing a common view in this passage, one which was best studied by Max Weber in *The Protestant Ethic and The Spirit of Capitalism*. There is no doubt that Calvin had an articulated political theology as set out particularly in the section of *The Institutes of the Christian Religion*[42] on 'Christian Freedom, Ecclesiastical Power and Political Administration', and certainly specific ideas within Calvinism, particularly on the idea of calling and his claim in *The Institutes* that 'we should use God's gifts for the use for which he gave them to us, with no scruple of conscience no trouble of mind. With such confidence our souls will be at peace with him, and we will recognise his liberality towards us.'[43] The lawful use of God's gifts in Calvin's view is entirely morally legitimate. This doctrine, particularly in the context of wealth, had enormous political implications: 'Thus let every man live in his station whether slenderly or moderately or plentifully, so that all may remember God nourishes them to live, not to luxuriate.'[44] But again I believe that Calvin's political theology utilises a conception of the role of God in history. This may seem a paradoxical claim, since Calvin's theology was anchored in the awful decree (Calvin's own words) of divine election, whereby God predestines some to salvation and some to damnation. For Calvin, because of sin we are all 'Children of God's wrath' and we cannot seek in ourselves his righteousness. God is free to bestow grace on all he chooses irrespective of human merit. If salvation is predestined, then in what sense, for Calvin, can there be such

[41] E. Troeltsch, *The Social Teachings of the Christian Churches* trans. O. Wyon, 2 vols. George Allen and Unwin, London, 1931, p. 576.
[42] J. Calvin, *Institutes of the Christian Religion* 1536 edition, trans. F. L. Battles, Collins, London, 1986. M. Weber, *The Protestant Ethic and The Spirit of Capitalism* George Allen and Unwin, London, 1930.
[43] Ibid. p. 180.   [44] Ibid. p. 181.

a thing as salvation history, because it is in history that human merits and deserts are obtained and are thus indifferent from the point of view of salvation when this is understood as predestination? We must recognise that our salvation consists in God's mercy alone, but not in any worth of ours, or in anything coming from us. It might be thought, therefore, that, while Calvin does have a political theology, this must be deduced from his doctrine of God rather than being mediated through some account of history as salvation history.

However, I think, as both Hodgson and Gilkey have argued in their books that I have mentioned, that this would be a mistake in that the idea of election or predestination does not exclude the idea of providence. Calvin argues that Scripture teaches that 'All events are governed by God's secret plan and not by chance or human agency acting independently of such a plan', and furthermore that this providence is not some kind of passive sort as he argues some Stoic thinkers believed, but rather is engaged, as he says, in 'ceaseless activity'. Events have a meaning and this meaning is to a large extent concealed in God's secret plan. This issue is largely one of perception. While God actively orders everything according to his purposes, yet individual events will seem to us to be fortuitous (XVI 9) in the sense that the reason and necessity behind such events is hidden from us. He uses quite a potent analogy here in Book XVII: our eyes are blinded and our ears deafened in a storm, but above the storm clouds, serenity reigns. This complexity in providence is linked to the many sidedness (Ephesians 3.10) of God's wisdom. This providence is not just general, somehow oper-ating at a macro-level, but is as he says a 'special providence'. As Gilkey argues for Calvin:

all that happens to us and all that occurs in us is under God's control and is directed to his purposes. However difficult or calamitous events may seem to us they have for faith an ultimate if presently hidden meaning. That is to say, despite their apparent chaos they lead in the end to our salvation for that – if we do have faith and so are certain of our election – is God's will for us. Calvin gives a nice example of how seriously he takes the doctrine of providence in history. If God had not ordained the intentions of Judas in betraying Jesus, then this betrayal would have been contingent and thus the necessary work of redemption through the passion, death and resurrection of Christ would have depended on 'God's good fortune'.[45]

Indeed, the idea of providence and history as the sphere within which God's providence is revealed is central to Calvin's idea of God as the Creator. This is made clear in chapter xvi of the *Institutes* where we see that he rejects the idea of God as momentary creator which in his view can only be the opinion of unbelievers. Rather, as the title of the chapter makes clear, 'By His Power God Cherishes and Guards the World which he made and by his Providence Rules Its Indivdual Parts'. Calvin takes the idea of God's providential action in nature and history to be central to an understanding of the creative nature of God: 'Unless we go further, to his Providence, we have not yet really grasped what it means that God is the Creator' (*Institutes* xvi.i).

This doctrine obviously stands in great tension with his account of human freedom which figures large in the *Institutes*, and this is a tension which I cannot try to resolve here. However, again Gilkey, it seems to me, has developed Calvin's doctrine here, however obscure we may find it, namely, that human voluntary action consists in willing, or perhaps better internalising, what it is in fact ordained that man will do. The doctrine also seems to imply a further problem with which Calvin grapples in the *Institutes*, namely, that it looks as though God has ordained evil, too, and a just God cannot punish men for what he has himself ordained. However, this issue to which he has several rather unconvincing answers is not central to my theme of the connexion between Calvin's idea of God, his conception of history and his account of politics.

The link lies in the fact that history has a meaning as part of both general and particular providence, and salvation is its goal; and it follows from this that the sanctification of men does not imply a strategy of withdrawal from a morally indeterminate world full of chance (indeed, Calvin quotes with approval Basil of Caesarea to the effect that fortune and chance are heathen words) and ambiguity into a private world of piety;

---

[45] Gilkey, *Reaping the Whirlwind* p. 176.

rather, the believer with confidence arising from faith in his election can act with confidence in historical and social events which are part of God's providence. In acting in the social and political world, governed as that is in the end by God's providence, believers are acting to bring that world itself into a new relationship with God. Since, however, it is believers who are saved, this relativises obedience to the state because, while he does believe that political organisation is necessary, the state cannot ultimately justify unconditional obedience since 'our consciences have to do not with men but with God alone'. The example that he gives is that of Daniel who denies that he has committed any offence against King Darius when he has not obeyed his 'impious edict'. For Calvin, the king had exceeded his limits, and had not merely been a wrongdoer against men, but in 'lifting up his horns against God he had himself abrogated his power.'[46] This point is reiterated in his *Commentary on the Acts of The Apostles* as Quentin Skinner has pointed out: 'It is better to obey God, rather than man'[47] and if a king or a prince or a magistrate conducts himself in such a way as to diminish the honour and right of God, he becomes nothing more than an ordinary man.

The doctrine of election and the role of providence in history also go to underpin Calvin's account of individualism. These two doctrines give an enormous confidence to the believer to act on his own conscience, given, as Gilkey argues, a tremendous confidence to go into the world to 'remould it to God's glory'. The idea of election and the confidence that God was at work in the historical process gave a degree of serenity to the individual, so that whatever might befall him in his station he could have ultimate confidence in his victory over the world. Gilkey puts the point better than I can:

Grounded in the eternal divine will, critical of the given forces of the world, empowered to transformative activity in that world and invulnerable to its hazards, these were individuals with immense inner

---

[46] For a stringent view of this, see *Institutes* pp. 225–6.

[47] Q. Skinner, *The Foundations of Modern Political Thought* vol. 2, Cambridge University Press, 1978, p. 220.

authority, power and energy, subordinate to nothing on earth, and threatened with no earthly calamity.[48]

Little wonder, therefore, that individuals empowered in this way could achieve for Calvinism what Troeltsch said they achieved.

Again, therefore, it is arguable that a rather skeletal theology of history acted as a kind of mediating link in Calvin's thought between an account of the nature of God and an account of the political sphere and the role of the individual within it. Calvin's political theology is situated in this kind of context. He drew from his experience in Bucer's Strasbourg[49] in developing his political thought. Bucer had argued that the situation for Christian thinking about politics was rather different in the sixteenth century from that in New Testament times. At that stage, political institutions were non-Christian. However, now, civil authorities can be seen as part of God's agency: 'when he had converted the authorities, he wished them truly to serve him with their office and power, which derives from him and is connected to them only for the good of Christ's flock'. Political authority is essential, and the aims and legitimacy of political authority are linked to Christian purposes as Torrance argues: 'to foster and maintain the external worship of God, to defend sound doctrine and the Church, to adapt and convert to human society, to form our manners to civil justice, to reconcile us to one another, to cherish peace and common tranquillity'.[50] Both civil and political power were to be used to promote virtue: in civil authority ultimately by coercion; and in the ecclesiastical by means of its teaching office. They differ in the means they are to use and, indeed, importantly in the breadth and depth of their moral base.

Unlike in the times of the prophets and kings of the Old Testament, by Calvin's time, as he argues, God's agents do not receive his word directly from God's lips, and thus the moral basis of action by both civil and ecclesiatical power is to be

---

[48] Gilkey, *Reaping the Whirlwind* p. 176.

[49] See A. McGrath, *Reformation Thought* Blackwell, Oxford, 1988, p. 150 citing also W. P. Stephens, *The Holy Spirit in the Theology of Martin Bucer*, Cambridge University Press, 1970 and T. F. Torrance, *Kingdom and Church: A Study in the Theology of the Reformation* T. and J. Clark, Edinburgh, 1956.

[50] Torrance, *Kingdom and Church* cited in McGrath, *Reformation Thought* p. 152.

found in Scripture and natural law. The civil power has wider discretion since they can frame laws within the limits of natural law; whereas ecclesiastical authorities are bound by the deliverances of Scripture. It has to be said, however, as Höpfl has argued,[51] that, while the natural law does play a central role in Calvin's moral theology, it is made subordinate to Scripture, and, indeed, as Calvin's life went on he tried more and more to produce scriptural warrant for quite detailed positive laws and rules about which natural law was too general to pronounce.[52] So, to what extent did the moral superiority of Scripture over natural law promote a case for theocracy? Certainly, as Höpfl has argued, if by theocracy is meant government in accordance with the will of God, then Calvin was a theocrat. If theocracy means that the authority of the civil power derives from God rather than the consent of the ruled, then he was a theocrat (and one who, given his doctrine of providence and history, saw the hand of God in the rise and fall of princes and governments). Finally if theocracy means rule according to biblical injunction not constrained by tradition, reason or natural law, then there is a good case, as we have seen, for regarding Calvin as a theocrat, since, although the civil power has to govern within the parameters of natural law, the natural law was subordinate to Scripture for its interpretation and thus to the ministry rather than the civil power.[53] Thus natural law had to be constrained by biblical narrative.

Although, as McGrath has argued, in practice in Geneva the magistracy was able frequently to weaken the power of the ministry and thus lessen the degree of theocracy, nevertheless, in terms of Calvin's political theory, it is difficult to see it other than as theocratic.

These views about the nature of history which we have been considering obviously came under attack during the period of the Enlightenment, particularly as the rise of science began to displace the idea of teleological explanation in the natural world. A good many theologies of history during the pre-

[51] H. Höpfl, *The Christian Polity of John Calvin* Cambridge University Press, 1985, pp. 179–84.
[52] Ibid.   [53] Ibid.

Enlightenment period did not draw a sharp distinction between God's action in history and his action in the natural world – both are the work of creation and both are characterised by a theistically based account of teleology. This is shown in a particularly quaint way in Augustine's preoccupation with freaks of nature in *De Civitate Dei*. If, however, the basis for understanding the natural world changes from a teleological to a mechanistic one, then this is going to have profound implications for an account of the historical world and the world of social institutions including politics. One strategy to be adopted in this context would be a retreat from a theology of the public world based, in turn, upon a theology of history and a move towards a more private view of the nature of religious belief. In Peter Hodgson's and J. B. Metz's view this is precisely what happened as a result of the influence of the Enlightenment, and there was such a retreat into a private account of religion and many theologians avoided working with historical categories. Hodgson gives Schleiermacher as a good example of this, so that, as a result of his work, dogmatic theology and historical theology became separated, the former becoming confessional dogmatics, interpreting the faith of the church, the latter becoming a descriptive discipline; but neither really addressed the problem of political theology in the context of the role of political institutions within an historical process. The major thinker who challenged this retreat into privatism, having been brought up in a pietist context himself, was Hegel.

HEGEL

I want now to turn to Hegel and to the link that he sees between God and history and the role of politics within the historical process. At the heart of Hegel's account is a challenge to what might be called the classical view of God. Hegel argued that the classical theist conception of God is defective because he finds it very difficult to explain creation if we accept the view that God is as he is usually assumed to be within classical theism, namely, changeless, fully complete, the *actus purus*, that he is simple, without body, parts and passion, as *The*

Book of Common Prayer has it. On this view, God is completely independent of the world, but the world is utterly dependent on God. In Hegel's view, this makes it impossible to understand in general terms the nature of creation because, as he says in his inimitable fashion: 'If God is all sufficient and lacks nothing, why does he declare himself in the sheer other of himself?'[54] If God is as he is understood within classical theism, it makes creation appear whimsical on the part of God. If God is fully perfect and complete, then he can have no intention, no purpose, no desire that he needs creation to fulfil. If, however, one sees creation as something within which God acts, including the realms of human history and human institutions, then, in Hegel's view, this conception of God needs to be modified. The point could be put in another way, as it has by Peter Hodgson when he argues that, under the circumstances of classical theism, it is very 'difficult to grasp how distinguishable acts such as creation, redemption and sanctification could be predicated of God.'[55] This kind of reflection led Hegel to the view that, if we are to have a theology of history as part of creation, and an account of the nature of human institutions within the historical process, then we have to revise our concept of God. As he argued, notoriously, in the *Lectures on The Philosophy Of Religion*, 'Without the world, God is not God.'[56] If a political theology relating to the nature of social and political institutions depends on a general theological understanding of history, then, in Hegel's view, this is going to require us to reflect on the nature of the idea of God which will allow us to have such a general approach to history. It is not the case, for Hegel, that we can think about human society and human history within which societies develop from a theistic perspective without radically altering our idea of God. Colletti, the Italian philosopher, argues that, for Hegel, human institutions

---

[54] G. W. F. Hegel, *Philosophy of Nature* vol. 1 trans. M. J. Petry, George Allen and Unwin, London, 1970, p. 205.
[55] Hodgson, *God and History* p. 53.
[56] G. W. F. Hegel, *Lectures on the Philosophy of Religion* vol. 1, ed. P. Hodgson, University of California Press, Los Angeles, 1984, p. 308.

are sacramental and are theophanies[57] because they reveal
God's action in the world, but in order to have this understanding for Hegel this has to be based upon a general account of the
nature of God and the world. So a theology of history cannot
proceed from a conception of the nature of God which is fixed
on other grounds and then an understanding of God so arrived
at, as it were, applied to an understanding of history. The two
are much more dialectically related than that. Hence political
theology, if it has this necessary historical dimension, cannot be
a matter of deducing from a predetermined concept of God a
doctrine about the nature of human history and human society.
Our concept of God and God's action in creation, and therefore
in human society and history, are united in an indissoluble way.

   This is not the place to enter into a full discussion of Hegel's
philosophy/theology of history which is too large and complex
to be described briefly. Indeed, we have to be aware of Hegel's
wry answer when the French philosopher Victor Cousin asked
him to put his system into a nutshell and he answered that these
things did not allow themselves to be put into nutshells!
However, there are a few salient points to make. First of all, in
the context of Hegel I have moved from talking about a
theology of history to a philosophy of history, and this shift is
important. In Hegel's view, the task of philosophy was to put
into a rational and exoteric form the basic assumptions of
Christian belief: to change the *Vorstellung* of religion which deals
in symbols, parables, myths, imaginative representations, narratives, stories and the like into *Begriffe* – that is to say rational
exoteric concepts, understandable and assessable by public
reason rather than private faith and judgement. This is very
important for Hegel in that, if a set of beliefs are to lie at the
basis of community life, then these beliefs cannot depend on
private faith and the life of private discipleship, but must be
open to all, or at least all of those who, as he says in the
preface to *The Phenomenology of Spirit*, are prepared to take on
'the exertion of the concept'. This was a central idea in his life

---

[57] L. Colletti, *Marxism and Hegel* trans. L. Garner, New Left Books, London, 1973,
   p. 269.

right from the time that he wrote *The First System Programme of German Idealism.*

This led Hegel to a fundamental reappraisal of Christian beliefs and doctrines, particularly with regard to the Incarnation, the Death and Resurrection of Christ, the Kingdom of God and the Trinity because, as he argues in *Lectures on the Philosophy of Religion*: 'Philosophy does nothing but turn our representations into concepts.' Christian beliefs as conventionally understood stay at the level of picture thinking or *Vorstellung* and not concepts, and this makes the appreciation of them private and leads to easy distortion. I cannot really discuss the nature of Hegel's transformation of basic Christian ideas in the context of this chapter, but what I will do is to say a little about his conception of the Incarnation of God in Jesus and his understanding of the Trinity, because these bear most directly upon his account of the relation between God and history within which political institutions play their part.

Hegel argues in *Lectures on The Philosophy of Religion* that any knowledge we have of God has to turn upon our understanding of our own consciousness: 'God is not to be considered in isolation because that is not possible. One knows of God only in connexion with consciousness.' In Hegel's view, it is central to the general concept of consciousness that there is a distinction to be drawn between self and other whether the other be other non-conscious objects in the world or other centres of consciousness – that is other people. I can only be conscious of myself as a person in so far as I distinguish myself from both forms of otherness. Self-consciousness does not just exist, it is not a *status* it is rather an *achievement*. It is a process of development, and this process is one of suffering and travail. In relation to objects, I show my self-consciousness by treating them as instruments of my will in property and in labour. In relation to others, I become self-conscious only in so far as a dual process is at work, namely, my differentiation of myself from other conscious beings, and in so far as these other *loci* of consciousness recognise me as a centre of consciousness and thus as a person. If this is what we mean by self-consciousness, that it is an *achievement* and not a *given*, then, in so far as we recognise

God as a self-conscious being who acts upon the world, it is true of God as well because the criteria in terms of which we recognise God as a conscious being have to depend upon the criteria that we use to recognise ourselves as conscious beings too. If God is conceived in terms of a kind of Christian Aristotelianism, then, in Hegel's view, we cannot account for the nature of the self-consciousness of God. God's consciousness has to be developed through both differentiation and recognition, and this occurs, as it does for individuals, through the world of objects and other self-conscious beings. This argument which is developed with great subtlety in *The Phenomenology of Spirit* and also in *Lectures on The Philosophy of Religion* forms the basis of Hegel's reworking of the doctrine of the Trinity and Incarnation:

God has two revelations, as nature and as spirit, and both manifestations are temples which he fills and in which he is present. God as an abstraction is not the true God; His truth is the positing of His other, the living process, the world, which is his Son when it is comprehended in its divine form.[58]

Hegel does not deny that God can be considered independently of the world, in what he calls his eternal idea, but, in Hegel's view, God understood in this way which he thinks corresponds to the first person of the Trinity is purely abstract and lacks self-consciousness. This corresponds in some ways to the idea of the primordial as opposed to the consequent nature of God as it is understood by some contemporary-process theologians. However, as with individuals, God's self-consciousness has to be developed and this is understood in terms of creation. The world of objects and persons provides the processes through which God's self-consciousness develops. In this sense, for Hegel, God has a 'career' (*Lebenslauf*), to use his own terms. The Incarnation of God in Jesus the second person of the Trinity along with creation generally is an image, a symbol, a *Vorstellung* of this necessity on the part of God. Writing of the Incarnation, Hegel says:

[58] Hegel, *Philosophy of Nature* p. 204.

It is essential to this form of nonspeculative consciousness that it is before us; it must essentially be before me – it must become a certainty for humanity. For it is only what exists in an immediate way, in inner or outer intuition, that is certain. In order for it (this divine – human unity) to become a certainty for humanity, God had to appear in the world in the flesh . . . for only in this way can it become a certainty for humanity.[59]

At the same time, the import of the Incarnation has to be properly understood – namely the unity of God and humanity and the developmental and progressive nature of this. So the certainty – present in the embodiment of God in the singularity of Jesus – has to be generalised by thought, since the 'substantiated unity of good and humanity is what humanity implicitly is, hence it is something that lies beyond immediate consciousness, beyond ordinary consciousness and knowledge'. Once this is understood, for Hegel, we need to understand the Incarnation of God in the world of social institutions. Hegel thus had a very strongly incarnationalist theology: 'The third element, then is this consciousness – God as the Spirit. The Spirit existing and realising itself in the community.'[60] To understand the relationship of God and history through the generalisation of the Incarnation is a central task for philosophy:

This reconciliation is philosophy. Philosophy is to this extent theology. It presents the reconciliation of God with himself and with nature, showing that nature, otherness, is implicitly divine, and that the raising of itself to reconciliation is on the one hand what finite spirit implicitly is, while on the other hand it arrives at this reconciliation or brings it forth in world history. This reconciliation is the peace of God, which does not 'surpass all reason' but is rather the place that through reason is first known.[61]

The Holy Spirit, the third person of the Trinity, is the consciousness we attain through our own reflection and understanding of the nature of humanity as achieved in art, religion and in the life of institutions. It is in philosophy that we understand how God works in relation to both the natural world and the world

---

[59] Hegel, *Lectures on the Philosophy of Religion* p. 454.
[60] G. W. F. Hegel, *The Phenomenology of Spirit*, trans. A. V. Miller, Clarendon Press, Oxford, 1977, p. 473.
[61] Ibid. p. 489.

of human institutions and human society in this way. The Trinity is realised when the stage of Absolute Knowledge is attained when we see the world clearly and rationally from this point of view. This realisation and this understanding involves a working through the processes of nature and history to see how God does develop this self-consciousness, and this involves seeing them as teleological processes. Philosophy uses the work of science and historians to trace this dialectical and teleological development. The *telos* in question is the attainment of absolute knowledge and self-consciousness which, for Hegel, is also a way of describing freedom since freedom for him involves acting in a rational way according to the greatest degree of self-consciousness that can be attained in specific circumstances. History, then, is part of the self-realisation of freedom and the institutional and political structures which facilitate the development of this consciousness and this freedom, and in its ultimate form, which Hegel thinks the modern world has attained, will issue in what he calls *Sittlichkeit* or 'ethical life' which provides the institutional embodiment for the achievement of a form of community within which this full self-consciousness is attained.

History, for Hegel, is a dialectical and progressive process in which God, on his understanding of God, becomes incarnate and thus self-conscious in and through human life and history. Human societies and forms of politics, embodying as they do different and possibly incommensurable values and views of human purposes and fullness, are, in fact, related in a progressive way. In Hegel's view, we are not presented just with different given social systems, different language games, each with their own organisation and logic which are internal to them. There is rather a way of holding them together in a meta-narrative of a philosophy and theology of history which allows us to see societies and the concomitant forms of politics as embodying to a greater or lesser degree fundamental developments in human consciousness and human purposes.

This influences in a major way Hegel's attitude towards the politics of his own time articulated in the *German World* as he calls it, but perhaps more appropriately understood as the

Western post-Napoleonic European forms of society and culture. In Hegel's view, a philosophy/theology of history reveals a process through which self-consciousness and individual freedom is developed. Ancient societies embodied what he calls an unmediated unity, a sense of community in which individuals had no real sense of their status as individuals with a sense of their own rights, status dignity and worth. Morality was not autonomously chosen or endorsed; it was a matter of habit, custom and tradition. This corresponds at the level of *Vorstellung* with prelapsarian innocence in the Garden of Eden. But, in the same way that eating of the tree of knowledge gave Adam and Eve a knowledge of right and wrong, and a sense of self-consciousness revealed by the sense of their own nakedness, so the unmediated harmony of ancient societies broke down under the weight of a growth of individualism and self-consciousness. Socrates was, for Hegel, a pivotal figure here in questioning and thereby disrupting the customary, second-nature morality of the Greek *polis*. This process of individualism has proceeded apace within Western history, culture and society: in Roman Law, in the Christian religion particularly in its Protestant form, in property ownership, in Kantian moral philosophy, in the French Revolution, in the development of the market economy. All of these have marked enormous gains in human development and are rational within the terms of the societies in which they developed. They are also rational in a sense as understood in Hegel's theology in that they contribute to a real dimension of human consciousness and freedom. At the same time, though, there is also loss. A loss of a sense of harmony, of community, of being at home in the world, a loss of reconciliation. Human fulfilment has to rest on the development within history of institutional and cultural forms which will preserve the gains of individualism, but will also lead to a modern 'mediated' sense of community. In the same way in the biblical story the sin of Adam is redeemed by Christ so that the Holy Spirit can be seen as creating a new spirit, a new sense of mutual integration; so, too, the historical process which is part of God's incarnation will lead in the same way. In Hegel's view, the modern European state and its associated forms of art, religion and culture, including philosophy, provide the vehicle for a new mediated harmony in human life, and thus history is redeemed not from the outside or in the beyond (*jenseits*) but within the process of history itself. His books on *The Philosophy of History* and *The Philosophy of Right* reveal in rich detail the whole account of this process and his interpretation of the modern state as a central element within which history is redeemed.[62]

Of course, Hegel's argument raises enormous questions about the nature of human reason and its capacity to provide an explanation which encompasses the whole of history. Modern relativists take from Hegel the view that social and political practices are rational within their own context, but Hegel wants to go very much further than this and argue that there is a rational structure which links in a developmental way the nature of such practices – this rational structure being rooted in his philosophical theology. This point has been well put by Hilary Putnam when he argues:

there is a limit notion of rationality in Hegel's system; the notion of that which is destined to be stable, the final self-awareness of spirit which will not itself be transcended. When present day relativists 'rationalise' Hegel by throwing away the concept of true rationality, they turn the doctrine into a self-defeating cultural relativism.[63]

This is really the crux not just for Hegel but for any theology of history. To make such an account of history plausible there has to be some basis for the belief that human reason can, in some sense, stand at the end of and encompass the totality of history. It is also central to this view that the world of human institutions can be understood and comprehended in theological terms or, as with Hegel, in theological terms which have been transformed into philosophical ones.

However, before leaving our rather heterogeneous examplars of a theology of history or of providence in history, it is perhaps worth summarising the basic problems with a theology of history as they have been identified by thinkers after Hegel.

---

[62] For further discussion of this project of reconciliation, see R. Plant, *Hegel* 2nd edition, Blackwell, Oxford, 1983; R. Plant, *Hegel* Orion Books, London, 1997; M. Hardimon, *Hegel's Social Philosophy; The Project of Reconciliation* Cambridge University Press, 1994.

[63] H. Putnam, *Reason, Truth and History*, Cambridge University Press, 1981 p. 158.

These issues, which will be discussed in more detail in the next chapter, are as follows.

First of all it can be argued with great force that theologies of history are not independent of a particular conception of God. Particular ideas about the nature of God can, and indeed do, yield rather different theologies of history. This will become apparent in the next chapter when we look at the contrast between Hegel and Barth. If there are no obvious rational or other authoritative grounds for settling disputes about the fundamental nature of God, then there can be no ultimately natural basis for choosing one theology of history necessarily linked to a particular concept of God rather than another.

It is also argued in a way that parallels the earlier question that a theology of history presupposes some kind of absolute standpoint from the vantage-point of which the *telos* of history can be discerned, and in terms of which particular historical events find a particular place. It is argued that such an assumption transcends human finitude. Reason cannot attain such a standpoint, and thus it becomes impossible to undertake a theology of history.

Linked to this is a further issue which has to do with the limits of reason. A theology of history has to make assumptions about the capacity of reason to grasp the totality of human experience in the social, economic, political and natural realms, and the fact that we have lost confidence in the capacity of reason to achieve such totalising possibilities. It is, of course, also assumed that the nature of social and political reality is such that it can be comprehended under normative categories of the sort that would be centrally involved in a theology of history.

In this sense, a theology of history is logocentric. That is to say, it has to assume that human knowledge can 'map' on to reality in a determinate way. However, modern philosophy, whether in the Wittgensteinian or continental forms, casts severe doubts on whether or not there can be a foundational universal way of understanding the nature of reality. This point is again linked to the idea of an absolute standpoint, and as we shall see in more detail in the next chapter, has been subjected to searching philosophical criticism.

Finally, in this sketch of the issues facing the claim that it is possible to develop a theology of history, the point is frequently made that, following the particular horrors of the twentieth century, it is literally incredible to think that history could be regarded as providential. This raises deep and highly controversial issues about how unique the horrors of the twentieth century are. Many of those who have formulated philosophies and theologies of history from the Old Testament period onwards were very clear about the dereliction of their own times, and Hegel, following Schiller, said that history was a slaughter bench. So, if theologies of history could in the past be formulated, while at the same time acknowledging the horrors of their time, what is it specifically about the twentieth century that makes the difference?

CHAPTER 4

Totality, finitude and history

Truth in essence can only be one.
(Pannenberg, *Basic Questions in Theology*, II)

What then is truth? A mobile army of metaphors, metonymies, and anthropomorphisms – in short, a sum of human
relations which have been politically and rhetorically
enhanced, transposed and embellished, and which after
long use seem binding to a people.   (Nietzsche, *Werke*, III)

Interpretation can never be brought to an end, simply
because there is nothing absolutely primary to interpret,
because at bottom everything is already interpretation.
(Foucault, *Nietzsche: Cahiers du Royaument No. 6*)

In the last, chapter we reviewed three approaches to the
theology of history. The theology of history is a clear candidate
for the mediating link between universal and particular in
political theology, since such theodicies could claim to promote
a universal explanation or meta-narrative of the historical
process while at the same time being enmeshed in the particularities of specific societies, their histories and their practices.

In this chapter, I want to push the discussion a bit further by
taking up the point made towards the end of the previous
chapter about whether a theology of history makes too extreme
a set of demands on human finitude. I shall do this first of all by
looking at the work of Pannenberg in this respect, since to some
extent his own views about a universal or theology of history
arise out of a response to Hegel. As he himself says: 'We must
ask how is it possible today to develop a conception of universal
history which in contrast to Hegel would preserve the finitude

of human experience?'[1] Pannenberg sees a universal history as being vital for Christians who wish to act and judge in the public world if their acting and judging is to be informed by their religious beliefs, and it is this aspect of his thought that I want to explore first in that there is little point in agonising about the possibility of a theology of history unless such a theology is thought to meet some basic need in the life of the Christian community.

In some ways, Pannenberg takes his cue here from von Rad whose work was discussed in the context of prophecy. As Pannenberg notes with approval, von Rad took the view that what made prophecy possible in Israel was a theology of history which provided the basis for the judgements that prophets make. Pannenberg cites the following from von Rad: 'In principle Israel's faith is grounded in a theology of history. It regards itself as based upon historical facts and reshaped by these facts in which it saw the hand of God at work'.[2] Pannenberg puts the point in a much more general way when he argues:

If we recognise the close association of revelation and history and try to see the Christ revelation in terms of its actual connection with world history, then we can live and act as Christians in our own particular historical situation without any break. We do not have to switch to another system when we are concerned with the actual demands of our historical circumstances and the decisions to be made within them.[3]

This is of crucial importance in that it links in a conceptual way the substance of religious belief with the demands of political practice. It would enable Christians *qua* citizens to avoid what Hilary Putnam calls a sort of moral double-entry bookkeeping in which identity-creating beliefs are separate from judgements one makes in the public sphere as a citizen.[4] Putnam links this to religious thought particularly, and goes on

---

[1] W. Pannenberg, 'Hermeneutic and Universal History' in *Basic Questions in Theology* vol. 1, SCM Press, London, 1972, p. 135.

[2] W. Pannenberg, 'Kerygma and History' in *Basic Questions in Theology* vol. 1, SCM Press, London, 1967, p. 88.

[3] Pannenberg, *Faith and Reality* p. 89.

[4] Putnam, *Reason, Truth and History*, p. 150.

to say that 'it is just because we feel uncomfortable that there is a real problem for us in this area'.[5]

As we shall see more fully later, some versions of liberal pluralism in political theory turn on the idea that foundational, comprehensive, metaphysical beliefs, of the sort that Christian beliefs are should *not* be part of public deliberation in a liberal society, and thus, in a sense, institutionalise precisely the separation to which Putnam alludes and which Pannenberg is anxious to overcome.

As we saw in the second chapter, on one view, the prophets of the Old Testament were able to act without this break because they belonged to a faith and a society which, as von Rad argued, was part of a general sense of God working in history. Lacking a theology of history, we cannot act in this way and we seem more bound up with difference and diversity. If we lack a theological understanding of history and politics, then we shall not be able to act as Christians in the public world, and this, in turn, will sanction a rather privatised approach to the nature of the faith which I spoke about in the earlier chapters, and which certainly stands in sharp contrast to Old Testament understandings of the relationship between religious faith and the public realm. Pannenberg's way of putting the point also links up to what I said earlier about the relationship between universal and particular. A theology of history looks as though it is the only mediating link between our understanding of the universal scope of the *Divine Logos* and the fact that we are called upon to act within specific historical circumstances. This is in additon to the fact that we are ourselves encumbered selves, to use the language of communitarian political philosophers and narrative theologians, that is to say selves with identities which are to a degree constituted by the historical forms of community of which we are a part.

Before looking specifically at Pannenberg's views on the theology of history, it is worth spending a little time to indicate that his approach here is intrinsic to the aspiration that he has

---

[5] Ibid.

to universalism in theology. As he argues in 'The Crisis of the Scriptural Principle':

This universality of theology is unavoidably bound up with the fact that it speaks of God. The word 'God' is used meaningfully only if one means by it the power that determines everything that exists . . . It belongs to the task of theology to understand all being (*alles seienden*) in relation to God, so that without God they simply could not be understood. That is what constitutes theology's universality.[6]

This, in turn, is linked to Pannenberg's idea of truth because, for Pannenberg, truth 'in essence can only be one'.[7] So a theology of history or a universal history is part of the overall universality of theology and its striving for the unity of truth. He discusses the question of how such a conception of truth is possible, and argues that the objectivity of human thought and thus its truth depends crucially upon God as the common ground between human subjectivity and non-human reality: 'The agreement of human thought with extra-human reality, and thus its truth, is possible only on the presupposition of God.'[8] In this sense, therefore, to use different vocabulary, Pannenberg's conception of truth is both universalist and logo-centric – human thought tracks the nature of a pre-given God-created reality.

It is important to recognise that this conception of truth does not in any sense exclude history. He is not invoking a Platonic notion of truth as unchanging and non-developmental. This may appear paradoxical, since, if we recognise the historicality of the basic categories of thought (as for example Plato and Kant did not), then does not this fragment the very truth whose unity Pannenberg wants to preserve? In so far as Pannenberg has a solution to this problem, it is by following in the footsteps of Hegel and, indeed, he believes that Hegel's conception of truth as process, development and historical coheres with a biblical account of the nature of truth. As we saw in the previous chapter, for Hegel truth is historical, and until we

[6] Pannenberg, 'The Crisis of the Scriptural Principle' in *Basic Questions in Theology* vol. 1, p. 1.
[7] Pannenberg, 'What is Truth?' in *Basic Questions in Theology* vol. 2, p. 1.
[8] Ibid. p. 18.

arrive at the end of history we cannot absolutise any particular stage of human history as embodying *the* truth. It is only with Absolute Knowledge that we arrive at an encompassing sense of all truth, and this is possible only at the end of history. This fits, in Pannenberg's view, with a biblical view of truth:

It does so firstly, by the fact that the truth as such is understood not as timelessly unchangeable, but as a process that runs its course and maintains itself through change. Secondly, it does so by asserting that the unity of the process, which is full of contradictions while it is underway, will become visible along with the true meaning of every individual moment in it, only from the standpoint of its end.[9]

It is here that the link is made with Pannenberg's own theology of history. He argues that because he had to conceive himself as standing at the end of history in order to speak the final truth about history, Hegel made too extreme a set of demands on human finitude and also closed off the future. Human finitude means that we cannot conceive ourselves as standing at the end of history and involves our openness to the future.[10] So, how does Pannenberg resolve the paradox of the historicality and yet the unity of truth if Hegel's own solution oversteps the bounds of reason and, indeed, our self-understanding as humans, and thus open to the future and to possibility?

Pannenberg believes that Hegel goes wrong in thinking that a universal history is possible only if its end is known in some kind of absolute and detailed sense. However, Pannenberg argues in favour of a view of history in which it is claimed only that the end of history is provisionally known, and, in reflecting upon this provisional character of our knowledge of the end of history, the horizon of the future could be held open and the finitude of human experience preserved. The figure of Jesus is crucial here in Pannenberg's argument. He argues that, for the Christian, history can still be whole although its end has yet to come, in the sense that Jesus, against whom all events are meaningful, has already appeared in history. That which gives meaning to the historical process has already pre-occurred, and

---

[9] Ibid. p. 22.
[10] Ibid. p. 25. See also W. Pannenberg, *What is Man? Contemporary Anthropology in Theological Perspective* trans. D. A. Priebe, Fortress Press, Minneapolis, 1970, p. 3.

in the historical process, and thus within finitude, that which is still an open future for us, into which we are still entering, has already made its appearance in him. The specific nature of the history of Jesus is to be ultimate in that way. Hence, this special event makes what is otherwise unconcluded history into a whole. History partakes of the nature of revelation only in terms of its end as it has appeared in Jesus Christ. Only from Jesus and towards him do the epochs and all the individual instances of history take part in divine revelation.

The task, then, as he defines it, is to consider how the 'light that shines from Jesus' makes all that has happened whole and comprehensible in world history. Only such a history can undergird Christian political practice in the same way as an understanding of the history of Israel under God provided the prophets with a basis for their political involvement. These themes are taken up in some detail in Pannenberg's *Faith and Reality*. However, all I can do in this chapter is to indicate how centrally he takes the idea of a theology of history for political theology and how he seeks to avoid Hegel's difficulties with the idea. On the views I have been considering, a theology of history is central to political theology just because there is the need for a mediating link between an account of the nature of God which in some sense makes universal claims about the nature of God and particular doctrines such as Incarnation, Resurrection, Atonement, Trinity and Kingdom, with the specific circumstances within which political theology has to operate. If political theology is to address the nature and circumstances of particular societies which clearly have a history, then it might be thought that a theology of history is indispensable as a way of linking up an account of the nature of politics with an account of the nature of God. This certainly seems to be the view that Pannenberg takes in his essay 'Kerygma and History' in *Basic Questions of Theology* volume 1, where he talks of the general and particular being mutually supportive in history.

As Pannenberg argues in 'Redemptive Event and History': 'Jesus is the anticipated end and not the middle of history.'[11]

---

[11] Pannenberg, *Basic Questions in Theology* vol. 1, p. 24.

Unlike Hegel, who may have regarded his thought as standing itself at the end of history, the incarnation reveals the end *in medias res*. God will remain active in the events subsequent to the life and death of Jesus, but there will be no new disclosure of God that will surpass the Christ event.[12] Pannenberg has interesting things to say about the general issue of the end of history, which I shall consider later when I raise questions about the feasibility of a theology of history, but, for the moment, Pannenberg's claim is that only the Christ event makes it possible to have a sense of *all* history as a unitary whole. It is worth pointing out, since we shall come back to it, that Pannenberg is deeply critical of Barth's idea of primal history, or redemptive history or *Heilsgeschichte*, which is, for Barth, a thin line within actual history. Pannenberg argues that the retreat from a theological attempt to deal with the *totality* of history in Barth is understandable, but nevertheless a wrong turning. He argues that the Barthian position is that secular historical–critical research as the scientific verification of events did not seem to leave room for redemptive events. Therefore, the theology of salvation history fled into a harbour supposedly safe from the historical flood tide by defining redemptive history as a thin line within the totality of history. Pannenberg, however, insists that:

It belongs to the full meaning of the Incarnation that God's redemptive deed took place within the universal correlative connections of human history and not in a ghetto of redemptive history, or in a primal history belonging to a dimension which is oblique to ordinary history.[13]

It is worth pointing out that this issue is controversial in Barthian interpretation. Kurt Nowak argued that it was philosophical idealism that had enabled German intellectuals to look at the growth of scientific approaches to history and the relativism that accompanied that with a degree of equanimity.[14]

---

[12] Ibid. p. 67.   [13] Ibid. pp. 41–2.

[14] K. Nowak, 'Die antihistorische Revolution: Symptome und Folgen der Krise historischem Weltorientierung nach dem Ersten Weltkrieg in Deutschland' in *Umstrittene Moderne: Die Zukunft der Neuzeit ir Urteil der Epoche Ernst Troeltschs* ed. H. Renz and F. W. Graf, Gerd Mohn, Gutersloh, 1987, pp. 133.

Idealism provided a standpoint in terms of which this historical process could be understood in its totality. With the collapse of philosophical idealism after the First World War, this optimism was no longer open. As a consequence, theologians such as Barth beat a retreat into the inner citadel of a revelation which had only an ambiguous relationship to history, as he makes clear in the 1919 edition of *Der Römerbrief*.[15] There is a good discussion of these items in Bruce McCormack *Karl Barth's Critically Realistic Dialectical Theology*.[16] These points will assume greater salience later when we look at Barth's critique of Hegelian approaches to a theology of history.

Without a theology of history to enable us to lay some kind of theological hold upon society and institutions Christianity will become:

spiritually a withdrawal from the concerns of the world; especially from its social economic and political problems. In that case, the natural institutional form of Christian spirituality in society will be either private activity or purely religious communities. If on the other hand, the end of the world and its history which has come in Jesus is viewed positively as the fulfilment of the world and history, Christian spirituality will be intent on transforming every aspect of the present and bringing it to fulfilment.[17]

I do not think that this idea of theology as a unifying and focalising account of the world of nature within which persons and societies operate and the history of those persons and those societies has been exhausted, but it does give rise to many difficulties. As an example of the way in which it has not been exhausted, I want to refer briefly to an essay which Professor Wiles published a few years ago[18] as a tribute to the centenary of the publication of *Lux Mundi*. In that essay on R. J. Illingworth's

---

[15] K. Barth, *Der Römerbrief* TVZ, Zurich, 1985, p. 25. See also the 1922 edition where he talks about a glacial crevasse, a polar region, or a desert zone separating the non-historical world of revelation and history.

[16] B. McCormack, *Karl Barth's Critically Realistic Dialectical Theology: Its Genesis and Development 1909–36* Clarendon Press, Oxford, 1995. See particularly p. 146.

[17] W. Pannenberg, *Faith and Reality* p. 128.

[18] M. Wiles, 'The Incarnation and Development' in *The Religion of The Incarnation. Anglican Essays in Commemoration of Lux Mundi* ed. R. Morgan, Bristol Classical Press, Bristol 1989.

contribution to *Lux Mundi*, which was essentially about the compatibility of the religion of the Incarnation with a modern evolutionary view of science, Illingworth rejected any attempt to somehow argue that a *logos* theology can be independent of an account of the natural world. Rather, an evolutionary account of nature has to be incorporated into a unified theology which sees the world as part of the immanence of God. At the centre of this idea, and resting upon Illingworth's view of the Incarnation, is the idea of the *unitary* nature of theology which, by extension, would apply also to the social and political world. Professor Wiles is sympathetic to Illingworth's approach here, while remaining very conscious of the difficulties:

> If traditional Christian truth and modern scientific knowledge are both to be embraced, that can only be done (it has come to seem to many) by rejoicing with the neo-orthodox in the paradoxical character of their relation to one another, or by insisting with the neo-Wittgensteinians in the role of traditional doctrine as a grammar of faith which needs no further justification. Illingworth would have had no truck with such escape routes, and nor should we. If there is such a thing as a distinctively Anglican theology, it should express itself in the repudiation of such alternative approaches and the continued pursuit of a more unitary vision.[19]

The neo-orthodox view of Barth rejoices in the paradoxical nature of the religious vision alongside the scientific and historical; the Wittgensteinian position insists upon the idea of a proliferation of language games each with their own logic grammar and norms of rationality with no overarching standards of rationality to provide a unified conception of life. If we value a unified approach to theology, as Wiles and Pannenberg do, then part of that unity should be concerned with linking an account of the Christian faith not only to the natural world but also to the worlds of history and politics. If there can be a political theology, then on this unitary view about the nature of theology it would have to be linked to an account of a theology of history, just because, as I have said, this seems to be the obvious way in which an account of the universality of God links to the specificity and contextual nature of political

---

[19] Ibid. p. 83.

theology. The doctrine of God and an account of God's action in history would be a way of founding Christian political judgement. However, to echo Wiles' question in relation to Illingworth, how is such a unitary vision possible? This is particularly acute in the fields of society, history and politics just because of the specificity and fragmented nature of those worlds.

Two points might be made at the start of this attempt at an appraisal. The first is that, as we have seen, Christian theologies of history are many and various. We have looked at Augustine, Calvin, Hegel and Pannenberg. While Hegel and Pannenberg share a good deal in common, the others are, nevertheless, a rather heterogeneous group, and it could be true to say that Christian theology has not developed a view of the theology of history which could be regarded as even methodologically authoritative never mind in terms of its substance. The second point is that, in modern articulations of the demand for a theology of history as in Pannenberg, Cobb and perhaps, by implication, Wiles, such demands are highly programmatic and skeletal. While it may be true to say that Christian thought must in some sense appropriate the historical world of social and political institutions if Christians are to avoid moral double-entry bookkeeping, nevertheless this has to go beyond a mere aspiration if it is to be of any use. Yet neither Pannenberg nor Cobb have produced such a theological account of history and nor has anyone else in the contemporary world. Hegel, of course, did, but there is no continuing contemporary exemplar of such a view from a theological perspective, and yet it is regarded as crucial to the rescue of Christianity from either privatised spirituality or a narrow view of redemptive history understood from within a limited community of belief. It is quite instructive to compare, for example, Pannenberg's highly skeletal remarks in his essay 'Christian Morality and Political Issues' in *Faith and Reality* with, say, the richness of an achieved theology of history in the work of Hegel. The same would be true of the contrast with Cobb's very stimulating but still highly programmatic 'The Politics of Political Theology' in *Process Theology as Political Theology*. We still seem to be a very long way from the promise of Pannenberg's *Faith and Reality*, given the separation of faith from an understanding of the social and political world and the need to pass from one to the other to act as a believer in politics, that: 'The reason for that kind of transition disappears once we have understood the inner association of revelation and history. Even modern history, from which the situations of our own present activity are derived, is then encompassed in the divine revelation.'[20] We do, however, need to probe deeper to see whether the reason why this supposedly necessary project remains an aspiration rather than an achievement is that there is something flawed in the whole idea of a theology of history.

So, is a theology of history possible as the mediating link between universal and particular? I want to discuss the force of four sorts of objection to the approach:

1 the disputed relationship between the nature of God and the historical process;
2 the intensely problematic nature of the 'end of history';
3 the link between the idea of a comprehensive history and foundational and realist metaphysics;
4 the problems posed for a theology of history by the radical evils of the twentieth century.

The first has to do with the concept of God, and a good place to start is to reflect on the work of Hegel which I have already discussed. There could be no more intimate link between God and history than that argued for in Hegel's work. The difficulty, however, is first that his conception of God underpinning the link between God and history is very controversial, and this can best be seen by looking in detail at the contrast between Hegel's and Karl Barth's concept of God and the different implications which these views have for history.

Karl Barth stands at the opposite end of the spectrum from Hegel and those who look for a unified theory in terms of the doctrine of God that he holds, and this seems to be bound up with a very different account of salvation history. As opposed to Hegel, who argued that 'without the world God is not God',

---

[20] Pannenberg, *Faith and Reality* p. 89.

Barth holds that: 'He would be no less God even if the work of creation had never been done, if there were no creatures and if the whole doctrine of providence were therefore irrelevant. Hence, there can be no place for this doctrine in that of the being of God.'[21]

World-relatedness is not an intrinsic part of the nature of God, for Barth, and this leads him to a very different conception of history from a theological point of view. Barth argues that there are two histories: the history of the world or of creation and what he calls sometimes the history of the covenant or salvation history. For Barth, salvation history is a thin line which occurs within general history. Both are part of the general rule which God exercises over the world, but salvation history is just one thin line traceable within general history and neither is in any sense constitutive of God as history was for Hegel. In addition, as McCormack points out this produces a fundamentally different conception of eschatology for Barth. As he argues: 'For Barth, eschatology tends to be associated with protology. Redemption does not bring about any greater blessing than was enjoyed in the original created relation.'[22] The point I want to make at the moment, however, is not to get into a detailed comparison of Hegel and Barth, so much as to show that an understanding of the theology of history within which a theological account of institutions would have place also requires us to come to a view about the general nature of the relation between God and the world within theism, and this, in its turn, is going to have enormous implications for the general idea of God. In this sense a political theology rooted in a theological understanding of history is going to be doubly controversial. It is surely contentious enough in its understanding of history and human society, given that there are many possible interpretations of these things. However, it is going to be controversial, too, in that a theology of history is likely to involve different, and perhaps radically different, accounts of the nature of God. The question of how disputes of this sort

---

[21] K. Barth, *Church Dogmatics* vol. 3/3 trans G. W. Bromiley and R. J. Ehrlich, T. and T. Clark, Edinburgh, 1961, p. 3.
[22] McCormick, p. 268.

could be settled within Christian thought is in itself a matter of acute controversy. Unless they can be rationally settled, however, it is difficult to see that there could be an authoritative theology of history to fulfil the role which Pannenberg envisages it should have in Christian political practice.

The second problem is that meta-narratives, such as a theology of history would be in relation to history and politics, all seem to presuppose in some sense an account of the end of history. It is difficult to see how there can be a theology of history which is not teleological in a macro sense of that word; that is to say that there is a goal towards which history is developing and that the actions of individuals and the role of institutions, as in Calvin and Augustine, play a part, if not always a conscious part, in that development. Knowledge of *telos* has to imply a sense of standing at the end of history.

I want now to explore this idea in greater detail. In order to focus more sharply on the idea of an 'end' in history, I shall dwell initially upon the work of a group of philosophers from the analytical tradition: J. L. Austin, J. Feinberg, D. Davidson and A. Danto. I shall start with the idea that all history, not just theologies and philosophies of history, requires some account of the end of history. The argument is connected to the idea due to Feinberg and developed by Davidson that action sentences and the identification of agency embody what Feinberg initially called 'the accordion' effect,[23] that is to say that the description under which an action is identified can be wider or narrower. Feinberg argues that the description of an action can be 'squeezed to a minimum' or 'stretched out'. So he says: 'He turned the key, opened the door, startled Smith, he killed Smith – all of these are things that we might say that Jones did with an identical set of bodily movements.' He comments 'we can, if we wish, puff out an action to include an effect'.[24] Much the same

---

[23] J. Feinberg, 'Action and Responsibility' in *Philosophy in America* ed. M. Black, Cornell University Press, Ithaca, 1965, pp. 134–60; see also D. Davidson, 'Agency' in *Actions and Events* Oxford University Press, 1980; J. E. Atwell, 'The Accordion Effect Thesis' *Philosophical Quarterly*, 19 (1969), pp. 337–42.

[24] Feinberg, 'Action' p. 146.

point was made by J. L. Austin in his classic paper 'A Plea for Excuses':

How far . . . are motives, intentions and conventions to the part of the description of actions? And more especially here, what is *an* or *one* or *the* action? For we can generally split up what might be named as one action in several different ways, into different *stretches phases* or *stages*.[25]

Thus the description under which an act is identified can be developed. In doing certain things, what might be called basic acts like moving our hands, we bring things about and these can then be incorporated in the description of the action, for example:

1 Luther moved his hand (basic action);
2 he nailed a piece of paper to the door of his church in Wittenberg (squeezed down description);
3 Luther caused the Reformation (vastly developed description).

So, unless we limit the description of what Luther did to his 'basic action' of moving his hand in a particular way, then the other things his action brings about will become built into the description and identification of what Luther did. Where, though, lies the limit to what Luther brought about, and thus to the ultimate characterisation of his action?

What, then, is the relevance of this to history and to the idea of the end of history in particular? First of all, it could be said that historical writing embodies this aspect of action statements to a very high degree, and this means, of course, that the historian is in the position of identifying activities in the past in the light of events, those things that the action brought about, that are in the future in relation to such actions (although, of course, they are still in the past for the historian). If this is a

---

[25] J. L. Austin, 'A Plea for Excuses' in *Philosophical Papers* Clarendon Press, Oxford, 1969, p. 201. See also 'Three Ways of Spilling Ink' in the same volume where Austin argues that: 'There is a good deal of freedom in the "structuring" of the history of someone's activities by means of words like "intention" just as when we consider a whole war we can divide it into campaigns, operations, actions and the like; but this is fairly arbitrary except in so far as it is based upon the plans of the combatants. So with human activities, we can assess them in terms of intentions, purposes, objectives and the like but there is much that is arbitrary about this', p. 285.

central feature of historical writing – that the description identifying the action can in fact be expanded to incorporate future events into the description of the action – then the question arises as to whether there are any objective limits to the extension of these descriptions – that is to say to the accordion effect.

Interestingly enough, Davidson argues that the possibility of such expansion is 'without clear limit'[26] and when Feinberg discusses the nature of the expansion he says 'We can, if we wish, puff out an action to include the effect'.[27] This seems to make the matter pretty arbitrary, as Austin noted in his paper – what we do and do not wish to do. So I need to go back to the more general point about whether there can be an objective way of determining the limits of the accordion effect. Without some limit to the descriptions of action, the identification of historical activities is going to be to some degree arbitrary. The only way it might be argued that we could remove this element of arbitrariness would be if in some sense the future was foreclosed and we could know all the consequences of action and, in the light of that, pick out the appropriate description since we would be in possession of what might be called the ultimate context or the ultimate perspective, namely, the end of history. In the same way as it is possible finally to assess the significance of actions within an individual's life only at the point of death when all possibility of further agency is precluded, as Dilthey, Heidegger and Sartre have argued, so, too, in history we need some sense of the final context if we are to provide a complete description of an activity. The idea of a complete description is the crucial one here, and while, of course, philosophies and theologies of history will purport to give complete descriptions of actions, nevertheless the same point applies to any kind of idea of a complete history whether or not it is supposed to be a theology or philosophy of history. As Danto argues: 'Completely to describe an event is to locate it in the right stories and this we cannot do. We cannot for the

[26] Davidson, 'Agency', p. 58.
[27] Feinberg, 'Action', p. 146.

same reason that we cannot achieve a speculative philosophy of history.'[28]

The idea of an objective and complete history therefore requires the fulfilment of the same condition that is usually taken to be a necessary condition for speculative philosophy or theology of history, namely, the complete account of the future:

Any account of the past is essentially incomplete. It is essentially incomplete, that is, if its completion would require the fulfilment of a condition which simply cannot be fulfilled. And my thesis will be that a complete account of the past would presuppose a complete account of the future, so that one could not achieve a complete historical account without achieving a philosophy of history. So that if there cannot be a legitimate philosophy of history, there cannot be a legitimate and complete historical account.[29]

The same point would apply to a theology of history. Hence, there is a crucial role to be played by the idea of an end to history. It is important for the idea of an objective or complete history, just as it is for a philosophy or theology of history.

Danto regards it as clear that we cannot achieve this without the idea of the end of history, which also implies an absolute epistemological and metaphysical standpoint. So why is this impossible? We need to explore it in detail because, as I have argued, the idea of a theology of history has been taken as crucial to the project of political theology. The reasons why such an account might be thought to be impossible are to do with the claimed contingency of language, society and selfhood, the loss of a sense of the unity of reason yielding an explanatory meta-narrative together with the growth of the ideas of perspectivism and relativism. These issues now need to be discussed in more detail both because of their insight on the idea of a theology of history and because they will recur throughout the rest of the argument of the book.

The initial problem with a theology of history lies precisely at the point at which Pannenberg starts, namely, that it requires some conception of an absolute standpoint and some kind of absolute knowledge. If, as the 'accordion effect' shows, actions

---

[28] A. Danto, *Analytical Philosophy of History* Cambridge University Press, 1965, p. 272.
[29] Ibid.

and events, of which actions are a subset, always occur under a description, and if this description can be expanded to include consequences of the actions and events, and this process is without clear limit, as Donald Davidson claims, then any reflective theology of history will have to justify a position from which the development of the accordion effect can, in fact, be foreclosed. This, however, goes beyond the bounds of human finitude for the reason given by Danto, which is that a final description of the past can only be given by claimed knowledge of the future and this is cognitively unavailable to us.

Part of the reason for this is that such an absolutist standpoint would presuppose a representational and realist view of language in which our language and descriptions are supposed to map on to a given reality. This position Pannenberg clearly and fully accepts, for, as he says in his essay 'What is Truth?': 'The agreement of human thought with extra human reality, and thus its truth, is possible only on this presupposition of God.'[30] The contrary view, represented by some of the philosophers I have mentioned, is to regard the 'given' as a myth. What is given is social practices of describing and asserting with truth being seen in some sense as coherence rather than as correspondence with a given reality. The basic objection to such foundationalist representationalism is given by Davidson in his paper 'A Coherence Theory of Truth and Knowledge'. Davidson argues that this kind of representationalism must be wrong:

We have been trying to see it this way: a person has all his beliefs about the world – that is, all his beliefs. How can he tell if they are true or apt to be true? Only, we have been assuming, by connecting his beliefs to the world, confronting certain of his beliefs with the tribunal of experience. No such confrontation makes sense, for of course we can't get outside our skins to find out what is causing the internal happening of which we are aware. What we have shown is that it is absurd to look for a justifying ground for the totality of beliefs, something outside this totality which we can use to test or compare to our beliefs.[31]

---

[30] Pannenberg, 'What is Truth?', p. 18.
[31] D. Davidson, 'A Coherence Theory of Truth and Knowledge' in *Truth and Interpretation: Perspectives on the Philosophy of Donald Davison* ed. E. de Pore, Blackwell, Oxford, 1986, p. 312.

There is no Archimedean point from which we can see the world or 'the given' from outside a particular set of beliefs, and thus there cannot be a justified claim to absolute knowledge if this means depicting the 'given' more adequately than any other conceptual scheme, because there is no such theory-independent and belief-independent *given* to which we can compare our beliefs. On the representational/foundationalist view, reality is what gives language sense; on the alternative view, as Peter Winch has opined, 'what is real and unreal shows itself in the sense that language has'.[32] Given that truth on this sort of view is related to coherence of beliefs and to social practices within which beliefs and the language to formulate them are agreed and developed, it follows that there can be competing or alternative accounts of 'truth' which cannot be attributed in virtue of an appeal to reality.

Such a view has radical implications, some of which were prefigured by Nietzsche and others which have been developed by philosophers such as Derrida, Foucault and Rorty, but in all cases the idea which seems central to the view that there can be absolute knowledge or an absolute standpoint from which to view history has to be rejected. The idea of a universal history or a theology of history presupposes, therefore, that there is a set of propositions about the nature of the *logos* in history which are foundational and which represent reality in a final and exclusive form.

However, this idea of a general goal of history is, in the view of many thinkers, fraught with fatal difficulties, particularly since it seems to presuppose some leaping over the boundaries of human finitude because it seems to imply some kind of absolute knowledge or be making some kind of absolute claim. As we have already seen, Pannenberg is troubled by this issue, but believes that he has solved it. One of the major sources for the radical critique of such a view is the later writings of Wittgenstein.

---

[32] P. Winch, 'Understanding a Primitive Society' in *Ethics and Action*, Routledge, London, 1972, p. 12; see also R. Rorty, 'The Contingency of Language' in *Contingency, Irony and Solidarity*, Cambridge University Press, 1989, pp. 3–22.

On a reasonable interpretation of Wittgenstein's view, there can be no absolute standpoint because metaphysical theories cannot provide a foundation for language. The meaning of a language and the ways of life in which languages are embedded do not rest upon some kind of antecedent metaphysical foundation. On the contrary, what is true and false, the real and the unreal, a standard of right and wrong, are internal to a language and cannot be determined independently of it. The concept of a reason has a place within a practice, but there is no transcultural standpoint which can define the absolute standpoint of reason independent of social practices. With a game, for example chess, a particular move can be right or wrong, a good or bad move, a justified or an unjustified one. The game of chess itself, however, is neither rational or irrational, justified or unjustified. These are internal questions, not external context-free, absolutist ones. If we are involved in a process of justification, we can go so far within the context of the practice within which we operate, but the context bounds the range of justification. The context, the practice, is itself neither rational nor irrational:

> If I have exhausted the justifications I have reached bedrock and my spade is turned. Then I am inclined to say: 'This is simply what I do.'[33]
>
> What has to be accepted, the given, is form of life.[34]
>
> What people accept as justification is shown in how they think and live.[35]

Forms of life, linguistic practices and contexts are what give meaning to the reasons we invoke for doing something or describing an action and its effects in one way rather than another. There are no a priori reasons for action, no a priori principles of practical reasoning, which can be identified independently of the particularities of culture and practices. The principles by which we live do not depict or track some kind of antecedent moral order so much as embody the commitment and the contexts in which we live. Within the religious practice

---

[33] L. Wittgenstein, *Philosophical Investigations* Blackwell, Oxford, 1958, para. 217.
[34] Ibid. para. 226e.   [35] Ibid. para. 325.

or language game, to live one's life as if it were under the prospect of final judgement, and to describe actions in ways that make them amenable to such judgement, are reasons for acting in one way rather than another and for describing action in one way rather than in another. Outside this context, both the reason and the action which is described according to these standards of reason may seem to be bizarre and unintelligible.

This claim, aspects of which will recur later in the book, might be thought to imply that the practices and language games in question are arbitrary. One must be careful, however. They are certainly arbitrary in the sense that they could have been different and there is no metaphysical argument to show that they have to be as they are. However, in Wittgenstein's view, this is really to misuse the word 'arbitrary', because not to be arbitrary would imply the possibility of fulfilling some kind of metaphysical standard which, in fact, is just not available to us. Language games are not arbitrary, however, in the sense that whole ways of life embody them, and these provide the context within which things events and actions have meaning and significance. They are not arbitrary in the sense that they cannot be changed at will because such a change could involve massive, and in some contexts unimaginably massive, changes in social life. This is a point which Wittgenstein makes clear at several points in *Remarks on the Foundations of Mathematics* because he wants to deny that conventionalism implies some sort of commitment to arbitrariness.

This point also implies that, since practices are not given support by metaphysical theories, they are not refuted either by their failure to measure up to some metaphysically inspired standard. There is no absolute standard of reason situated outside language games and between practices in terms of which such practices can be grounded, evaluated, discussed or put into some hierarchy of ascending order of adequacy. We cannot give some contextless account of reason, nor can we take reason out of one context, for example, natural science, and make it paradigmatic for all others, for, as Winch argues:

Criteria of logic are not a direct gift of God, but arise out of and are only intelligible in the context of ways of living or modes of social life.

It follows that we cannot apply criteria of logic to modes of social life as such. For instance, science is one such mode and religion another, and each has criteria of intelligibility peculiar to itself . . . we cannot sensibly say that either the practice of science itself or that of religion is either logical or illogical, both are non-logical.[36]

The consequences of this approach for the idea of an absolute position from which the totality of history is to be comprehended are twofold. First of all, we cannot make sense of an idea of reason which transcends all contexts which a rational grasp of the totality of history would do in a paradigmatic way. Second, reason is fragmented into particular contexts and language games. There is no rational standpoint from which we could reify the whole of history. There is no single language game which can provide some ultimately real meta-narrative of the world from which we can see the world and history from an absolute standpoint. At the best, rival language games seek to out-narrate one another, not refute one another. If they disappear from human life, it is because they have been forgotten, not because they have been refuted. The idea of a universal history or a theology of history presupposes, therefore, that there is a set of propositions about the nature of the *logos* in history which is foundational and that therefore grounds this account of history and the political theology which is part of it.

Nietzsche also saw the issue very clearly, again in respect of Hegel:

The historian creates an artistically, not historically true picture. In this sense to think objectively of history is the quiet work of the dramatist: namely to think one thing into another and weave the element into a whole: all with the presumption that the units of plan must be put into things if it is not already there. There could be a manner of writing history which contained not the slightest drop of empirical truth and could still claim to be called in the highest degree objective.[37]

---

[36] P. Winch, *The Idea of a Social Science* Routledge, London, 1958, p. 100.
[37] F. Nietzsche, 'Vom Nutzen und Nachteil der Historie für des Leben' in *Werke* ed. G. Colli and M. Montinori, Walter de Gruyter, Berlin, 1967, p. 92.

The point, however, for Nietzsche, is that the foundation of history is *posited*, it is not *tracked*; it is a matter of *will* not of *reason*. As he argued in *The Gay Science*, 'There are no eternal horizons or perspectives'. Nietzsche would no doubt approve of Wittgenstein's use of Goethe's dictum: *Im Anfang war die Tat* in *On Certainty*.

This is an important if rather pithy point to the argument. Nietzsche, in saying that I can posit a meaning for my own life and for history, wants to link this kind of approach to *will* rather than to *reason*. It is imposed rather than discovered. An idea of the ultimate meaning of a process is one that reflects *will*, of endowing the historical process with meaning rather than one that is *logocentric*, attempting to describe and discern in the historical process some pattern of meaning which *it* has. We shall now move on to a discussion of the kind of metaphysical realism which seems to be represented by a theology of history.

Theologies of history and the political theologies they generate, however, claim not only objectivity and truth, but a truth of some kind of absolute sort, since they claim to know the *telos* or the end of history which endows history with meaning and gives a place to political institutions. This sort of idea of the eschatological end of history transcends the human point of view. However, if human truths are relative to language games, then a claim to absolute knowledge about the end of history involves a mistaken view about human cognitive capacities.

Foucault, too, in *The Archaeology of Knowledge* not only wants to stress, as he does, the breaks, the thresholds, ruptures and displacements that take place in history and that place a huge question mark over some kind of theology of history, but he also wants to question all totalisations and teleologies of the sort that a theology of history turns upon. Instead of a meaning of history which is being played out under providence, he wants to question, following Nietzsche, the possibility of history in this sense at all. Rather, a genealogy of history reveals just forms of domination influenced, above all, by chance. Compare the following from Foucault with Augustine's *De Civitate Dei*:

The inverse of the Christian world is spun entirely by a divine spider, and different from the world of the Greeks, divided between the realm of will and the great cosmic folly. The world of effective history knows only one kingdom, without providence or final cause, where there is only 'the iron hand of necessity shaking the dice box of chance.'[38]

Far from the *Civitas Dei* being intertwined with the *Civitas Terrena*, there is only the one world of chance and the patterns of domination which emerge from it. I want to discuss in more detail post-modernist critiques of theology and political theory in the next chapter, but clearly these sorts of arguments against the possibility of meta-narrative place a large question mark beside the claim that political theology can take place only against the background of meta-narrative of history as deployed in theologies of history.

I will say just a little more, however, about the main lines of this more thorough perspectivism. Derrida wants to argue in favour of decentering discourse. There is, in his view, no origin, no end, no place outside discourse from which to fix, make determinate and establish metaphysical boundaries for the play of linguistic signifiers. He rejects the idea, which he takes in its different forms to have governed Western thought, that there is a metaphysical presence which abides through various metaphysical applications:

The history of metaphysics, like the history of the West, is the history of these metaphors and metonymies. Its matrix . . . is the determination of Being as *presence* in all senses of the word. It could be shown that all the names related to fundamentals, to principles or to the centre have always designated an invariable presence – *eidos*, *arche*, *energeia*, *ousia* . . . *aletheria*, transcendentality, consciousness, God, man and so forth.[39]

He goes on to say that, with the dawning of the idea that there is no centre to existence, 'everything became discourse' and 'the absence of the transcendental signified extends the domain and the play of signification infinitely'.

This means, for Derrida, that language is a closed system of signs and every sign is but a closed circle of other signs – an idea which, despite a different philosophical perspective, is not all

---

[38] M. Foucault, 'Nieztsche, la généalogie, l'histoire' in *Dits et Ecrits* vol. 2, ed. D. Defert and F. Ewold, Gallimard, Paris, 1985, p. 148.

[39] J. Derrida, *Writing and Difference* trans. A. Boss, Routledge, London, 1978, p. 79.

that dissimilar a point from that made by Wittgenstein in the *Tractatus* that 'if the world had no substance then whether one proposition had sense would depend on whether another proposition was true'.[40] The consequence of this deconstruction of systems of thought which seek to depict the substance of the world, is to empty the world of any metaphysical presence, as Peter Hodgson says, and it turns history into a labyrinth. We lack any kind of objective frame of reference and certainly do not have one for founding a universal history as a way of dealing with the public world. This seems to sanction a retreat into self and a kind of aestheticism. This point comes out very clearly in Nietzsche's *Will to Power*: 'There are no facts in themselves for a sense has to be projected into them before they can be facts.'[41] There is no objective structure to the world or to history, and all that one can do is to use the power that one may have in one's situation to impose a structure of signs, a language game which does not depict an objective reality so much as to allow one to exercise power in this way if one can. All that are left are self-interest and self-assertion, and whether one can use a structure of signifiers to serve such purposes. The upshot here being that knowledge cannot be separated from power.

This leads fairly naturally to Foucault's idea of regimes of truth and the relationship between this idea and power, on the one hand, and a thoroughgoing relativism, on the other, which Charles Taylor[42] argues is inherited from Nietzsche's *The Gay Science*. It is part of Foucault's argument that there is no standard outside ourselves in terms of which we can evaluate ways of life or sets of values. These norms and ways of life are not rationally legitimated by some kind of metaphysical theory or meta-narrative of human history. They are, rather, secured by power. This is really why he calls them regimes of truth. They are not just language games or narratives or traditions, but, rather, regimes of ideas which are legitimised by power. Within these

---

[40] L. Wittgenstein, *Tractatus Logico Philosophicus* Routledge, London, 1961, Proposition 2.021.
[41] F. Nietzsche, *Will to Power* trans. W. Kaufmann and R. J. Hollingdale, Random House, New York, 1968, p. 556.
[42] C. Taylor, 'Foucault on Freedom and Truth' in *Philosophical Papers* vol. 2, Cambridge University Press, 1985.

structures there are ways of making judgements, there are modes of rationality and criteria to distinguish between truth and falsity, but, as with Nietzsche, truth is subordinated to power:

Each society has its own regime of truth, its 'general politics' of truth ; that is the types of discourses which it accepts and makes function as true; the mechanisms and instances which enable one to distinguish between true and false statements, the means by which each is sanctioned, the techniques and procedures accorded value by the acquisition of truth; the status of those who are charged with saying what counts as true.[43]

From this it follows, as a result of the relativism that goes with it, that changes in regimes of truth are not in any sense a move towards a recognition of truth, or a growth of freedom. Rather, such changes are the result of changes in power. For Foucault, the power exercised here should not be interpreted as a kind of power which is exercised intentionally, but is, rather, part of the common situation and common activity in which people find themselves. Of course, in earlier forms of society that power might have been exercised intentionally, from the top down, by the king, the priest or whatever; however, in our sort of society, power, undergirding regimes of truth, is micro-power and is as much exercised through language as anything else.

Against a *logocentric* philosophy of history or theology of history which sees history moving in an ideal way towards a *telos*, Foucault argues, following Nietzsche, that a genealogy of regimes of truth is what is required to illustrate their relation to power, rather than an idealising theology or philosophy of history:

Genealogy must record the singularity of events outside of any monotonous finality; it must seek them out in the most unpromising places, in what we tend to feel is without history . . . not in order to trace the gradual curve of their evolution, but to isolate the different scenes where they are engaged in different roles. Genealogy rejects the metahistorical deployment of ideal significations and indefinite teleologies.[44]

---

[43] M. Foucault, *Power and Knowledge* ed. C. Gordon, trans. G. Gordon, L. Marshall and R. Soper, Pantheon, New York, 1980, p. 131.

[44] M. Foucault, 'Nietzsche, la généalogie, l'histoire', p. 136.

Genealogy rather than a philosophy or theology of history and regimes of truth is what we need. The upshot of which is as Putnam argues that 'past practices are not more rational than they appear to be, but that all practices are less rational, are in fact, mainly determined by unreason and selfish power'.[45] History is therefore not a teleological process of growing into greater truth or greater freedom, but a more-or-less discontinuous series of discourses, ideologies or regimes of truth which succeed one another for no overarching rational reason, but which nevertheless represent and are built upon regimes of power. Again, this kind of thought clearly represents a major challenge to a theology of history if this is seen as a necessary background to a fully developed political theology.

I want to explore a little more the fragmentation question which goes alongside this rejection of representation and foundationalism. The idea of an absolute standpoint, and in particular the idea of a theology of history, must make some very comprehensive claims about the scope of human reason, since a theology of history in particular would become all encompassing. Such a view of reason is clearly wholly incompatible with the sort of critique that I have described. Rationality is both limited and fragmented on such a view. There is no Archimedean point on which reason can stand, and what is rational and irrational depends upon the particular framework of coherent beliefs and social practices of which they are a part. That is to say, rationality is internal to particular language games and social practices, and there is no overarching reason or standards which could be used to arbitrate between different points of view and coherent belief systems.

Reason is context-based, not Archimedean. Belief systems can only out-narrate one another, they do not get refuted but rather forgotten when they have lost their point and purpose. So, where CS is a conceptual scheme, Rorty says: 'CSj pictures more adequately than CSi just means that CSj is better suited to our needs than CSi.'[46] This reference to needs might, however,

---

[45] Putnam *Reason, Truth and History* p. 162.
[46] Rorty, 'Representation, Social Practice, Truth' in *Objectivism, Relativism And Truth: Philosophical Papers* vol. 1, 1991, p. 155.

give the defence of a theology of history some grounds for a counter-attack on the post-modern fragmentation of reason into different language games to which it is internal. It might be argued by the theologian that, in fact, the needs of human nature or the needs of sustaining a human community more widely can actually give us transcultural standards and norms in terms of which we are able to think about historical development and the extent to which historical developments across cultures do or do not fulfil the basic needs of human existence. Essentially this is the Hegelian response. Hegel himself saw human nature as being marked by the twin desires for both freedom and a sense of community. He was able to interpret the historical process in terms of ways in which those forms of freedom were, or more likely were not, compatible with some forms of community. So common human needs and aspirations would give us a universal in the midst of all the flux and complexity of history. It is also certainly the case that a thinker like Pannenberg believes that there are indeed such basic structures to human existence which would make it possible to have a firm position from which to consider the role of different historical circumstances in contributing to human flourishing and fulfilment. There is a parallel movement in political theory in the earlier work of someone like Jürgen Habermas who, in his book *Knowledge and Human Interests*, has linked knowledge to human interests just as much as Rorty, Davidson and others, but he also wants to link that to some attempt to provide an objective and universal basis for these interests. So why could not the nature of the self and/or the nature of community not form the basis for thinking about the pattern of history?

The answer to this question, for Rorty, is that the ideas of both the self and community are so contingent and lacking a real or essential nature that they cannot in their respective ways form a benchmark for judging the extent to which different historical forms contribute to a universal account of human flourishing either as a solitary self or in community. Equally there is no universal telos of human life rooted in the structure of selfhood or community towards which history is moving for exactly the same sort of reasons.

These reasons are large and complex, and I shall survey only some of them. The first is that Wittgenstein, for example, has produced very powerful arguments against an essentialist nature of the self and of the idea that there is some kind of prelinguistic core nature to the self which is then, as it were, a universal underlying the differences of expression in different linguistic, social and cultural contexts.

The idea that self and context can be separated received its most paradigmatic statement in the work of Descartes who argued in *The Meditations* that it was possible to doubt the existence of the external world, the existence of other human beings and indeed the existence of one's own body – but not the experiences and contents of one's own mind. On this view, therefore, it is possible to see the nature of the self as being independent of the social, linguistic and cultural context of which it is a part. Wittgenstein denies this central Cartesian idea, and with it the representationist view that it is possible to think that psychological vocabulary in some way names or refers to a mental reality which exists in a clear and differentiated way prior to the acquisition of the appropriate language.[47] The argument against the possibility of a private language depends upon rejecting the idea that one could ever learn the language to characterise one's experience purely by reflecting upon the private, pre-linguistic nature of that experience. The effect of the argument, which turns crucially upon the idea that language necessarily involves rule following and that we could never follow a private rule, is to show that there is a non-contingent relationship between self and society and the linguistic practices of that society. Given this point, it follows that the terms in which we describe our states of consciousness such as desires, wants, needs and interests are drawn from a common stock of descriptions which are part of a common set of linguistic practices. As we shall see in the next chapter, this view is both crucial to and typical of post-liberal theologians such as George Lindbeck and also the narrative theologies of

---

[47] See Wittgenstein, *Philosophical Investigations* para. 258; S. Kripke, *Wittgenstein on Rules and Private Language* Blackwell, Oxford, 1986; F. Kerr *Theology After Wittgenstein* Blackwell, Oxford, 1986.

theologians such as Hauerwas and Frei. For the moment, however, we need to concentrate on the importance of this for the possibility of a theology of history. The main point at this stage in the argument is that there is not a universal core to selfhood which can in some sense be defined and characterised independently of particular linguistic practices and thus be able to act as the basis for a theological or philosophical anthropology to provide the ground for an absolutist stance in the theology of history.

The critic might, however, argue that even if self and society are related via language in the way posited, that does not mean that there cannot be universals relating to fundamental human purposes, since it could be the case that all languages and all forms of human society in fact articulate the same basic general truths about what human beings need in order to flourish, and which could then form a general standpoint from which to construct a universal history. Is this the case? Or is it rather, as Lyotard, the post-modern philosopher, argues, that the 'social subject itself seems to dissolve in this dissemination of language games' and thus can provide, neither, a universal sense of self, nor a universal set of reasons for action and a universal set of values such as justice – a concept that has been crucial to the tradition of political theology?

The critic of universalism in relation to society and social values will argue that values are embedded in particular ways of life which are not universal and may be incommensurable one with another. Each of these perspectives constitutes a major challenge to the idea of a theology of history as a basis for political theology. Questions about politics on this view are questions about particular societies, particular values and particular forms of language. The goods with which politics deals are deeply embedded in, and derive their meaning from, the contingent forms of community of which they are a part. Take, for example, Michael Walzer's views in *Spheres of Justice* where he argues that even the necessities of existence have local and particularistic social meanings: 'A single necessary good and one that is always necessary – food for example – carries different meanings in different places. Bread is the staff of life, the Body of Christ, the symbol of the Sabbath, the meaning of hospitality and so on.'[48] He goes on to argue that one cannot assume that underlying these different social meanings for bread there is a basic or primordial one to do with physiological need: 'If the religious use of bread were to conflict with its nutritional uses – if the Gods demanded that the bread be baked and burned rather than eaten – it is by no means clear which use would be primary.'[49]

Social goods have social meanings; there is no neutual account of human nature or the goods that human beings desire which could be used as a standard to determine which forms of human society meet human needs and desires most fully or constitute a richer and more persuasive focus of human fulfilment. Such goods are contingent and particularist, so the argument goes. They are not deducible from a single universal standard nor are they easily linkable to form a universal standard (an argument which will be revisited in the chapter on natural law and in the final chapter), and thus neither human nature nor a universal theory of human goods can be used to ground a theology of history. Values and ends made universal by abstracting from every specific context become for all practical purposes, meaningless.[50]

The same point is also true in relation to issues about the commensurability of values. If we accept the possibility of a theology of history and an end point or proleptic end point in the historical process, then it would seem to be entirely plausible to think that the process of history, either in completion or prolepsis, would imply a reconciliation of all values with one another – not just personal values of integrity, virtue, truth-telling, promise keeping and the like, but also public values such as liberty, equality, community etc. There is, however, the view, particularly associated with Isaiah Berlin, that values such as liberty and equality, valuable as they are, cannot be reconciled with one another or put into some kind of authoritative ranking. If this is so then choices have to be made between the demands

---

[48] M. Walzer, *Spheres of Justice* Martin Robinson, Oxford, 1983, p. 8.
[49] Ibid.   [50] Ibid.

that they make. These will be tragic choices often and, as choices, they will also be highly contingent. That is to say, the choice-based ranking cannot be regarded as tracking some kind of external reconciling procedure. Social and political life on this basis is agonistic.

So, for all these many reasons which lie at the heart of contemporary philosophical debates, the hope of John Cobb and Wolfhart Pannenberg that political theology can only proceed if we have a theology of history looks to be a vain hope – as, for that matter, is a philosophy of history. The conclusion at this stage of the argument is drawn well by Rorty:

> We do not need to replace religion with a philosophical account of a healing and unifying power which will do the work once done by God.
>
> I should like to replace both religious and philosophical accounts of a suprahistorical ground or end of history convergence with a histor- ical narrative about the rise of liberal institutions and customs. Such a narrative would clarify the conditions in which the idea of truth or correspondence with reality might gradually be replaced by the idea of truth as what comes to be believed in the course of free and open encounters.[51]

If this is, indeed, the agenda which political theology has to face, and there is a lot of argument to go in the book before we see clearly whether it is, then it raises in a fundamental way one of the issues raised in the discussion of liberalism in chapter 1, namely, in a liberal society which accepts the degree of plural- ism and particularism which has been the focus of the past few pages, and in circumstances in which there is no overarching way of resolving these problems, then we have to ask how Christians who believe that their faith has political implications should relate to such democratic and deliberative politics. Is it reasonable in a situation of pluralism to bring religious and metaphysical views into the public arena in a liberal society?

Before finally leaving the issue of a theology of history, however, I want to refer to one set of much less theoretical arguments against the possibility of history but ones which have

---

[51] Rorty, *Contingency Irony and Solidarity* p. 68.

probably shaken the confidence of those minded to see the possibility of a theology of history as central to political theology. These have to do with the question of whether it is possible to pursue a theology of history against the background of some of the singular horrors of the twentieth century. These arguments can be found in many post-war works on theology . Let me take just two examples. The first is from Alasdair Heron's essay 'The Person of Christ' in *Keeping the Faith*, one of the two volumes published to commemorate the centenary of the publication of *Lux Mundi*, a book deeply influenced by the domesticated Hegelian idealism developed in Oxford by T. H. Green and others, and which influenced Gore the editor and one of the main contributors to the book, and Illingworth the most competent philosopher of religion among its contributors. Heron argues in respect of the attempt to incorporate history and society into a unified theology:

> The road back to *Lux Mundi*'s vision of a world suffused by the light of the divine immanence is barred to us by an angel with a flaming sword – and the flames are not those of the transfiguration but of Auschwitz and Hiroshima, of Vietnam and Afghanistan. The harsh reality is that not only nature is red in tooth and claw: so too are human power, human politics, human striving for a better world. For those who have ears to hear, the cry of desolation uttered by Christ on the cross is as essential a key to our understanding our human predicament as the Prologue to the Fourth Gospel.[52]

And the same point is made by Gillespie in his fine book *Hegel, Heidegger and the Ground of History*:

> reason does not permeate all reality but rests upon an underlying darkness that is the true source of human motion and life. The 150 years since Hegel's death have witnessed the ascendancy of this darkness . . . Who today after Nietzsche and Freud, after Hitler and Stalin, after Verdun and Dachau can still believe in the triumph of reason. How can we avoid the conclusion that not reason but unreason rules in history?[53]

---

[52] A. Heron, 'The Person of Christ' in *Keeping the Faith: Essays to Mark the Centenary of Lux Mundi* ed. G. Wainwright, SPCK, London, 1989, p. 122.

[53] M. Gillespie, *Hegel, Heidegger and the Ground of History* University of Chicago Press, 1984, p. 114.

So, the idea of a theology of history appears to be very deeply problematical, and we need to consider alternative ways in which it might be thought Christian belief and social and political realities can be brought closer together. In the same way as Theodor Adorno once said that there could be no poetry after Auschwitz, so there can be no theory of history.[54]

---

[54] For a discussion of this theme in Adorno see G. Steiner, *Language and Silence* Faber, London, 1967.

CHAPTER 5

Narratives and foundations

For wisdom dealt with mortal powers,
Where truth in closest words shall fail,
When truth embodied in a tale
Shall enter in at lowly doors.

And so the Word had breath and wrought
With human hands the creed of creeds
In loveliness of perfect deeds,
More strong than all poetic thought;

Which he may read that binds the sheaf,
Or builds the house, or digs the grave
And those wild eyes that watch the wave
In roarings round the coral reef.

(Tennyson, *In Memoriam*)

If the foundations be destroyed, what can the righteous do? (Psalm 11)

It doesn't matter how you slice the salami, it's still the same salami. (Anon, New York)

Given the difficulties in undertaking a theology of history in the modern world, it might be thought that the basis for political theology has to be sought elsewhere: in systematic theology, so that the political implications of Christian belief could be derived by a process of inference from some sense of the foundations of theology as a doctrine of God. It might be thought that a doctrine of God would then yield an account of creation, within which would stand an account of the human person, and from this an account of society and politics. On this sort of view, the universal would be connected to the particular through a process of inference from what were to be taken as foundational propositions to be found in either a biblical or natural theology and their concomitant doctrine of God. Universal and particular would be linked through a greater and greater specification of the consequences of this foundational set of beliefs. Political theology would, as it were, lie downstream of a set of propositions taken as more basic, and from which the propositions of political theology could then be derived. To some extent, and at least in one reading of the tradition, this might be seen as the traditional Catholic approach to political theology. This is certainly how Hauerwas, who is not a disinterested observer, describes the strategy:

Catholics often assume that one must start with fundamental theology, which investigates the conditions of truthfulness, the metaphysical propositions (natural theology) which make theology at all possible. Then one proceeds to systematic theology, which deals with revelational claims such as Trinity, redemption, Christology, church and so on. Finally, one turns to ethics on the assumption that only when one's basic beliefs are clear and well-founded can one consider their moral implications . . . Even though Protestants have been less confident in natural theology or a natural law ethic, they also assume that theology begins with prolegomena.[1]

There is, in fact, an interesting kind of parallel in this respect with political philosophy. It has often been argued that political philosophy has to begin with some universal account of human nature, which might well include some account of man's place in the cosmos, and then go on to draw out of this some account of human purposes and human flourishing. In turn, from this could be derived some normative account of the role of society and politics as the environment within which human beings with this nature could flourish. In this sense, an account of human nature is thought of as foundational for politics in the same way as a doctrine of God and man is thought of as foundational for political theology within the systematic theology position.

However, in political philosophy, as we have already seen, this approach has come under severe attack over the past

---

[1] S. Hauerwas, *The Peaceable Kingdom* SCM Press, London, 1984, p. 54.

generation, particularly as the result of the work of Alasdair MacIntyre which, partly through the work of Hauerwas, has also become influential in theology. In the context of political philosophy, MacIntyre has argued that there is no way in which an account of human nature can be given which abstracts it as a foundational basis for any sort of theorising about human nature and human life, because, in his view, human nature is differently conceived within different and incommensurable political and moral traditions and there is no neutral account to be given between these different traditions. As he argues:

I cannot look to human nature as a neutral standard asking which forms of social and moral life would give it the most adequate expression. For each form of life carries with it its own picture of human nature. The choice of a form of life and the choice of a view of human nature go together.[2]

Human nature cannot be some kind of neutral foundation for a political theory. I believe that this claim is relevant to political theology in the following way. The systematic theology approach as set out by Hauerwas is not dissimilar in its central logic. The doctrine of God, whether based upon Natural or biblical theology, will yield a doctrine of what it is to be a person. and from this a theory of Christian ethics and politics. This presumes that the doctrine of God and man articulated within theology is in some way politically neutral, from which some kind of authoritative Christian ethics and politics can be deduced. However, it does seem to me that there are good grounds for doubting this. The detail of this argument is to be found in David Nicholls' fine book *Deity and Domination*[3] in which, as the result of a survey of the work of many theologians, he concludes that our understanding of the nature of God as Father, as Lord, as Judge, as Sovereign and so forth is not politically neutral, but, rather, that our understanding of God is shot through with ideas and analogies drawn from different forms of political life and different political experiences.

To take such a view is not to accept a form of Feuerbachian

2 A. MacIntyre, *A Short History of Ethics*, Routledge, London, 1967, p. 268.
3 D. Nicholls, *Deity and Domination*, Routledge, London, 1989.

reductionism[4] because, for Nicholls, the relationship between symbols and anologies used about God is far too dialectical to admit of reductionism, as he makes clear in the conclusion to *Deity and Domination*. Nevertheless, these political images are part of how believers understand God, and part of the terms in which we worship God and pray to God. These terms are indispensable, but they are not wholly compatible and yet there is no way of standing behind such images to produce a neutral, universal and objective way of determining the validity of such images. This is 'a wild goose chase' in Nicholls' view. As a result of his argument, he comes to the conclusion that: 'There is no possibility of simply working out the political implications of neutral theological understanding enjoying immunity from political taint.'[5] From this, he draws the conclusion that Christian ethics and political theology cannot be a matter of deducing from some politically neutral account of the nature of God the nature of a Christian political theology.[6]

On this view, therefore, it is not possible to employ a politically neutral concept of God, purged of social and political analogies and symbols from which could be derived a foundationalist or universalist political theology. Equally, we cannot argue that we can look at the different moral, social and political implications of the conceptions of God to try to determine which concept of God is most adequate in the sense of implying the most acceptable social and political consequences. On this point, Nicholls is surely right when he argues that:

Appeals 'downwards' from images and concepts of God to the kind of moral consequences – individual and social – which they entail is no solution. Different religious traditions assess these consequences differently and they cannot therefore constitute an agreed criterion to which appeal may be made. Within a particular tradition, however,

---

[4] For a subtle discussion of these themes see D. Pailin, *The Anthropological Character of Theology: Conditioning Theological Understanding* Cambridge University Press, 1990, see pp. 34ff.

[5] D. Nicholls, 'Christianity and Politics' in *The Religion of the Incarnation* ed. L. Morgan, Bristol Classical Press, Bristol, 1989, p. 180.

[6] Ibid.

where general agreement does exist, such appeals may be of considerable value in determining the appropriateness of competing images.[7]

The point is more or less exactly parallel to that of MacIntyre in the passage cited earlier with respect to *human* nature: 'The choice of a form of life and the choice of a view of human nature go together.'[8] Even if this could be done, there would still be two interrelated acute difficulties. The first I have already referred to several times, namely, that of the problem of universals and particulars, and again the problem here also has its parallel in political philosophy where the issue has become acute. Many political philosophers, the so-called communitarians such as Michael Sandel and Michael Walzer, argue that the attempt on the part of political philosophers to set out universal standards and principles of political morality and political principles such as equality, social justice, and so forth, is misconceived just because such principles are not sensitive to the specific historical circumstances of particular societies and the beliefs and values that people actually hold, and which play a crucial, if not determining, part in forming their identity as persons. We saw some of these themes worked out by Walzer in earlier chapters. Walzer has a particularly fine evocation of the issues at stake here in the opening pages of *Spheres of Justice*:

One way to begin the philosophical enterprise – perhaps the original way – is to walk out of the cave, leave the city, climb the mountain, to fashion for oneself (what can never be fashioned by ordinary men and women) an objective and universal standpoint. Then one describes the terrain of everyday life from far away, so that it loses its particular contours and takes on a general shape. But I mean to stand in the cave, in the city, on the ground. Another way of doing philosophy is to interpret to one's fellow citizens the world of meanings that we share. Justice and equality can be conceivably worked out as philosophical artifacts, but a just or egalitarian society cannot be. If such a society isn't already here – hidden as it were, in our concepts and categories – we shall never know it concretely or realise it in fact.[9]

We can only reason, for example, about how certain kinds of goods should be distributed when we understand the meaning

---

[7] Nicholls, *Deity and Domination* p. 241.
[8] MacIntyre, *A Short History of Ethics* p. 268o.
[9] Walzer, *Spheres of Justice* p. xiv.

that such goods have for people in the circumstances of particular societies. General principles, however subtle the philosophical arguments may be in favour of them, are going to be inert in relation to the particular circumstances of specific societies with the beliefs and values which societies may have, and the sense of identity which people have as the result of these values (which was the point Walzer made about Jonah, as we saw earlier).

Again, there is a parallel with systematic theology in its approach to political theology. Even assuming that it was possible to read off political values and principles from some kind of general or foundational doctrine of God and man within systematic theology, it would still confront the problem which Walzer identifies which parallels the difficulties we saw in the second chapter in relation to prophecy. How would these very general political values, which is almost certainly what they are going to be, actually relate to the specific circumstances of particular societies, even those which have a Christian background? It would, of course, be difficult for a Christian to see political theology within Walzer's perspective because Walzer rejects the idea of a standpoint which transcends the practices of particular societies, and yet a Christian doctrine of God and man within systematic theology is just such a transcendent perspective. Nevertheless, if we reject the possibility of a theology of history acting as some kind of mediating link between the particular and the universal, such as theologies and philosophies of history claim to establish, Walzer's point still has force, namely, that a political theology articulated from such a transcendent standpoint as a by-product of natural or biblical theology is still going to raise big questions about how such general principles relate to the beliefs and values of particular societies.

This is not a purely theoretical issue and it leads on to a further criticism, namely, that the universalist political theology which might emerge from such a systematic theology may be too general in a way that makes a Christian political commitment more or less indeterminate. This will form a theme of several later chapters. For the moment, I just want to indicate what the issue is here by using three separate examples. Three of the general principles that have been central to the political witness and interventions of the Christian churches in the twentieth century have been concerned with social justice, poverty and the idea of the common good. The problem with asserting a Christian concern with these things is that just on their own in an unqualified way the ideas of social justice, common good and poverty are very indeterminate.

Social justice is multifaceted: it can be concerned with distribution of social goods according to merit, need, entitlement, rights and so forth. These different principles will yield quite different distributions and might well imply different views of the roles of the state, the market and the voluntary sector as the agent of distribution. Invoking social justice without further qualification takes us virtually nowhere. Assume for the moment that a concern for social justice can be grounded as part of political theology within a systematic theology; can this theological grounding actually take us further in giving a more precise account of the nature of social justice that is in question? That is to say, can a concern with distribution according to need or desert or whatever be grounded within a broad theological framework? I doubt very much that it can at the level of systematic theology, in which case we are faced with a dilemma. From a universalising systematic theology we might be able to ground a general Christian concern for social justice, but such a general grounding may completely underdetermine Christian political praxis. If we are to have responsible Christian praxis informed by a theology, then it is going to have to be much more specific than this. However, the very generality of doctrines of God and man within systematic theology, even assuming that these might in some sense be morally and politically neutral (*pace* David Nicholls), are highly unlikely to be able to make these specific links. If, however, the links cannot be made, then we are back with the gap between universals and particulars which a theology of history was at least prepared to address.

Similar problems arise in relation to poverty and the bias to the poor. The question of who the poor are and, therefore, to whom we should have bias is highly controversial, particularly in relation to the question of whether poverty is *relative* or *absolute* and the relation of both to inequality. These issues are not technical questions to be solved by social science, but involve deep questions of moral and political principle. However, I doubt whether within a systematic theology these issues can be resolved just because they are so specific and involve among other things the beliefs and values of particular societies.

Exactly the same problems arise in relation to the nature of the common good which the Anglican liturgy enjoins us to seek: Christian political practice seems to involve the idea that it should be theologically informed. As we shall see in much more detail later, the idea of the common good is complex and controversial at the political level. It may mean a set of substantive goods and values which people are supposed to hold in common, in which case the question arises about the degree to which such an idea has salience in a pluralistic society in which people may differ quite fundamentally over their concep-tion of the good. Alternatively, the common good may be seen not so much in terms of an agreement on substance as a framework within which people with different conceptions of the good are able to get along in a way marked by a mutual recognition and respect for differences, as, for example, Charles Larmore argues.[10] It is quite possible, therefore, to entertain at least two radically different general conceptions of the common good. The question is whether a universalist/foundationalist theology can ever become specific enough to enable a cogent arbitration to be made between them in the light of such a theology. Christian practice seems to involve the idea that it should be theologically informed. However, if such practice as rooted in systematic theology is not specific enough, can there really be a political theology of the common good which can inform a specifically Christian praxis?

An additional doubt here is, in some ways, parallel to the previous point, but perhaps makes it in a rather different way,

[10] Larmore, *Morals*.

namely, that however abstract a conception of God may be, there may be quite salient and social and political implications built into that abstract characterisation. If competing abstract characterisations of God at the foundational level are incommensurable, and disputes over the appropriate characterisation of God cannot be resolved, then the social and political doctrines which flow from those incommensurable characterisations will also be irresolvable if indeed they are grounded in the disputed nature of God. Let me take a very specific example to illustrate this difficult point. As we saw earlier, Hegel and Barth had very different conceptions of God for which they could claim support from Scripture and, in the case of Hegel, from metaphysics. In Hegel's view, God's self-consciousness cannot be conceived independently of the world, human life and human history. Any attempt to understand the nature of God in abstraction from the created world makes it impossible to understand God as possessing self-consciousness and it makes creation appear whimsical and arbitrary.[11] The first argument is that self-consciousness for Hegel has to be understood as an *achievement*, not a *status*, that is to say it has to be developed in relation to 'otherness' where the 'other' includes other persons as centres of self-consciousness and the world of natural objects and phenomena. This is how we develop our own self-consciousness, for Hegel, and we cannot have a concept of self-consciousness which is applicable to any other being which does not utilise the same criteria for its ascription – that is, we can only come to some kind of judgement about the nature of God's self-consciousness if that is rooted in what we understand by self-consciousness in general and how it is achieved. Hence, it cannot be the case, for Hegel, that the world of nature and human history is somehow contingently related to the being of God. God's self-consciousness is also non-contingently related to otherness, alienation and the overcoming of this estrangement. On the contrary, as Hegel notoriously argues in his *Lectures on the Philosophy of Religion*: 'Without the world God is not God.' Creation therefore, for Hegel, was an inner necessity on

---

[11] See Plant, *Hegel on Religion*.

the part of the development of God's self-consciousness. So, too, is Incarnation. Obviously, on this view of the necessary immanence of God in relation to God's own self-consciousness, the nature of man and how this nature is developed in history and in and through institutions is central not only to human development, but also for understanding the nature of God.

Barth, on the other hand, takes a resolutely different line, with major consequences for the relative position of history and institutions within his and Hegel's theology. In contrast to Hegel, Barth argues that 'God would be no less God even if the work of creation had never been, if there were no creatures and if the whole doctrine of providence were therefore an irrelevance. Hence, there can be no place for this doctrine in that of the being of God.'[12] From this it follows, for Barth, that neither what he calls general history, nor, for that matter the thin line of salvation history (*Heilsgeschichte*), is part of the self-revelation of God, as both are for Hegel, and nor do they reveal any necessary features about the nature of God. This obviously makes their theological understanding of history and institutions radically different. The point for note at the moment, though, is that, if we take the doctrine of God as being in some sense foundational for political theology, then radically different conceptualisations of the nature of God will yield different accounts of the nature of political theology and a theology of history. If there is no way of arbitrating between these foundationalist conceptions of God, then the political and social theologies which they generate will also be incommensurable if they are really rooted in such conceptions. Equally, precisely because of this last point, we cannot use the social and political implications of a concept of God to arbitrate disputes about our understanding of God for exactly the reasons given by David Nicholls earlier.

There are other difficulties, too, with the systematic theology approach which have assumed importance in recent years in the work of narrative theologians. These theologians include J. B. Metz in *Faith in History and Society*,[13] G. Lindbeck in *The*

---

[12] Barth, *Church Dogmatics* pp. 48–9.
[13] J. P. Metz, *Faith in History and Society* trans. D Smith, Burns and Oates, London, 1980.

Nature of Doctrine: Religion and Theology in a Post-Liberal Age,[14] S. Hauerwas in *The Peaceable Kingdom*[15] and J. Yoder in *The Politics of Jesus* and *The Royal Priesthood*.[16] In the background here, in the case of Hauerwas and Lindbeck, are the later writings of Wittgenstein and the work of Alasdair MacIntyre, particularly *After Virtue*[17] and *Whose Justice and Which Rationality?*,[18] and Hans Frei, *The Eclipse of the Biblical Narrative*,[19] *Theology and Narrative*,[20] and *Types of Christian Theology*.[21] There are, of course, major differences between these thinkers, and in the case of Lindbeck, his interest is not primarily in Christian political theology and political ethics so much as the nature of doctrine, but for the purposes of this chapter I shall treat the differences as being less important than the similarities. What they have in common is a rejection of the approaches so far outlined, i.e. theology of history and systematic or foundational theology and an insistence on the importance of practice and narrative as opposed to some kind of universalist and foundationalist approach to political theology. They all contest the model that is common to the two approaches that I have outlined so far. The model presupposed in what has gone before is one in which theology and doctrine are construed as cognitive structures which will lead via inference to a political theology as a set of propositions that will guide political practice. In rejecting such a view in favour of a narrative view of Christian belief and the primacy of practice in Christian ethics and politics, they do produce rather similar arguments. In addition, it is worth remarking that some of these arguments find parallels in the writings of political

[14] G. Lindbeck, *The Nature of Doctrine: Religion and Theology in a Post-Liberal Age* Westminster Press, Philadelphia, 1984.
[15] Hauerwas, *The Peaceable Kingdom*.
[16] J. H. Yoder, *The Politics of Jesus* W. B. Eerdmans, Grand Rapids, Mich., 1972; *The Royal Priesthood* W. B. Eerdmans, Grand Rapids, Mich., 1994.
[17] MacIntyre, *After Virtue* 2nd edn, Duckworth, London, 1985.
[18] A. MacIntyre, *Whose Justice? Which Rationality?* Duckworth, London, 1988.
[19] H. Frei, *The Eclipse of the biblical Narrative* Yale University Press, New Haven, Conn., 1974.
[20] H. Frei, *Theology and Narrative: Selected Essays* ed. G. Hunsinger and W. Placher, Oxford University Press, 1993.
[21] H. Frei, *Types of Christian Theology* ed. G. Hunsinger and W. Placher, Yale University Press, New Haven, Conn., 1992.

philosophers such as Walzer and Rorty who have also been influenced by narrative approaches.

The first argument which is used extensively by Metz and by Hauerwas is that theologies of the universalist sort that I have described in fact abstract from the historical and situated sense of the self. As we saw in the last chapter, albeit in a different context, such a view of the self runs up against profound philosophical difficulties. This is argued by Metz in the section of *Faith in History and Society* which is titled 'Against the Theologies of the Subject that are Divorced from the Subject'. What Metz has in mind here are theologies which, either through theologies of history, or through universal principles, actually do not take into account the specific ways in which human nature is, to a large extent, constituted by specific historical situations. Examples here would be systematic theologies which purport to derive a doctrine of man from a prior doctrine of God and then seek to ground political theology in such a doctrine of man; and theologies of history which purport to link the universal and the particular but only through a view of the nature of God and man which is determined by the undergirding metaphysical framework within which the essence of God and man are, as it were, predetermined and then seen as realised or not in the processes of history and specific societies. Metz argues as follows:

[I]n this type of theology of the subject, history and society only appear as anthropological reductions. They can be regarded only as variables of a subject or an anthropology which tries to keep the subject out of its historical and social struggles for identity, as it were almost *a priori*, by means of a late and diminished form of metaphysics and which compensates for its suspected disassociation from history by a weakened idea of the historicity of the subject.[22]

Metz is therefore criticising the idea that we can formulate a conception of the self abstracted from all forms of context and particularity.

A very similar point was made by Bernard Lonergan in his *Collected Papers*, volume 2[23] in which he describes a transition in

---

[22] Metz, *Faith in History and Society* pp. 62ff.
[23] W. Ryan and B. J. Tyrrell, eds., *A Second Collection of Papers by Bernard J. F. Lonergan* Darton, Longman and Todd, London, 1974, pp. 69–86.

the contemporary world from a 'metaphysics of the soul to an analysis of the subject'. His point is glossed by Charles Davis when he remarks that:

The metaphysics of the soul is a totally objective account of the constituents of human nature, applying universally to all human beings, whatever may be the state of mind or degree of development. The study of the subject concerns oneself in as much as one is conscious.[24]

Lonergan envisages that the analysis of the subject reveals an existential self, free to create itself, that is to say, there is not a universal essence of the soul ultimately identical in every case. The difference with the narrative theologians is that, while they would agree with Lonergan's worries about the metaphysics of the soul and dismiss it, the subject is not an existential self-creation but rather formed by narrative which is a public, common and unchosen inheritance.

Hauerwas draws explicitly on the work of MacIntyre to make the last point clear:

What is crucial to human beings as characters in enacted narratives is that, possessing only the resources of psychological continuity, we have to be able to respond to the imputation of strict identity. I am forever what I have been at any time for others . . . there is no way of founding my identity – or lack of it – on the psychological continuity or discontinuity of the self. The self inhabits a character whose unity is given as the unity of character.[25]

This contrasts fundamentally with an idea of the person as subject that is determined independently of history and culture in order to produce its account of society and politics which is of a universal and transcultural sort; indeed, the sort of conception of the self that has often been presupposed in liberal political thought – particularly that inspired by Kant. This conception of the subject has been vigorously contested by Hauerwas. He argues that the crucial aspects of being a subject and being an agent are dependent on language and narrative. My capacity as an agent is dependent upon my descriptive

---

[24] C. Davis, *Religion and the Making of Society: Essays in Social Theology* Cambridge University Press, 1994.
[25] MacIntyre, *After Virtue* p. 217.

ability, the sorts of intentions that I can ascribe to myself, the sorts of motives I can entertain. This descriptive ability is not a kind of private power, but is rooted in the language of a particular community and the range of descriptions available within it. This follows from the Wittgensteinian critique of the idea of a private language which was discussed in the previous chapter. We learn to describe through appropriating the narratives and range of descriptions of the community of which we are a part. The self is narratively formed, and those narratives are going to be highly specific to particular communities and traditions. The narrative for the Christian is formed by the life, death and resurrection of Jesus and the tradition of the church. There cannot be some abstracted idea of the self or of human nature which can be determined independently of narrative and particular forms of language:

We are our character. But many feel that this is not enough. If we are to be genuinely free, a transcendental 'I' is required that ensures that we will never be contained by our character. The difficulty with this, however, is that such an 'I' must be impersonal, free from any history, which is exactly what makes us what we are.[26]

The same sort of point is made by Hans Frei who argues that: 'there is such a direct mutual determination of character and circumstance, all one can do is to tell the particular story of it'.[27] This leads Hauerwas to argue that I am only able to locate my action within an ongoing history and within a community of language users. My actions are mine not because I have caused them as if they were external to me, but rather because I am able to fit them into an ongoing story. My power as an agent is therefore relative to the power of my descriptive ability. Yet that very ability is fundamentally a social skill, for we learn to describe through appropriating the narratives of the communities in which we find ourselves. The self is narratively formed, and these narratives are going to be highly specific to particular communities and traditions, hence a foundationalist theology cannot produce out of a doctrine of God an historical doctrine of man which can therefore act as some kind of foundation for

---

[26] Hauerwas, *The Peaceable Kingdom* p. 39.
[27] Frei, *Theology and Narrative* p. 37.

political and social theology. Metz, too, calls the attempt to do this *Idealistic* in the sense that such general theologies involve an abstraction of persons from the very circumstances which give persons a sense of identity and worth.[28]

It is worth noting here not only the parallelism with some modern writers in political theory such as Rorty, Walzer and Sandel, who also stress the narrative constitution of the self or what Sandel[29] calls the 'encumbered self', but also the impact of such a situated view of the self on liberal political thought.

Liberal political theory has stressed its universalism and foundationalism which seems to ascribe a common structure to the self and the universality of that structure. But in its perfectionist form it has also made autonomy one of its central virtues. The emphasis by both narrative theologians and narrative political theorists on the 'situated self' challenges all of these: universality because the selves are constituted by different and incommensurable narratives; foundationalism because the self is a product of narrative not some extra narrative foundation; and autonomy because of the way the self is constituted and of its narrative context. As Hauerwas argues, bringing these points together: 'Since our existence is historically determined we should not be surprised to discover that our moralities are historical: they require a qualifier. We are unable to stand outside our histories in mid air, as it were.'[30]

Lindbeck makes a not dissimilar point, but in a rather different context. It has been argued by theologians, he says, and F. Schleiermacher, R. Otto and M. Eliade are the best examples, that religion is to be seen as a way in which human beings articulate certain kinds of fundamental and universal experiences which are common across human nature and across time, whether this is a sense of absolute dependency as in Schleiermacher, or the idea of the Holy in Otto, and so forth. This view that different religions, as it were, articulate some kind of basic general or universal prelinguistic religious experience, which can be described independently of the different

---

[28] Metz, *Faith in History and Society* p. 65.
[29] M. Sandel, *Liberalism and the Limits of Justice* Cambridge University Press, 1982.
[30] Hauerwas, *The Peaceable Kingdom* p. 29.

forms that it takes, is a basis for some kind of claim to universality in religion. However, Lindbeck rejects this view. On the view that he wants to defend, which is clearly heavily dependent on some version of Wittgenstein's argument about the impossibility of a private language, such approaches are misconceived. Instead of religious discourse giving shape to some pre-existing prelinguistic and universal religious inner experience he argues that:

the means of communication and expression are a precondition, a kind of quasi transcendental (i.e. culturally formed) a priori for the possibility of experience. We cannot identify, describe, or recognize experience qua experience without the use of signs and symbols . . . In short it is necessary to have the means for expressing an experience in order to have it.[31]

These means of expression are then part and parcel of particular religious narratives. To become religious means to become skilled in the language, and he draws from this the conclusion that being religious is not a matter of entertaining propositions and drawing inferences from them, but is rather a matter of how to be religious in such-and-such ways. His approach rejects a kind of cognitive universalism in religious belief, whether this is based on the supposed cognitive content of religious claims, or whether these claims are supposed to articulate some universally shared sense of religious experience. What is important, then, is the narrative and the way the narrative is bound up with the life of the religious community, or what he calls the cultural linguistic system. Doctrines are not, as it were, basic propositions of the system from which inferences are to be drawn, but act more like the grammar or the rules of the system. Doctrines provide the grammar for religious interpretive systems, as he calls them, and these, as in Wittgenstein (to imagine a language is to imagine a form of life), cannot be detached from the life of religious discipleship and treated as cognitive claims in some kind of universalist sense.

Indeed, he links this issue with J. L. Austin's idea of *performative utterance*. It is not the case that religious claims derive their

---

[31] Lindbeck, *The Nature of Doctrine* p. 36.

truth from comparison with some kind of reality to which they correspond, rather, as he says:

a religious utterance acquires the propositional truth of ontological correspondence only in so far as it is a performance, an act or a deed which helps to create that correspondence. The truth of religious beliefs is not therefore an attribute that they have when considered in and of themselves, but is only a function of their role in constituting a form of life, a way of being in the world.[32]

Hence the systematic approach to a political theology which sees political theology as a set of inferences drawn from basic propositions established in basic theology, whether Natural or biblical, is to mistake the nature of religious claims and more importantly the religious life. It follows from this, he argues, that religious claims are altered and modified neither by difficulties in the truth claims of those beliefs, nor as the result of changes in pre-linguistic religious experiences, but rather because a religious interpretive scheme embodied, as always, in religious practice or belief develops anomalies in its application in new contexts: 'Prophetic figures apprehend, often with dramatic vividness, how inherited patterns of belief, practice, and ritual need to be and can be reminted.'[33]

Frei, by whom MacIntyre has been influenced, and who did not regard himself straightforwardly as a narrative theologian, still makes the same general point as Lindbeck when he argues that:

There is, it seems to me, a variety of descriptions for any linguistic phenomenon, and hence, above all, no ontological super-description or explanation for it. Furthermore, the 'grammar' (used according to the rules of such a construct) is more readily exhibited or set forth than stated in the abstract.[34]

Indeed, Frei's editors for the book, George Hunsinger and William Placher, made a good case in the 'Introduction' for claiming that Frei is seen as a post-modern theologian who, along with Barth, they argue 'rejects universal rules of hermeneutics and scholarly method and attends to the particularities of the texts and the communities before them.'[35]

---

[32] Ibid. p. 65.   [33] Ibid. p. 39.
[34] Frei, *Theology and Narrative* p. 33.   [35] Ibid. p. 19.

In the case of political theology, which Lindbeck does not discuss, this means, it seems to me, to constitute a rejection of the systematic theology approach. This seems to be clear from what he says when discussing other aspects of the implications of his doctrines and his rejection of theological liberalism. When he discusses the problem of preaching the gospel in a dechristianised world, he argues that the attitude of what he calls liberal foundationalism is misconceived. Such liberals, he argues, think that the problem here is to identify what the modern world is concerned about and then to translate the gospel answers into a currently understandable conceptuality. However, this is mistaken, in his view. He argues that the task of preaching the gospel is more like the ancient churches approach to catechism rather than translation of a set of universal propositions into a modern idiom. Instead of redescribing the faith into modern terms, it is a matter of teaching the languages and practices of the religion to potential adherents. It is a matter of initiating them into the narrative and practices of a way of life. As far as political commitment is concerned, this would seem to imply the falsity of a liberal version of the approach.

It is also argued by the narrative theologians that the systematic approach in fact relativises the truth of the narrative to the representational truth of the propositions of the systematic theology or a metaphysical theory underlying theology. Religious truth and the narrative events in which it is embedded become an examplar of a set of metaphysical truths which are not embedded in a narrative and can be known on grounds not connected with the narrative. On the narrative view, however, there is much more a performative rather than a representational view of the truth. As George Lindbeck argues: 'a religious utterance acquires the propositional truth of ontological correspondence only in so far as it is a performance, an act or a deed which helps to create that correspondence'.[36]

This is a crucial reason for rejecting foundationalism in the view of these thinkers. They reject the idea that the Christian

---

[36] Lindbeck, *The Nature of Doctrine* p. 95.

faith can, in fact, be translated into the metaphysical conceptual structures of philosophy and defended with reference to those structures. They also reject the idea that the social and political implications of Christianity can be derived from such metaphysical claims rather than from claims about the salience of the narrative which defines Christian belief. This is an important issue, and I shall spend some time on it with reference to the work of Hegel, Strauss and T. H. Green because, in the work of Hegel and Green at least, this translation of faith into philosophy has a direct bearing on the nature of society and politics. These thinkers provide the greatest possible contrast to the narrative approach, but equally they embody views which have been very influential in political theology and, indeed, at least in the case of Hegel and Green, the links between philosophy, theology and social and political understanding form an indissoluble whole.

Throughout his life, Hegel was concerned about what he saw as the social fragmentation of the modern world which he thought had very deep roots in the history of Western culture. Since the decline of the Greek *polis*, which he saw, particularly in his early writings, as an image of a cohesive community, the Western world had experienced a growth of individualism which he saw as linked to a wide range of historical phenomena: the rise of Roman Law, the rise of Protestantism, the growth of the economic market and industrialisation and urbanisation of modern society, and the impact of philosophical theories, particularly Kantian moral philosophy and the French Revolution. Hegel was convinced that modern Western society had a deep need to restore a sense of community and ethical life, and, in order to do this, the moral values that actually existed in society, particularly Christianity, needed to be reinterpreted to create an outlook which could form the basis of social cohesion. As we saw in the third chapter, as a religion, Christianity, while a true picture of the immanent relationship between God, man and the world as represented in the Incarnation, remains at the level of *Vorstellung*, of picture thinking. It is shot through with analogies, parables, stories, symbols and so forth and rests upon subjective faith or, to put the point in the terms of the present discussion, on narrative and stories. If Christianity was to play a continuing role in the value system that could create a coherent society, narrative had to be transcended by philosophy: to transform *Vorstellung* into *Begriffe*, into a conceptual structure which would rest upon reason rather than faith. Faith and narrative forms of religion are esoteric and rest upon private judgement and attitude. This standpoint has to be transcended dialectically into a philosophically defensible conceptual structure which would be available to public reason, and thus provide a coherent framework of values for political society, at least for all those willing to take on what he calls 'the exertion of the concept'. This dialectical transformation does *not* mean that narrative is lost, but it does mean that it is a *bridge* to this public exoteric understanding.

So transformed, the Christian religion which appears to be other-worldly, involving the worship of a transcendent God whose relation to human life and history in all its particularity seems to be obscure, has to be turned into a philosophical structure which, as we saw in chapter 3, stresses the immanence of God in human life and history and which as we saw Colletti argues, treats history and the institutions of society as sacramental[37] – as demonstrating the development of God's self-consciousness in and through all the modalities of human life. Once the world is interpreted in this way, it will provide a basis for common understanding and common culture: in a word a common life.

These points were taken up and developed by Strauss, albeit in a more radical way and without such an emphasis as in Hegel on the social and political implications of such views. Strauss gives a clear account of the more radical Hegelian transformation of Christianity into a rational, exoteric philosophical form when he argues as follows:

Humanity is the union of the two natures – God becomes man, the infinite manifesting itself in the finite, and the finite spirit remem-

---

[37] Colletti, *Marxism and Hegel* p. 269: 'These institutions, which to us seem to be historical institutions, institutions that were born at one time and and are destined to pass away at another, to Hegel appear . . . as the presence of God in the world – not profane realities but "mystical objects", not historical institutions but sacraments.'

bering its infinite . . . It is Humanity that dies, rises and ascends to heaven, for from the negation of its phenomenal life, there ever proceeds a higher spiritual life; from the suppression of its mortality as a personal, national and terrestrial spirit, arises its union with the infinite spirit of the heavens. By faith in the Christ, especially in his death and resurrection, man is justified before God; that is by the kindling within him the idea of Humanity, the individual participates in the divinely human life of the species . . . This alone is the absolute sense of Christology: that it is annexed to the person and history of the individual, is a necessary result of the historical form from which Christology was taken.[38]

The narrative of Jesus as the Incarnate Lord has to be transformed into a philosophical doctrine about the indwelling of God in the whole of humanity – a view which clearly has potential for social and political theology. This process of transforming intuition, perceptions and representations into concepts (*Verarbeitung von Auschauung und Vorstellung in Begriffe*) allowed Hegel to provide an account of what Colletti calls the Bourgeois – Christian Society in which 'the reconciliation of the two worlds, which with Christ has taken place only in a single point, must pervade reality as a whole'.[39]

These themes are taken up by T. H. Green in the late nineteenth century and linked again as they were explicitly by Hegel and implicitly in the passage quoted from Strauss to problems of modern society. In his Lay Sermons, given in Balliol College Hall, and other writings Green argued that the historical and narrative bases of Christianity in the Bible were coming under threat, partly from biblical critics such as Strauss and Baur, and from modern science which, for example, cast doubt upon the biblical account of creation. Green was convinced that Christianity could not survive in its narrative and historical form, but its essence could be secured by transforming it into a philosophical theory which could also ground moral and political principles just as much as Christianity in the traditional narrative form had done. So this metaphysical system served two purposes for Green. First of all, it would

---

[38] D. F. Strauss, *The Life of Jesus Critically Examined* trans. G. Eliot, SCM Press, London, 1973, p. 780.
[39] Colletti, *Marxism and Hegel* p. 267.

render philosophically defensible and perspicuous the beliefs held by Christians but which were represented in both a misleading and contested narrative form within the life of Christian discipleship. In addition, however, because the essential elements of Christian doctrine and morality could be transformed into a philosophical account of the nature and purpose of human life and institutions, it could still provide a public, rational basis for common understanding of the basic structures of human life and society and for ideas about citizenship and the common good.

We can illustrate both of these themes from Green in ways that point the contrast very clearly with the views of narrative theologians. As far as the first point about the philosophical basis of Christianity is concerned, Green writes as follows:

> At a time when every thoughtful man accustomed to call himself a Christian is asking the faith which he professes for some account of its origins and authority, it is a pity the answer should be confused by the habit of identifying Christianity with the set of written propositions which constitute the written *New Testament*.[40]

And:

> Philosophy on its part is seen to be the effort towards self-recognition of that spiritual life which fulfils itself in may ways but most completely in the Christian religion and is related to religion as flowers to a leaf.[41]

So far as the second point is concerned, we can point to the following argument which leads him to link an account of Christianity so transformed into a public philosophy with moral and social consequences in the following passage:

> Our formula then is that God is identical with the self of everyman in the sense of being the realisation of its determinate possibilities . . . that is that in being conscious of himself man is conscious of God and thus knows what God is but knows what he is only in so far as he knows what he himself really is.[42]

---

[40] T. H. Green, 'Essay on Christian Dogma', *The Works of T. H. Green* vol. 3, ed. Nettleship, R. L. Longman Green and Co., London, 1911, p. 101.
[41] Green, 'Popular Philosophy in its Relation to Life' in *Works of T. H. Green* p. 121.
[42] Ibid. p. 227.

This point is linked by Green to morality in his Sermon *The Word is Nigh Thee:*

If there is an essence within the essence of Christianity, it is the thought embodied in the text I have read; the thought of God not as 'far off' but as 'nigh'; not as master but as father, not as terrible outward power forcing us we know not whither, but as one of whom we may say that we are reason of his reason, and spirit of his spirit, who lives in our moral life and for whom we live in living for the brethren as in so living we live freely.[43]

The fulfilment of the duties of citizenship are seen by Green as involved in 'living for the brethren' and the conception of shared obligations is rooted in the idea that we all share in the life of God. These arguments were taken up by other Idealist philosophers of religion, particularly by Edward Caird and Sir Henry Jones, and linked to social and political thought and, indeed, to a significant set of developments of liberal political theory at a formative time in the late ninteenth and early twentieth centuries, and had a significant influence on the development of New or Social Liberalism.[44] Thus the inherited narrative which has become contested could be transformed into a philosophical account which could become the base of a common social and political life.

Alasdair MacIntyre makes the point rather well when he argues that:

T. H. Green tried to inaugurate a new concept of citizenship which would link men of different social classes. The concept was based upon the notion that there was a good common to members of all classes, a goal the existence of which could be established from German Idealist metaphysics which could be made visible in actual measures of educational reform and social welfare.[45]

The point about 'German metaphysics' should not, however, be misconstrued. For Green, such metaphysics is not, as it might seem, a rather distant and arcane theory, but makes a philosophical rendering of what he takes to be the essence of

---

[43] Ibid. p. 221.
[44] For a fuller treatment see A. Vincent and R. Plant *Philosophy, Politics and Citizenship* Blackwell, Oxford, 1984.
[45] A. MacIntyre, *Secularisation and Moral Change* Oxford University Press, 1967, p. 28.

Christianity as it was lived in what was still a Christian society which was in danger of being eroded because the narrative and historical bases of that position were under attack.

It would also be a mistake to think that these ideas are completely *passé*, rooted in late nineteenth-century concerns and in an arcane metaphysics. Whatever one might think about the metaphysical theories, the normative impulse behind them is still salient, as Donald MacKinnon has made clear. He argues that:

We cannot deny a sort of attraction to the view which would make Christianity in some sense independent of certain events having taken place; or indeed would enable us to treat these events as mere illustrations of some more general principle of spiritual life which in their bare bones they dramatically illustrate. (One thinks here of the handling of the Christian tradition by those who have studied deeply in the school of Hegel, or who have made their own existentialist ethic of freedom, derived supposedly from the work of Martin Heidegger.) Moreover, we have to reckon with elements in the tradition itself which seem to encourage us to free our religious imaginations from too tight a bondage to Jesus in the days of his flesh. There is the Johannine theology of the Paraclete, and above all perhaps, that obscure saying of St Paul which so baffled exegetes when he writes (in II Corinthians) of 'knowing Christ no longer *kata sarka* (after the flesh)'. Were not the Hegelians justified in construing the *noli me tangere* of the risen Christ to Mary Magdalene in the record of the fourth Gospel as a concrete mythical expression of the demand that Christians discard the bondage of a false attachment to the details of a particular history, and adhere within themselves to a way of life which they must realize in circumstances altogether strange to those who first listened to Jesus?[46]

It is obvious that narrative, post-liberal or post-modern theology poses a considerable challenge to the position I have just described. The challenge is of two sorts.

First of all, the narrative theologian will reject very clearly the idea that the narrative of the Christian faith, as found for example in the gospels, can be seen either as a bridge or a ladder to a philosophical position which then can be understood and defended independently of the narrative. As Hauerwas

---

[46] D. MacKinnon, *The Borderlands of Theology* Lutterworth, London, 1968, p. 83.

argues 'there is no point that can be separated from the story
. . . stories are not substitute explanations we can someday
hope to supplant with more straightforward accounts'.[47] Narrative is the only means of knowing God. As Hauerwas says:

> Narrative is not secondary to a knowledge of God; there is no point
> that can be separated from the story. The narratives through which
> we learn of God are the point. Stories are not substitute explanations
> we can some day hope to supplant with more straightforward
> accounts. Precisely to the contrary, narratives are necessary to our
> understanding of those aspects of our existence which admit of no
> further explanation i.e. God, the world, and the self.[48]

Hegel and Green, to the contrary, believed that one could come
to understand the nature of the Christian God through reflection on the nature of human consciousness, and reason from
that to an account of the sort of consciousness that God has,
and his relationship to the world and human history as a being
whose self-consciousness could only be realised in the created
world and human history. This was, for them, not only a true
account of the essence of Christianity, but also it insulated
Christianity against attacks on the veracity of its narrative and
biblical form by transforming it into a socially and politically
relevant metaphysic. This, however, leads us back to what, as
we saw earlier, is called the metaphysics of the soul as opposed
to the analysis of the subject. If human self-consciousness is
narratively formed, is related to particular stories and circumstance then there is no general theory of the self that could lead
us to an account of the nature of God. It is true that Hegel had
an ineliminable place for narrative in the formation of the self,
and this is the main theme of his *Phenomenology of the Spirit*, but
narrative had to be transcended. Metz, too, criticises the
approach taken by Green and Hegel, and in a modern idiom by
Rahner, as transcendental/idealistic, and argues that it does not
do justice to the narrative nature of Christianity. He accepts the
kind of pull of this idea, as we saw did Mackinnon:

> One suspects that the process of transcendentalization of the Chris-
> tian subject may have been guided by a tendency to unburden and to
> immunize. Should this process of transcendentalization not give

---

[47] Hauerwas, *The Peaceable Kingdom* p. 26.   [48] Ibid. p. 26.

Christianity a kind of omnipresence which would ultimately remove it from every radical threat in the sphere of history?[49]

Narrative and history were fundamentally challenged in the nineteenth century, and what Metz calls this idealisation of Christianity transformed it into a more metaphysical doctrine considered to be immune from this attack. But he goes on to argue that the nature of Christianity is destroyed by the very process of transcendentalisation. The underlying reason for this is the same as for Hauerwas; there is no such universal subject whose fundamental nature can be identified independently of the narrative and, furthermore, translating Christian belief into the categories of theological reflection turns the Christian religion and its linked theology into a set of inert philosophical categories rather than the practically oriented, narratively formed phenomenon that it is: 'This practical structure of the idea of God is the reason why the concept of God is basically narrative and memorative (narrative and memory are not added as an ornament to a "pure" idea of God).'[50]

Metz goes on to say that 'stories of conversion and exodus are therefore not simply dramatic embellishments of a previously conceived pure theology.' This links up to Lindbeck's idea of truth outlined earlier where he situated the notion of truth in a performance and praxis oriented way rather than a reflective, philosophical one:

Christ does not become universal via an idea, but via the intelligible power of praxis, the praxis of following Christ. This intelligibility of Christianity cannot be transmitted theologically in a purely specula-tive way. It can only be transmitted as narrative and practical Christianity.[51]

Narratives are not a contingent embellishment of pure ideas. They are not symbols. Rather, what God is is revealed wholly and only in narrative, and narrative is linked to the life of Christian discipleship.

This relates back directly to political theology in the following

[49] Metz, *Faith in History and Society* p. 163
[50] Ibid. p. 51; cf. Hauerwas, *The Peaceable Kingdom* pp. 56–7.
[51] Lindbeck, *The Nature of Doctrine* p. 95.

way. Hegel and Green, together with those who followed them, saw the need for abstracting a universal reflective essence from Christianity as the only way of ensuring that it could form the basis of a common world which could be shared by both Christian and non-Christian. Since the rational essence of Christianity as the true religion reveals in symbolic form the real nature of ultimate human purposes both privately and in the public world, it follows that, once this religion is translated philosophically into a universally valid conceptual form accept-able to public reason, it would then form the basis of a common life. This issue is vitally important, since the privatisation of Christianity has occurred as a result of a belief, unlike the beliefs held in the early church and by the medievals, that the public world cannot be understood in terms of theological categories. Hegel and the post-Hegelians such as Green believe that it could be so understood if religious belief could be changed from a contingent and contested narrative and trans-formed into a philosophical and rational theory which would enable Christians to act with confidence in a public world which could be understood in terms of these categories.

If, however, we take the narrative route and see Christianity as rooted in, and intelligible only within, a specific narrative, then this would be bought at the cost of denying the possibility of a common public world given that, in a pluralist society, this narrative is shared and lived by only some. This would mean that there can be no common world, because there is no standpoint outside competing narratives to which they can be assimilated and within which their essence can be understood. Those thinkers who put the central emphasis on narrative do not flinch from this point. Yoder, from the standpoint of Christian narrative theology, makes the point explicitly as does MacIntyre when he argues in *After Virtue* (p. 263) that a pluralist society embodying competing and incommensurable narratives would be embodying a dark age where, to invoke Matthew Arnold in *On Dover Beach* 'Ignorant armies clash by night'. The point is made trenchantly by Yoder: 'There is no public that is not another particular province . . . all communities of moral insight are provincial . . . there exists no non-provincial general community . . . [and] therefore we must converse at every border.'[52] The implications of such a view for political theology and, indeed, the unity of society are profound, but I shall seek to draw out these in the next chapter.

It is important to realise at this juncture that there is another side to the narrative point which strikes at the heart of the Hegel/Green claim that a rationalised form of Christianity could provide a common ethos for modern society. First of all, as MacIntyre argues: 'most contemporary philosophers would treat that metaphysics as a pretty weak candidate to offer for the intellectual foundation for a new religion'.[53] A religion, that is, that would provide a common ethos for society. This point is also made by Rorty and by Hauerwas, although not particularly in relation to the idealist metaphysics of Hegel and Green, but more generally they reject the idea that the common basis of society can be found in a philosophical theory. So this is an argument that Hegel and Green's whole project, in trying to produce a rational form of Christianity as basis of social solidarity, is mistaken not just because of the violence that it does to the narrative and specific nature of Christian belief, but because the whole social and political orientation has to be rejected because a philosophical theory of whatever sort cannot hold society together. If society can have a common culture, it is not based on something antecedently shared whose nature and justification relies on philosophy. The sources of social solidarity and the legitimacy of political institutions rest rather, upon shared traditions, values and narrative. If these are not shared, they cannot be invented by philosophical argument about certain general features of human life which are antecedent to narratives, largely because such philosophical theories are too abstract, because in so doing such theories 'assume a stance external to our commitments and cares, which are the lifeblood of any morality'.[54] Again the point mirrors the argument in the second chapter about particularity versus universality in relation to the prophets.

[52] Yoder, *The Royal Priesthood*; see also p. 129.
[53] MacIntyre, *Secularisation and Moral Change* p. 29.
[54] Hauerwas, *The Peaceable Kingdom* p. 18.

MacIntyre goes on to show that the ideas of common human nature and common good, which Green thought had been legitimised by his philosophical transposition of Christianity, were, in fact, inert in relation to determinate political issues. As he points out, many of Green's followers were divided over education, over social welfare, particularly over the issue of state provision versus private charity and the unconditional nature of dole, over social work and over *laissez faire*, and, he argues, 'as they did the notion of a religious unity imposed on these secular issues by Green's idealistic metaphysics disappears'.[55] This point provides evidence from the standpoint in specific historical circumstances of the narrative theorists' claim that abstract philosophical systems cannot provide a basis for determinate political action whether such philosophical systems are regarded as reformulations of Christianity or not. Additionally, they cannot if they act as reformulations of Christianity, because, as a set of reflective categories, they mistake the praxis and narratively oriented nature of Christianity.

This dilemma, then, is pretty acute. If a liberal political order is to have a sense of legitimacy when faced with other vigorous and competing ideologies, and if such legitimacy cannot be secured across society by common values and common purposes identified across competing narratives and salient to them, then where does liberalism stand? Hauerwas argues that liberalism detaches people from the stories which give them identity and purpose.[56] This may be so, but if the alternative is a criterionless clash of competing narratives, wherein can lie the legitimacy of a liberal public order from a Christian point of view?

This final point is critical in relation to Western liberal societies. Such societies are marked by quite a high degree of moral pluralism, with such plural moral views being related to specific cultural and religious narratives in a multi-racial and multi-cultural society. So the problem for liberal societies is, if there is no overall narrative to bind such societies together,

---

[55] MacIntyre, *Secularisation and Moral Change* p. 28.
[56] S. Hauerwas, *A Community of Character* University of Notre Dame Press, 1986 pp. 78, 217, 220.

what kind of political and constitutional order can allow different narratives to flourish and provide a sense of specific identity
for members of particular communities, and wherein would the
moral legitimacy of such a set of arrangements lie if moral
resources are always specific to particular narratives and communities? This point will be addressed in the final chapter, but
for the moment, in *A Community of Character*, Hauerwas argues
that the constitutional arrangements of a liberal society get a
spurious moral legitimacy because they are based upon thin
and general moral conceptions which detach the notion of
citizenship in a liberal society from the specific narratives that
give individuals a sense of their own history and identity. As he
says: 'The unity of the self is not gained by attaining a universal
point of view but by living faithful to a narrative that does not
betray the diversity of our existence'.[57] Nevertheless, this alternative looks rather bleak, namely, that modern society is an
arena of competing and incommensurable narratives with no
overall moral resources to bind society together. As Yoder
argues, 'there exists no non-provincial general community'.[58]
Or, as A. K. Sen argues: 'There is a tendency here to split up
the large world into little islands that are not within normative
reach of each other.'[59]

[57] Ibid. p. 149.
[58] J. Yoder, *The Priestly Kingdom* Notre Dame University Press, 1984 p. 46.
[59] A. K. Sen, *Reason before Identity* The Romanes Lecture 1998, Oxford University Press,
1999, p. 7.

CHAPTER 6

Natural law and natural order

Nature provides no standards or ideals. All that exists, exists at the same level, or is of the same logical type.
(M. MacDonald, 'Natural Rights')

Where there is no transcendent point of reference, there is no datum for the natural order in the immanent sphere; this becomes the field of an unguided scramble for power.
(V. A. Demant, *The Idea of a Natural Order*)

In this chapter I shall focus on the ideas of natural law and natural order as a possible foundation for Christian political theology. This is an important issue in several respects. As we saw in the second chapter, there is a plausible case to be made that at least some of the prophets of the Old Testament operated implicitly with a conception of a law of nature which applied not just to Israel as the result of its covenant with Yahweh, but to the nations generally. As we saw then, John Barton argues that:

The prophet Isaiah, working in Jerusalem in the eighth century B.C. already had a developed understanding of the basis of morality which has more affinities with western theories of natural law than has usually been thought and less in common with the notion of impera- tives as 'revealed' or positive law given by God as the terms of a covenant or contract with the people of Israel, than is supposed by many Old Testament specialists.[1]

This point has been taken up and developed further in the context of the claimed link between natural theology and

[1] J. Barton, 'Ethics in Isaiah of Jerusalem' in *The Journal of Theological Studies*, 32/1 (1981), p. 1.

biblical theology in James Barr's *Biblical Faith and Natural Theology*.[2] Certainly, the idea of natural law has played a central role in western Christian thinking about the nature of politics and its link to political belief.

The idea of natural law is also important as a possible basis for political theology because it would justify a strategy whereby Christian beliefs about politics could be made compatible with some sorts of secular beliefs about politics, since each would be sanctioned by natural law. On this view, natural law consists in a set of rules rooted in the nature of what it is to be a person pursuing a set of basic or natural goods which would ensure the flourishing of such persons with that nature. Forms of social and political order receive a sanction from natural law if they facilitate the achievement of these goals and goods. Natural law can be understood or discovered by reason, reflecting on the circumstances of human life and human nature; equally, however, as a law sanctioned by God, it can be known by faith and revelation. The natural law can be discovered through these two modes, and what is discovered – namely, the basic laws of our nature and our good – is the same. The extent of the natural law derived from faith or revelation may go further than that revealed by reason, but there is a common content and that content can be shared by the believer and the unbeliever alike.

There is a plausible case for claiming biblical sanction for this view, although, as we shall see later, this is controversial. In the *Epistle to the Romans*, chapter 2, St Paul says:

For there is no respect of persons with God.

For as many as have sinned without the law shall also perish without the law: and as many as have sinned in the law shall be judged by the law;

(For not the hearers of the law *are* just before God, but the doers of the law shall be justified.

For when the Gentiles, which have not the law, do by nature the

---

[2] Barr, *Biblical Faith and Natural Theology* pp. 94–5. Barr argues that the implication of Isaiah's prophecies involve the idea that they are 'a way of declaring that God acts on the same eternal principles which humans can discover in nature by the operation of reason'.

things contained in the law, these, having not the law, are a law unto themselves:

Which shew the work of the law written in their hearts, their conscience also bearing witness, and *their* thoughts the mean while accusing or else excusing one another.)

On the interpretation of this passage which I am adopting at the moment, there is a case for arguing that the laws of God which are known by faith and revelation to the Christian are known, at least in part, by nature and reflection by those who do not share this revelation. D'Entrèves, in his basic work on natural law, makes precisely this point in explaining why Christians were attracted by the idea of natural law:

However different their conception of man, Christian writers like St Ambrose and St. Augustine had developed the notion of *lex naturalis in corde scriptura* and of an *innata vis* to attain knowledge of it. There could be little difficulty on the part of Christians in accepting a notion which seemed so pertinently to confirm the Apostle's saying of the Gentiles.[3]

And he then goes on to quote part of the section of the Epistle to the Romans cited above. Consistent with this approach, it is worth noting that St Paul's condemnation of homosexuality in Romans 1.26 is that it is against nature (*physis*) not because it was condemned in the Old Testament as in Leviticus 18.22 and 20.13 as James Barr has argued. If something is against nature, then this is something that can be known, at least potentially, by reflection as much as by faith. On this basis, the law of nature and the idea of a shared natural order underpinning at least a limited morality could form the basis of common ground between the Christian and the non-Christian in thinking about issues of political morality. This can be looked upon in a positive light with the natural law forming the basis of a common life, or it could be regarded, as by Hauerwas for reasons which we shall consider later, as an 'accommodationist strategy'.[4] Whichever way it is seen, it is a very important possibility for political theology which we need to explore.

I shall say a little here about the nature of the role that

---

[3] A. P. D'Entrèves, *Natural Law: An Introduction to Legal Philosophy* Hutchinson University Library, London, 1951, p. 35.
[4] Hauerwas, *The Peaceable Kingdom* pp. 59–60.

natural law theories have played in Western political thought. This tradition is long and complex, and my aim is only to set the scene rather than to provide a detailed scholarly account of the development of natural-law theories. I shall also concentrate on natural-law theories in the Western philosophical and theological tradition, but the point that I have now made twice should be borne in mind, namely, that there is a case for thinking that this tradition goes back much further in the work of the Old Testament prophets.

In the Western tradition, the idea of natural law became clear and definite in the writings of the Stoics, although there is a literary version of it to be found in Sophocles' *Antigone*. Following Antigone's disregard of his injunction not to honour the body of her dead brother Creon says:

> CREON: Now tell me in as few words as you can,
>   Did you know the order forbidding such an act?
>
> ANTIGONE: I knew it, naturally. It was plain enough.
>
> CREON: And yet you dared to contravene it?
>
> ANTIGONE: Yes
>   That order did not come from God. Justice,
>   That dwells with the gods below, knows no such law.
>   I did not think your edicts strong enough
>   To overrule the unwritten unalterable laws
>   Of God and heaven, you being only a man.
>   They are not of yesterday or today, but everlasting.

Here we have the roots of the idea that there is a moral law that transcends the laws of particular societies and which can legitimise acts that transgress the positive or given laws of particular societies if they are inconsistent with this set of basic rules.

The Stoics, who formalised these ideas to a great extent, held the view that human fulfilment consists in living life in accordance with nature: human, social and natural (as Seneca argues in *De Vita Beata*).[5] For the Stoics, morality is unintelligible if

---

[5] Seneca, 'De Vita Beata' in *Seneca: Moral Essays* Harvard University Press, Cambridge, Mass., 1932, pp. 99–179, e.g. 'Beata est ergo vita conveniens naturae suae . . .'.

divorced from cosmology (a view clearly held by Zeno, Cleanthes and Chrysippus), for human nature is part of the order of nature governed by a divine *Logos* which provides the law to which human beings ought to conform. The only basic moral question is the extent to which we as rational beings assent to live according to this natural law or struggle against it. If everything is the will of the divine *Logos*, then virtue lies in learning to want what we have or are going to have (a point made by Seneca in *De Vita Beata*).[6] Only one thing is within our power, namely, to assent to what is. For the Stoics, this means that emotion which leads us to struggle against the natural law and natural order is an evil. So a necessary component of virtue is *apatheia* (Cicero in *Tusculanarum Disputationum*).[7] A life purged of emotion will lead us rationally to assent to what is. For the Stoic, human life is sacred: it is created by the divine *Logos* and is the meeting place of the divine ar argued by Seneca in *Ad Lucilium Epistulae Morales*.[8] The natural law and natural order are universal and transcend the laws of particular societies, a point made in a famous passage in Cicero *De Republica*:

True law is right reason in agreement with nature; it is of universal application, unchanging and everlasting; it summons to duty by its commands, and averts wrongdoing by its prohibitions . . . It is a sin to try to alter this, nor is it allowable to repeal any part of it, and it is impossible to abolish it entirely . . . And there will not be different laws at Rome and at Athens, or different laws now and in the future, but one eternal and unchangeable law will be valid for all nations and all time, and there will be one master and ruler, that is, God, over us all, for he is the author of this law, its promulgator, and enforcing judge. Whoever is disobedient is fleeing from himself and denying his human nature.[9]

In *De Officiis* Cicero recognises that not all civil or positive law embodies the universal law, but it should do so. It is the norm

[6] Ibid. p. 138.
[7] M. T. Cicero, *Tusculanaram Disputationum* ed. J. E. Keyes, Harvard University Press, Cambridge, Mass., 1927, p. 211.
[8] Seneca, *Ad Lucilium Epistulae Morales* ed. R. Gummere, vol. 2, Harvard University Press, Cambridge, Mass., 1920, p. 447ff. Seneca refers to 'divina ratio'.
[9] M. T. Cicero, *De RePublica* ed. C. W. Keyes, Harvard University Press, Cambridge, Mass., 1928, III xxii, p. 211.

whereby the legitimacy of civil law is to be judged. In *De Finibus*, he argues that living virtuously means living in accordance with an understanding of the natural course of events.[10] From this natural law it was possible to derive practical precepts for action, as Finnis argues in *Natural Law and Natural Rights*.[11] The Stoic conception of natural law, therefore, in the words of John Milbank: 'aspired to a universal ethic, based on reason, transcending all political boundaries and towards a universal and ontological peace'. As Milbank points out, as Hegel had done before him in The *Phenomenology of Spirit*, this universalising ethic, implicit in the natural-law approach as they understood it, meant that Stoicism was:

unable to conceive of any new, non-political practice, and so the realization of peace had to remain 'inward' and its political transcription could only take the form of a respect for the free space of others, and a formal acknowledgement of equality. This incipient 'liberalism' broke with the *sittlich* form of antique ethics, where roles were prescribed by the community and collective concrete agreement was sought after.[12]

This is an important point, as we shall see later, because what the contrast pointed to by Milbank and Hegel shows is that the problem with a wholly general natural-law ethic which does not give specific moral weight to the *ethos*, the narrative and *sittlichkeit* of a particular community, may actually be inert in politics, although its promise, that of a common morality rooted in a universal form of natural law, is affirmed with quite the opposite intention. As we shall see, this is important when we come to look at the narrative and communitarian critique of natural-law theories.

The Christian conception of natural law owes most to St Thomas Aquinas, particularly *Summa Theologiae* parts I and II.[13] Aquinas argued that by reflecting on our own nature we could determine certain ends which relate to specific forms of

[10] M. T. Cicero *De Finibus* Loeb Classical Library, particularly Book II, ch. 34, and Book IV, ch. 14.

[11] J. Finnis, *Natural Law and Natural Rights* Clarendon Press, Oxford, 1980, p. 375.

[12] Milbank, *Theology and Social Theory*.

[13] St Thomas Aquinas, *Summa Theologiae* Blackfriars, Eyre and Spottiswoode, London, 1963.

disposition or inclination, *inclinatio*, which we find within ourselves. In 9.94a.2, Aquinas distinguishes between three sorts of
goods revealed in *inclinationes* which, as A. J. Lisska has convin-
cingly argued, should be treated as dispositional properties
essential to human nature: 'The end to be attained is always
determined by the properties of the human essence or human
nature.'[14] These goods are as follows:

1 The disposition to seek survival 'everything according to its
  own nature tends to preserve its own being'. This disposition
  as well as the associated ones of nutrition and growth (to use
  Lisska's words) are shared with animals.
2 Dispositions towards procreation, sexual relations (between
  male and female), the care of children.
3 Dispositions 'to those goods based upon the rational properties of human nature' – for example, to 'know the true
  propositions about God and concerning those necessities
  required for living in a human society'.

All of the dispositions towards these types of goods, rooted in
human nature or human essence, fall within the purview of
natural law. The goods are themselves natural and universal,
rooted as they are in the fundamental dispositional properties of
our nature. These inclinations are ordered and some are
subordinated to others: so, for example, we educate children so
that they can pursue the goods associated with rationality and
so forth.

The natural law is accessible to reason but, at the same time,
it is a precept of divine law given in Scripture. Aquinas argues
in *Summa Theologiae* that it is the rational order of divine wisdom
in so far as that wisdom directs the acts and motions of
everything (ll 93.1) and this is reflected in the *lex naturalis* which
he sees as the 'sharing of the eternal law by intelligent creatures'
(ll 91.2). This *lex naturalis* is further specified in a particular
society by *lex humana*, which allows us to move from common
and indisputable principles to making specific arrangements
(91.3). At this juncture, it is perhaps worth quoting Aquinas at

---

[14] A. J. Lisska, *Aquinas' Theory of Natural Law: An Analytic Reconstruction* Clarendon Press,
   Oxford, 1996, p. 100.

some length to indicate his conception of the relationship between divine and natural law:

> Supposing the world to be governed by divine Providence . . . it is clear that the whole community of the universe is governed by divine reason. This rational guidance of created things on the part of God . . . we can call the Eternal law.
>
> (Now) since all things which are subject to divine Providence are measured and regulated by the Eternal law . . . it is clear that all things participate to some degree in the Eternal law, in so far as they derive from it certain inclinations to those actions and aims which are proper to them.
>
> But, of all others, rational creatures are subject to divine Providence in a very special way; being themselves made participators in Providence itself, in that they control their actions and the actions of others. So they have a certain share in the divine reason itself, deriving therefore a natural inclination to such actions and ends as are fitting. This participation in the Eternal law by rational creatures is called the Natural law.[15]

Since the natural law is discernible by reason as well as through revelation, every person is responsible for his actions when not acting on the law.[16] This potentiality for disobedience is eradicable only by divine grace for Aquinas.

Reflecting on our God given, but rationally discoverable inclinations and the goods towards which they incline us, leads Aquinas to be able to specify a set of more specific precepts built upon our recognition of these inclinations and their associated goods. Once these precepts are determinate, they have to be applied, and this leads on to Aquinas' conception of *prudentia* which is a crucially important element not only in his own natural-law theory, but indeed in any such theory. Laws and precepts are bound to be general and they will have to be interpreted and applied in particular cases. As Finnis points out, it is essential to Aquinas' case that the exercise of *prudentia*, of this interpretative capacity that leads to the application of natural law, does not involve any kind of general or metaphysical knowledge. *Prudentia* can be virtuously exercised by anyone who is well disposed to the natural ends of human existence

---

[15] Aquinas, *Summa Theologiae* 1a.12.
[16] Ibid. 1.11.94, 13.3.6.

revealed through reflection on the nature of our inclinations. There is a point of general importance here to which I adverted at the end of my first chapter and to which I shall return, namely, that any general theory of political morality or political theology is going to have to find a role for political *judgement*, for the application of general rules, precepts or views of the good to particular cases. Aquinas wrote a *Commentary on the Nicomachean Ethics* of Aristotle in which he argued for the centrality of prudence and the attentiveness we must have to the particularities of actions. For example, he draws an analogy between the role of a doctor and someone called upon to make moral decisions. There are general rules and principles in medicine, but individuals respond to possible cures in different ways and cures have to take circumstances into account:

The moral agent in acting prudently must attentively consider the action to be undertaken at the present time, but only after all the particular circumstances have been taken into consideration. In this kind of way, a medical doctor must act in order to bring about a cure.[17]

As Joseph Boyle says in a comment on the role of prudence in Aquinas:

Prudentia is Aquinas' rendering of *phronesis* which is usually translated as 'practical wisdom'. Aquinas regards practical wisdom as an intellectual virtue, as a disposition of practical intelligence to do its proper work well. That work is to make concrete moral judgements.[18]

Prudentia / phronesis are essential ways in which the universal and the particular are combined for Aquinas.

I want now to emphasise an important issue in the interpretation of Aquinas which is important for the whole modern strategy of seeing natural law as the possible basis for a common social and political life which could be affirmed by both the believer and the non-believer alike. This depends upon an understanding of the place of religion in the context of natural law. To put the point oversimply at this stage, is it the

---

[17] St Thomas Aquinas, *Commentary on the Nicomachean Ethics* trans. C. I. Litzinger, Chicago University Press, 1964, p. 259.
[18] J. Boyle, 'Natural Law and the Ethics of Traditions' in *Natural Law Theory* ed. R. P. George, Clarendon Press, Oxford, 1992, p. 13.

case that the natural law consists of a determinate set of laws which can be discerned in two distinct ways: one by reason and the other by faith? If this is so, then it is possible that natural law could form the basis of a common life, because the dictates of natural law could be affirmed by people who come to understand it in these two different ways. D'Entrèves has posed the question well in his *Natural Law*:

If so great a body of wisdom had been discovered without super-natural help, if a basis was to be provided for human relations independently of the higher requirements of Christian perfection, surely there must be a knowledge of ethical values which man can attain with the sole help of his reason. There must be a system of natural ethics. Its corner-stone must be natural law . . . This entirely new function for the idea of the law of nature is nowhere more apparent than in the teaching of St Thomas Aquinas . . . Thus the possibility was opened up of giving a rational explanation and justification of ethical imperatives as well as all those institutions which earlier Christian thinkers had conceived as the result of sin and as its divine remedy. . . A positive value could be given to the state as the highest expression of natural morality. . . Yet natural law was not only the foundation of morality and of all social and political institu-tions. It is also the paramount standard by which these institutions could be judged.[19]

On the face of it, natural law is to be known by the operation of reason – 'the light of natural reason', but at the same time we need to explore a little the disputed relationship in Aquinas between a rational apprehension of natural law and religious faith. If they are completely intertwined, then the idea that natural law could become the basis of a wholly rational, naturalistic ethics looks doomed, and yet D'Entrèves, who has defended precisely this interpretation, argues that 'Natural law is unintelligible unless we realize its close link with the divine order on which the whole of creation ultimately rests.'[20] This is not just an arcane point in the interpretation of Aquinas, it is also concerned, as I have said, with any kind of subsequent strategy in political theology which sees natural law as both being compatible with Christian understanding and being able

[19] A. P. D'Entrèves, *Natural Law* p. 38.
[20] Ibid. p. 39.

to be affirmed by a person who has the light of reason but no religious faith.

Finnis has argued that there is no necessary link between Aquinas' account of natural law and his theism. Finnis takes up this point by responding to Kai Nielsen's critique of natural-law theories in 'The Myth of Natural Law'.[21] Nielsen had argued as follows (in a way that rather reflects the previous point cited from D'Entrèves): 'Traditional concepts of natural law are completely dependent for their viability on the soundness of such claims (as that natural theology is intelligible . . . and that God exists)'.[22]

Finnis argues against this that it cannot be true for Aquinas. First of all, Aquinas believes that the natural law is self-evident to reason and is not derived from anything, and yet, for Aquinas, the existence of God is not self-evident to the human mind – it can be known either by demonstration or revelation. Secondly, Aquinas believes that friendship with God is our last end and that this is not available by the light of reason but by revelation. Thirdly, we can only attain the end of friendship with God by grace and not by rational striving. Finally, the will of God, so far as it concerns mankind, cannot be known by reasoning. So we are left with a view that is rather at variance with D'Entrèves' claim about the link between natural law and religious faith. This leaves ambiguous the capacity of natural law to provide a basis for common political endeavour for the religious believer and the atheist.

I now want to consider a number of the deep objections that have been made against natural-law theories of the sort developed by Aquinas on the assumption, for the moment, that the more conventional reading of Aquinas is correct, rather than Finnis' revisionist proposals. The problems with natural law on the conventional view are certainly manifold, and believed by many philosophers to be fatal to the whole approach. They are that:

---

[21] K. Nielson, 'The Myth of Natural Law' in *Law and Philosophy* ed. S. Hook, New York, 1964, p. 130.
[22] Ibid.

1 natural-law theories presuppose a realist metaphysics and a belief in essences;
2 natural-law theories presuppose a correspondence theory of truth;
3 natural-law theories presuppose a philosophical anthropology underpinning both; an account of human essence and a theory of natural goods;
4 natural-law theories breach the fact/value dichotomy;
5 natural-law theories commit the naturalistic fallacy;
6 natural-law theories do not take account of moral diversity;
7 natural-law theories are inert in relation to specific moral and political issues and judgements.

The first two issues may be taken together in that a realist and essentialist metaphysic is bound to imply a correspondence theory of truth. In so far as natural-law thinkers believe that natural law is rooted in the essential nature of man, then the language in which such laws are described has to correspond to precisely this essential nature. It may be, of course, that for a thinker like Aquinas these essential features of human life are revealed dispositionally (as inclinations), but nevertheless these dispositions are not just occurrent, they are rooted in the essential nature of human personality. An essence is a synthetic necessary property making something what it is. This is a point of fundamental importance, in that the ends and purposes of human nature which among other things politics is supposed to serve are based upon these dispositions and inclinations which are, as McCloskey says: 'inherent in human nature'.[23] So moral, psychological and metaphysical language has to map on to and exemplify the nature of the essence of humanity both in its inclinations and ends.

We saw in the previous chapters that such an approach poses quite major problems for modern philosophy, and I do not propose to go through these arguments again. The arguments of Davidson and Rorty and, in the background, Wittgenstein, seem to many contemporary philosophers to make it impossible to assume, as Aquinas does, that language represents an

---

[23] H. J. McClosky, 'Respect for Human Moral Rights' in *Utility and Rights* ed. R. G. Frey Blackwell, Oxford, 1985, p. 126.

external reality which is, as it were, already individuated – as, for example, Plato thought in the *Timaeus* and *Cratylus*. Rather, our language, the conception of what is real and unreal that is revealed in the sense which language has, and our sense of self, are all contingent. They may be given as part of a specific way of life, they may be what we do, and this deeply embedded in the ways we understand one another within particular cultures, but such uses of language cannot be given any metaphysical foundation beyond the social practices. There will be varying social and linguistic practices in particular societies. No doubt, if one believes with Aquinas in a God's-eye view, then there can be such essences and correspondences in the world and in language, but the problem is that, if the philosophical basis of natural law has to be in theology or in a specific moral and religious tradition, then it cannot apparently play the role of providing a cross-cultural and transnational moral framework and a common life based upon it which can be accepted by the religious believer and the religious sceptic alike. So, to base the metaphysics of natural law on theological beliefs alone would, on the face of it, undermine, at least in part, one of the central purposes of natural-law theory. I shall return to this argument when I consider natural law and cultural and moral diversity.

This point can also be put in another way. If natural law's objectivity is based upon its God-givenness, then that objectivity only counts if there are equally objectively compelling reasons for belief in God. The claimed objectivity of natural law cannot be based on faith or commitment. It has been a standard argument against relativism that, if relativism is held to be objectively true, then it is self-defeating because one cannot be an objectivist about relativism. The argument, however, also works in the other direction, namely, that one cannot be a fideist in relation to objectivity. The claims of natural law to reveal a universal and foundational form of human nature and human good cannot rest upon faith alone.

It might, of course, be argued that natural law should be seen as being part of a specific moral tradition rather than as something that stands behind or above tradition – a view defended by Joseph Boyle in 'Natural Law and the Ethics of Traditions' in *Natural Law Theory*. This view might well avoid some of the metaphysical and epistemological problems of which mention has already been made. The difficulty with this approach, however, is fairly obvious. Natural-law doctrines claim universality, but how could this be maintained if natural law is seen as one tradition among others? Boyle faces this problem clearly when he says:

Perhaps the universality of some natural law prescriptions and the claim that the knowledge of these prescriptions is accessible to all human beings, have implications incompatible with this kind of dependence of enquiry upon cultural contingencies. But it is not clear why . . . The natural law claim that its most basic prescriptions are accessible to all . . . may seem more difficult to accommodate within a view in which the cultural contingency and particularity of enquiry is acknowledged . . . Why should it be impossible that the same proposition or prescription can be expressed in different languages or arrived at by enquiries with very different starting points and presuppositions? Or why should it be impossible that two distinct propositions or prescriptions should make reference to the same moral reality?[24]

The difficulty with this view raises issues which will be discussed towards the end of the chapter when the contrast between the natural-order approach and Walzer's *Spheres of Justice* will be discussed. The main difficulty is that, if natural law, understood as one among other moral traditions, posits certain general or natural human goods and inclinations, then it might be argued that the meaning of these goods is given within particular contingent moral traditions and practices and that these meanings will be so diverse that we cannot guarantee that, in fact, they do refer to or posit the same thing. At the most there will be a purely formal identity of goods and principles – for example that murder is wrong; but what counts as murder is going to vary quite substantially across different traditions and ways of life. If natural law claims to be a specific moral tradition rooted in the cultural contingency that traditions have, while at the same time providing an account of goods and principles which can be accepted across traditions, then this congruence is

---

[24] J. Boyle, 'Natural Law and the Ethics of Traditions' pp. 6–7.

likely to be bought at the cost of vacuity. These points also bear upon the issue of how far natural-law theories can actually cope with moral diversity and difference.

It is important, however, to consider two well-known modern philosophical critiques of natural law which rely on more general logical consideratons: the fact/value dichotomy and the naturalistic fallacy. Although in some ways allied, the issues raised by these two arguments are, in fact, rather different. The criticism made on the basis of the fact/value dichotomy is clear enough. If natural-law theory seeks to derive an account of human goods and human obligations from essential facts about human nature and human inclinations, then such a view commits a fallacy because, as Hume showed, no statements containing normative principles can be derived from factual statements. It might, of course, be argued by natural-law theorists that natural-law propositions about human nature have normative factors built into them and they can therefore function as premises in moral arguments that lead to moral conclusions. This argument has been defended by Veatch[25] who has made two points: firstly that we should not take the question of inferring a conclusion from a set of premises in too rigorous a manner; secondly that, in any case, natural-law doctrines about the nature of the person have values built into them. The first part of Veatch's answer to the fact/value dichotomy seems odd if natural law is to provide a universal and objective ethic, since, if leeway is allowed in what is to count as an appropriate inference from a set of premises, then it is not at all clear how its objectivity and universality is to be preserved. The second part of Veatch's argument is more interesting and salient. It may well be the case that natural-law conceptions of the person do have values built into them, but then the question arises about the objectivity of the claims about these values and their derivation. The central point here is that, for the critic, the claimed naturalness of inclinations and goods cannot be the source of their value, that claim has to be justified in some other way – for example by an appeal to God's

25 H. Veatch, 'Natural Law and the Is – Ought Question' *Catholic Lawyer*, 26 (1981), p. 265.

purposes in creating human beings that way. Then the justification of these value components of the account of our nature
will rest upon something beyond this naturalness and this gives
rise to two problems. The first is that the recognition of this
would undermine the idea that the precepts of natural law can
be shared by both the theist and the non-theist, since for the
latter the value components of natural-law theory cannot rest
upon their naturalness, nor upon the theistic presuppositions of
the theory. Secondly, the objectivity of these normative components will depend crucially upon what is claimed about the
relationships between these value assumptions and the nature
of God and how these relationships are justified.

The argument about the naturalistic fallacy has much the
same effect, but its structure is different. The natural-law
thinker wants to assert an identity between goodness and those
ends which reflection reveals are the objects of our most basic
and natural identities. The claim made is, however, disputed by
G. E. Moore's 'open question' argument – that is to say it is
perfectly intelligible to ask: is this x (where x is an end revealed
by our inclinations) good? The very fact that this is an intelligible question – indeed, it is often a source of moral difficulty –
shows that it is not definitionally true that what is good is what
is identical with that end. There is a logical gap between the
identification that x is a natural end of human life and the claim
that x is good. The issues to which these lead then parallel the
case of the fact/value problem.

I want now to turn to the question of moral diversity which I
raised earlier in the context of tradition. If natural law is
assumed to be based upon an account of the essence of what it is
to be a person, and upon the natural goods which are the
objects of the inclinations of such persons, then it would seem
clear that such a doctrine is going to involve a high degree of
abstraction, generalisation and universalisation. So, both the
conception of the person and the account of those goods, is
going to be either of a very high degree of generality or
alternatively is going to involve universalising the more specific
feature of human nature as these are understood and concep-
tualised within a particular moral tradition such as Catholicism.

In the first case, such an approach would run directly counter to these sorts of philosophical and theological doctrines considered in the last chapter, which argued that the self is narratively formed, that we discover what we are as part of inherited moral traditions, that we can only ascribe states of mind, emotions and intentions to ourselves via the descriptive resources available in a specific and contingent moral vocabulary.

Many of the basic philosophical and theological issues here will be considered again later in the book, but for the moment I want briefly to advert to just one thing: namely, the view most associated with Michael Walzer that such general values and principles will be inert in practice and will only provide us with reasons for actions when these general values are construed in the context of particular and rich moral traditions. We need to be able to judge and to act on moral principles, and this can only be done if these principles are rooted in social meanings which are part of the linguistic and descriptive environment. There is no clear response to this issue within the natural-law tradition. What is needed is a theory about how general goods can be given a specific and rich particularistic specification while retaining their claimed universality and objectivity.

Hence the philosophical and theological problems of the natural-law view are extremely acute, and there is a view amongst even sympathetic commentators that it can no longer provide a moral basis for a political theology, since the whole metaphysical context in which it arose has just become less and less salient and, indeed, in the view of various critics, unintelligible. For example, Hittinger produces a critique of 'new' natural-law theory on the grounds that any defensible natural-law theory has to treat nature as normative.[26] This view is, however, completely at odds with the points made in relation to the fact/value dichotomy and the naturalistic fallacy. The central dilemma here has been well focussed by Jeffrey Stout when he argues as follows:

Natural law theory in its traditional form was intertwined with the realist metaphysics of traditional natural philosophy. It sought to

[26] R. Hittinger, *A Critique of the New Natural Law Theory* Notre Dame University Press, 1987, p. 8.

provide a correspondence to the cosmos that would explain what makes moral sentences true. The idea seemed plausible so long as natural philosophy conceived of the cosmos in a moralised teleological fashion. But when the teleological cosmos gave way to the impersonal and infinite universe of modern science, scientific and ethical realism tended to break apart.[27]

So, it appears that the metaphysical and theological background of natural-law theories makes it very difficult to see how such a conception could become the basis of a shared political ethics. Many of these problems are overcome if natural-law theories are seen as part of a specific moral tradition within which these nomative elements make sense, but this tradition-relative approach precisely undermines the claimed objectivity and universality of the natural-law approach.

This point provides a direct link to more modern thinkers than Aquinas about the idea of natural law and natural order, and I want to introduce these topics by citing two passages which I believe will resonate with precisely the points I have just been making. The first is very well known and is from T. S. Eliot's *The Idea of a Christian Society*:

The Christian can be satisfied with nothing less than a Christian organisation of society – which is not the same thing as a society consisting exclusively of devout Christians. It would be a society in which the natural end of man – virtue and well being in community – is acknowledged for all, and the supernatural end – beatitude for those who have eyes to see it.[28]

Picking up this point in a chapter called 'The Idea of a Natural Order' in his book *Theology of Society*, Canon Demant argues that a conception of the natural order, of the essential nature of man and of what man is 'in the order of creatures' could be used as a basis for co-operation between Christians and non-Christians in working for a society which will reflect the essential nature of man better than that of the recent period in the West. This natural order can be known either through faith or through rational reflection and as a result he argues

[27] J. Stout, 'Truth, Natural Law and Ethical Theory' in *Natural law Theory* ed. R. P. George.
[28] T. S. Eliot, *The Idea of a Christian Society and Other Writings* Faber and Faber, London, 1939, p. 34.

that he can count on the support 'of all who believe that man has a real structure and who, through the discernment of conscience or insight into the forces of history, have some convictions concerning the permanent needs of men through all phases and periods'.[29]

The relevance of this argument to the previous one should be obvious. This modern account of the natural order as something which can be affirmed by the Christian and the non-Christian alike has a resonance to the medieval conception of natural law in the sense that a shared conception of the natural and the precepts that are held to follow from that can be understood as providing a basis for co-operation between Christian and non-Christian alike. The Christians' vision will be broader, as it was for Aquinas, in that our friendship with God can be known only by revelation and not reason, but at a more restricted level the shape of a natural order can be understood on rational grounds alone and thus potentially by the believer and non-believer. Hence the Eliot/Demant approach puts into more modern dress the possibility not of an exclusive political theology based upon a specifically Christian approach to understanding the world, but of a shared conception rooted in the idea of natural law and natural order which is compatible with Christianity (while not exhausting its nature), while at the same time being affirmable on rational grounds. I do not want to underplay the central role of Christianity in Demant's account of natural law for, as we shall see, it is central, but the strategy set out in 'The Idea of a Natural Order' is clear enough. Writing this chapter in 1945, he argued that the horrors of totalitarianism and the spiritual failures of liberalism (on which more below) have led to a situation in which:

There is a revived desire today to find out whether there is a norm of social ordering underlying all the special achievements of an age, a people, or a culture and what its content is . . . Men therefore want to know whether there are some permanent elements of human morphology according to which they can try to build more securely the next phase of civilised life. Such a demand comes at the end of a period of

---

[29] V. A. Demant, *Theology of Society: More Essays in Christian Polity* Faber and Faber, London, 1947, p. 70.

unparalleled confusion, dislocation and violence. This period has been marked by an evolutionary or dialectical relativism which assumed that all was in flux, including man's fundamental nature, and in its latest phase by a colossal attack in the name of historic destiny upon all genera; truths about man. Both the eviscerated liberal societies and the violent dictatorial ones represent conflicting movements of a phase in which it was virtually disbelieved that man is a real kind.[30]

So the idea of a natural order and natural law which will reveal the real nature of man and provide a 'criterion for placing the different activities of man in their instrumental order'[31] can provide an alternative basis for an understanding of politics than those forms of relativism which have led to a weak kind of liberalism, at its best, and a will to power form of totalitarianism, at its worst. At the same time, at a restricted level this is a conception of man, society and politics which all can share. Such a conception of the natural order is universal and, although its roots, as we have seen, are pre-Christian, in Demant's view it is obvious why ideas of natural law and natural order became salient for Christian social and political understanding. The appeal of natural law lay in the fact that the early church found itself located in different historical communities and this posed a tension for the church: the tension between particular historic communities each with its own particular life and ethos and the church as the 'custodian of the universal, common elements in human existence. That is why, at one stage, Christianity, becoming a formative influence in society, welcomed and adopted the pagan ideas of natural law that belonged to man as man – distinct from his status in a particular historic setting.'[32]

Demant seeks to give a scriptural basis to this view in his essay by dwelling upon the idea that, in the context of Jesus' teaching, 'the world comprehends Him not'. In Demant's view, Jesus spoke to men in a particular setting, but he did not speak to them through it 'nor would any other historic setting have received him' because the world demands that it should com-

[30] Ibid. p. 71.
[31] V. A. Demant, *God, Man and Society* SCM Press, London, 1933, p. 42.
[32] V. A. Demant, 'The Idea of a Natural Order' in *Theology of Society* p. 73.

prehend Him in one setting or another. The truth, for Demant, is that: 'The Gospel speaks to each man that word of truth about himself which is not given in and through and by his setting in nature, history and society.'

So, there is a natural order, and Demant argues that this leads to an approach which may allow us to rank the distinctive modes of human activity in an instrumental order. This is set out in section 3 of his essay on 'Natural Order and Social Structure' (in which, interestingly, he links the conception of Natural Order to Aquinas' account of *synderesis* which underlies both conscience and natural reason and is seen by Aquinas to be a natural habit). It is clear that Demant does not see this ranking of the modes of human existence as normative in the sense that he is setting out a set of *oughts*, but, rather, is describing what *is*. Since these orders are rooted in the natural order which can be understood by reason, his ordering of these modes sets them out for what they are even if, because of sin or disordered intellect, we fail to grasp this. The ordering is instrumental, and all elements of the order are wholesome and legitimate if they fulfil subordinate roles. He takes the family to be elemental in that it is the context in which the higher powers of man, including the rational and the spiritual, are nurtured. It is also the context in which ideas about authority and obligation are learned. The elemental nature of the family, Demant argues, is metaphysical not moral, in the sense that there may be other bonds between people in the spiritual and rational spheres which involve a greater sense of achievement than this bond of the family which is 'so close to nature'. Economic affairs have a physical but not a metaphysical priority in human life, as does politics. Both are essential to the sustaining of physical life and security, but, in terms of the fundamental nature of man, they do not have metaphysical priority which is accorded to cultural goods that are more essentially spiritual and universal than economics or politics. These arguments may seem very arcane and abstract, but, in Demant's view, they have clear practical implications. So, for example, given the metaphysical priority of cultural goods as being closest to the 'natural order of man's inner structure' as a spiritual and rational being with a universal nature, it follows that the natural order is violated when:

provision is not made for people to teach and carry on the religious, educational, aesthetic and scientific arts; if any class is so exhausted in one or more of the practical tasks that it has no opportunity, energy, or guidance for cultural pursuits; if the cultural domain is treated as an adjunct for political consolidation, as this sphere is in totalitarian societies; or if it is prostituted to keep the economic process going as it largely is in the democracies.[33]

The same is true in the context of economics and politics. Politics is metaphysically subordinate to culture, but nevertheless is instrumental to the achievement of cultural goods. As he has argued, culture is deformed if it is put to a political use, as in Nazi Germany. At the same time, though, politics has a spiritual dimension. While it is not the function of politics to determine the cultural and ethical ends of men, nevertheless it is a prerequisite for them, 'enabling men with diverse non-political purposes to live with that degree of solidarity which common citizenship requires.' Economic activity is deformed when it becomes an end in itself. It is instrumental to the ultimate goods of men. It is also deformed when it is assumed that it is beyond any kind of human control and co-ordination (as in free-market capitalism, as we shall see in later chapters); it is equally deformed when 'the limitations of that control are similarly denied.[34]

So, for Demant, there is a natural order leading to a hierarchy of human goods which is universal and rational for those who wish to see it, and thus it can form a basis of both Christian and non-Christian political judgement and critique.

I now want to turn to Demant's critique of liberalism which, though initially a political theory, which historically accepted the idea of a natural law and a natural order as in Locke's *Second Treatise of Civil Government*, has in fact jettisoned that view and in Demant's view provides a kind of criterionless account of politics with no moral foundation. It has replaced true judgement about the nature and the ends of man with a kind of relativism and moral subjectivism which leads to a politics of

[33] Ibid. p. 87.   [34] Ibid. p. 87.

negotiation and bargaining rather than truth. For Demant, the relativism and subjectivism of modern liberalism was, in fact, the degradation of liberalism which led him to describe liberalism in 'The Idea of a Natural Order' as 'eviscerated'. By this he means that liberal political ideals have been undermined by liberals' own philosophical dogmas: 'modern liberal thought tried to preserve the truth without its foundations'. This is a very interesting point which will be taken up more fully in the final chapter, but, for the moment, I will outline Demant's critique of criterionless or foundationless liberalism. Initially, liberalism affirmed the dignity of the human person and the ideal of human freedom, but the relativism and subjectivism of modern liberalism has undermined the nature of these commitments. Without the idea of some kind of natural law or natural order, it is not clear in what it is that human dignity resides. Human dignity becomes a matter of individual choice and preferences.[35] Similarly, he argues that freedom has been restricted to freedom from interference with no concern about the ends or purposes to which this negative liberty of being free from coercion should be directed.[36] Both of these views are defective for Demant, because they undermine liberalism itself. Liberalism has lost sight of ideas about human purposes and human virtues. So, for example, instead of seeing human dignity as being grounded in a conception of human spiritual and rational purposes, it is now seen as a by-product of relativism. That is to say, lacking a common sense of human purposes, human dignity is rooted in the role of the person as a centre of choice and agency, in the agent as the author of his/ her own morality and purposes. As far as freedom is concerned, Demant argues that 'Instead of claiming liberties for the pursuit of positive social purposes directed by man's spiritual relationships, it encouraged demands from this or that encroachment.' However, such a view of freedom will not work in his view, since we have to be able to justify the reasons why we wish to be free from encroachment. An answer to this question presupposes some account of human purposes which is best given by

---

[35] See the discussion of M. MacDonald in chapter 9.
[36] See the discussion of liberal theories of freedom in chapter 8.

natural-law ideas and the idea of a natural order.[37] In *A Christian Polity* he argues that in the Middle Ages (the time of the dominance of natural law theories) the idea of freedom was justified in the name of justice: 'Men wanted to be free to fulfil certain purposes. It was the purposes that mattered and freedom from hindrances was but the necessary condition.'[38] This is an important argument because, as he goes on to say: 'Having no purpose for which liberty is striven for, there is no criterion to judge the interests which make use of such freedom as exists.'[39] Which in turn leads him to argue that 'whenever men seek only freedom from something, freedom of choice, subjective freedom, they always put themselves at the mercy of whatever secular forces happen to be dominant at the time'.

So ideas about human dignity, human rights and freedom become rootless in liberalism, since the foundations for them in an account of human purposes are destroyed by the very moral subjectivism and relativism which liberals espouse. In Demant's view, this opens the way for totalitarianism of the sort that dominated European politics in mid-century. He argues, following his natural-order doctrine, that, since man does actually have purposes which within liberalism are given only subjective value, he will yearn for something more, for a framework of value and purpose which can be provided either by the state-based totalitarianism of Italian Fascism or the race-based sense of sharing purposes in the *Volksgemeinschaft* of National Socialism. This is not just wishful thinking on Demant's part, since both Mussolini and Hitler saw their doctrines as counteracting the atomistic individualism of modern liberalism. So, for example, Mussolini argued as follows:

It (fascism) is opposed to classical Liberalism, which arose from the necessity of reacting against absolutism, and which brought its historical purpose to an end when the State was transformed into the conscience and will of the people. Liberalism denies the State in the interests of the particular individual. Fascism reaffirms the State as the true reality of the individual. And if liberty is to be the attribute of

---

[37] Demant, 'The Idea of a Natural Order' p. 64.
[38] V. A. Demant, *A Christian Polity*, Faber and Faber, London, 1936, p. 81.
[39] Ibid. p. 84.

the real man, and not of the abstract puppet envisaged by individualistic Liberalism, Fascism is for liberty. And for the only liberty which
can be the real thing, the liberty of the State and of the individual
within the state. Therefore, for the Fascist, everything is in the State,
and nothing human or spiritual exists, much less has value outside the
State.'[40]

Hitler, too, talked about the matter in *Mein Kampf*.[41] Of course,
for Hitler and Mussolini, these doctrines were a matter of *will*
not of tracking some kind of antecedent moral order. So there
can be no doubt that, for Demant, the lack of a universal and
objective foundation for political judgement was not just an
intellectual gap but was highly dangerous, not least for those
living in liberal democracies, since liberalism's own commitment to subjectivism and relativism had made the idea of
foundations and truth in politics problematic, not least for
liberalism itself. These are still central problems in liberal
political thought, as we shall see more fully in the final chapter.
For the moment, however, I might indicate the salience of
Demant's argument by quoting from a contemporary critic of
liberalism who incorporates a gesture towards the political
weakness of liberalism if we abandon the idea of objective
human purposes: 'If one's convictions are only relatively valid,
why stand for them unflinchingly? . . . if freedom has no
morally privileged status, if it is just one value among many,
then what becomes of liberalism?'[42]

For Demant, the only solution to this problem was to recover
the idea of natural law and a universal natural order instead of
what a contemporary philosopher has called the 'bleached'[43]
theory of human nature and human agency to the invocation of
which modern liberal society has been reduced. The problems

---

[40] B. Mussolini, 'The Doctrine of Fascism' in *Social and Political Doctrines of Contemporary Europe* ed. M. Oakeshott Cambridge University Press, 1939, p. 166.

[41] See Stern, *Hitler* p. 60: 'One man must step forward in order with apodictic force to form granite principles from the havering world of the imaginings of the broad mass and to take up the struggle for the sole correctness of these principles until from the shifting waves of a free world of ideas there rises up a brazen cliff of a united commitment in faith and will alike.'

[42] Sandel, 'Introduction' to *Liberalism and Its Critics* p. 8.

[43] R. Wollheim, *The Thread of Life* Cambridge University Press, 1984, p. 202.

Demant found in liberal doctrine remain a powerful diagnosis and prescription for the intellectual crisis of modern society and its need for criteria of political judgement and engagement. Some of these issues will be taken up more fully in the next chapters which deal with issues to do with social justice, freedom and the common good and the general problem of political reasoning in modern society which I pursue in my final chapter. For the moment, however, I want to do two things. First of all I want to explore some parallels between Demant's arguments about the spheres of human goods and their ordering and those of Michael Walzer developed in *Spheres of Justice*. This will help us to focus more precisely on the issues at stake in this debate. I shall then go on to discuss some of the features of the modern world which have led liberals to take the path which Demant has criticised, since this will also provide an account of the sort of critique to which the natural-law/natural-order approach is susceptible and which Demant did not fully confront.

As we saw earlier, Demant argued that it was possible on his natural-law/natural-order approach to generate an account of the relationship between the different activities of man in an order based upon a metaphysical theory about the true nature and ends of man. This would allow the working out of what is subordinate to what within the natural order which can also be understood at least partially by reason and without divine revelation. Without such a conception of order and hierarchy between activities, Demant argues, we shall have a disorderly society with the particular risk that the sphere of economics, despite its metaphysical subordination to politics and culture, will come to dominate. This concern with the appropriate relationship between the fundamental forms of human activity mirrors in an interesting way an argument set out by the liberal communitarian philosopher Michael Walzer in *Spheres of Justice*. Walzer is as concerned as Demant about the crisis of liberal political thought; but the big difference is that Walzer wants explicitly to eschew any appeal to metaphysics or the idea of a natural order to support his view. It is striking how historically and culturally unspecific Demant's arguments are in his work on ordering of human goods and activities such as the family, politics, economic, culture etc., despite his argument that the natural-order approach allied with sociological method will yield what he called a Christian sociology. The reason is deep but obvious, namely, that the natural order *qua* natural is ahistorical and transcends the particularity of culture, and this goes back to the point made earlier when the natural order is looked at from the Christian point of view, 'that the world comprehended Him not'. The natural law and natural order are embedded in culture and history, but transcend it and can be set out independently of it. Walzer rejects such a universalising approach for two closely interrelated reasons. The first is that any such approach will involve taking a very abstract view of human practices and human goods. Any list of universal goods and their relationships will be abstracted from any particular historical and social meaning and will be, to all practical purposes, meaningless. The second is that goods and activities have social meanings, that is to say meanings which are embedded in the beliefs and values of the particular society of which they are a part. Goods have no general transhistorical meaning outside of the specific social meanings that they bear. This leads Walzer to reject a universalising metaphysical approach to the ordering of goods. Goods have the relationships which they have in a particular society. They are not separated from one another or differentiated into different spheres by general, universal metaphysical principles, but by social mechanisms which he calls 'blocked exchanges' which prevent goods from one sphere with the specific social meanings that they have spilling over or colonising goods from other spheres with their distinctive social meanings. The universalising approach of the natural-order view would, in Walzer's view, be inert in creating boundaries around goods of the sort that both he and Demant want to see. They would be inert because they are abstract, and if they are interpreted and made more palpable, or, in his terminology, turned from *thin* to *thick* principles, then they will, in fact, draw from the social meanings which such goods have in a particular society. Even if we accepted the natural-order approach which would be abstract and thin, Walzer argues we could not in any sense deduce the implications of this for how we should live. As he argues:

They (universal principles RP) provide a framework for any possible (moral) life, but only a framework with all the substantive details still to be filled in before anyone could actually live in one way rather than another. It is not until the conversations become continuous and the understandings thicken that we could get anything like a moral culture, with judgement, value, the goodness of persons and things realized in any detail.[44]

While it may be possible to imagine that some general moral precepts may emerge through history,[45] they can be given no general metaphysical deduction and, even if that were possible, which it is not, we could not deduce from such universal principles the appropriate arrangement of such goods in particular societies without 'stepping into the thicket of moral experience' where goods have social meanings. This point is linked by Walzer to the idea of human dignity and respect and in particular to the potential that human beings have as culture-producing creatures, a feature of human life which Demant himself made so much of:

We are all culture producing creatures, we make and inhabit meaningful worlds. Since there is no way to rank and order these worlds with their understanding of social goods, we do justice to actual men and women by respecting their particular creations . . . Justice is rooted in distinct understandings of places, honours, jobs, things of all sorts that contribute to a shared way of life. To override these understandings is (always) to act unjustly.[46]

Demant might well agree that justice consists in the right ordering of the spheres of human activity and the proper boundaries between them. The difference is that Walzer does not think that this can in any sense 'track' a metaphysical theory which would underlie this. Such judgements have to draw upon the social meanings which such goods have and the place that they have in a particular society.

It is also important to understand that Walzer here is not just

[44] Walzer, *Interpretation and Social Criticism* p. 25.
[45] Ibid. p. 24.
[46] Walzer, *Spheres of Justice* p. 314.

rejecting the natural-law/natural-order approach as a foundation for such judgements. Although he does not say so explicitly,
he would also reject any approach based upon a philosophy or
theology of history in terms of which goods emerge as more or
less important through some kind of teleology of human history
as, for example, found in Hegel's *Phenomenology of Spirit*.

So we seem to be faced with a major set of problems in terms
of providing general criteria for social and political thought
from a Christian perspective. As we saw right at the beginning
of these chapters, the general issue might be put in terms of the
relationship between the universal and the particular: the
universality of the Christian message and the historic and
particular circumstances of politics in specific societies. As we
saw earlier, the theology of history cannot provide us with
criteria, since the intellectual problems are so great; the
natural-order approach certainly addresses the universal side of
the problem, but, as Walzer shows, it is difficult to provide any
accommodation for the particular; the narrative-theology
approach seems to dissolve the problem into a situation in
which there are no overarching standards of rationality, rather,
they are specific to particular narratives, and no universal
foundations, since narratives do not have foundations. If we live
in a narratively ordered world in which there are competing
and incommensurable narratives with no possibility of judgements based on history or natural law to arbitrate, are we not
left with precisely the problem which Demant lays at the door
of liberalism: that there is no transcendent and no truth and
that politics is reduced to bargaining between people with
different interests and points of view rooted in different narratives? The difficulty is, though, as Demant argues, that such a
view of politics seems to make it very weak in the face of
totalitarianism in his day and fundamentalism in ours. It further
raises the question of what place a Christian voice has in the
negotiating and bargaining which it might seem that is all that
there is left to politics with the collapse of the grand narratives
of history and natural law.

PART II

The site of political theology

As citizens we have no right or claim to appeal to motives or ideals specifically Christian, or to lay down lines of policy which have no meaning except from the stand point of the Catholic Church. We must recognise these facts even where we do not like them.

(N. Figgis, *Churches and the Modern State*)

Introduction

We have now completed the attempt to answer the first question to be posed in this book: is political theology possible? As we have seen, the answers to this question are controversial and will vary according to the theological stance taken. There can be no wholly definitive or authoritative political theology and, indeed, no authoritative political praxis associated with it, since the methodological controversies are so profound.

However, this is only one side of the dialectic between political theology and religious belief in a liberal society, since it is also vitally important to address the question of what is the *site* of political theology, that is to say, what kinds of issues and questions in a liberal democratic society could or should political theology seek to address? This is a complex issue, since however controversial or fragmentary political theology will have to be, lacking as it does an authoritative paradigm, we also need to have some understanding of what sort of political issues and questions we could reasonably expect religious belief to be able to address and at what level of generality or, indeed, specificity.

One obvious answer to this question is to say that political theology should address itself to those issues in liberal democratic societies that are a matter of collective moral concern and might be thought to embody a sense of collective moral responsibility. However, in the context of a liberal society with a market economy and democratic political organisation, this is not really possible in a straightforward way. The reason for this has to do with moral pluralism and with the allied, but not identical, idea of moral subjectivism and individualism. Each of these ideas in rather different ways, which will be explained in the four chapters in this section, encourage the idea that a liberal political, economic and social order should make rather limited demands on ideas of collective morality and collective moral responsibility. So, for example, ideas about the common good, of social justice, or the moral basis for rights, of the nature of the morally correct limits and boundaries of markets, become deeply problematic if it is acknowledged that these ideas, if they have legitimacy at all, have to find it in a deeply individualistic moral culture. The task of liberal political thought has often seemed to be how far it is possible to provide a basis for liberal politics while making the most minimal demands on morality. This is really the position which Demant argued would become definitive of liberal political thought. Because of its moral individualism liberalism has shed the idea of the constraints on individual action other than those of mutual toleration; the idea that freedom has to be connected with human purposes and human flourishing; the idea that social justice is a necessary feature of a humane form of economic organisation; and the idea that community and the common good are essential features of a good society. This view of liberalism becomes criterionless and fails to be an adequate vision to engage the range of human sympathy.

This is not to say that these points are lost on liberals, but they do want to interpret the values which are, for Demant, rich and morally substantive in a way that makes the most limited moral demands, because how could we justify more in a society of moral individualism? This kind of moral diversity has to be accepted as a fact about modernity, and these ideas about freedom are literally demoralised. Freedom becomes negative freedom, that is to say freedom from coercion – it does not involve a *positive* moralised conception of the ends which a free person ought to pursue. The common good, if the idea is to be used at all, becomes identical not with substantive purposes and moral goals which citizens hold together, but rather with the framework of law and rights which guarantees to each individual maximal mutual freedom from interference. Social justice, if again it is thought to be a concept of any salience, becomes a doctrine about mutual non-coercion in economic exchange, rather than a substantive collective notion about the human ends which the economy should serve and how it might be reshaped to achieve those purposes. Equally, community becomes deeply problematic as a *political* concept. That is to say, individuals from their own subjective point of view may choose to belong to all sorts of communities as part of the civic culture of a liberal society, but community cannot be a project for the political sphere, since it presupposes that there are overall political norms and values which go beyond the procedural principles of liberalism. This view has been well articulated by Charles Larmore:

Greek and medieval thinkers generally argued that moral principles must shape the powers of government. But they entertained very sanguine prospects about the possibility of reasonable agreement about the good life. For them, it was axiomatic that here, too, reason tends naturally toward single solutions. The result was that, in their different ways, Greek and medieval thinkers usually assigned to the state the task of protecting and fostering substantial conceptions of the good life. The proper ends of government must look very different to liberal thinkers for when unanimity about the good life is more likely to be the fruit of coercion than of reason.

To avoid the oppressive use of state power, the liberal good has therefore been to define the common good of political association by means of a minimal moral conception.[1]

This poses a major challenge for political theology in modernity. Many of the models of political theology interrogated in Part I of this book sit rather uneasily with Larmore's assumptions. The prophetic tradition, as we saw, required either a specific social ethos (in this case defined in terms of covenant) as the basis of social and political criticism or the idea of a natural law known by all by reflection, a view which we have just considered in much more detail. The systematic theology tradition embodies the view that there is a human essence which can be specified via the doctrine of creation and that this will yield specific and substantial ideas about human flourishing. The narrative-theology approach believes that

[1] Larmore *Morals*, pp. 122–3.

minimalist ideas of political moral order abstract precisely from the specific forms of life with which people identify and relate. If the liberal agenda in political theory is adopted, then it would seem either religious believers, with comprehensive and substantive moral beliefs that are not widely accepted in a modern society, have to be prepared to limit the public and political demands of their own beliefs and treat much of what they believe as private beliefs, while utilising other aspects of their belief system to justify the acceptance of the minimal moral assumptions of the liberal state. Or religious believers become, in some sense, internal exiles in that sort of society, holding fast to a narrative of belief and practice, living by it within its own community but not participating in the normative justification of liberal practices.

Some will argue that this is too bleak and unnuanced a picture. It can be argued that the liberal idea of a politics based upon a minimal moral conception is itself deeply flawed. Normative justification in liberal society has to take on issues of substantive moral ends. If this is so, it is claimed, then religious beliefs can play a significant role in this enterprise and in particular that liberal doctrines to be at all justifiable have to draw upon what are, in fact, quite rich doctrines about human nature and human flourishing and that religious believers can rightly contribute to that debate.

We now need to consider these issues in some detail. First of all we shall look at the moral issues raised by the market economy so central to liberal societies and which, in the hands of some thinkers, can be regarded as the institutional embodiement of moral subjectivisim. We shall then look specifically at ideas about freedom, social justice and the common good in the liberal tradition. Subsequently, issues about the nature, scope and justification of the idea of human rights will become the main focus. Part II will then conclude with a chapter on the individual and community in liberal political thought. Throughout I shall try to link questions about the nature of the liberal perspective on these issues with some of the theological issues that we have been considering so far.

CHAPTER 7

Markets, morality and theology

The outcomes of the market are, in principle, unprincipled. (F. Hirsch, *The Social Limits to Growth*)

So far we have looked at the theme of political theology, from
the standpoint of theology and we have considered some of the
difficulties involved in arriving at what might be seen as a
cogent approach to the development of a political theology. I
now want to change perspective and discuss the ways in which
general issues of moral principle arise in relation to our understanding of modern society and politics, and in this context I
shall concentrate in this chapter and the next on the state and
its role in the economy. I want to focus on this theme largely
because it has been so central to the concern of the churches in
the past twenty years with the emergence of a much more pro-
market and limited government approach in Western societies.
Relatively recent illustrations of this concern would be the
publication of *Faith in the City* by the Church of England,
Centessimus Annus by Pope John Paul II commemorating the
centenary of *Rerum Novarum* promulgated by Leo XIII, and the
recent document on *The Common Good*, published by the Catholic Bishops of England and Wales.

This change of focus from theology to politics and economics
is important because one has to have some sense of what the
scope of theological concern in relation to political and
economic life might be, and also what aspects of politics and
economics to which it might make sense for a political theology
to apply itself. In broaching this topic, what I have in mind is
the extent to which the church can rationally develop theo-

logical judgements about fundamental forms of modern social organisation when there is a current argument as to whether some, at least, of these forms may seem to be wholly beyond the possibility of moral and thus theological assessment. An example might make clear what I have in mind here.

In the early part of this century, Charles Gore, Henry Scott-Holland and William Temple incurred the criticism of Canon, and then Bishop Hensley Henson, because both Gore and Temple wrote and acted on the assumption that the modern economy was subject to moral constraints and these moral issues in the economy could link up with a theological perspective on economic life. This led both Gore and Temple not only to write about the modern economy from a theological perspective, but also to use their theological insights to guide political intervention.

Henson, on the contrary, believed that the market economy was an autonomous sphere governed by inexorable laws and that it was more nearly akin to a natural order which spiritual and theological insights could not address. He cites 1 Corinthians 15 as an example of the distinction which Paul draws between terrestrial and celestial bodies, and that spiritual values apply only to the celestial ones.[1] This point is picked up in his Gifford Lectures on *Christian Morality*, in which he argues that Christian morality is personal and cannot be applied to collective or social entities. To be sure, individual Christians as capitalists and workers can seek in their lives to exemplify Christian values, but, in Henson's, view this is categorically different from believing that Christian morality can be used to appraise the structure and outcomes of collective or social entities. If this is so, then the project of political theology is fatally flawed from the outset, since theological insights and theological judgements can only be applied to the private and the personal. Henson's argument thus reflects some of the themes we have already discussed, namely the extent to which the social and public world can be understood in terms of theological categories. If it cannot, as Henson argues, because

---

[1] See verse 40.

the economy, at least, is autonomous and detached from moral constraints, then this will sanction the privatisation of Christianity to the moral conscience of the individual Christian.[2]

This argument trades upon two assumptions. The first is Henson's own reading of the nature of Christian morality and the assumption that it is addressed to the private conscience of the individual Christian. It is, however, the second assumption on which I wish to focus in this chapter and the succeeding one, namely, that the economy is a kind of natural and autonomous entity which is governed by quasi natural laws and is not susceptible of moral appraisal as a social or collective entity. If this assumption is correct, then there can be no place at all for a political theology which seeks to provide a critique of markets and their outcomes and the relative roles of the state and the market. My own view is that this argument is profoundly mistaken, but the argument that it is mistaken is complex and will be discussed along a range of rather different dimensions in this chapter and the one which follows. At the moment I shall concentrate most on the related ideas that, contrary to what Henson argues, the economic market has moral underpinnings, runs up against moral boundaries and involves clear moral limits so that, even if one were to believe, as he does, that markets themselves are an autonomous quasi natural form, nevertheless one has to confront the question of the appropriate role and limits that a market and market relationships should have in society. In the next chapter on social justice, I shall attempt to show that Henson's view of the economy, which bears some striking resemblance to the ideas of F. A. von Hayek, who has greatly influenced economic thinking in the past twenty years, is false, that moral ideas such as social justice do have a central role to play in economic thinking, and that one cannot rule out a theology of markets and politics just on the grounds of this attempt to demoralise

---

[2] For some discussion of these themes, see O. Chadwick, *Hensley Henson: A Study of the Friction Between Church and State* The Canterbury Press, Norwich, 1994; A. Suggate, *William Temple and Christian Social Ethics Today* T. and T. Clark, Edinburgh, 1987, p. 230ff.; E. R. Norman, *Church and Society in England 1770–1970* Clarendon Press, Oxford, 1976; J. Oliver, *The Church and Social Order*, Mowbray, London, 1968.

the collective or corporate nature of market transactions and their outcomes.

So my argument is an attempt to complete the circle for political theology in that in the first part I argued that it is a complex and controversial task to develop a coherent account of the nature of political theology, but that nevertheless the Christian religion has to be seen as having implications that go beyond the individual; my strategy now is to argue that there is nothing about the collective entities of state and market that makes them somehow immune in principle from theological understanding, interpretation and critique.

I need now to substantiate my claim that markets cannot somehow be bracketed off from the moral realm and treated as autonomous entities, and I shall turn first to what I shall call the moral underpinnings of markets. In this context I shall focus on contract and property, although other features could have been taken as important, too. It would be impossible to think about markets without the idea of contract, since market transactions are of a contractual or quasi-contractual sort. Given this, it is also obvious that contracts depend upon a set of indispensable moral attitudes such as trust, promise-keeping and truth-telling. As Emile Durkheim, the French sociologist, once remarked 'Not everything in the contract is contractual.' That is to say, for contractual relationships to work effectively and efficiently, there has to be in place a set of moral attitudes and relationships to underpin contract. These moral underpinnings as much as enterprise and self-interest are necessary conditions for the effective operation of the market order. These features are now referred to by economists as part of social capital. If morality comes to be seen as a form of self-interest, and as reduced to instrumental and subjective calculation of self-interest, this would be disastrous for the market itself. If the culture of a society with a strong market order within it came to be dominated by subjective and self-interested conceptions of morality, then there is at least some danger, if there are no other countervailing moral constraints, that the moral inheritance on which the market rests could, in fact, be eroded by the culture of self-interest. So my argument is that, while the emergence of the capitalist market economy may well have depended on its emancipation from some theologically sustained values, such as the rejection of usury and the doctrine of the just price, nevertheless the market cannot operate effectively without sustaining some common moral values which, in turn, underpin contractual relationships.[3] If the market does rest upon such a moral background, then this is part of the market order to which religious belief might address itself.

This issue is one which goes back quite a long way in western history. Some sophists in ancient Greece argued that morality is both subjective and self-interested, and that it would be foolish to act justly if one could get away with acting unjustly when it was in one's interests to do so. Many cultural thinkers across the political spectrum have argued that the capitalist market order emerged from within Western European Christianity which protected moral values from the corrosive effects of such self-interest. However, with the growth of secularisation, which, in turn, is closely associated with capitalism, the values of truth-telling, promise-keeping and trust, which were an inheritance from the Christian tradition, have become eroded in the sense of their being regarded as collective values turning our understanding of morality away from one of common values towards self-interest. In these circumstances, the moral framework of values on which capitalism has historically drawn to preserve the values that are essential to its own effective conduct has become eroded by the very development of capitalism itself.[4]

No doubt the maintenance of these values could be turned into a formal legal matter, so that there could be legal sanctions against a failure to keep to these moral requirements. There are however, two difficulties with this assumption that the moral underpinnings of markets should be preserved by legal sanction.

---

[3] Durkheim quoted in F. Hirsch, *The Social Limits to Growth* Routledge and Kegan Paul, London, 1977, p. 141. For up to date secular discussions of the arguments see F. Fukuyama, *Trust: The Social Virtues and the Creation of Prosperity* Hamish Hamilton, London, 1995.

[4] For a full discussion of how, if at all, trust once eroded as a virtue based in habit and common belief could be reconstructed and reconstituted on a material choice basis which assumed self-interest on the part of individuals see M. Hollis, *Trust Within Reason* Cambridge University Press, 1998.

The first is that the law cannot be very effective where there is a collapse of the moral assumptions which the law has to protect. The law does not exist in a vacuum. It has to be sustained by widely accepted moral values. However, if such values are turned into matters of self-interest, then the authority of the law in its role of protecting basic values will be undermined. This has become clear recently in the context of the regulation of financial markets. Some defenders of the market have become uneasy about the regulation of these sorts of markets, for example to produce legislation against insider dealing, because they see them as embodying the idea of a victimless crime in which someone can be guilty of an offence caused by the unrestrained pursuit of self-interest without there being an identifiable victim of this self-interested activity. What seems to be lacking in such arguments though, is that the integrity of the market itself can become the victim of self-interest if it is not constrained by regulation of this sort. If, however, the idea of there being victimless crimes was taken as a reason for easing such regulation, then the point that I made earlier would become salient: that is, that the law in this area would fall victim to self-interest so that the maintenance of the integrity of the market itself, as opposed to identifying individual victims, is not seen as an important issue. The law can maintain this kind of function only if it is assumed that there is a general morality relating to the underpinning of the market which has to be preserved. If, however, there were to be this change of attitude, namely, that all that matters is that the self-interest of an identifiable victim has been been harmed, then it is difficult to obtain social consent for having laws which protect some idea of the moral integrity of the market.

In order to secure such consent, there has to be some wider appreciation of the moral integrity of the market. Of course, it might be argued that this could still make sense in terms of the long-term self-interest of market actors, or alternatively by appealing to some idea of universalisability: what would be the consequences if everyone acted like that? However, both of these strategies based upon self-interest still presuppose that there is some constraint on self-interest in market transactions either of the long-term sort or of the universalisable variety. The potential problem, though, is that the prospect of short-term gains may well override such constraints unless there is some deep-seated morality in society: what Hegel calls *Sittlichkeit* - ethical life or civic virtue which acts as a countervailing power to self-interest.

The second problem involved in turning these ethical matters into ones of formal regulation is that it is more costly and inefficient. If there are internalised values of a non-self inter-ested sort, which constrain behaviour in the market, then it is arguable that this is a much less costly form of regulation than what would otherwise be a growing problem of the need for more and more regulation.

The second aspect of the moral underpinning of the market is in many ways parallel to the first and was well recognised by Adam Smith: that is, the maintenance of some sense of civic virtue and social obligation in respect of the market. On a purely self-interested approach to morality, attitudes could arise in relation to economic behaviour which would actually damage the market.

This could occur in two ways. First, on a self-interested view of morality there would be every incentive for the trader to seek to secure a monopoly of the goods and services that he or she has to sell. Monopolies again are harmful to the free market, as defenders of the market such as Hayek recognise, and in some cases, as in the newspapers and the media, are inimical to the flourishing of society as a whole. But what argument could be put to a trader that he or she should not try to secure a monopoly if it is in his or her interests to do so? Again, the only appeal would be to some sense of the integrity of the market as a whole, or to the principle of universalisability, or to Adam Smith's own impartial spectator theory. The point is that laws against monopoly have to have some sort of moral justification, and it is difficult to see where this could come from unless one assumes that morality is relevant to the market economy in a way that basically Henson denies. The regulation of the market will become more and more problematic if there is not some concern to cultivate a sense of social and civic responsibility, which, as I have suggested, may become more and more difficult if we accept the argument that morality is confined to the private sphere and cannot address the civic behaviour on which markets crucially depend.[5]

A parallel point may be made in respect of the market in relation to the state. From the point of view of self-interest, the individual trader may, in a wholly rational, instrumental way become a rent seeker from the government – seeking, that is, to secure privileges from government in terms of subsidies, tariffs or legal benefits. On a free-market view, such rent-seeking behaviour is harmful and government should seek to resist it. However, the same problem which I have already identified returns at this point. The state has to act to resist such behaviour in terms of seeking to protect the integrity of the market, and in terms of a sense of fairness and justice to other actors in the market. In order to do so, it has to appeal to a sense of fairness and civic virtue which goes beyond self-interest; that is, to say again, the integrity of the market and its regulation by the state will be difficult to maintain if morality is collapsed into self-interest.[6]

Much the same arguments apply in the case of trust. Trust has come to the fore recently as an area of concern in relation to markets and has been the subject of a substantive book by Francis Fukuyama.[7] It has also been prominent in the debate in the Far East in the context of emerging dynamic market economies and how these can fit into a more traditional culture without eroding that culture, in particular the religious and cultural beliefs which are necessary underpinnings of trust which, in turn, is a central moral underpinning for the market. Exactly the same points apply in relation to trust as we saw earlier. Trust is essential to the efficient operation of the market, and in their early stages capitalist markets were able to rely on trust which, in turn, was rooted in a moral inheritance which, it is argued by critics, capitalism has eroded. On this view,

---

[5] For a fuller discussion of these issues see R. Dahl, *Dilemmas of Pluralist Democracies* Yale University Press, New Haven, Conn., 1982.
[6] Ibid.   [7] Fukuyama *Trust*.

therefore, capitalism depletes the moral inheritance and a sense of virtue on which its own efficiency rests.

These general points that I have been considering are exacerbated by the fact that many of the justifications of the market order by liberal economists and social and political theorists rely heavily on the idea that morality has now to be seen as subjective and potentially self-interested.[8] On this view, not only the market but, indeed, the extension of the market is justified by the fact that morality is best regarded as a matter of subjective preference. In a market we do not have to appeal to a common or objective morality or to a shared moral inheritance. Rather, the market manages subjective preferences. Value is reducible to preference, and in a market preferences are recorded and, if the price is right, the preferences are satisfied. Price, too, is subjective; it records the value that an individual chooser places on commodities. In this sense, a market is moral subjectivism writ large. Any attempt to constrain markets by moral values such as social justice betrays on this view a kind of pre-modern outlook, and does not take seriously the fact of moral diversity rooted in the subjective judgements of value exercised by free individuals. This point relates to the extension of markets in the following way. Collective public provision rather than market provision has to invoke some kind of notion of value – for example the priority of meeting needs which transcends individual choice and preference; whereas, on this view, the nature of needs and the obligation to satisfy them are matters of moral controversy which free individuals can disagree about profoundly. This point was well put by John Gray:

Needs can be given no plausible cross-cultural content, but instead can be seen to vary across different moral traditions. Even where moral traditions overlap so as to allow agreement to be reached on a list of basic needs, there is no means of arriving at an agreed schedule of urgency among conflicting basic needs . . . There is an astonishing presumption in those who write as if hard dilemmas of this sort can be subject to a morally consensual resolution. Their blindness to these

---

[8] See F. A. Hayek, *Law Legislation and Liberty* vols. 1, 2, and 3, Routledge, London 1972–9; J. M. Buchanan, *The Limits of Liberty* University of Chicago Press, 1975.

difficulties can only be accounted for by them failing to take seriously the realities of cultural pluralism in our society or what comes to the same thing, taking as authoritative their traditional values.[9]

On this view, therefore, morality is relative to particular moral traditions and practices – the sort of narrative communities discussed earlier – and, because we lack a sense of common morality, collective provision, which implies a sense of common values and common obligations, should make way for market provision in which individuals will be able to choose and by choosing put a value on whatever it is that they want, whether these goods are normal consumer goods or welfare goods such as health and education. In the next part of the chapter I shall consider this issue of the extension of markets justified by this approach, but for the moment I want to dwell on the point that moral pluralism and subjectivism poses quite severe difficulties for the operation of markets if it is taken as a full account of the nature of morality. This marries up the point about subjectivism and the moral underpinnings of markets. If it is true that markets depend upon certain moral underpinnings, such as promise-keeping, trust, integrity and so forth, there are obvious dangers in reducing all moral values to subjective preference, since such preferences will not be circumscribed by constraints other than self-chosen ones – such as the deferment of gratification into the future, and certainly not by some kind of agreed common moral order within which preferences are constrained and limited – irrespective of whether such a moral order is regarded as being rooted in the idea of a natural law/order or in the formative narratives of a particular society. As we shall see in the next chapter, economic liberals who hold the views about values that I have described invoke the subjectivity of value to reject the claims of social justice in relation to the economy. If, however, the market needs moral underpinning, it is problematic to say that all values are subjective in an unconstrained way as the argument about social justice implies. Equally, it would be inconsistent to invoke

[9] J. Gray, 'Classical Liberalism, Positional Goods and the Politicisation of Poverty' in *Dilemmas of Liberal Democracies* ed. A. Ellis and K. Kumar Tavistock, London, 1983. pp. 181–2.

the argument about the subjectivity of value to render the appeal to a collective value like social justice illusory, while at the very same time wanting to insist that some collective values, namely, those which bear upon the moral underpinning of markets, should not be seen as subjective.

I now want to change direction a little. So far I have been concerned with trying to identify morally important beliefs which have to be in place for the market to operate effectively, and to show that these beliefs have to apply to collective elements of the market, to contract and to property, and that a wholly privatised morality, whether reduced to self-interest or not, will not be able to address these cogently. I now want to turn to the idea of the moral boundaries or limits to markets. As we have seen, Henson takes the view that the economy is autonomous, but, even if we were tempted to believe that such a view is true, there would still be a problem about the kinds of goods that should be conceived of as commodities to be privately owned and traded and exchanged in markets together with the associated issue of what sorts of human relationships should be seen as embodying market values. This is a central moral issue. The point here is this: do we have a sense of where the limits of commodification lie and where the boundaries of market values and relationships should give way to other sorts, whether they are political relationships, community ones or non-monetary voluntary ones, or to other kinds of values? There may be areas of human life in which markets and market values are wholly inappropriate and market-type relationships such as contracts equally wrong. Not only might our humanity be damaged by such extensions of this supposedly autonomous sphere, but, equally, the legitimacy of the market itself might be damaged if it were to transgress these boundaries. Those who take the view I have outlined earlier, namely, that morality is wholly reducible to subjective preference will, as I have argued, claim that markets should be extended to more and more areas of life because we lack the moral resources to legitimise collective judgements about the nature of common values, common obligations and common views about the nature of fundamental relationships. The realm of commodities, on this view, could only be circumscribed if we have common moral views, whether rooted in some notion of our common humanity which would rule out seeing some values as reducible to commodities or the moral traditions of a particular society which would also constrain reducing things to commodities in this way. If morality is subjective, we do not have the resources to do this, and the extension of the market will allow subjective choosers to make these judgements for themselves.

In order to focus this general issue more, let me take two examples. The first is to consider whether the sale of human organs should be permitted: that is, should there be a market in bodily parts? On a strictly capitalist view of the market, it would be very difficult to see why not. The scope for such a market could clearly be quite wide. There could be a market in blood and blood products, in kidneys, in sperm, in renting out a uterus for surrogate pregnancy and so forth.

On a market view, at least two considerations would favour the extension of the market into these areas. The first is that there might well be a clear demand for these products, since there is an unsatisfied demand from those awaiting transplants, for example. Secondly, if markets are to be construed as mechanisms for the exchange of property rights, then it might be argued that if a person owns anything he or she owns his or her own body and its parts. Indeed, some theories of capitalist property rights from Locke through to Nozick rest on the idea of self-ownership. The case for a market in organs and tissues has been put forcefully put by advocates of the free market. The Institute of Economic Affairs has long argued for a free market in blood products to run alongside the donor system, and a broader case has been put by Simon Rottenberg in his essay 'The Production and Exchange of Used Body Parts' in his contribution to the *Festschrift for Ludwig von Mises*. All of these would see a clear role for markets and for enterprise and entrepreneurship in these fields. We have to ask whether this extension of the market would run up against some widely held moral boundary and, if so, on what sort of principle such a boundary rests; and, secondly, whether the extension of the market into such fields, which would sanction seeing the body as a commodity, would in some sense weaken the market just because it was seen to have crossed such a boundary.

In his well-known book on the blood-donor system, Richard Titmuss argued that, if blood could be bought and sold, then anything could be.[10] If human tissue is to be regarded as a commodity and in terms of other economic categories and relationships such as property and contract, then anything could be. There would be no limits to commodification and thus to the scope of the market and enterprise. Nevertheless, an issue of importance that cannot be evaded here, but which I will take up in more detail at the end of the chapter, is how such a limitation on the growth of the market could be justified, and, in trying to answer this question, we come up against some of the issues that preoccupied the previous two chapters. Is it possible to give some general moral reason why this might be thought to be a wrong extension of markets, or is the reason much more parochial and based upon the values found within a particular society and how it conceives the social meanings of goods, as in Walzer?

An answer utilising general or natural moral principles would most obviously invoke ideas like human dignity and respect for persons. It might be argued that, by reflecting on what might be implied in the principle of respect for persons, we would come to a general view that people should not treat themselves as commodities with their bodily parts being bought and sold. Persons should be treated as ends in themselves, and they should not treat themselves as means to the ends of others, even when it might be a life and death situation for the other person. This was certainly the basis of Kant's objection to what we might term the commodification of the body when he discussed this issue in the parallel cases of whether one might sell teeth (to make dentures for the rich), hair and sexuality when he discussed the recruitment of castrati for choirs. He argues that, in respect of a person: 'Humanity in his own person (*homo noumenon*) can so far restrict the right to make use of his body, that all use of it as a thing is forbidden to him . . . He is

[10] R. Titmuss, *The Gift Relationship* Penguin, Harmondsworth, 1970.

therefore not the *dominus* of his body, since he may not treat it as *res sua.*'[11]

For Kant, such considerations rule out selling teeth and sexuality (and also put limits over the authority of others over his body, for example in manual labour). The point I want to make here, though, is more about the form of Kant's argument, which is general and metaphysical, about the nature of selfhood, humanity and freedom. It owes nothing to more narrative or communitarian ideas about what it is to be a person within a particular moral tradition. On the view that Christian public ethics are linked to general moral ideas, whether we call these part of natural law or derived from an idea of a natural order, this would be the place to start answering the question. Communitarian political theorists, together with narrative theologians, would start in a different place. The communitarian would consider the social meanings which such goods would have in a particular society to see whether one could provide an interpretation of such goods in a way that was consistent with the values which pervade that society. There would be no general or a priori answer to this question rooted in some general notion of humanity. The same point would hold for the narrative theologian if invited to reflect on this issue. One would have to consider what image of the body was conveyed in the Christian narrative and what that view might sanction for Christians, but, equally, as we saw in the last chapter, such a view would not, for the narrative theologian, be part of the public deliberation in the sense of pursuing an accommodationist strategy on this. So, this particular example throws into relief the different approaches to the nature of theological ethics when they are asked to confront a public problem of this sort.

The second example I want to take to illustrate the issue of the moral limits to markets is concerned with the possible consequences for ideas like service if a commodified and contract-based culture goes beyond its appropriate limits. In the view of the advocates of the extension of the market and quasi market mechanisms into more and more areas of public life, the

[11] I. Kant, *Lectures on Ethics* ed. P. Heath and J. B. Schneewind, Cambridge University Press, 1997, p. 341.

service ethic is something of a myth. The public-choice school of economists argues that those who work in welfare, health and educational areas are, in fact, motivated in the same way as those who work in markets, that is to say, by utility maximisation or self-interest.[12] The fact that someone earns his or her living as a doctor, teacher, nurse or social worker does not mean that they have stepped into a different moral realm in terms of motivation and attitude in which they are motivated by the demands of caring, service and vocation, unlike people in markets who seek to maximise their utilities. They do, in fact, maximise personal utility by using the public sector and the public funds at their disposal to increase their scope of responsibility, the scope of bureaucracy, their status and their income; and they do this first of all free from the threat of bankruptcy which stalks the market, and free from direct accountability, since professional knowledge and professional status allows them to some extent to evade accountability.

Given this diagnosis, there is a case for trying to limit discretionary forms of delivery of service either by privatising public services, or developing internal markets, or trying to tie service providers down to performance indicators and greater specification of duties in contracts to secure more definite and less discretionary forms of delivery by producers of services. If people are motivated by subjective utility maximisation rather than the service ethic, then, the argument runs, they have to be constrained by market or quasi-market mechanisms. This point was well put by Nigel Lawson in his pamphlet *The New Conservatism* in 1980:

We are all imperfect – even the most high minded civil servant. Academic work is still in its infancy on the economics of bureaucracy; but it is already clear that it promises to be a fruitful field. The civil servants and middle-class welfare professionals are from selfless Platonic guardians of popular mythology: they are a major interest group in their own right.[13]

---

[12] See W. Niskanen, *Bureaucracy – Servant or Master?* Hobart Publications, London, 1973; N. Lawson, *The New Conservatism*, Centre for Policy Studies, London, 1980.
[13] Ibid.

The academic work to which Lawson refers is from the Public Choice School of economics which has been heavily influenced by the assumptions of economic liberalism that we have been discussing. The conclusion, as he makes clear, is that public service should be demythologised into the utility max-imising behaviour of producer interest groups, and their be-haviour constrained in the same way as behaviour in the market is constrained by the customer.

This argument has many important aspects that cannot be discussed here. However, I do want to question one basic assumption, which seems to be involved in this analysis, which implies that the service ethic can be a feature only of voluntary organisations in which people are not paid and therefore have no incentive to turn themselves into producer interest-groups as maintained by the 'public-choice' model. This analysis assump-tion turns on accepting the argument that utility maximisation is the basic form of human behaviour, or at least of behaviour for which one is paid. This assumption is, in itself, highly disputable; and I have suggested earlier that, if it is accepted, then some assumptions about civic virtue, which may be absolutely necessary to the market itself, are put into jeopardy.

It can also lead to some changes in behaviour among those in the public sector, which might, paradoxically, harm the service offered to the client, patient or customer, for, if the service ethic is displaced by a contractual or a market one, there is a danger that people whose self-understanding is that they are offering a service, but are being constrained to behave as if they were in a market or a quasi-market, might then act only within the terms of the contract and the strict interpretation of what it requires. This had, I think, already happened in schools. It would not then be open to government to appeal to an ethic of service to provide more than is specified in the contract, since the whole point has been to displace the ethic of service and replace it by contract or quasi-market relations.

Again, a market-oriented approach may lead to effects that are unintended. Can we, in fact, manage a society in which the ethic of service is displaced to the voluntary sector? Just as in the market, where appeal is made to virtues which may not be subsumable under those of private utility and private interests, so, too, in the state sector, the introduction of markets, quasi-markets and the dominance of contract might well deprive us of ethical principles such as service and vocation, which are essential to the efficient delivery of services. We have to be very careful about the market again crossing an important moral barrier and replacing one ethic by another.

There is another deep issue here. In the public sector, which is part of government and should therefore be subject to the rule of law, we are concerned with things such as equity and treating like cases in like manner. These are not values served by markets, and there is no particular reason why they should be. However, they are central to government and to the rule of law. There is a clear danger that the introduction of market principles into the public sector might undermine these basic moral and political principles of public provision and, again, this provides some basic idea of moral restraint on what the role of the market might be in this context.

The main point of this chapter however, does not lie in the detailed discussion of its themes, so much as in the contention, *contra* Hensley Henson and, indeed, *contra* Hayek, that the market is an autonomous entity in a sense beyond good and evil in its autonomy. Markets are human creations; they have to be embedded in moral networks if they are to work effectively, and it is in virtue of the fact that markets have this inescapable moral dimension that religious belief can address them. Markets raise basic questions about the nature of value, about the character of human goods and the nature of human motivation, and thus form part of a public world to which religious belief can address itself.

The extension of markets and quasi-markets has widespread effects on how we understand society. First of all, in the ways that I have indicated, it can transform public values into private ones because it transforms the citizen with a set of public rights and entitlements into a private consumer. It extends the process of commodification, and this, in turn, will have complex effects. Instead of a range of human goods embodying different types of value, commodification will homogenise values into ones which can be given some kind of financial embodiment and thus attenuate our understanding of the range of human value. It will also have the effect of subjectivising value in terms of those goods which are transformed into commodities. Given that the value and price of commodities are the result of subjective preferences, then the extension of the realm of commodification will be also, and by necessity, an extension of the idea of subjective preferences. So, for example, more and more goods are seen in terms of 'life-style choices', which is a practical way of making the philosophical point. Alongside this extension of commodities and market relations will go an extension of those areas in which it is assumed that the instrumental reasoning of rational economic man will work. If utility maximisation is the best way of explaining behaviour in a market, then it may well be the case that the extension of the sphere of commodities will also be accompanied by an extension of these motivational assumptions. Hence, not only will commodification displace other ways of thinking about value, it will also have the effect of displacing other types of understanding of human nature than rational economic self-interest.

From the point of view of theology, it might be argued that this displacement and erosion of the complexity of human value and motivation, which may well harm the market order, itself needs a countervailing influence. It would be central I think to this view that only a sense of the transcendent can, in fact, provide a secure basis for the argument that there are definite limits to the sphere of commodities and to the sphere of rational self-interest. If we do not have an idea of transcendent value, then other sorts of value are always going to be subject to market transformation and commodification. It might seem that the only secure way to defend the idea that there are values beyond choice is to assume that spheres of value do not possess just contingent social meanings and the effects of choice, but mirror some kind of moral reality of the sort that we saw argued for in the chapter on natural law with all the difficulties that such a perspective carries with it.

Perhaps the best way of finishing this chapter is with a quotation from Francis Fukuyama who emphasises very strongly the ways in which markets can only work effectively if they are embedded in a rich background culture:

The liberal democracy that emerges at the end of history is therefore not entirely 'modern'. If the institutions of democracy and capitalism are to work properly, they must coexist with certain pre-modern cultural habits that ensure their proper functioning. Law, contract and economic rationality provide a necessary but not sufficient basis for the stability and prosperity of post-industrial societies, they must as well be leavened with reciprocity, moral obligation, duty towards the community and trust which are based upon habit rather than rational calculation. The latter are not anachronisms in a modern society but rather the *sine qua non* of the latter's success.[14]

The recognition of the way the economy has to be embedded in a moral order undermines the idea that it is an autonomous entity beyond moral appraisal and constraint. As Charles Gore argued, such a conception of the economy allows Christianity to breathe more freely in the atmosphere. This is, of course, all very well, but what kind of moral principles might be thought to apply to an ethical economy? This will form the subject-matter of the next chapter. In addition, of course, Fukuyama's way of making the point, namely, that economies rely on trust and other forms of social capital which are pre-modern, makes the issue of how to sustain that background in which the market is embedded very fragile in the modern world. Is the defence of the embeddedness of markets in a moral culture a matter of trying to shield the remaining remnant of a pre-modern order, or are there ways in which the moral content can be defended and renewed on a more rational and deliberative basis rather than as a matter of custom and habit which seems destined ultimately to be undermined?[15]

[14] Fukuyama, *Trust* p. 11.
[15] Hollis' book *Trust Within Reason* is a brilliant exploration of these themes.

CHAPTER 8

Social justice, freedom and the common good

The very structure of democratic capitalism – even its impersonal economic system – is aimed at community, not of course in the nostalgic sense of *Gemeinschaft*, but at a new order of community, the community of free persons in voluntary association.

(M. Novak, *Free Persons and the Common Good*)

In the Eucharistic liturgy we are enjoined to seek the common good. The aim of this chapter is to attempt to see what can be made of this notion in a complex market-driven society marked by a high degree of individualism and moral pluralism, and what contribution theology might make to an understanding of what the common good might mean. I shall concentrate first of all on issues of political economy and the possible sense that could be given to the idea of a common good in a market society before moving on to discuss the possible contribution of theology.

I shall begin by looking at the idea of social justice, and I need to explain why I am starting with this rather than with the concept of the common good itself. The reason is that it would not, as we have seen, be very plausible against the background of the pluralism of Western societies to argue that the common good can consist in a rich, deep and elaborated form of substantive agreement on values and human purposes. Such a thick account of the common good or the common purposes of society, it is argued, looks both implausible and potentially dangerous in a society marked by moral diversity in which individuals believe strongly that judgements about substantive and, indeed, ultimate values are for them to make by exercising their own judgement. While many Christians may deplore this, for good or ill, it is claimed to be a basic fact of life in modern society, and any search for an acceptable notion of the common good which could be endorsed from the standpoint of different moral positions has to take this fact very seriously indeed. From this perspective, Professor West seems to be clearly right when he argues that: 'We must start with the liberal premise: the search for a common good must start with particular goals and the values which many different persons and groups pursue, and seek in mutual respect, some accommodation.'[1]

Towards the end of this chapter and for most of the final section I shall return to West's idea that Christian political thought on this issue has to start with this liberal premise which would not be all that obvious to both the Christendom approach of Demant or the narrative approach of Yoder and Hauerwas. Assuming, however, that we do regard this as a plausible stance to take in the light of the pluralism of modern society, there are then clear limitations on the scope of an idea of the common good, for, to quote West again:

No longer can we impose on all society the goals and values, however reasonable or good, which for one group in society seem to define the meaning of the whole. Where religious authorities attempt to do so – one might mention the diverse cases of Iran and South Africa – the consequences are monstrous.[2]

This is why an alternative starting-point, such as some version of the Christendom approach to an understanding of the common good, can seem to critics to be both implausible and dangerous. If we accept that we live in a society in which individuals believe that they have a right to their own conception of the good, then any conception of the common good is going to fall a long way short of some common purpose for

---

[1] C. C. West, 'The Common Good and the Participation of the Poor' in *The Common Good and US Capitalism* ed. F. Williams and J. Hauck, University Press of America, Maryland, 1987, pp. 46–7.
[2] Ibid.

society as a whole. It will also fall far short of the idea that the common good lies in tracking some kind of transcendent moral order which is the same for all societies. Reflection on this fact has led many philosophers and theologians to believe that, if there is a common good to be found, then it has to lie not in the search for a substantive common purpose, but, rather, in the common needs or basic goods which people have to have in order to be able to act as moral agents at all, that is, to pursue any conception of the good whatever it might be. This has led to a focus on the idea of the common good as lying in the range of goods and services, benefits and opportunities which all citizens need to have in order to pursue their conception of the good, whatever it might turn out to be. In this sense, there is still the idea of an order of goods which are basic or primary and which lie behind or are presupposed by the pursuit of other goods. In this sense, therefore, the liberal moves from the idea of common human purposes to be identified in a unified way by reason, to the idea that, even though reason cannot identify a set of common human purposes, it can, in fact, identify a set of conditions for the pursuit of any sorts of purposes: that is to say, primary goods or those things that would satisfy basic needs. If there are such generic goods which are necessary conditions of agency, then these can be seen as constituent parts of a political common good. So, in a liberal society, we move away from the idea of thick or substantive moral agreement to the idea of the conditions under which agency or autonomy can, in fact, be exercised. So, while it may be said that liberal political thought moves away from a more classical view of human nature and the purposes which human beings have to fulfil if they are to flourish, nevertheless there is this thinner conception of the self as an autonomous agent. The next issue to arise and which would also be part of the common good is how such basic goods are to be distributed. Hence the issue of social justice becomes central to the idea of the common good. This is why Michael Novak has been led to the view that, when the concept of the common good is used in a liberal society, it is usually conflated into social or distributive justice: 'in short, the invocation of the phrase is generally intended to have as its operative meaning:

redistribution'.[3] There is clearly a logic about this for the reasons that I have already given. Indeed, Hayek has argued that a substantive notion of the common good and common purpose is at home in a tribal society with a shared history, with common understanding together with little sense of diversity and individualism.[4] This is why, from this perspective, the modern invocation of this view as a religious ideal rooted in the Old Testament prophets is misguided, because, in so far as they had a sense of the common good, it was rooted in the shared values of a tribal society bound together by an ethos and a common purpose. We are emphatically not in that position. Hence, the tendency to move the idea of the common good one stage further back: that is away from a substantive shared good to a concentration on whether there are goods we have to have in common as moral agents and the appropriate distribution of such goods, and thus the link between the idea of the common good and social justice. Nevertheless, exactly the same forces that have led to this pushing back of the scope of the common good have led thinkers such as Hayek to argue that distributive justice is as much an illusory ideal in relation to the economy as a thicker notion of the common good is implausible for society as a whole. In the first part of the chapter, I shall explore the idea of social justice in more detail to see why economic liberals such as Hayek think that social justice is a mirage, and therefore cannot be part of the articulation of the idea of a common good for a pluralist society.

This economic liberal or neo-liberal approach (I shall use the terms interchangeably) is both intellectually and politically important: intellectually because it provides a powerful and coherent account of the proper way to understand the nature of the market economy particularly in a global context; politically because it is espoused by many politicians on the Right in Britain, Western Europe and the United States, and because its claims have been promoted by distinguished think tanks such as the Institute for Economic Affairs, the Adam Smith Institute and, in some respects, the Social Market Foundation. It also

---

[3] M. Novak, *Free Persons and the Common Good* Madison Books, New York, 1989, p. 20.

[4] See F. A. Hayek, *Law Legislation and Liberty* vol. 2, *The Mirage of Social Justice passim.*

informs the thought of those who argue that we must abandon welfare capitalism in favour of a more competitive, less secure version. The neo-liberal argument about the very restricted role of morality within markets helps to legitimise this approach. It is particularly important in the context of the task that I have set myself – the exploration of the idea of the common good in a market society, or, perhaps, to put the point differently, the possibility of an ethical economy – because, in certain important respects the neo-liberal regards the economy as a *morally free zone*. What I mean by this is that the neo-liberal wishes to resist the idea that certain moral notions, such as those of social justice, common good and community – notions which represent some kind of collective moral standard which the society should aspire to reach – are logically inappropriate to apply to the outcomes of the market. To put the point crudely at this stage, collective moral notions such as social justice or common good cannot be used as a yardstick to assess the outcomes of the market economy. Thus, the market is a morally free zone in this respect.

It is important to stress precisely what my point is here, because I do not wish to be misunderstood. I am not denying that the economic liberal believes that individual moral integrity is vitally important in economic transactions – a point I discussed in the previous chapter. Rather, I am concerned with *collective* moral notions in relation to the economy, particularly the ideas of social justice and the common good which obviously go beyond the issue of the moral integrity of individual economic factors. In the previous chapter, I contrasted the approach of Henson with that of Gore and Temple. Because Henson believed that the economy is in some sense autonomous, rather like the order of nature, its structures and outcomes were not susceptible to moral constraint. He did, however, as I pointed out, make the point that the individual Christian should act conscientiously and righteously in his private dealings. This is, however, fundamentally different from the question as to whether the economy falls within the purview of a social morality associated with transpersonal ideas like social justice and the common good. Nevertheless, Henson's point is still highly relevant in this context too. Before Gore and Temple embarked upon their argument that an ethical economy has to go beyond the righteousness and fair dealing of individual Christians and had to confront issues about social morality, they each felt the need to confront Henson's point. So, for example, Gore, in a report which he drafted on *The Moral Witness of the Church on Economic Subjects*[5] which was presented to the Convocation of Canterbury on 16 April 1907, put the issue between him and those who took Henson's line as follows:

Abstract laws of supply and demand, in combination with a certain theory of population (Malthus) were supposed to rule out in the scientific treatment of commerce and industry all questions of justice and mercy to wage earners and all moral considerations in the relations between employers and employed . . . the Christian Church allowed itself to be silenced by the terrors of supposed inexorable laws.[6]

Temple makes much the same point in his essay 'Discipleship and Economics' in which he responded to the views he was criticising in the following way:

Those laws (of Political economy) are as fixed and immutable, it is said as the laws of mechanics, they are set forth in the exact science of Political Economy; and that Christianity has no more to do with them than it has to do with Geometry . . . (the Christian) is not to suppose that these laws can be modified at the dictates of the Christian conscience.[7]

In the previous chapter we saw some reason to doubt this account of the immutability of economic laws and the exactness of the science of political economy. Nevertheless, this still leaves untouched the question of how far the outcomes of the economy can be judged by collective moral standards such as social justice and the contribution of the economy to the common good and the role of the churches, if any, in trying to contribute to an account of what such yardsticks might be.

As I have suggested, the growth of economic liberalism over

[5] *The Moral Witness of the Church on Economic Subjects*, a report presented to the Convocation of Canterbury April 1907, SPCK, London, 1907.
[6] Ibid.
[7] W. Temple, 'Discipleship and Economics' in *Personal Religion and the Life of Fellowship* Longmans, Green and Co., London, 1926, p. 59.

the past twenty-five years, both as an intellectual movement and as political practice, poses a rather similar challenge to those who believe that the outcomes of the economy should be subjected to a form of collective moral restraint rooted in ideas about social justice and the common good as faced Gore and Temple. The aim of this chapter will be to consider the arguments of economic liberals in favour of the view that social justice is a *mirage*, to use Hayek's description, and that the idea of the common good should be given a much more restricted moral meaning than that which tends to be favoured by current Christian commentators on political economy.

I want to start with the neo-liberal critique of the idea of social justice. This seems appropriate because the churches seem particularly wedded to the idea of social justice. It looms large in church pronouncements about politics and society and was central to *Faith in The City*.[8] Clearly, the idea of social justice, for those who believe in it, could well be thought of as at least a component part of any full conception of a common good in society. So what do we make of Hayek's claim that social justice is a mirage?

It is central to the neo-liberal view that injustice arises only as the result of intentional action. If I intentionally infringe your rights, that is an injustice, but, if a hurricane destroys your crops, that is not an injustice but rather misfortune or bad luck. Similarly, something like genetic handicap is misfortune rather than injustice, since no one is intentionally distributing such handicaps. If, however, an intentional action of mine causes you disability, then this does become injustice. The political rub here is that, while it might be regarded as a central role for the state to rectify injustice, it is not the role of the state to seek to rectify the consequences of misfortune. The appropriate response to misfortune is charity and benevolence, which are discretionary virtues that cannot be part of the state's own actions given that these, for example in the sphere of taxation, are coercive. In the view of the neo-liberal, the aggregate outcomes of market behaviour, the so-called 'distribution of

---

[8] *Faith in the City*, Church House Publishing, London, 1985.

income and wealth' which prevails at any one time, cannot be regarded as either just or unjust, since that outcome was neither intended nor foreseen by anyone. There is no distributor and thus no distribution. In a market, millions of people buy and sell for all the individual reasons that they have, and those actions are intentional.[9] The aggregate outcome of such actions is not intended, nor is it foreseen. It is an unintended consequence of individual behaviour in a market. Given that injustice can only apply to intentional acts, the outcomes of a market cannot be regarded as just or unjust. They are rather the unforeseen, unintended and undesigned consequences of millions of individual acts of exchange. So long as exchange is uncoerced, the outcomes of exchange are fair and legitimate whatever the degree of inequality they might embody. This point is very important because it blocks a criticism of the market as producing socially unjust results. Those at the bottom of the pile have suffered bad luck or misfortune, not injustice, and the most appropriate claim that they have on others is in terms of charity and benevolence, not in terms of justice. If it seems realistic, indeed prudent, in political terms, to have a minimal welfare state and transfer payments to meet the needs of these unfortunates, then this implies a minimum safety-net for welfare to prevent destitution, not a welfare state the aim of which is to rectify inequality in the name of a more just distribution of resources and opportunities. The other important philosophical point to emerge from this, which, as we shall see, assumes more importance later on in my argument, is that the neo-liberal is interested in *procedures*, not in what might be called *end state principles*. That is to say, so long as market transactions are procedurally fair, that is to say, uncoerced, then the outcomes of uncoerced exchanges are legitimate whatever degree of inequality they may manifest. Of course, a good deal depends upon how one is to understand coercion in relation to freedom and this will be considered further later in the chapter.

The second argument used against the claims of distributive justice has to do with claims about the moral diversity of

---

[9] See Hayek, *The Mirage of Social Justice*.

modern societies. A conception of social justice embodies a distributive principle – for example that resources and opportunities should be distributed to meet needs, or that they should be distributed to reward merit or whatever. The neo-liberal will, however, argue that, in a morally diverse society, we have no way of agreeing first of all whether distribution should favour merit or desert, on the one hand, or need, on the other.[10] Even if we could resolve this dilemma, it would still leave untouched the deep moral issues involved in arriving at an agreed account of merit, if that is what we want to reward, or need, if that is what we prefer, and there is no way of ranking merits or needs in terms of priorities or urgency. Merely to invoke the ideal of social justice without tackling such large and complex questions is to give an illusion of political concern in a way that cannot lead to practical application in a diverse society. Moral diversity is, on this view, so thoroughgoing that social justice cannot form part of an account of a common good and such a conception of a common good cannot survive in a situation of moral pluralism. It is possible, of course, to argue that there is a core analytic definition of justice which would be 'to each his/her due'. This, however, will not work because, while all parties to a dispute about the concrete meaning of justice would agree on this core definition, and, indeed, if they did not, it would not be clear how they would know they were disagreeing about justice as opposed to entertaining two quite different concepts, nevertheless the analytical definition is too thin and unspecific to be action funding. That is to say, following John Rawls, that we can distinguish between a *concept* of justice, i.e. to each his due, and different *conceptions* of justice which provide specific interpretations about what is, in fact, a person's due. Conceptions of justice differ and, indeed, are part of the moral pluralism of contemporary society. Only in pre-modern, morally homogeneous society did the concept of justice yield one and only one specific conception of justice. The neo-liberal will argue that social justice might have had a role to play in homogenous, pre-modern societies with little in the way of market development

[10] Ibid.

because, against the background of an homogeneous morality, it might make sense to have agreed distributive principles. However, it would be no good for a Christian to invoke the fact that in the Old Testament there seems to be at many points an endorsement of what we might call social justice, because the prophets were preaching a doctrine of justice against a background of common understandings and a common moral framework, even if part of their message was that the society in question was not living up to its own conception of its moral values. We no longer live in such an homogeneous, pre-modern, what Hayek calls tribal, order – a point which was made in chapter 2 on prophecy and political theology.

The point about moral diversity and moral subjectivism also implies, for the neo-liberal, a commitment to a free market economy unconstrained by a commitment to social justice because, in a sense, the market is best seen as a kind of institutional embodiment of the subjectivity of value and individual preference. Value and price represent aggregate preferences for the free market liberal. There can be no content to the idea of a just price or a price fixed by a political mechanism. A value and a price are subjective to each individual and are revealed in an incorrigible way through their individual preferences.

In a situation of moral diversity, it is best to arrange society in more and more procedural terms: that is to say, a set of rules which will provide a framework for uncoerced market transactions, a full role for a market unconstrained by collective moral notions such as social justice or the common good, a safety-net welfare state (if at all), and the transfer of activities as far as possible from the public to the market sector. Public provision, as we saw in the previous lecture, implies what for the economic liberal is false – namely, a set of common purposes in society which would underpin such public provision. Such provision, as far as possible, should be transferred to a market in which individuals will be able to utilise resources as best they can to pursue their interests and aims in their own way, so long as, in doing so, they do not infringe the freedom of others.[11]

[11] See J. M. Buchanan, *The Limits of Liberty*.

It is important at this point to say something about the neo-liberal view of freedom which again is procedural. The neo-liberal wants to resist two claims which are often made about liberty which have an immediate effect on markets. These are that freedom involves ability, resources and opportunities, on the one hand, and that freedom has something to do with a specific set of human virtues, on the other. These links between liberty and ability and liberty and virtue were crucial to many of the arguments for the welfare state developed by philosophical and theological idealists in late Victorian and Edwardian Britain, ideas to be found in T. H. Green, Henry Jones, Edward Caird, Charles Gore and William Temple.

The first of these claims has the most direct economic import. If we believe that being *free* to do something implies being *able* to do it and thus having the resources to do it, then part of the common good of human freedom would imply common access to resources and opportunities to secure, for all individuals, the same sort of level of liberty.[12] If the state is seen as a guarantor of freedom for individuals, then it would be part of the responsibility of the state to secure to individuals the resources and opportunities they need to be *able* to do what they are *free* to do. This link between freedom and ability is, however, rejected by the neo-liberal. The argument here is that no one is able to do all that he or she is free to do. However rich I am, I am unable to do all the things which no other person is intentionally preventing me from doing. The list of actions which I am not currently prevented from doing is potentially infinite and thus logically I am not able to do all that I am free to do. The neo-liberal wants to define freedom as the absence of intentional coercion, and, in this sense, I am free to do whatever other people are not intentionally preventing me from doing, and thus freedom and ability are two separate things. The political rub here is acute for, as Sir Keith Joseph argued, 'poverty is not unfreedom'.[13] The lack of resources is not a restriction on liberty, and the state, as the custodian of equal freedom, has no obligation to secure resources and opportu-

---

[12] See F. A. Hayek, *The Constitution of Liberty* Routledge, London, 1960, p. 17.
[13] K. Joseph and J. Sumption, *Equality* J. Murray, London, 1979, p. 47.

nities to individuals to increase their ability to act. In this sense, this view of freedom also implies that the defence and endorsement of liberty does not involve a commitment to a just distribution of resources.

The second point about freedom is that the neo-liberal wants to produce a non-moralised conception of liberty. It is defined as the absence of intentional coercion where coercion is understood as the physical prevention of someone doing what he would otherwise do. This makes restrictions on liberty a wholly empirical question definable in terms of individual physical acts of coercion. In the view of the neo-liberal, the physical nature of coercion is central to an objective and non-normative account of coercion, and thus of freedom as the absence of coercion. Coercion and unfreedom have to be linked to the idea of someone making it physically or practically impossible for someone to do something. If coercion is broadened from this idea, then it becomes something subjective and controversial because it would become linked to a person's interests, desires and values. So, for example, in the case where A threatens to destroy something of value to B in order to ensure that B does X which he would not otherwise do, then this is not a form of coercion because it is physically possible for B not to do X by sacrificing what he values. An example of this would be a situation in which someone was threatened with violence if he/she did not mock their own religious faith. On the present account, this threat is not coercive. If we were to regard this as a form of coercion, then it would become entirely subjective because what would make it coercion would be the value that B places on X. Hence, according to Hillel Steiner: 'Interventions of a threatening or offering kind effect changes in the individual's relative desires to do certain actions. But neither the making of threats or that of offers constitutes a diminution of personal liberty.'[14]

The point about offers is as important as that of threats. So, for example, on the above analysis, to offer a destitute person £100,000 for his kidney for transplantation would not be a

---

[14] H. Steiner, 'Individual Liberty' *Proceedings of the Aristotelian Society* (1974), p. 43.

coercive offer, since it is not impossible for him to turn the offer down. So neither threats not offers are coercive, because it is always possible for the individual to choose. All that threats or offers do is to change relative *desires*, they do not affect *freedom*. So, on this kind of view, it is crucial to define coercion in terms of impossibility which is empirically identifiable; once the idea of coercion is broadened, it becomes subjective, normative and disputed.

This argument also has a bearing on what might be called structural coercion – that is to say, that one's position in the economy in which one lacks resources is a form of coercion. This is not so, since, according to the first argument we looked at, so-called structural coercion is not intentional and, secondly, according to the present argument, poverty does not make it impossible to resist threats and offers. These sorts of arguments are used by neo-liberals to argue that lack of resources does not of itself lead to coercive exchange in the market. Clearly, for the neo-liberal, coercive exchange is morally wrong and is a situation in which moral appraisal is important in the economy at this level of individual exchange. It does, however, depend upon this very narrow definition of coercion.

This cuts any link between freedom and morality. To be a free person is to be free from coercion which is a physical and empirically detectable state of affairs – it does not imply having resources. Equally, nor does it imply a link between freedom and virtue. Freedom does not mean living in a particular kind of way or having a conception of those sorts of human virtues which makes freedom valuable to us. It is purely to be understood as freedom from coercion. Thus it is fairly easy to see the link between freedom in the neo-liberal's sense and the role of the market. The framework of law is there to preserve mutual non-coercion, and the market is there to provide what I called the institutionalised form of moral subjectivism which allows free and uncoerced individuals the widest play for their individual preferences. It also links to the criticism of social justice, in the sense that freedom has nothing to do with a just distribution of resources since the possession or absence of resources has nothing to do with liberty.

It is also worth pointing out that the neo-liberal uses the arguments about social justice and liberty to demoralise the idea of property. Property is vital to the economic market because market exchange is essentially an exchange of property rights. On the neo-liberal view, however, there is no case in terms of either social justice or liberty for redistributing property. It is central to the view of Hayek, for example, that property is best left with existing owners, however unequally it is distributed, because the market offers incentives to property owners to use their property in productive ways, and that this is in the interests of the worse-off members of society because it will enhance the trickle-down effect. The trickle-down effect is the claim that the benefits of a dynamic economy may first of all only be available to a few, for example air travel, TV sets, refrigerators etc., but that, with increased production, these goods will become cheaper and more widely available. Equally, with increases in wealth and income, real resources also trickle down in the same way.

I want now to say a little about bias to the poor in this context. The economic liberal or neo-liberal will acknowledge that those who believe in social justice are committed to it as a way of helping the poor by striving for a more just distribution of resources, whether at what one might call the starting-gate of market competition by making sure that individuals have more resources and opportunities to operate in the market, or at an end state in terms of redistributing market outcomes so that the disadvantaged will be better off. Nevertheless, they reject the idea that social justice is the appropriate strategy, mainly because they believe that its moral demands are illusory for the reasons I have mentioned. In the view of economic liberals we have to get greater clarity about the nature of poverty. In their view, what matters to the poor, or at least should matter to them, is not whether there is a growing gap between rich and poor, or a rise in inequality which is an inevitable consequence of an economy run on such lines, but, rather, whether the poor person is better off this year than he was last year. As Joseph and Sumption argue:

An absolute standard (of poverty) means one defined by reference to the actual needs of the poor and not by reference to the expenditure of those who are not poor. A family is poor if it cannot afford to eat. It is not poor if it cannot afford endless smokes and it does not become poor by the mere fact that other people can afford them. A person who enjoys a standard of living equal to that of a medieval baron cannot be described as poor for the sole reason that he has chanced to be born into a society where the great majority can live like medieval kings.[15]

In the economic liberal's view, poverty in this sense will be better cured by the trickle-down effect of the market than by collective action through misguided ideas about social justice to meet the needs of the poor. In short, they reject ideas about relative poverty where poverty is defined in relation to a norm of consumption which, in their view, makes poverty impossible to cure without greater economic equality, and they favour, on the contrary, a view which links poverty, as I have said, with the absolute position of the poor which they believe that the trickle-down effect will improve on a year-by-year basis even if it means a decline in the relative position. This means, effectively, a complete reversal of what might be called the social democratic approach in which what matters is the relative position of the worse off. So, on the neo-liberal view, if Christians are to have a bias to the poor, they should take issues like this into account and not be blinded by their commitment to ideas of social justice and believe falsely that poverty is relative and connected to inequality.

For the neo-liberal, the defects of social justice not only are confined to the level of theory, but also involve severe political drawbacks. These are largely connected to the point about the indefinite nature of social justice in a context of moral pluralism which was discussed earlier. On this view, it is impossible in a morally pluralist society to arrive at agreements about the nature of social justice, and this gives rise to acute political difficulties if we pursue some social justice strategy against this background. First of all, a government pursuing social justice in a moral vacuum in which there is not agreement about distribu-

<hr />

[15] See Joseph and Sumption, *Equality* p. 27.

tive principles will be obliged to invoke vague and indefinite notions, such as fairness, for example, in relation to incomes and incomes policies, if these are thought to be part of a social justice approach. Equally, a government will fall prey to powerful interest groups if it sees its main task as distributing resources and opportunities. Groups of people will pursue what they see, from their own subjective points of view, as their just entitlements, and will pressurise governments to ensure that these entitlements are met. So, against a background of scarcity, politics will become a bleak zero-sum game in which groups are competing for a just distribution of scarce resources without government being able to draw upon some agreed norm of distribution. In these circumstances, government is bound to fall prey to the most powerful interest groups or coalitions of such interest groups. And, far from social justice being a noble political ideal, it will become a fig leaf for a zero-sum competition between powerful groups taking a wholly particular and subjective view of their entitlements.[16] On such a view, the ideal of social justice is very far from being part of the common good; it is, rather, a way of fracturing society into competing interest groups.

Secondly, the pursuit of social justice in a situation of pluralism in which norms cannot be agreed will mean that officials in the public sector, whose job it is to dispense resources in the interests of social justice, will have to act in highly discretionary ways, since we cannot write the rules of law which would guide such officials in a situation where we lack clear criteria for distribution. This puts unaccountable discretionary power at the heart of government, and middle-class welfare professionals in a very powerful position. When this is linked with the economic liberal's critique of the service ethic, which we discussed in the last chapter, according to which professional groups in the public sector are engaged in utility maximising behaviour, the problem is exacerbated. The overall point here is that it is not possible to make a distributive state compatible with the operation of the rule of law, since there cannot be the

---

[16] See S. Brittan, 'Hayek, Freedman and Interest Groups' in *The Role and Limits of Government* Temple Smith, London, 1983.

appropriate degree of definiteness about the norms of social justice which would underpin such laws, and, since social justice means treating different individuals and groups differently, this undermines the universality and the impartiality of law. In this sense, the *Wolfhartsstaat* is incompatible with the *Rechtsstaat*. The most appropriate political response, therefore, is to demoralise the issue of economic outcomes and accept the consequences of uncoerced economic transactions as being 'in principle unprincipled', to use Fred Hirsch's phrase, and to accept that more and more decisions which, according to the canons of social justice, would be made by politicians and administrators in ways that cannot be normatively sanctioned or constrained, should be transferred to the market. This is a further form of the argument that there is no normative underpinning to public policy and that, in these circumstances, so far as possible, public policy should be privatised to the subjective preferences of the market unconstrained by illusory ideas about social justice.

So what on the neo-liberal view would a notion of the common good in relation to the economy consist in if it is not to consist in just economic outcomes? The answer is, in the most part, procedural. It consists in the maintenance of that framework of mutual non-coercion and the other aspects of law, for example to do with contract, which define the framework of the market. The market is also part of the common good in the sense that it provides the central institution within which individuals are able to pursue in their own way whatever they find valuable. The neo-liberal, as with other sorts of liberals, puts the *right* before the *good*. The framework of law is a procedural good, and we have to abandon the idea of a common good, whether this is seen in terms of social justice or the common needs which free persons have to have satisfied in a just manner in order to live an equally free life.

The second sense that the common good can have for the neo-liberal is in terms of what economists call public goods, that is to say, goods that we all want but which will not be produced by a market for technical reasons. Such goods, such as common defence or clean air, will not be produced by the market because there are no mechanisms available to exclude non-payers from the benefits of defence and clean air, and everyone will have an incentive to free-ride. Taxation, which is there to produce what we need to have in common for a market society to exist and flourish, should ideally, therefore, be limited to funding the framework of law, and the police, courts and so forth which are necessary to secure this, and the public goods which the market will not produce, since they can only be produced co-operatively and there are no mechanisms for excluding non-payers. An important point to note about public goods as part of the common good of modern society is that public goods are not to be understood as part of a collective moral ideal. They are, rather, procedurally and technically defined. They are those goods which people want (with their wants being taken as incorrigible) and which, for reasons of co-operative production and non-excludability, will not be produced by the market.

So the legitimacy of a liberal market society rests upon two things. First of all, it provides a framework within which individuals will be able to pursue their own subjective preferences. Given that morality is person-relative, each individual will see the legitimacy of the market order in terms of that order's framework which will allow him/her to pursue his/her own good in his/her own way. Secondly, a free market will be more productive than any other sort of economy in that it will produce more of the goods which each individual from his/her subjective standpoint wants and, while this economic growth can continue, the market will seem legitimate to members of a liberal market order who, over time, will get more rather than less of what each subjectively wants. This point applies, too, to those at the bottom of society. The trickle-down effects of economic growth will gradually mean that the worse off, too, will get more of what they want.[17] They will get this more through the market than through any attempt to seek social justice in the distribution of resources which will be both economically inefficient as well as being morally illusory. Thus,

[17] See Hayek, *The Constitution of Liberty passim.*

the want-satisfying quantities of the market order will, in fact, secure the loyalty of all sections of society, including the worse off.

This is what I meant by the neo-liberal arguing that a liberal market order is a morally free zone. It is morally free except in procedural terms – the provision of a framework of law and the provision of public goods; and, as we saw in the last chapter, in personal terms in that individuals have to act with integrity and non-coercively in the rather restricted economic liberal's account of coercion. It should be seen as free from the constraint of collective moral notions such as social justice and the social conditions of freedom which, in any event, do not have moral salience. On these assumptions, the churches and Christian social theology have no real moral purchase on the collective institutions of a liberal market order because, if the churches are to address such a public order, it cannot be in terms of technical economic issues, and must be in terms of moral values, but those moral values, in so far as they have a collective dimension, have no significance.

This applies, too, to the neo-liberal account of community. On the neo-liberal view, it is wholly wrong to see the state as embodying some form of community or as the guarantor of socially based forms of community. *Contract* rather than *community* is the dominant idiom for social life within this view. The state has no overall purpose beyond the maintenance of the market order within which free, that is to say uncoerced, individuals are free to pursue their own good in their own way. If free individuals choose to belong to communities which can sustain themselves without collective provision, that is fine, but it is a matter of choice, and the state is not itself a form of community, nor should the state use collective resources to sustain communities which have become unviable because, for example, the industries on which they are based are no longer viable. Living in a community is a matter of choice[18] and not one which should be underpinned or underwritten by collective provision to sustain such communities. If there is an analogy to

[18] M. Novak, *The Spirit of Democratic Capitalism* Institute of Economic Affairs, London, 1991, p. 129.

be drawn between the neo-liberal vision and other forms of social organisation, the appropriate one is that the state should be seen as a hotel.[19] In a hotel, anonymous individuals come together to pursue their individual ends. They do this within a framework of rules governing the mutual reasons for living together in the hotel. Which subjective ends I can pursue in a hotel – whether I can dine, for example, depends on the resources open to me. It is not the job of the hotel to impose some substantive common purpose on those within it, nor to redistribute resources from well-off guests to needy guests. The alternative image of society is more like that of a family in which, usually, the benefits of family life are shared, there is concern that all members of the family have the opportunity to pursue their own ends, and the family does have some common purpose. Ideas like a substantive common good, a sense of community and belonging, and a reasonably just distribution of resources imply that modern society can be seen like a family writ large. This is fantasy for the neo-liberal. We should embrace the subjectivism, the anonymity and the lack of a collective identity which is characteristic of modern society. Such an anonymous society, governed by procedural rules rather than common purposes, is the best condition for the achievement of subjective freedom and for a competitive economy that will allow more and more people to secure for themselves the resources necessary to live their own lives as they want to do. This is the 'Great Society' as Hayek calls it. In this sense, the economic liberal would argue that his conception of the common good still fits into the Christian tradition. The Second Vatican Council defined the common good in the following way: 'The common good is the sum of those conditions of social life which allow social groups and their individual members relatively thorough and ready access to their own fulfilment.'[20] The liberal sees this as being achieved best by a free market and a framework of mutual non-coercion rather than by distributive politics and social justice. What fulfils the individual for the thoroughgoing liberal is a matter of choice,

---

[19] I owe this analogy to Professor N. Barry of the University of Buckingham.
[20] Vatican Council II, 'The Church in the Modern World' 1965.

whereas, for the Catholic Church, it consists in freely following a moral order. The common good for the neo-liberal is not very substantive; it is, on the contrary, largely procedural.

So is this what we mean when we are enjoined to seek the common good? My own view is that it is not. However, if ideas such as the common good are to have purchase, it is essential that the argument of the neo-liberal, that there can be no substantial collective moral constraints on the market, has to be rebutted. As I have suggested earlier, this is critical for the churches, because it seems to me that the churches can only address the realm of economics in moral terms, and to be able to do this the economy has to be seen as an area in which general moral principles may be thought to have a place. So this part of the chapter will be devoted to trying to explain that the notion of an ethical economy, that is to say, one whose outcomes can be constrained by moral principles, is not an oxymoron. I shall do this first of all by trying to rebut the arguments about social justice and freedom which lie at the heart of the neo-liberal claim, and then go on to say something in more detail about the relationships between economics and ethics which seem to me to be central and which are, by and large, neglected in the neo-liberal picture.

On the issue of social justice, several arguments can be put which I believe considerably weaken the neo-liberal case. I am prepared to accept the neo-liberal argument that the overall outcomes of the market are not intentional. But this does not itself absolve us of responsibility in terms of the moral critique of its outcomes in terms of social justice. The neo-liberal argues that the outcomes of markets are not only unintended, but also unforeseen. This question about foreseeability is critically important to the issue of whether we bear moral responsibility for the aggregate outcomes of the market, since in everyday individual life we are held responsible for the unintended but reasonably foreseeable consequences of our actions, as, for example, in the case of manslaughter. Now it would be an odd argument in general for the neo-liberal to claim that the consequences of markets are unforeseeable, because, after all, for the past few years we have been treated to endless papers from politicians and think-tanks which argue for the extension of markets to more and more areas of our lives on the grounds of the beneficial consequences which might be thought to follow from this. So, in overall terms, it must be central to the neo-liberal case for the extension of markets that outcomes are foreseeable in aggregate terms, and the case for the extension of markets is put in those aggregate terms. My claim is that there is an aggregate judgement that one can make about free markets, namely, that those who enter the market with least are likely to leave it with least, and that for those at the margins of society the trickle-down effect without social intervention will not alter this. If this conjecture is right, then it follows that we can bear collective responsibility for those outcomes and that their consequences for those who are worse off can be compensated for.

This relates to another point about the neo-liberal critique of social justice, namely, that the question of whether justice or injustice applies can be settled by determining how a situation has arisen – specifically whether or not the situation has been produced by intentional action. I do not think that this settles the matter at all, in that the question of social justice is also concerned with our response to a situation irrespective of how it has been caused. Take the following example. Imagine that a young child has been blown by the wind (a non-intentional force) face down into a pool of water and is rendered unconscious. Without intervention, the child will die. I am the only person able to help the child, and can do so at no comparable cost to myself. If I fail to help the child, does it follow that I have not committed an injustice merely because the child has not been the victim of an intentional process? Surely not. If we do think that a failure to rescue the child is a failure not merely of altruism but of justice, in that the child will die without an intervention by me which would cost me very little, then, by analogy, we could argue that those who are rendered poor by the unintended consequences of markets suffer an injustice when there is the possibility of compensating them at no comparable cost to the rest of society. If these points are valid, then there is a case for arguing that the aggregate outcomes of the market are susceptible to collective moral criticism and collective moral constraint, and thus there is a purchase for the critique of economic outcomes in terms of social justice.

These points, however, leave untouched that part of the philosophical critique, that is to say, the claim about moral relativism and subjectivity. Even if social justice is a relevant consideration, there is still no way on this view that we can, in fact, make the claims of social justice more determinate as a set of distributive principles in a situation of moral diversity. This is certainly a serious problem and not one to which there is an easy or straightforward solution. It seems to me, however, that the neo-liberal is looking for too much – namely, some kind of philosopher's stone which would provide some kind of definitive principles of distribution. This is certainly unrealistic and, if this is the only answer to the neo-liberal's question, then it seems unattainable. However, the neo-liberal underestimates the re-sources of democratic politics, and I see no reason why, in a democratic society, rough-and-ready principles of distribution could not emerge out of democratic debate and dialogue. The neo-liberal is committed to saying, for example, that we have absolutely no consensus on those basic needs which, as a members of a modern society, we have in common. Is this really the case? Surely it is possible to identify a set of needs or primary goods which all citizens need to have equal access to, irrespective of whatever else we may differ on in terms of our ultimate goals. Health, education and a degree of financial security are surely part of such basic needs, and to assume that in a democratic society we cannot reach agreement over these, given the argument that distributive principles have some purchase on the economy, is surely taking the claims of moral subjectivism and the diversity of value too far. This point can perhaps be illuminated by referring back to the distinction drawn earlier between concept and conception. While there may be basic agreement about the analytical core to justice: to each his/her due, there will, nevertheless, be deep disputes about what specific conception of justice will fill out a particular conception of what is a person's due – is it to have one's needs met, and merits recognised or whatever? This argument about particular conceptions is a moral and political argument which should be a matter of deliberative and informed political debate. It is not a debate that can be settled a priori. What is important is to have established that the debate is worth having because, *contra* the neo-liberals, the idea of social justice does have moral salience. It is the role of the church to participate in this debate about particular conceptions of justice, and in order to do so it has not only to draw on its own theological resources while recognising that these are likely, for reasons already discussed, to point in more than one direction, but also it needs to get beyond just invoking justice as a *concept* and to engage in a detailed debate about *conceptions*.

I want now to turn to the neo-liberal's attempt to define liberty in non-moral terms and I do not think that this will work. The first point, recall, has to do with freedom and ability and the claimed categorical distinction between them which was used as an argument to resist the idea that poverty is a restriction on liberty. There are two counter-arguments here. The first has to do with the value of liberty. If one were to ask the neo-liberal why liberty is valuable to us, surely the answer would be that to be free from coercion, even as the neo-liberal defines it, would enable us to live lives shaped by our own purposes and interests. But, if the value of liberty lies in achieving our purposes, then it seems odd to deny that there is a relation between freedom and the resources necessary to achieve those purposes. The general philosophical point here is that it is not possible to separate out the meaning of a term from an account of those values and circumstances which give that term a central role in our lives. We learn the meaning of freedom in relation to the activities that make it valuable for us and, on a Wittgensteinian[21] view of meaning at least, it would be impossible to split the meaning of liberty from the circumstances in human life that make it of value to us and in which we learn the meaning of the term.

The second point is that I do not believe that it makes sense

---

[21] Wittgenstein, *Philosophical Investigations passim.*

to think of freedom in the absence of some general account of human abilities. Take for example the following question. Before the invention of aeroplanes, and thus the generalised ability to fly, I do not think that it would make sense to ask the question, were people free or unfree to fly? The question would be unanswerable and absurd, because there was no general ability to fly. I think, therefore, it can be argued that a general ability to do X is a necessary condition for asking whether a particular individual is free or unfree to do X.[22] If this is so, then there cannot be a categorical distinction between freedom and ability, and the neo-liberal's attempt to draw such a sharp distinction, to block the claim that freedom involves the resources necessary to realise abilities, has no force. In order to determine the most important types of freedom, we need an account of what are the most important general abilities that human beings have and value.

This leads me to my final point, which is due to Charles Taylor.[23] We cannot provide a non-moralised account of liberty. The notion of liberty has to be connected with what we believe are essential human purposes. If liberty merely means freedom from intentional coercion, then a society with very few rules restricting behaviour because it is a simple society may be thought to be more free than a modern society with a large number of such rules restricting and controlling, for example, traffic or financial markets. This would be absurd. It would be like arguing that ten years ago Albania was a freer society than Britain because, as a simple society, it had fewer pieces of law than Britain. Surely, what made Britain a freer society was not a question about how many rules each society had but, rather, what sorts of things people in Britain were free to do which Albanians were not – for example, leaving the country or criticising the government. So it is arguable that freedom has to do with some conception held within a particular society about what are the important human purposes, and this is a moral

---

[22] See J. P. Day, 'Threats, Offers, Law Opinion, and Liberty' *American Philosophical Quarterly*, 14 (1977), p. 260.
[23] C. Taylor, 'What's Wrong with Negative Liberty?' *Philosophy and the Human Sciences: Philosophical Papers* vol. 2, Cambridge University Press, 1985, p. 218.

judgement. Again, therefore, the neo-liberal's attempt to make its notion of freedom some kind of morally free zone will not work, and yet, as we saw, this conception of freedom was critical in the justification of unconstrained markets.

If these arguments are valid, then it is possible to argue that liberty is a moralised conception and that we need some account of valued human activities to make sense of human freedom. This allows a bridge to be built at least to some kinds of theological insights, which I shall merely indicate at this stage although I shall return to the point in my final chapter. The point is well made by Demant in his essay 'The Catholic Doctrine of Freedom':

Whenever men seek only freedom from something, freedom of choice, subjective freedom, they always put themselves at the mercy of whatever secular forces happen to dominate at the time. Having no purpose for which liberty is striven for, there is no criterion by which to judge the interests which make use of such freedom as exists.[24]

If liberty is linked to some account of what makes life worth-while, as the Albanian example implies, then, as we shall see, there is space for theological insights into the nature of these valued capacities. However, the same message for the churches applies in relation to liberty as it does for justice, namely, that it is just no good invoking liberty as a concept. It is integrally related to both an account of coercion and an account of what is valuable in human life. In democratic and deliberative debate about these things, the religious believer has to engage with the detail of this kind of moral debate. There is, however, a central issue here which will dominate the final parts of the book. It is true that we cannot demoralise the market, and that in a liberal democracy in which the market is central there has to be a debate about these basic moral principles in relation to justice, freedom and coercion. However, it can be argued by liberal political theorists that Christians (and for that matter other groups with comprehensive belief systems) should not use arguments and conceptions drawn from, and sanctioned by, these comprehensive belief systems in public deliberation in a demo-

---

[24] V. A. Demant, 'The Catholic Doctrine of Freedom' in *Christian Polity* Faber and Faber, London, 1936, p. 84.

cratic society. These belief systems are controversial down to their foundations, and in a plural society they should not be used as part of the public reason of a democratic society.

It is false, therefore, to see the economy as a sphere within which moral considerations do not play a central role, and I have argued this in respect of both social justice and freedom. There is, however, another point that can be made to illustrate the neo-liberal's neglect of the moral dimension of markets.

The point about morality also applies to general issues about legitimacy. The legitimacy of the market order, for the neo-liberal, is not that it embodies some general moral purpose, so much as its being a mechanism to ensure that as many people as possible get as much as possible of whatever it is they want, and this applies via the trickle-down effect to the worse off, too. However, if the legitimacy of the market depends upon constant economic growth and the claims of the trickle-down effect, and if more and more of our lives are taken over by such doctrines, then if growth fails we have virtually no resources in which to secure the legitimacy of a market society. So, if we face in the future severe constraints upon economic growth because of environmental factors, then where is a sense of social, economic and political legitimacy to come from if the morally free market has undermined all other substantive moral assumptions?

There is a very revealing discussion of this point in Hayek's *The Mirage of Social Justice* in which he argues that given that when the market is correctly understood it will be seen as not involving moral conceptions of justice including for example merit and desert.[25] He goes on to say that it may well be that there will be resistance on the part of people to accept such an impersonal and literally demoralised institution as the mediator of their life chances. He argues that the legitimacy of the market may well depend upon the maintenance of the fiction that the market does secure moral purposes. People otherwise may not feel loyalty to an institution which is so indifferent to their moral claims or capacities, and their loyalty may have to be

---

[25] F. A. Hayek, *The Mirage of Social Justice* Routledge and Kegan Paul, London, 1976. See also I. Kristol, 'When Virtue Loses All Her Loveliness' in *The Public Interest* vol. 21, pp. 250–1.

mobilised by means of a 'noble lie' about the real nature of society – not the first time in the history of social and political thought that the legitimacy of an institution is based upon people having false beliefs about it. This question about the moral framework of the market, which was also discussed in the previous chapter, would become very important in a situation in which limitations on growth, for whatever reason, actually removed the materialist defence of the market.

So, in the specific case of the market, there may be real challenges in relation to legitimacy in adopting what Larmore called the minimal moral-conception approach to the idea of a common good.

CHAPTER 9

Human rights, human dignity and the scope of responsibility

Who is my neighbour?   (St Luke)

The recurring theme of this book has been the question of
whether liberal democratic societies have or need to have a
secure moral foundation and, if they do, the role that Christian
social and political reflection could or should contribute to the
articulation of this moral base. We have also seen reasons
deployed by communitarian thinkers such as Richard Rorty
and Michael Walzer for thinking that the search for a universal
rational philosophical basis for politics is misconceived. In their
view, societies are based upon common self-understandings and
a lively sense of their own ethos, not upon some abstract
universal principles. At the same time, narrative theologians
have argued that, if liberal society is conceived as being based
upon some set of general philosophical principles, then theology
cannot contribute anything to the formulation and defence of
such principles. To do so would be to abstract from the
narrative of Christianity and use its insights in a way that
detaches them from the story, and to make what is a distinc-
tively Christian moral perspective an exemplar of some more
general moral and political position. In this sense, the narrative
theologian is opposed to an 'accommodationist'[1] strategy: of
using Christian moral resources, as it were, at the service of a
moral position which can be reached and accepted by others on
purely secular or humanist grounds.[2] At the heart of the
narrative position on these issues is the idea, indebted to

[1] Hauerwas, *The Peaceable Kingdom* pp. 59–60.
[2] Ibid. p. 59.

224

Wittgenstein, that one cannot separate off the grounds for a belief, and the ways in which such beliefs are acquired and taught, from the characterisation of the nature of the beliefs themselves. So, it is claimed, it is false to think that a set of beliefs can exist and mean the same thing to all those who assent to those beliefs, while being held on quite different grounds by different groups of believers and embedded in the different narratives. We shall return to this discussion shortly, but in this chapter I want to consider in some detail a particularly good and salient example of the accommodationist strategy, namely, the role of the idea of human rights.

A rights-based argument is one way in which one could respond to the claim that liberal democratic societies lack a moral foundation. It is claimed that the reason why such societies might be thought to lack a moral foundation is that they are marked by moral subjectivism in which each individual is regarded as the ultimate legitimate source of his or her own values. In parallel to this runs the argument about the instrumental nature of reason: that reason cannot prescribe ends; it can only prescribe means to ends which are, in their turn, subjectively chosen. Given this, there is clearly a deep problem about how to theorise the legitimacy of a society with this diversity and with this limitation on reason. There are two ways typical of modernity in which attempts have been made both to recognise the limits of reason and to accept value diversity as a consequence of our inability to justify moral cognitivism. These two approaches are, on the one hand, theories of rights and, on the other, utilitarianism. I shall concentrate on rights in this chapter, before moving later to an examination of the role of utilitarianism as a way of addressing the problem of social and political morality in the context of moral diversity.

It might be thought paradoxical to argue that theories of rights could help to fill the legitimation deficit of liberal societies, since a theory of rights surely has to have some kind of moral foundation, and yet precisely the problem with liberalism, according to its critics, is that we cannot have a cognitive moral theory (morality is seen as a matter of subjective preference) and we do not have a non-instrumental view of reason

(reason cannot establish moral truths). Yet, frequently, theories of rights have been introduced as attempts to provide a basic moral framework to regulate the relationships between members of liberal societies who differ profoundly about morality. This strategy involves 'putting the right before the good', in Rawls' felicitous phrase. We disagree about the good, and we cannot accept that an authoritative view of the good can be established. Nevertheless, it is argued, it may be possible to reason about the right, that is to say about the framework of rights, which is appropriate and legitimate to regulate the relationships of those who differ fundamentally about the good. This, for example, is the position taken by the American philosopher Alan Gewirth, and is certainly one of the most subtle justifications of rights that recognises the fact of moral diversity and pluralism.[3] At the same time, the whole rights-based strategy has been criticised by Alasdair MacIntyre, who, as we have seen, is a major inspiration to narrative theology, when he argues:

The best reason for asserting so bluntly that there are no such rights is indeed of precisely the same type as the best reason we possess for asserting there are no witches and the best reason we possess for asserting that there are no unicorns: every attempt to give good reasons for thinking that there *are* such rights has failed.[4]

Given the salience and popularity of the idea of rights, not just within particular societies, but also in international politics, it is therefore very important to consider in detail whether it is possible to devise a moral strategy for the justification of a rights-centred approach to politics.

Gewirth gives us a very useful conceptual structure which any fully worked out theory of rights has to fit: A has a right to Φ against B in virtue of Z. That is to say, we have to identify the agent(A) who is the bearer of rights, what it is about the agent(Z) in virtue of which he/she is the bearer of rights, also the person or persons(B) against whom the right is held and the nature of the right asserted(Φ).[5]

---

[3] A. Gewirth, *Reason and Morality* University of Chicago Press, 1978.
[4] MacIntyre, *After Virtue* p. 69.
[5] A. Gewirth, *Human Rights* University of Chicago Press, 1982.

So we shall begin with the agent, the person who is the bearer of rights. Given that the rights tradition in moral theory has had quite deep roots in natural-law theory, although it is by no means confined to that, it is understandable that a good deal of thinking about human rights has been rooted in an account of human nature and of how an understanding of that nature can support conceptions of rights. I have already discussed the ways in which natural-law theory gets into difficulties about the relationship between nature and the moral principles the moral order is supposed to support, and I do not want to repeat these. I shall, however, concentrate on one or two particular issues of special relevance to human rights. One of the most basic of these is a claim about the role of human nature in supporting claims about rights. It might be argued that, because human beings have certain capacities such as consciousness, the capacity for deliberation and choice, then these capacities give them a kind of dignity and worth which deserves respect, and that this respect should be institutionalised in terms of rights. The Catholic political philosopher Jacques Maritain provides a good example of this approach:

there is a human nature and this human nature is the same in all men . . . and possessed of a nature, constituted in a given and determinate fashion, man obviously possesses ends which correspond to his natural constitution and which are the same for all – as all pianos, for instance, whatever their type and in whatever spot they may be, have as their end the production of certain attuned sounds. If they do not produce these sounds, they must be attuned or discarded as worthless . . . since man has intelligence and can determine his ends, it is up to him to put himself in tune with the ends necessarily demanded by his nature.[6]

Such a conception of human nature is used by Maritain to justify a natural-law based theory of rights. There is, however, a very great deal that is morally and logically controversial about this.

The first is that his argument requires that *essence* precedes *existence*: the view that human nature has a fixed essence which

---

[6] J. Maritain, *The Rights of Man and Natural Law* trans. D. C. Anson, Ignatius Press, San Francisco, 1986, pp. 140–1.

particular human beings then realise. This view has, however, been severely criticised, first of all by the existentialists – particularly Heidegger and Sartre, whose *Existentialism and Humanism* is a vigorous critique of this view that there is a human essence which 'precedes that historic existence which we confront in experience'. In Sartre's view, the argument that essence precedes existence has to depend upon the existence of God as creator. If a piano (Maritain's example) or a paper knife (Sartre's example) has an essence, then it is because each is created according to a preconceived plan:

Thus the paper-knife is at the same time an article preconceivable in a certain manner and one which, on the other hand, serves a definite purpose, if one cannot suppose that a man would procure a paper knife without knowing what it was for. Let us say then of the paper knife that its essence – that is to say the sum of the formulae and qualities which made its production and its definition possible – precedes its existence.[7]

However, this relationship, between essences and the fact that something has been created for something which gives the notion of essences its sense, has now broken down in the case of God and man:

Atheistic existentialism of which I am a representative declares with greater consistency that if God does not exist, there is at least one being whose existence comes before its essence, a being which exists before it can be defined by any conception of it. That being is man or as Heidegger has it, the human reality (Dasein).[8]

So, Maritain's idea that man has an essence which can underpin a notion of natural law and natural right depends upon the idea of God as a creator and, thus, the remit of this argument runs only within the religious communities which take not only this view of God, but also that God creates man with a substantive essence, a view which is, in its turn, criticised by existentialist theologians. If ideas about rights are supposed to provide a firm foundation for both domestic and international politics in a situation of great moral diversity, any such strategy will be undermined by rooting a doctrine of rights in a

---

[7] J. P. Sartre, *L'Existentialisme est un humanisme* Les Editions Nagel, Paris, 1963, pp. 18–19.
[8] Ibid. p. 21.

view about the human essence and what this requires, since claims about the nature of that essence will be very dubious and controversial.

The second point about the argument from human nature is closely connected and has to do with the 'fact/value' distinction. Even if it was possible to determine the nature of the human essence, it would be logically illegitimate to deduce from statements about this essence any conclusion about the nature of the rights supposedly required by the possession of this essence. Either statements about human purposes and human flourishing are straightforwardly factual, and if so cannot in logic imply normative conclusions, or they are already statements containing normative elements and, if so, they will be logically unsupported since it is not possible to provide a cognitive basis to such normative conceptions. Reason cannot ground norms and norms cannot be read off nature – so either way there cannot be a cognitive theory of rights. As Margaret MacDonald says:

nature provides no standards or ideals. All that exists, exists at the same level, or is of the same logical type . . . standards are determined by human choice, not set by nature independently of them. Natural events cannot tell us what we ought to do until we have made certain decisions . . . natural events themselves have no value and human beings as natural existents have no value either, whether on account of possessing intelligence or having two feet.[9]

Norms cannot be deduced from facts. Normative judgements are rooted in personal decisions and preferences. Reason is purely instrumental to devising the efficient means to ends.

These two sorts of consideration, therefore, pose major question marks at the side of theories of rights which have wanted to base the moral justification of rights on ontological claims about the nature of the person, and it is worth remarking at this point that there seems to be a prima-facie case for thinking that Christian approaches to theories of right will be likely to be involved in making such ontological claims[10] and, in this sense,

---

[9] M. MacDonald, 'Natural Rights' in *Philosophy, Politics and Society* Series I, ed. P. Laslett, Blackwell, Oxford, 1956, p. 45.

[10] See K. Cronin, *Rights and Christian Ethics* Cambridge University Press, 1992, p. 253.

these structures are important. Within Christian thought it might be possible to link a normative conception of human nature with a conception of rights. This would avoid the fact/ value problem, since both the concept of human nature and the rights derived from it will be normatively toned. The problem is that, if, for the Christian, rights are rooted in a specifically Christian narrative and understanding, then part of the alleged usefulness of rights as a way of providing a framework for a liberal democratic order will have been diminished if this foundation is and can only be found in one specific normative tradition. I want to return to this question shortly, but before that, I want to explore a bit more fully the question of whether or not the idea of basing rights on some conception of human nature and human flourishing has been exhausted.

In the passage quoted from MacDonald's seminal essay on 'Natural Rights', she argues that 'Human beings as natural existents have no value . . . whether on account of possessing intelligence or having two feet'.[11] No empirical human quality can on its own justify claims to rights. These empirical features have to be put into a normative framework to relate to other normative concepts such as rights, but these normative perspectives, in turn, will depend upon choice or decision, not reason.

This argument is however, too rapid, because it seems to me that there are empirical characteristics of human beings which are more morally relevant than others, and that this is so without having to claim that these features are relevant because they already contain normative elements. Take, for example, MacDonald's own deeply felt views about the nature of morality. She argues that value utterances are more like records of *decisions* than propositions: 'To assert that "Freedom is better than slavery" or "All men are of equal worth" is not to state a fact but to choose a side.' It announces: *This is where I stand.*[12] So moral judgements are non-cognitive. At the same time, reason plays an instrumental role which she regards as more akin to, say, defending a judgement such that Keats is a better poet than

---

[11] MacDonald, 'Natural Rights' p. 45.   [12] Ibid. p. 49.

Crabbe or defending an account of events in a court. We *defend* decisions by utilising reason, but we do not *prove* the basis of our decisions. So, one way of putting these points together is to say that morality is a matter of choice, but the choice in question is not sheer arbitrary choice like tossing a coin, but a choice which involves a degree of deliberation, but which, at the same time, is quite unlike scientific deliberation.

Now, given MacDonald's views about the nature of morality, it does seem that some features of human activity and 'nature' could be argued to be more morally important than others. The capacities for choice and deliberation are in this respect, therefore, surely more important than having two feet. They are morally relevant in the sense of being necessary conditions of moral action (as characterised by MacDonald) in a way that having two feet are not.

So, it could be argued that we should not give up the idea of an ontological basis of rights too quickly, because it might seem that there are some human capacities which are morally relevant in ways in which others are not.

However, to be relevant for a rights-based theory such an account of human capacity would have to be not only morally relevant but universal, if it has to do the job of grounding a theory of human rights. In this sense, *human* rights, that is to say rights which we bear in respect of our specific human capacities, rather than as a member of this nation rather than that, or this culture rather than that, would be tracking some rational universal features of human nature – those fundamental moral capacities which would be the basis of a universal moral framework.

This is a tall order, and one which is rather counter-cultural in a post-modern intellectual context, but it is still worth exploring a bit further to see whether it can be achieved or whether this whole project is, as MacIntyre argues, like trying to prove the existence of unicorns and witches. Let us take the example of Alan Gewirth, the philosopher discussed by MacIntyre in his argument against rights, whose *Reason and Morality* is probably the most sophisticated and subtle defence of a metaphysical theory of human rights. Gewirth recognises the fact of moral diversity and the fact that, as human beings we have radically different goals and purposes to pursue, and to that extent his argument is at least implicitly critical of a thinker like Maritain who, as we have seen, argues that there is only a single set of rational human goals in the same way that there is only one purpose for a piano. Gewirth, however, focuses on the fact of moral agency – that human beings with diverse aims and purposes nevertheless have to be able to act as moral agents in order to affirm and follow this diversity of ends. Given that we are moral agents, what are the necessary or generic conditions of agency, that is to say: are there necessary conditions of moral agency – conditions that relate to moral agency in a way that having two feet, to use MacDonald's example, do not? Gewirth argues that there are, in fact, two necessary conditions of agency: *freedom* and *well-being* and that, as necessary conditions of agency, these form the basis of claims to rights. His argument is complex and his own schematic characterisation of it runs as follows:

every agent implicitly makes evaluative judgements about the good-ness of his purposes and hence about the necessary goodness of the freedom and well-being that are the necessary conditions of his acting to achieve his purposes. Second, because of this necessary goodness, every agent implicitly makes a deontic judgement in which he claims that he has rights to freedom and well-being. Third, every agent must claim these rights for the sufficient reason that he is a prospective agent who has purposes he wants to fulfil, so that he must logically accept the generalisation that all prospective agents have rights to freedom and well being.[13]

This argument thus links two parts of the formula for rights: A has a right to Φ against B in virtue of Z in that it specifies the agent and in virtue of what it is about the agent in terms of which or in virtue of which he/she is a bearer of rights.

On the basis of his argument about the generic condition of agency (which could also be transposed into a theory about basic needs), Gewirth is then able to elaborate a complex structure of rights which specifies in quite a lot of detail what is

---

[13] Gewirth, *Reason and Morality* p. 48.

required both negatively (not to be coerced, assaulted, interfered with) and positively (education, health and social security)
to secure the generic goods of agency.

At the moment, however, I am concentrating on the argumentative strategy rather than its detail. It does aim to show
that, despite first-order moral diversity, we should not abandon
the idea that there can be a universal and rational basis for
human rights which is not undercut by arguments about the
diversity of human goods and, indeed, the narrative patterns
within which such goods may have a home for particular moral
agents – Christians for example. So his argument is that there is
a structure of moral agency which transcends particular moral
narratives and which will enable us to construct a meta-theory
grounding universal rights in the nature of this agency, which
recognises that individual agents may, of course, pursue their
moral goods from within particular narrative communities. If
such an argument were to go through, then, of course, it would
be a way of reconciling the universal and the particular, the
foundational and the narrative: the structure of agency and its
generic goods would be constant; the particular forms of moral
agency could be narrative specific.

This would, however, be far too bland a way of reconciling a
cognitive theory of rights and a narrative or tradition-based
view of morality with its emphasis upon virtues specific to
moral traditions rather than universal rules. We need to follow
in some detail the argument as to why this bland reconciliation
may not work, since it will shed a good deal of light upon what
might be construed as a narrative theologian's critique of rights
and the political strategies which follow from this. I want to
look at the argument in what is, chronologically, the reverse
order. Gewirth's *Reason and Morality* was published in 1978. Its
argumentative strategy was subjected to a vigorous critique by
MacIntyres's *After Virtue* in 1981 with a rejoinder by Gewirth in
1985 in 'Rights and Virtues' in the *Review of Metaphysics*.
Gewirth defines morality in terms of universals which are
rationally compelling, rooted as they are in the necessary
conditions of agency; MacIntyre, in contrast, sees morality in
terms of virtues which, in turn, are related to practices and

traditions which are local and particular. These perspectives cannot be easily reconciled.

Consider Gewirth's 1985 criticism of MacIntyre's virtue ethics first of all. MacIntyre relates virtues to practices in such a way that a virtue is something the exercise of which will tend to 'enable us to achieve those goods which are internal to practices'.[14] Practices are, of course, always in the process of change and development, and with that change a development in the internal conception of virtue. An account of human virtue is *not* rooted in some kind of antecedent idea of human flourishing derived from a general / universal theory of human nature such as Aristotle's metaphysical biology, or in Maritain or Demant – as we have seen.[15] However, MacIntyre recognises that it is not possible to restrict the definition of virtues to the internal relations of given practices because, of course, some practices may involve virtues which cannot be regarded as being morally good: 'That the virtues need initially to be defined and explained with reference to a practice thus in no way entails approval of all practices in all circumstances.'[16] So what are the resources for the criticism of practices to which the virtues are internal?[17] It might be thought that this would be the point at which MacIntyre's argument for a basis on which practices could be subject to criticism might need the kind of objective moral universalism of which Gewirth's argument is an example. MacIntyre, however, argues that it is possible to develop different moral resources for a critique of practices and their internal virtues. To provide the moral resources, he considers two supplementary arguments which he believes rescue the practice-based argument from relativism without committing him to some kind of abstract universalism. First of all, he develops the idea that the virtues in particular practices have to be seen in the context of 'the good of a whole human life' – so that a virtue relating to a particular practice may become grotesque if taken as characteristic of life as a whole.[18] This idea of the good of a whole human life, however, should not be taken as implying

---

[14] MacIntyre, *After Virtue* pp. 193–4.   [15] Ibid. pp. 196–7.
[16] Ibid. p. 200.   [17] Ibid.   [18] Ibid. p. 275.

some sort of universal moral teleology of the sort to which he objects, because he relates this idea to that of tradition in his chapter 'Virtues, Unity of life and the Concept of a Tradition' and in the 'Postscript' to the second edition of the book in which he refers to a good for human beings the conception of which can only be elaborated and possessed within an ongoing social tradition. Such traditions accumulate experiences and resources to give a sense specific to that tradition of what is the good of a whole life. Life within a tradition makes answers to these sorts of questions rich and determinate at any particular point (although not permanently, since traditions change). So MacIntyre wants to secure the idea of a *telos* of a whole human life which will allow a moral critique of practices and their internal virtues while avoiding universalist foundationalism by referring to the issue of teleology to particular moral traditions which then provide the resources for the critique of practices.

This is a clear alternative to the rights-based strategy of Gewirth, who argues that it is possible to give an objective and universal answer to the sorts of questions that MacIntyre raises but, in Gewirth's view, fails to answer properly. Why does he take this view?

Gewirth produces a critique of the three stages of MacIntyre's argument: at the level of practices; the good of the whole life; and tradition. In terms of practices he, in fact, follows MacIntyre's own lead here, by arguing that a practice like torture can be related to the achievement of some internal good – so what would be the grounds for arguing that it is not morally virtuous? The answer then lies in the second stage of the good of a whole life – MacIntyre's argument would be that the idea of integrity would militate against the elevation of the sort of 'virtues' to do with the practice contributing to the good of a whole life. However, as Gewirth argues, this still leaves the question of the moral critique of this practice indeterminate, since Hitler or Stalin could be regarded as authentic and sincere in their quest for a good human life. So a move has to be made to the third stage, to a moral tradition within which the notion of a good human life has a determinate sense and would allow for the critique of practices. For Gewirth, however, this appeal to a moral tradition rooted in specific communities will not produce anything morally determinate:

But which community? Aristotle's perfect community required the enslavement of farmers and mechanics; the Nazi community required the murder of Jews and others; the contemporary Afrikaner community requires the subjugation, economic and personal as well as political of millions of blacks. For all his endorsement of a morality of laws, MacIntyre's specification of their 'point and purpose' together with his unclear evaluation of moral universalism, leaves available such violations of basic rights.[19]

He concludes by arguing that MacIntyre's strategy is no substitute for the more traditional view that derives the content of the 'virtues from moral rules about rights and duties'.

So, here is the nub of the issue at stake between universalism over rights compared with a virtue-based ethics which links virtue with tradition, practice and narrative which, as we have seen, has also been endorsed by narrative theologians. It also bears upon MacIntyre's own vigorous critique of Gewirth's argument about the necessary conditions of action in *After Virtue*, in which he argues that the link seen by Gewirth between the necessary goods of agency and rights is defective. He argues that the argument is defective since the idea of a right is *internal* to a moral and social practice, it is not something philosophically foundational that can ground the practice:

But the objection that Gewirth has to meet is precisely that these forms of human behaviour which presuppose notions of some ground to entitlement, such as the notion of a right, always have a highly specific and socially local character, and the existence of particular types of social constitution or practice is a necessary condition for the claim to the possession of a right being an intelligible type of human performance . . . lacking any social form, the making of a claim to a right would be like presenting a cheque for payment in a social order that lacked the institution of money.[20]

[19] A. Gewirth, 'Rights and Virtues' *Review of Metaphysics* 30 (Nov. 1985), pp. 758–9. For further discussion of Gewirth see R. Plant, *Modern Political Thought* Blackwell, Oxford, 1991, ch. 7; E. Regis, *Gewirth's Ethical Rationalism* University of Chicago Press, 1984; for Gewirth and MacIntyre see R. Hittinger, 'Natural Law and Virtue: Theories at Cross Purposes' in *Natural Law Theory: Contemporary Essays* ed. R. P. George, Clarendon Press, Oxford, 1992.
[20] MacIntyre, *After Virtue* p. 67.

I want to leave this argument for the moment, before returning to it later in the chapter, with some concluding remarks which will situate this issue more fully into the narrative theology debate. However, before moving on, it is worth remarking that it would be perfectly possible to avoid the general metaphysical claim about the grounds of rights that Gewirth wants to make, and treat rights as products of a particular moral tradition and the creations of particular political communities which have found it good to order the communities in this way. The problem with such an approach is that the idea of *human rights*, that is, rights held by human beings as such, then seems to go by the board in favour of rights created in particular communities.

I want now to move away from the metaphysical discussion about the grounds of rights to look at some other aspects of the formula for rights, namely, the nature of the right asserted and against whom it is asserted. There has been a long-running dispute amongst philosophers and political theorists about the nature of a right, whether it should be understood negatively or positively. A negative right would be a right to be free from coercion, interference, power, intimidation and so forth. In some respects, it could be seen as defining the requirements of the kind of negative liberty at which we looked in a previous chapter. A positive right would be a right to a resource of some sort: health care, education and social security for example. Civil and political rights could be cast in terms of negative rights, a right not be impeded or coerced when voting, or when owning property, or going about one's lawful business. A good example to point the contrast would be the right to work. On the negative view of rights, a right to work would be a right not to be impeded when going to work (by pickets for example), on the positive view, a right to work would mean a right to a job. Another example would be the right to life. On the negative interpretation, the right to life is a right not to be killed, on the positive view, it would be a right to the means to life, to health care, food, shelter etc. As I have said, philosophers have differed sharply over whether or not social, economic and welfare rights can properly be regarded as rights. For some, this is a logical or conceptual issue, for others, it is more empirical. One of the major theological writers about rights, Jürgen Moltmann, is nicely ambiguous on this point:

The fourth plenary meeting of the World Council of Churches in Uppsala in 1968 recognised that 'in the modern world wide community the rights of the individual are unavoidably tied to the fight for a better living standard for the socially disadvantaged of many nations. Human rights cannot be secured in a world of gross inequality and social conflicts.' Then came to the fore the knowledge that there are economic, social and cultural human rights about which the history of freedom in Western Europe has little to say. The International Covenants of 1968 also place the 'economic and social rights in the primary position and the Civil and political agents' only in the second place. Indeed in what other way shall a human being actualise his or her individual freedom rights if he or she does not find the economic and social possibilities for doing so

. . .

The right to life and the means which make continued living possible stand in the forefront. The St Plöten Report, therefore, just like the Roman Synod of Bishops places the right to life, nourishment and to work at the beginning of the catalogue of human rights.[21]

This argument could be construed in one of two ways. It could be seen as an argument to the effect that as a matter of fact civil and political rights cannot be exercised or enjoyed against a background of economic and material deprivation. So, for example, Henry Shue argues: 'No one can fully, if at all, enjoy any right that is supposedly protected by society if he or she lacks the essentials for a reasonably healthy and active life'.[22] This way of putting the point is consistent with the view that only civil and political rights as negative rights are genuine rights, and that a concern with economic and social circumstances may require a change in social policy so that citizens can enjoy their proper rights without at all conceding the argument that these social policies should themselves be seen in terms of rights.

The other way of looking at it, however, has been to argue

---

[21] J. Moltmann, *On Human Dignity: Political Theology and Ethics* SCM Press, London, 1986, pp. 5–6.
[22] H. Shue, *Basic Rights: Subsistence, Affluence and US Foreign Policy* Princeton University Press, 1980, p. 24.

that social/economic and welfare rights are, in fact, genuine rights alongside civil and political rights, a point of view which is most consistent with the overall thrust of Moltmann's points quoted earlier. Many political philosophers have, however, regarded allowing such rights as a logical error. We need to look at the argument in some detail, since social and economic rights are frequently involved in direct pronouncements on public policy and yet there is little or no realisation that the ascription of such rights is, in fact, highly controversial.

The critical case against the idea of social rights turns on three claims: about the nature of liberty; about the nature of obligation and responsibility; and about the nature of ability.

As I said earlier, one way of thinking about negative and positive rights, the former rights to be free from coercion, the latter rights to resources, is to see these different rights as defining the sort of protection these two accounts of rights require. In the view of the critic of positive rights to welfare, this conception of rights trades upon a false positive conception of liberty. I wrote at some length about liberty in the earlier chapter on social justice, so it will be necessary to rehearse the points at issue here reasonably briefly. The critic argues as follows: if rights protect liberty, then there are no positive rights since positive liberty is a false conception. Freedom is the absence of coercion, not the possession of resources. To assume that freedom and possession of resources go together is to assimilate freedom and ability, but this is false, since no one is able to do all that he is free to do. I am *free* to do the indefinitely large number of things that I am not prevented from doing, but I am *able* to do only a proportion of these things. So freedom and ability are different concepts, and yet positive rights trade upon this false association of freedom and ability.

Secondly it is argued that, even if freedom and ability were to be conceptually linked, we could not, in fact, agree in a pluralistic society on what kinds of abilities were central to freedom and therefore what sorts of abilities should issue in rights.

So it is argued that the claim that there are genuine social and economic rights depends upon a faulty account of liberty.

For reasons given in chapter 8, it is difficult to accept this argument. First of all, freedom and ability cannot be separated in the way desired by the critic. If we ask the question in relation to negative liberty: why is negative liberty or being free from coercion valuable to me? The answer to this question must surely be that, if I am free from coercion, then I shall be able to live a life shaped by my own purposes or projects. But this links the worth of liberty with the idea of what I am able to do with liberty. If this is so, then the categorical difference between freedom and ability is not so wide.

Secondly, it is arguable that a generalisable ability to do X is a necessary condition for determining whether A is free or unfree to do X. It is only because people in general are able to sign cheques that we are able to determine that A is free to do so. If the general ability to do X is a necessary consideration of determining whether someone is free or unfree to do it, then freedom and ability cannot be categorically different.

Finally, in the argument due to Charles Taylor which was considered earlier: if negative liberty is a correct characterisation of freedom as the absence of coercion, then the question of whether society A is more free than society B then depends upon a quantitative judgement, namely, whether society B contains more or fewer coercive rules than A. This detaches the question from the moral question of whether what people in society A are able to do is more important than those in society B, and yet this is critical to the judgement, since society B may have fewer coercive rules because it is a much more simple society. So, although people are able to do more important and valuable things in society A, B might be regarded as more free, because as a simpler society it has few rules.

The final point is about moral diversity and the identification of these abilities which positive rights theorists argue lie at the basis of positive rights. This issue takes us straight back to the issues raised in the earlier debate about Alan Gewirth's arguments. The pluralist/communitarian and, indeed, the narrative theology view will argue that the diversity of moral traditions both within and between societies makes it impossible to identify outside of tradition and narrative context those forms of ability which are fundamental; whereas the cognitivist such as Gerwith argues that it is crucial that we should be able to do this in a rational, universal and foundational way, and that the abilities in question are those to do with freedom and well-being which are the necessary goods of agency.

So it is very unclear that the argument from the nature and legitimacy of negative liberty is enough to block the case for social and economic rights as rights.

This does not, however, exhaust the argument, since the critic will also take the view that the idea of positive rights to resources has irrational consequences for the nature of obligation. The basis of this argument is the Kantian distinction between perfect and imperfect duties. Perfect duties are duties which it is always possible to perform and which are clear and categorical, none of which conditions apply to imperfect duties. In the view of the critic of positive rights, negative rights correlate to perfect duties just because the obligations required by negative rights are duties of abstinence and forbearance. The right to life on this view is the right not to be killed, and the correlative duty is not to kill; the right to privacy is the right to be free from interference, and the correlative duty is not to interfere and so on. Since the duties relating to these rights are basically to abstain from action, such duties are always capable of being performed since they are costless and not subject to scarcity. The obligations are perfect: they are categorical in that we do not have to exercise discretion as to when we shall exercise the obligations, since there is no constraint of scarcity. Since such obligations are acts of omission, we are always clear about what they are. We know exactly what is the obligation not kill, there is no ambiguity or unclarity about it.

It is also possible to argue quite coherently that the obligations in respect of human rights are held by all other persons. Since the duty is one of forbearance, it makes sense to say that every other person has a duty to forbear from interfering with the negative rights of all other persons. So mutual leaving alone is a perfectly possible set of rights and obligations to ascribe to all people everywhere. Since the obligations are costless and negative, the idea of a set of universal perfect duties and related rights makes perfect sense.

The situation is, however, quite different with positive rights, in the critic's view. First of all, since positive rights are rights to resources such as health care or education, the corresponding duties cannot be clear and categorical. We know what the negative duty of not killing means in respect of the right to life; if, however, the right to life is construed as a right to the means to life, then that duty seems unclear and open ended. Does it, for example, imply the provision of all the resources necessary to keep someone alive? If not, where and on what basis do we arrive at a stopping place? We shall have to develop principles of rationing for such resources, and this then means that neither the right not the duties are categorical.

Secondly, in the case of positive rights, it is not clear who bears the obligation and *thus the responsibility when it is not discharged*. In the case of negative rights, it makes sense to say that all can bear the obligation and the responsibility, since they imply costless duties of forbearance, but, since positive rights, by definition, involve costs, it is not possible to believe that these rights could be allocated equally to all individuals.

There are some complex issues here. Even if we were to argue in the context of domestic politics, the obligation to meet the costs of the social rights of citizens becomes transmuted into the obligation to pay the taxes to meet these costs, this does not meet the case claiming social and economic rights as human rights, as Moltmann clearly does. If we say, again with Molt-mann, that social and economic rights are human rights, that is applying to all people everywhere on the basis of their dignity as persons, then the critic will argue that all other people have a correlative duty (subject to the 'I ought implies I can't' principle) to meet these social-rights-based obligations. In the view of the critic, this extends human moral responsibility in a wholly irrational way. It does make sense to talk about universal obligations in respect of negative rights for the reasons I have given, but it does not make sense in regard to positive rights. I would become morally responsible for all the costs of social and economic rights which I am currently not meeting. I become responsible for all the bad consequences for anonymous other people in respect of the obligations I am not discharging in respect of their positive rights.

There are some rather deep theological as well as philosophical issues here which relate to sins of omission and, because of the theological salience of these points, it is worth dwelling on them for a while. In the Anglican context in the General Confession for Evening Prayer, we are enjoined to confess the fact that 'we have left undone those things we ought to have done'. However, for this to make sense we have to have some general conception of what we ought to have done. There are at any single moment an infinitely large number of actions we are currently not doing. Which of these activities ought we to have done? What are the consequences of our not doing them, and what is the degree of our responsibility here?

If Christian ethics is allied to doctrines about human rights and in particular social and economic rights, then, in the view of the critic, the ethic and the responsibility ascribed in the Prayer Book becomes totally irrational. We shall always have an indefinitely large number of duties to an indefinitely large set of anonymous others to whom we owe such duties. The contrast here with the negative rights theories was made by Trammel:

It is an empirical fact that in most cases it is possible for a person not to inflict serious physical injury on another person. It is also an empirical fact that in no case is it possible to aid everyone who needs help. The positive duty to love one's neighbour or help those in need sets a maximum ethic which never lets us rest except to gather strength to resume the battle. But it is a rare case when we must really exert ourselves to keep from killing a person.[23]

Essentially, the idea at stake here is that our common humanity and our common recognition of human dignity require us to respect rights and to bear the obligations that follow from those rights. Some of the obligations in respect of negative rights are perfect and costless, others are imperfect and costly, but we still bear responsibility when we could discharge such a positive

---

[23] R. Trammel 'Saving Life and Taking Life' in *Killing and Letting Die* ed. B. Steinbeck Prentice Hall, New York, 1980, p. 168.

obligation and fail to do so. If all of this follows from the idea of human dignity in relation to rights, and if one believes, with Moltmann, that for a Christian this sense of the dignity of man comes from humanity's relationship with God, then it follows that these obligations are part of the Christian ethic[24] part of Christian responsibility and thus of sin.

However, in the view of the critic of social rights, all of this is quite irrational because there are no such rights, partly for the reasons given and partly for the fact of scarcity to which we shall come shortly. For the critic, positive duties can arise only out of explicit or quasi contractual relationships. The duties of a doctor to the patient, or of parent to child, are understood on a quasi or implicit contract base: if I am promised in a contract the sum of £100, then I have a right to receive that resource as part of the contract. It follows from this that positive obligations are internal to contractual relations. A sense of common humanity, or for that matter a sense of citizenship, are not rich enough or explicit enough to ground positive obligations – although they can ground the perfect obligations that generally follow from negative rights and negative freedom. In respect of positive rights, however, we need a much more specialised moral framework, since positive obligations have to be discretionary because of scarcity, and this moral framework is provided, for the critic, by contract. A failure to honour a contract is a breach of obligation and thus a 'sin' in relation to a clearly prescribed duty. Failure to respond to the obligations set out by a spurious set of social rights is not however a moral failing or a sin on this view.

Before we move to an evaluation of the force of this argument which is very important but largely ignored by those who wish to link Christian ethics to human rights and thus to link ideas about duty and sin to such rights as providing the framework for what we ought to do (which is necessary condition for identifying sins of omission), I want to look at the final point of the critique to do with scarcity since this has entered the argument in relation to the issue of the imperfect and discre-

---

[24] Moltmann, *On Human Dignity* p. 11.

tionary nature of the obligations to do with the critique of positive rights. The argument here has been admirably focussed by Charles Fried:

A positive right is a claim to something – a share of a material good or to some particular good like the attention of a lawyer, or a doctor, or perhaps to a result like health or enlightenment – while a negative right is a right that something not be done to one, that some particular imposition be withheld. Positive rights are always asserted to scarce goods and consequently scarcity implies a limit to the claim. Negative rights, however, the right not to be interfered with in forbidden ways do not appear to have such natural, such inevitable limitations. If I am let alone, the commodity I obtain does not appear of its nature to be a scarce or limited one. How can one run out of not harming each other, not lying to each other, leaving each other alone?[25]

From these points about scarcity, Fried draws the conclusion that there is a categorical difference between negative and positive rights:

It is logically possible to treat negative rights as categorical entities. It is logically possible to respect any number of negative rights without necessarily landing in an impossible or contradictory situation . . . Positive rights, by contrast, cannot as a logical manner be treated as categorical entities because of the scarcity limitation.[26]

So, fundamentally, scarcity accounts for the basic differences between the two sorts of 'rights' and the discretionary nature of positive obligations.

This set of arguments is important and needs to be taken very seriously, partly because they are important in political theory, but also, as I have said, if Christian ethics is aligned with a rights-based approach, then it is important to get clear from that perspective exactly what the commitments of a rights-based argument might be thought to be.

I want to begin with the most recent point about scarcity, since it underpins much of the rest of the argument. It would be absurd to deny the fundamental importance of the issue of scarcity, but we have to be very careful before we assume that it draws a sharp distinction between negative and positive rights,

---

[25] C. Fried, *Right and Wrong*, Harvard University Press, Cambridge, Mass., 1978, p. 113.
[26] Ibid.

because it could be plausibly argued that, if the issue of scarcity undermines the categorical nature of positive rights, it does so equally in respect of negative rights too. Scarcity no doubt exists as a constraint on positive rights; but it also exists in respect of negative rights, but here it is scarcity in respect not of resources but of virtuous motivation. Respecting negative rights entails abstaining from action which would infringe such rights and, as such, it entails the absence of coercion, violence, assault, interference etc. There is, of course, as Christians with a sense of the idea of the fallenness of human nature would be the first to acknowledge, a shortage of such forms of forbearance. Given that people do coerce, interfere, assault etc., then the protection of negative rights implies costs, for example of police forces and courts, and thus the possibility of scarcity. At this stage of the argument, therefore, it might appear that scarcity is a constraint as much upon negative rights as positive ones. The negative rights theorist, though, has a response to this. The claim is that the costs associated with the idea of negative rights are contingent. That is to say, the issue of scarcity is not logically implicated in the nature of the right; it is, rather, a matter of enforcing the right that leads to scarcity; whereas a positive right to a resource builds the issue of scarcity directly into the nature of the right.

There are, however, two interrelated problems with this response. First of all it is possible to argue, as Fried does, in response to this sort of objection that it is possible to preserve the categorical nature of a negative right by denying that the issue of protection or enforcement has anything to do with the matter at all: 'The fact that I have a right to freedom of speech against the government does not also mean that I have a right that the government protect any exercise of that right' (pp. 110–11). The reason why Fried takes this draconian step is because, as he recognises, a right to the protection of a negative right would be a right to the resources of the community and, as such, would be a positive right. This is, however, a very high price to pay for preserving the idea of a negative right. It is not clear what the point would be in specifying a set of negative rights which did not include enforceability conditions. Fried wants to make the conditions of enforceability a purely contingent matter, not logically connected to the nature of negative rights, but we have to ask what then would be the point of such a list of rights?

There is, however, a second and much stronger way of making the point, and that is logically to tie the idea of a right to its enforceability conditions. There is a good case for this. We have all sorts of preferences, interests, needs, desires and claims, only some of which are considered to be grounds of rights. We single out those claims and interests which we believe should give rise to enforceable obligations on others and call them rights. If the idea of enforceability is what makes a right a right, then in what sense is it possible to treat the conditions of enforcement as a contingent feature of rights? If this is so, then all rights, negative or positive, will run up against scarcity because of the costs entailed by enforceability conditions. Thus, if the negative-rights theorist believes that scarcity destroys the categorical nature of rights, then it is not clear why it does not do the same for negative rights too.

It seems to me that the solution here is not to be too abstract and categorical about rights, and to bring them more fully into relationship with political processes, particularly democratic ones. Issues of scarcity are part of the stuff of politics and in the same way as we can reach acceptable judgements in society through democratic discussion about the level of resources which should be committed to protect civic and political rights (the negative rights in the critic's view) so, through the same process, we can arrive at a rough and revisable consensus about the resources necessary for positive rights such as health care, education and so forth. This will make both sets of rights more or less as much or as little categorical as one another.

I now want to turn to the final aspects of this dispute, namely, the argument that positive obligation can arise only out of contract and therefore that a failure to aid is only an injustice if it is a failure in a duty that was required in contract. Again, this is an area, it seems to me, where theological approaches to human rights issues have not been as alert to the complexities and controversies as they ought to have been. The critic's view is straightforward: positive rights to resources and aid can arise only out of contract and I only have an obligation to provide resources and aid if I have been party to such a contract and hence I can only commit an injustice in relation to positive duties within this contractual relationship. A culpable failure to do what I ought to have done is specified by a contractual or quasi-contractual relationship. Contract, therefore, provides the moral framework for positive obligation. I want to explore some of the problematic issues here before moving on to some more general observations on contract and covenant as the basis for a Christian view of ethics which will take us back to some of the issues mentioned at the end of the chapter on prophecy.

The problem with the contractual approach to obligation is that of harm. If I fail to act in a positive manner to your needs, this will cause you harm. You need X which I have, I withhold X and you are harmed. The negative-rights theorist will argue that the fact that you have a need for X which I recognise does not create an obligation on me to provide X, that obligation can arise out of contract alone: *contra* Simone Weil, needs do *not* create obligations. It is only if they are set in a contractual context that they do. However, this leads to a rather paradox-ical, or at least , morally controversial result. Imagine that you have this need to which I do not respond because I do not have a contract with you. You are harmed by my lack of response but I have committed no injustice. On the other hand, another person, B, equally withholds X from you and you are badly harmed again, but he/she has committed an injustice because he/she was part of a contractual relationship. Now, leaving aside contract, it is a matter of empirical observation that you have been similarly harmed by our equal failure to act. Or, to put the point another way, our sequential failures to act each time caused the harm in question. If we assume for the moment that moral responsibility follows from the ascription of causal responsibility, and the causal circumstances are the same in each case, then in what sense does contract come into it? Contracts are a set of marks on a paper (on one view) and they cannot make any difference to causal responsibility and should not make any difference to moral responsibility.

This is one way of making a criticism of the contract view, but there are others too. The critique we have been considering is very severely physicalist, that is to say, it is not concerned with the framework of rules within which responsibility for obligations is assigned. It concentrates instead upon causal circumstances. In doing so, it can encourage the increase in proliferating responsibilities if it can be shown that my failure to act could have prevented some harm possibly to some anonymous other person.

Another way of looking at the issue is not to reject the idea that obligations have to be assigned by rules, but to argue that the rules of explicit contract are far too constraining. In fact, on this view, the appropriate rules and obligations are specified by rights and obligations to which rights give rise. So the issue between the negative- and positive-rights theorists is not whether obligations arise out of rules, but how extensive the rules are: the narrow rules of contract or the wider set of rules specified in a framework of both positive and negative rights.

Later, I want to explore the relationships between these issues about rules and contracts and Christian ideas about covenant and contract. Before moving on to these theories, however, I want to look at the critique of the human rights approach, developed by narrative theologians, which takes up in a theological context some of the theories that were discussed earlier in the debate between Gewirth and MacIntyre. In most respects, these disputes mirror ones we have already encountered in the earlier discussion of natural law, but it will be useful to refocus them on issues to do with rights.

The first point to be made by the narrative theologian is that a theory of human rights cannot provide the moral basis of principle for society just because it is so abstract. Ideas like human dignity or even the generic conditions of agency are 'bleached' conceptions, they are abstracted from the nature of persons as those persons exist in communities shaped by traditions and held together by narrative. Stanley Hauerwas describes the position thus by criticising a more general moral strategy of which a theory of rights would be a part:

contemporary discussions of morality which neglect or, at any rate, make virtue secondary are attempts to develop ethical theory not founded on such a moral community. Morally and politically, we act as though we were members of no community, share no goods and have no common history. Thus, the challenge is to provide a theory of how moral objectivity can be achieved in such a society. By providing an impersonal interpretation of 'moral rationality' in which the emotions and history of the agent are relegated to the 'private', recent moral theory has tried to show how moral argument (and even agreement) is possible between people who otherwise share nothing in common. Thus, it is thought, 'morality' can be grounded in human nature, only now 'nature' is limited to 'rationality', abstracted from any community's history.[27]

Hauerwas acknowledges the importance of this project – indeed, he regards it as an extraordinarily important project 'to secure societal co-operation between moral strangers'. Nevertheless, it is a project which he argues must be resisted because it fails to account for the actual nature of our moral agency, as we saw in chapter 5, and makes differences morally irrelevant, whereas, for Hauerwas, they are crucial.

In any case, it is morally rather inert. It depends, as Hauerwas says, upon abstraction, whereas the sources of thick moral agency lie in narrative and their accompanying traditions. The 'social generalities', as he calls them in *The Peaceable Kingdom*, will not be morally motivating, since there is no place outside history where we can find a secure place to anchor our moral convictions. To take his own example, what was wrong with apartheid was not that it offended against some universal account of human nature and human rights, but because one could not be a Christian at the Lord's Table and treat other people like that. The source of the moral concern is to be found within the particular community, with its narrative which provides the sources of moral concern and for moral agency, not in Gewirthian a priori reasons for action. A similar view is taken, for example, by Richard Rorty, in respect of the concern we should show in the USA to the deprivation of urban blacks. It is not that their human rights or human dignity conceived in an abstract rational way is being infringed, but rather that, in a

---

[27] Hauerwas, *A Community of Character* p. 120.

society with a sense of the 'American Dream',[28] the possibility of participating in that dream is being denied to others.

It is for reasons of this sort that Hauerwas and other narrative theologians are very unwilling to share in the accommodationist strategy for social ethics that a theory of rights is supposed to provide. Recall Gerwirth's strategy as an exemplar of this strategy: we have to accept the fact of moral pluralism, that people disagree fundamentally about the good, but it is possible to put the right before the good, to determine a set of rights which people can be regarded as possessing while disagreeing about substantive morality. While this is, for Hauerwas, a project which should not lightly be dismissed, it is equally one in which the Christian should not be involved, just because it distorts the nature of morality and requires Christians to regard the moral dimension of their beliefs as an exemplification of something else, namely, a theory of human rights and human dignity which can be characterised and accepted by others on quite other grounds. This, however, raises the deep question which we looked at earlier, namely, whether it can make sense to say that A and B believe in X (which is supposed to have constant content) even though the grounds for believing in it are incommensurable: for example, Christian and humanist accounts of the notion of human dignity.

It is worth remembering that these issues have led to distinctions being drawn in Roman Catholic moral theology between a Faith Ethic (*Glaubensethik*) and an autonomous morality on which all might agree. The former stresses Christian ethical distinctiveness and accepts the point just made that there is an internal relationship or epistemological dependence between typical Christian moral positions and other aspects of the Faith. It is not the case that there are moral principles which can be supported from different epistemological perspectives, but rather that 'some moral positions held by Christians cannot be critically . . . arrived at or supported without the framework of faith'.[29] This, of course, is rather parallel to the point of the

---

[28] Rorty, *Contingency, Irony and Solidarity*.

[29] V. MacNamara, *Faith and Ethics* Gill and Macmillan, Dublin, 1985, p. 96.

narrative theologian, and the position could be supported by a Wittgensteinian view of meaning as taken into theology by a thinker such as Lindbeck.

The autonomist position would be part of what Hauerwas calls the 'accommodationist strategy'. There are moral principles which have a meaning that is independent of the different epistemological perspectives of those who assent to the principles. The role, for example, of Christian belief in respect, say, of principles about human rights is to provide motivation for acting on the principles but not for characterising their meaning. Such an approach in the work of Cronin 'is in line with traditional "natural-law" theory which insists upon a common grasp of moral truth by all people independently of divine revelation.'

Related to this is the possibility of arguing rationally with other humans, believers and non-believers alike, regarding the requirements of the moral imperative.[30] Again we see the features of this divide in Christian moral, social and political thought which we shall seek to evaluate in the final chapter.

I now want to go back to issues about covenant and contract in relation to rights because they can be seen to be linked to some of the issues at stake between what might be called narrative and natural theologians on the issues to do with rights. As we have seen, rights have to be seen in the context of sets of rules, and the complexity we encountered was to do with how extensive these rules should be, with critics of positive rights, for example, arguing that such rights could arise only from within a contractual relationship. Given that the biblical tradition and Christian theology has had a lot to say about the nature of covenant, what, if any, light could covenant conceptions shed on issues to do with rights?[31] Again, it is difficult to escape from the fact that such models get enmeshed in exactly the same sort of considerations that we have just been looking at: that is to say, between *Glaubensethik* and autonomist ethics or

---

[30] See Cronin, *Rights and Christian Ethics* p. 236; O. O'Donovan *Resurrection and Moral Order: An Outline of Evangelical Ethics* Apollo, Leicester, 1994, p. 20.

[31] J. Allen, *Law and Conflict: A Covenantal Model of Christian Ethics*, Abingdon Press, Nashville, 1984, p. 45.

narrative and universalist ethics. The thinker sympathetic to the 'natural' approach might have to use the covenantal language of the Old Testament as a way of providing part of the moral case for thinking about rights in relationship to God's covenant. He/she will want to stress the universalism of the covenantal relationship that God's covenant, properly understood, was being with humanity not just with the people of Israel. We saw some of these issues arising in relation to the prophetic tradition in the second chapter with Barton, for example, stressing the extent to which Isaiah and Amos could be seen as being at least implicitly universalist in their ethical perspective. Such views could also be supported by reflection on the story of Noah, for example when Allen claims that all of humanity is to be understood as one covenant community. Indeed, Cronin argues that the covenant relationship is the best resource, at least within the Christian tradition, for thinking about the idea of human dignity rather than seeing that dignity as rooted 'in our special endowment as rational animals'.[32] On this view, therefore, the covenantal relationship is universal and, in so far as moral principles such as rights and duties can be drawn from this relationship, they are universal.

As we saw, however, the covenantal relationship and the interpretation of this by the prophets was regarded by Michael Walzer, in a morally particularistic way, as defining the relationships of a particular community, and such a view would no doubt be endorsed by both the narrative theologian and the *Glaubens ethik* thinkers. Thus, on this view, invoking the notion of covenant within the Christian tradition will not help at this stage of the argument to resolve the problem about the nature of rights, since the implications of the idea of the covenant, too, are linked to fundamental disputes about the distinctive and narrative nature of Christian ethics.

Finally, we should consider the question of the general relationship between rights-based conceptions and the whole of morality. It is frequently argued that a rights-based morality will

[32] Cronin, *Rights and Christian Ethics* p. 216.

reinforce a proprietorial and self-regarding conception of the person and that it will, in fact, displace the notion of virtue in both general and specific virtues like charity, benevolence and altruism in particular. At this stage, I shall not address the questions directly – since they will become important in the next chapter on the individual and community in a liberal society – but, in concluding the argument about rights, it is worth 'flagging up' the issue to some extent.

In the view of the critic, the idea of a rights-based morality, even if it is confined to the political sphere, embodies too attenuated a conception of the person, and one which will, over time, transform the public realm into one that is dominated more and more by private conceptions, and thus to construe the common good as a nexus of rights is a fundamental error, particularly from a Christian point of view, since it is central to Christian ethics, so it is argued, to endorse a very different conception of both the nature of the person and the public realm. The best modern protagonist in this view of rights is Joan Lockwood O'Donovan. In her essay 'Subsidiarity and Political Authority', she argues that the idea of rights and individual autonomy which yields theories of rights is not compatible with the ways in which we either do or ought to conceive certain sorts of goods, both private and public, and that, in conceiving these in a rights-based way, we are fundamentally undermining a proper understanding of these goods:

The public realm suffers from moral monism, being enslaved to one universally acclaimed good, that of individual self-determination. The public hegemony of this good is both disclosed and maintained in the public hegemony of the language of individual rights. Increasingly, in liberal democratic polities, all communal and institutional aims, aspirations, and claims must be articulated in the individualist language in order to be heard. But this language is unsuited to express the purposes and structural laws of diverse communities. It is equally unsuited to express the goods and law of marriage – personal communion and sexual fidelity, or the bonds and duties of family life – parental care and filial obedience, or the purpose and normative structure of economic activity – production to fill material needs and stewardship of natural resources, or of education – the communication of truth under conditions of openness and sincerity . . . their various norms cannot be comprehended by the language of moral individualism.[33]

Her argument is that such human practices not only cannot be understood in terms of rights and autonomy, but also they can only be understood if they are regarded as embodying: 'transcendentally given and permanently binding constraints on human action; that they have purposes and structures which are not entirely subject to historical and cultural arbitrariness, are not manipulated by the will of individuals and groups'.[34] This truth, which obviously mirrors the sorts of claims made by Demant in his argument about natural order which we considered in chapter 6, is, she argues, denied by what she calls the civil religion of individual rights. Such a civil religion will, in fact, transform the nature of central human institutions and practices and, far from being neutral between conceptions of the good and favourable to pluralism, such an approach transforms society to its own form of moral monism – namely, individual autonomy.

To take a specific example which relates to a point made in chapter 7, an emphasis upon individualism and rights is as likely as the market to transform an ethic of public service into one of private right and, in this respect, far from the civil religion of individual rights articulating a common good it, in fact, transforms a common good into a private one:

On the basis of their ever more explicit contractual relations with the state, as formalised in bills and charters of rights, citizens have growing incentives to demand legal redress of the failures of Government and public agencies to furnish the expected goods and services. Such political contractualism spells the most extreme reduction of public law and the common good it enforces to private law and private good.[35]

On this view, it is impossible to keep a boundary between spheres of life which should be protected from individualism and subjectivism, and the progressive transformation of public

---

[33] J. L. O'Donovan, 'Subsidiarity and Political Authority in Theological Perspective' in *Studies in Christian Ethics*, 6/1, (1998), pp. 29–30.

[34] Ibid. p. 32.

[35] J. L. O'Donovan, 'Historical Prolegomenon to a Theological Review of Human Rights' *Studies in Christian Ethics*, 4/2, (1996), p. 63.

goods into private ones, other than by some accepted view of their relation to a sense of the transcendent. In the same way as Pannenberg, as we saw earlier, believed that belief in God was basic to the idea of truth, so in this argument a recognition of the transcendent is a necessary condition of a correct under-standing of the appropriate moral nature of different spheres of human life. It is, however, clear from this argument that the givenness or embeddedness of practices or spheres, as Walzer, for example, argues, is not sufficient to prevent their trans-formation by what are seen as the corrosive acids of individu-alism. In the next chapter, therefore, we need to turn to an examination of the relationship between individual and com-munity in liberal thought.

CHAPTER 10

Self and community

> The distinction between the individual and his creed is a
> foundation truth of democracy, and any community that
> seeks to blur it will not do itself any favours.
>
> (Salman Rushdie, *The Observer*)

In this chapter, I shall focus on the issue of the relationship
between the individual and community within liberal political
theory. The claim that liberal societies are neglectful of the
idea of community is an old one.[1] Certainly, religious believers
have shared this critique of liberal society, as we saw in the
first chapter. Having said that, it is also true to say that the
Christian tradition is not univocal on this point. There have
been strong defences of what might be thought of as liberal
individualism from within the Protestant tradition particularly
and, of course, this tradition contributed enormously to the
growth of the idea of individualism in Western societies. A
good and, indeed, famous example of a defence of liberal
individualism and its proper relationship with the Christian
faith can be found in *Das Wesen des Christentums* by Harnack.
Writing in the third chapter, composed exactly one hundred
years ago in the winter session of 1899–1900 at the University
of Berlin, Harnack said:

---

[1] See, for example, S. Holmes 'The Permanent Structure of Antiliberal Thought' in
Liberalism and the Moral Life ed. N. Rosenblum, Harvard University Press, Cambridge,
Mass. 1991, pp. 227–54. A number of other works have been published recently that
bear upon this issue. See particularly: Kautz, *Liberalism and Community*; A. Gewirth,
The Community of Rights University of Chicago Press, 1996; E. Fraser, *The Problems of
Communitarian Politics* Oxford University Press, 1999; D. Phillips, *Looking Backward: A
Critical Appraisal of Communitarian Thought*, Princeton University Press, 1993.

The Kingdom of God comes by calling to *individuals*, making entrance into their *souls* and being grasped by them. The Kingdom of God is indeed God's *rule* – but it is the rule of a holy God in individual hearts. It is God himself in his power. Everything dramatic, all public historical meaning vanish here . . . It is not a matter of angels and devils, principalities and powers, but of God and the soul, of the soul and its God.[2]

He goes on to say: 'Now for the first time everything external and everything merely future is cast off: it is the individual who is redeemed; not the people or the state.'[3]

It is certainly true, therefore, that there is no easy or natural affiliation between religious belief and the communitarian critique of liberalism although, clearly, narrative theologians whose work was discussed earlier will share some affinities with such communitarian critics of liberal society. There is, however, this complexity in the religious response to liberalism. A very good example of a very thoroughgoing individualism is the essay by E. Grässer, 'Jesus und das Heil Gottes: Bermerkugen sur sog 'Individualisierung des Heils' in which he argues uncompromisingly as follows:

Jesus' message of salvation brings about a complete shift from the collective to the individual. The individualising tendency is tangible everywhere. The prefiguration of the Old Testament–Jewish relation to God constituted through the relation of Yahweh to the people through covenant, cult and Torah, loses its normative power. Jesus penetrates critically through and behind this to the sole decisive situation and relation, God–individual, Father–son of God (= man).[4]

It will be recalled that we saw in chapter 2 in the work of M. Walzer, who for these purposes can be taken as a communitarian critic of liberalism, that it was precisely these normative structures of community, covenant and relationships in society that made prophecy and social criticism possible. These relationships constituted a normative framework without which moral exhortation in the form of prophecy would not, in fact, be possible. It would be, as Walzer says of Jonah: 'The prophet

[2] A. von Harnack, *Das Wesen den Christentums* Siebenstern, Gütersloh, 1977, p. 43.
[3] Ibid. p. 45.
[4] E. Grässer, 'Jesus und das Heil Gottes' in *Jesus Christus in Historie und Theologie: Festschrift für Hans Conzelmann* ed. G. Strecker, J. C. B. Mohr, Tübingen, 1975, pp. 182–3.

comes and goes, an alien voice, a mere messenger, unconnected to the people and the city.'[5] On this sort of approach, the community and the appeal to community is a normative framework within which morality is learned and which it alone can give individuals moral tools and resources to interpret and criticise that moral outlook and moral tradition that one has inherited. This point is well made by Schneewind when he argues that, far from moral and political reasoning embodying what in another context T. Nagel has called 'the view from nowhere', moral reasoning requires a *tradition* of moral wisdom which should not be seen as a deposit of unchanging moral truth, but which provides reasons for development, change and criticism. Such moral traditions cannot, however, exist in an abstract way; they have to be instantiated in real communities in which such moral wisdom is acquired and transmitted.[6] So the appeal to community provides a normative framework without which individuals will not have the moral resources to think about and act the moral life.

Of course, as we have already seen, there is more than one view about all of this from the standpoint of Christian moral thought, and certainly Harnack and Grässer dispute it. In addition, there is also the point that we have already encountered in chapter 2. If morality is regarded as being embedded in specific frameworks and traditions which are carried by communities, how could morality aspire to be universal when that which bears morality, namely the community with its specific narrative, is particularistic. This point is not lost on communitarians such as Hauerwas, who argues that: 'Most ironically, Christian theology attempted to deny the inherent and community dependent nature of our moral convictions, in the hope that our ethics might be universally persuasive.'[7]

So, there is a lot to investigate here. I shall look at the central

---

[5] M. Walzer, *Interpretation and Social Criticism* p. 77.

[6] J. B. Schneewind, 'Moral Knowledge and Moral Principles' in *Revisions: Changing Perspectives in Moral Philosophy* ed. S. Hauerwas and A. MacIntyre, Notre Dame University Press, 1983.

[7] S. Hauerwas, *Against the Nations: War and Survival in a Liberal Society* University of Notre Dame Press, 1992, p. 41.

issue of how communitarian and liberal thinkers differ about the relationship between the self and the community and how the community acts as the basis for a normative order for the communitarians. I shall then move on to an analysis of what community might actually mean. It is one thing to invoke the idea of community as playing a central and indispensable role in moral reflection, but, if this is the role that it is to play, we need to be much clearer than we are about what community might actually mean. It may be true as Nancy Rosenblum has argued,[8] that, despite the obvious centrality of the idea of community to communitarian thinkers, they do not offer us a theory of community. Communitarians, however, with their view that moral and, indeed, other kinds of reasoning are possible only against the background of an authoritative moral order, are likely to argue that it is not possible to provide a general or universal account of the nature of community. As the argument of this chapter proceeds, it will become clearer why it may not be possible to produce a general account of the nature of community, but not necessarily for the reasons advanced by the communitarians.

John Rawls advances the proposition that: 'the self is prior to the ends which are affirmed by it',[9] and in many ways this provides the crucial issue about which communitarians and liberals differ, and which has deep ramifications across a whole range of issues in moral and political philosophy. For Rawls and for the liberal, the individual moral agent is prior to any sort of social identity. The individual entertains and chooses between and among particular conceptions of the good. There are, to be sure, primary goods which are the goods anyone wants, whatever else that person may want. They are, so to speak, necessary goods required to achieve any recognisable human end. These more substantive ends are, however, a matter of choice, and that is why a thick theory of the good cannot be a basis for politics in the modern world. The right has to be put before the good; the framework for choice has to be in place and be justified independently of any of the specific and differentiated

---

[8] Rosenblum, *Another Liberalism* ch. 7.
[9] Rawls, *A Theory of Justice* p. 560.

goods that individuals may have. Of course, individuals may choose, as part of their conception of the good, to attach themselves to and endorse the values of particular communities and, indeed, religious communities. However, the basic moral and political framework of society is *not* justified by the specific values of these chosen communities. We have a moral identity as agents or selves which can choose between particular conceptions of the good; our fundamental moral identities, so far as they concern the justification of basic political rights, duties and rules, are not drawn from the values of particular communities: 'Thus a moral person is a subject with ends that he has chosen, and his fundamental preference is for conditions that enable him to frame a mode of life that expresses his nature as a free and equal rational being as fully as circumstances permit.'[10] Our moral identity lies in the common capacity for choice, not in the moral substance of what is chosen for 'it is not our aims that primarily reveal our nature'.[11]

The communitarian rejects such a view of the self and the conception of how the self relates not only to the substance of the moral values affirmed by an individual, but also of the conception of the relationship between the individual and the communities in which such values are embedded. This alternative has sometimes been put in terms which suggest that the self is socially constituted. The self is not unencumbered, as it appears to be for Rawls and other liberals.

This is an argument deployed by many philosophers: M. Sandel,[12] A. MacIntyre,[13] C. Taylor[14] and M. Walzer,[15] and I shall take Sandel's book as the best exemplar of the thesis. Sandel puts forward the alternative conception of the self when he writes about community in the following way:

On this strong view, to say that the members of society are bound by a sense of community is not simply to say that a great many of them profess communitarian sentiments and pursue communitarian aims, but rather that they conceive their identity . . . as defined to some

---

[10] Ibid. p. 561.   [11] Ibid. p. 560.
[12] Sandel, *Liberalism and the Limits of Justice*.
[13] MacIntyre, *After Virtue* pp. 204–5.
[14] C. Taylor, 'Atomism' in *Philosophical Papers Vol. 2* Cambridge University Press, 1985.
[15] Walzer, *Spheres of Justice*.

extent by the community of which they are a part. For them, community describes not just what they *have* as fellow citizens but also what they *are*, not a relationship they choose (as in a voluntary association) but an attachment they discover, not merely an attribute but a constituent of their identity.[16]

There is a denial of the Rawlsian self not least because communitarians argue that individuals only have the capacity for deliberating about moral choices because they have acquired or inherited these resources as members of particular moral traditions embedded in particular forms of community. There can be no radical exercise of moral agency which involves standing back from the totality of this community-borne moral resource, and, therefore, the community is partly a theory about how the self is constituted, but it is also a normative theory about how the community instantiates and bears normative value. At the same time, such communities are specific, and their moral culture is not based upon universal moral premises philosophically grounded. They are, rather, given and embedded in particular ways of life, but it is only by being a member of such ways of life that one can learn to be a moral agent at all.

While communitarian thinkers invoke the idea of community, they are, as philosophers, somewhat unspecific about the nature of the relationship between self and community in relation to particular communities (the large exception being Michael Walzer). It would, therefore, be useful to look at the way Hauerwas conceives of this relationship specifically in the context of a Christian community. He argues thus:

The question of what I ought to *do* is actually about what I am or ought to be. 'Should I or should I not have an abortion?' Is not just a question about an 'act' but about the kind of person I am going to be . . . notions like 'abortion' are not simply given; their meaning and intelligibility depend on narrative construal . . . A community's moral prohibitions, therefore, are not so much 'derived' from basic principles as they exhibit the way the community describes what its habits and commitments entail. You do not first have the principle 'life is sacred' and then deduce that abortion is wrong. Rather you learn about the value of life, and in particular human life that comes in the forms of our children, because your community and your parents

16 Sandel, *Liberalism* p. 150.

acting on behalf of your community, do not, practice abortions . . . The stances that comprise a living tradition, if they are serious are meant to tell us the way things are – that is we learn from them the conditions of truth. Re-examining the prohibitions required by particular narratives is one of the ways the narratives are tested against our ongoing experiences. In this way the narrative is challenged and renewed.[17]

All the essential ingredients of communitarianism in both philosophy and theology are embodied in this passage. The self does not choose general principles from which specific judgements flow, rather, the self is embedded in a narrative community, moral issues cannot be identified in an abstract and universal way outside a narrative; narrative communities change as the result of internal critique, not as the result of failing to meet some alleged philosophically grounded general standard.

There are, however, difficulties associated with this kind of critique of the liberal theory of the self and how that theory underpins other aspects of liberal society. These problems have to do with the nature of the link between self and community and the nature of community itself. There is no doubt that many of the central communitarian thinkers are very ambiguous about the strength of the claim about the way the self is constituted by the community. Taylor, for example, argues that: 'Our experience is what it is, shaped in part by the way we interpret it; and this has a lot to do with the terms available in our culture.'[18]

Similar qualifications are entered by Sandel in the passage cited earlier. If the thesis is that the self is not wholly constituted by the community, then it does leave scope for that part of the self which is not, as it were, so constituted to take a critical stance towards the pattern of community life which has helped to constitute the self. As Gewirth argues: 'These restrictions seem, then , to leave an important place for the individual autonomy of thought and action.'[19]

---

[17] Hauerwas, *The Peaceable Kingdom* p. 119.
[18] C. Taylor, *Hegel and Modern Society* Cambridge University Press, 1979.
[19] Gewirth, *The Community of Rights* p. 91.

This is a very important qualification to the constitution of the self thesis because it also brings into play one of the other frequently cited problems about communitarianism. This is particularly the case when, as Gewirth points out, we may find ourselves as embedded in communities which one might want to believe embody a rotten conception of human life and morality, for example Nazism, Stalinism, Maoism and apartheid. He also points out that Aristotle, whose views on community and morality are frequently cited by communitarians, was committed to the slavery which was not an incidental aspect of the community of which he was a part, nor, for that matter, was it an incidental feature of his own philosophy.[20] The question was discussed at some length in the debate between MacIntyre and Gewirth which I discussed in the previous chapter, and there is no need to repeat it here. It does, however, mean that if communitarians are not claiming the very strongest form of their thesis that the self is constituted by community *simpliciter* then there is scope for the moral critique of the way of life and the social roles of a community bond upon this remaining capacity for autonomous deliberation.

A similar problem arises about how communitarians envisage the relationship between the identity of the self if an individual is part of several communities: family, church, business, neighbourhood, sporting etc. It would be overoptimistic to believe that the values of diverse communities serving different human interests could just be assumed to be compatible. Is not the capacity for at least a degree of autonomy necessary to stand aside to a degree and order and prioritise the possibly incompatible demands of different communities?

Finally, at this stage of the argument we need to point to the contrast between communitarian theories and the human rights views we considered in the previous chapter. Communitarianism is a doctrine of moral particularism, unless it is assumed that different communities with their different thick and rich narratives will turn out to be talking in different ways about the same thing. This is a view which will be investigated in the final

---

[20] Ibid.

chapter of the book – it does seem to me, however, that, whatever the difficulties about human rights theories, it is difficult not to agree with Gewirth when he argues that: 'The particularism stressed by some communitarians, with their dedication to the values of local or partial communities, must here be corrected by the universalism of the principle of human rights.'[21]

We now need to turn to the other side of the communitarian equation, namely, the concept of community itself. Here I believe there are many complexities. Sometimes the idea of community is being invoked as a sociological term pointing out, as it were, the undeniable empirical fact that individuals do have ties to one another through family, school, work, neighbourhood and through language itself, and that these are part of the context of human existence. All of this could be argued without utilising the concept of *community* as opposed to that of *society*. The point here is that community, as we shall see, is an evaluative and not just an empirical concept and, furthermore, it is an evaluative conception in rather controversial ways. The invocation of the term by communitarian thinkers is rarely accompanied by an attempt to analyse some of the profound complexities which the evaluative notion of community raises. The same is true with regard to the use of the idea of community as a narrative framework. If community itself is, as I shall argue, a normative concept, how far can the appeal to community itself constitute the ultimate normative basis for moral reasoning?

I hope that the discussion will promote a better understanding of the concept of community. The analysis offered will not dissipate the ambiguity at the very heart of the concept, but it will, I hope, show that there is something explicable and, indeed, predictable about this ambiguity. The analysis is equally intended to be critical of the uninterpreted use of community as a legitimating notion. I shall be pointing out that beneath this use are important ideological undertones of one sort or another, and that the term is thus used to give an air of consensus, a

---

[21] Ibid.

spurious consensus that evaporates once the inherently normative structure of the concept is realised.

One way of trying to account for the vagueness of the
concept of community is to concentrate on it as an *evaluative*
concept that plays a major legitimating role in our talk about
institutions. The word is one of those descriptive/evaluative
terms that have been given a good deal of attention in recent
moral philosophy.[22] When the term is used in ordinary discourse, it is used not only to describe or to refer to a range of
features in social life, but also to put those features into a
favourable perspective. Community is a valued and valuable
achievement or social state. This point has been clearly taken
up in two recent treatments of the concept: 'Community is both
empirically descriptive of the social structure and normatively
toned.' It refers to a unit of society as it is and to aspects of that
society that are valued if they exist and are desired in their
absence.[23] And, 'Sociologists no more than other individuals
have not been immune to the emotive overtones the word
community constantly carries with it. Everyone – including
sociologists – has wanted to live in a community; feelings have
been much more equivocal concerning life in collectivities,
networks and societies.'[24]

Just as the pejorative force of the term *fascist* can best be
understood by looking at the history of Europe over the past
fifty years, the commendatory force of the term *community* can
be best understood by looking at the last two-hundred years. In
this time, the notion of community has been used almost
universally by social and political philosophers to point up some
of the drawbacks and claimed baneful characteristics of liberal
society and to point the way towards new and more human
forms of social relations. Indeed, Wolin has argued that this
view of community characterises modern political thought:
'The political thought of the 19th and 20th centuries has largely

---

[22] See John Searle, 'Meaning and Speech Acts' *Philosophical Review,* 51 (1962); and
Geoffrey Warnock, 'Hare on Meaning and Speech Acts' *Philosophical Review* 80 (1971).
[23] S. Greer and D. W. Minar, eds., *The Concept of Community* Aldine Press, Chicago, 1969,
p. 9.
[24] C. Bell and H. Newby, *Community Studies*, George Allen and Unwin, London, 1972,
p. 21.

centred on an attempt to restate the value of community, that is the need of human beings to dwell in more intimate relationships with each other, to enjoy more affective ties, to experience some closer solidarity than the nature of urban industrial society seemed willing to grant.'[25] This view of the role of community has also been a major feature of Nisbet's various interpretative essays on this theme.[26] Thus, an understanding of the history of the concept of community is necessary for a full grasp of the high degree of consensus that exists about the positive evaluative meaning of the term.

However, it might be argued that such a consensus does not help us in any way to understand the concept's current ambiguity, especially since it seems to imply there *is* no ambiguity. The critic might also point to a descriptive/evaluative term such as *industrious*, which is not notably ambiguous in its meaning. The word is clearly commendatory, and there would be wide agreement about the type of behaviour commended. In this case, the fact that the word is both evaluative and descriptive does not make it ambiguous, so why should it in the case of community? The answer lies in the complex relationship between the evaluative and descriptive meanings of the word. The high degree of agreement about the commendatory force of community is lacking in the case of its descriptive meaning. Community has a complex and often incompatible range of descriptive meanings. Conventionally, the term is used to refer to: locality; interest group; a system of solidarity; a group with a sense of mutual significance; a group characterised by moral agreement, shared beliefs, shared authority, or ethnic integrity; a group marked by historical continuity and shared traditions; a group in which members meet in some kind of total fashion as opposed to meeting as members of certain roles, functions, or occupational groups; and, finally, occupational, functional, or partial communities. Clearly, not all of these meanings are

---

[25] S. Wolin, *Politics and Vision* George Allen and Unwin, London, 1961, p. 363.

[26] See R. Nisbet, 'Moral Values and Community' in *Tradition and Revolt* Oxford University Press, New York, 1970; Nisbet, *The Sociological Tradition* Heinemann, London, 1967; Nisbet, *The Quest for Community* Oxford University Press, New York, 1970.

compatible, but each has its defenders. What makes community particularly ambiguous is the relationship between this descriptive complexity and incompatibility and the evaluative meaning of the term. While there is formal consensus that to talk about community is to talk in a commendatory way, there is no such consensus about what precisely is being commended in terms of empirically detectable features of social life. The positive evaluation of community takes place within different ideological/ normative groupings, and what is being commended often differs between these groupings. Raymond Williams has drawn attention to this point: 'Community can be the warmly persuasive word to describe an existing set of relationships, or the warmly persuasive word to describe an alternative set of relationships. What is most important, perhaps, is that unlike all other terms of social organization (state, nation, society, etc.) it seems never to be used unfavourably, and never to be given any opposing or distinguishing terms.'[27] It has often been remarked that both conservatives and socialists value community very highly,[28] but what they understand by the social relationships that would embody a sense of community differs very widely.

In this way, the concept of community might be thought to be much more indeterminate than democracy, for example. Quentin Skinner has argued that there is a consensus over the evaluative meaning of democracy, and a similar consensus about the formal specification of its descriptive meaning, namely, 'rule by the people'.[29] Of course, there will be difficulties about the interpretation of the notion of rule by the people, and these disputes will be very severe. However, they do seem to occur within the limits set by the formal specification of the descriptive meaning of the concept. Given the list of possible meanings for community cited earlier, which is by no means exhaustive, and the evident incompatibilities among them, it might be thought that disputes about descriptive features are so severe as to rule out any agreement over even the formal

[27] R. Williams, *Key Words*, Fontana, Glasgow, 1976, p. 6.
[28] Robert Paul Wolff, *The Poverty of Liberalism* Beacon Press, Boston, 1968, pp. 183–4.
[29] Q. Skinner, 'The Empirical Theorists of Democracy and Their Critics' *Political Theory*, 1 (1973).

specification of the descriptive meaning of community. If this is granted, then community would become an 'essentially contested' concept in W. B. Gallie's sense of the term. Gallie has listed various criteria that mark out a concept as essentially contested, and these criteria seem to apply very clearly in the case of community:[30]

1 An essentially contested concept must be appraisive; it must be concerned with some kind of valued achievement. As we have seen this is characteristic of community.

2 This achievement must be of an internally complex nature. Again we have seen that community has many incompatible meanings.

3 In explaining the worth of a concept, a person must be able to make reference to its constituent parts, rival claimants putting these in different orders of priority. This is a clear feature of debates about community. The traditional conservative, for example, may put great emphasis on locality and attachment to place, whereas the liberal may be much more inclined to think of community in terms of interest or occupational groups and assign very little if any importance to locality.

4 The accredited achievement must allow considerable modification in the light of changed circumstances. Thus it is precisely the applicability of the concept of community to changed circumstances to, for example, functional or occupational groups that is disputed between the conservative, the liberal, and the Marxist.

5 The users of an essentially contested concept must be aware of rival interpretations and maintain their particular one. In debates about community different users of the concept seem to be aware of the disputed nature of the concept.

6 The concept must be derived from an original exemplar. If this condition is not satisfied then those arguing about the concept might be thought to be arguing about different things under the same name. There must be some paradigm case, perhaps drawn from the remote past, that all parties

---

[30] W. B. Gallie, 'Essentially Contested Concepts' in *Proceedings of the Aristotelian Society*, 56 (1956).

using the concept in their different ways are willing to regard as falling under the concept. In the case of community there do seem to be clear attempts to secure paradigm cases. The Greek city state was widely propounded by the German philosophers and literary figures such as Hegel, Schiller, and Hölderlin to be a prime example of community; the feudal village has been seen in much the same way, particularly by William Morris, some of the Guild socialists, and, in a quite different way by Peter Laslett. Others have turned to works of fiction as portraying incontestable paradigms of community. W. J. M. Mackenzie, for example, cites Mrs Gaskell's *Cranford*, Trollope's *Barchester*, Winifred Holtby's *South Riding*, Faulkner's *Yoknapatawpha*.[31]

7 There must be the probability that the continued competition between users enables the original exemplar's achievement to be sustained. This again is a necessary condition for the debate about community not to be a debate about different things under the same name.

Thus, it can be argued that community fits quite neatly into this analytical schema, and this approach to the explication of social and political concepts has indeed recently been revived and defended by Alasdair MacIntyre and in a more extended way by William Connolly.[32]

It could also be argued, however, that Gallie's sixth criterion concerning an original exemplar might be much too strong so far as community is concerned. The heterogeneity of the examples mentioned above might lead one to question whether there is, in fact, an agreed exemplar here. As William Connolly has argued: 'sometimes contestants argue not just over the weighting and specifying ingredients in an agreed and original exemplar, but over which experience or construct counts as the

---

[31] See R. Plant, *Hegel*, Blackwell, Oxford, 1983; E. P. Thompson, *William Morris: From Romantic to Revolutionary* Gollancz, London, 1956; P. Laslett, *The World We Have Lost* Methuen, London, 1965; W. J. M. MacKenzie, *Politics and Social Science* Penguin, Harmondsworth, 1967, p. 218.

[32] A. MacIntyre, 'The Essential Contestability of Some Social Concepts' in *Ethics*, 84 (1973); W. E. Connolly, *The Terms of Political Discourse* D. C. Heath, Lexington and Toronto, 1974.

best exemplar',[33] for example, the Greek *polis*, a medieval manorial estate, a nineteenth-century Cheshire village, or a working-class neighbourhood in a large British town between the wars. It does seem to be that there *can* be disagreement over the original exemplar, and, if so, it follows that this exemplar is not like some golden thread running through all the different debates about community and making them, as it were, debates about community. This feature of community would make it perhaps more radically contestable than any other central social and political concept.

However, there are those who would argue that this approach to community, or for that matter to any other concept central to social and political life, commits us to an extreme form of Protagorean relativism and to the abandonment of any claim on the part of the social sciences to be free from ideological taint. If the concept of community is radically contestable in the way indicated and if it can only be given a fixed definition against a particular ideological or normative background, then any theory developed within the social sciences that makes use of such a concept is going to embody ideological/normative assumptions. This is certainly a difficulty that worries many social scientists, and, in order to avoid it, many have claimed that it must be possible to produce a straightforward descriptive definition of those concepts that are central to the social sciences. In support of just this kind of conclusion Felix E. Oppenheim has recently argued that 'for the purpose of a scientific study of politics, we must at least attempt to provide basic political concepts with explications acceptable to anyone regardless of his normative and ideological commitments so that the truth or falsity of statements in which these concepts thus defined occur will depend exclusively on intersubjectively ascertainable evidence'.[34]

One can certainly sympathize with this. If the basic concepts of the social sciences are ineradicably normative and ideological, then this will have very severe consequences, at least in so far as social scientists wish to be allied with the natural sciences

---

[33] W. E. Connolly in a private communication to the author.
[34] F. E. Oppenheim, 'Facts and Values in Politics' *Political Theory*, 1 (1973), p. 56.

as the positivist programme would require them to be. However, in the light of what has already been said, the question to be asked is whether an agreed core of descriptive meaning to social and political concepts, and *ipso facto* to community, is feasible. My answer to this will be a *very* qualified yes, but I shall also argue that such an agreed descriptive meaning is so formal that it will be of no use in social and political analysis, and that, once a move is made beyond this formal agreement, then we are back with contestability an ideology once again.

So far as community is concerned, an important attempt has been made to produce a consensus-descriptive meaning for the concept by a theorist who is quite well aware of the way in which normative or ideological factors can enter into the definition of social and political terms. David B. Clark argues that a core descriptive meaning of community must be established if the concept is to be of any use in social and political science: 'A good deal more confusion seems to have arisen as a result of researchers concentrating all their attention on the social expression of community without having first clearly defined that is its essential nature. The two fundamental communal elements of any social system are a sense of solidarity and a sense of significance.'[35] In this passage, Clark seems himself as having set out the necessary and sufficient conditions for the use of the term *community*, and feels that this definition, if it could be sustained, would meet Oppenheim's requirement that a term in social and political theory must have a clearly defined non-ideological meaning. Behind the surface play of difference, interpretation and ideology there is an essential core meaning to the term, namely, solidarity and significance. This core meaning is, to use Lukes' terminology, the underlying concept of community, that which all views or expressions of community have in common.

Lukes[36] links his account of the relationship between the underlying or primitive concept and the various views yielded by that concept with Rawls' distinction between *concept* and

---

[35] D. B. Clark, 'The Concept of Community: A Re-examination' *The Sociological Review*, 21 (1973), pp. 403–4.
[36] S. Lukes, *Power: A Radical View* Macmillan, London, 1975.

conception, a distinction fully adumbrated in his *A Theory of Justice*. According to Rawls, 'it seems natural to think of justice as distinct from various conceptions of justice and as being specified by the role which these different principles have in common'.[37] A concept of X, where X is a concept characteristic of social and political life, is defined as what all conceptions, views or expressions of X will have in common. In the case of justice, there are many divergent and incompatible conceptions of justice – deserts, merit, need, moral worth, historical entitlement – but what they have in common as conceptions of *justice* is, in Rawls' view, the idea that there are 'no arbitrary divisions between persons in assigning the basic rights and duties of social life'. All conceptions of justice have this feature in common, and this common core constitutes the essential nature of the concept in question. Thus, according to Clark, divergent uses, conceptions, views or, to use Clark's term, expressions of community, such as locality, interest group, ethnic integrity, shared traditions, total interaction, shared authority, do not mean that community is essentially a contested concept incapable of other than ideological definition. Rather, all these conceptions presuppose a core descriptive meaning: 'a social structure is a community if and only if it embodies a sense of solidarity and significance'. In this way, then, we have cut through contested ideological accounts by distilling what all these conceptions have in common, and have arrived at a purely descriptive account, an account that would, on the face of it, satisfy Oppenheim's criterion of applying to 'intersubjectively ascertainable empirical evidence'.[38]

However, the extent to which this is a gain is not at all clear. Leaving aside the question of whether Clark's list of descriptive features is exhaustive (one might, for example, want to say something about size; also, with the proposed definition, a family would be a community, and yet it would seem better to keep those two concepts separate), it does not seem that the advantage gained by specifying this supposedly incontestable core to the concept is very great. As they stand, the features

---

[37] Rawls, *A Theory of Justice* pp. 9–100.
[38] Oppenheim, 'Facts and Values in Politics' p. 56.

constituting Clark's necessary and sufficient conditions for the use of community are entirely formal and abstract: there are no definite requirements expressed or implied for the institutional structure of a community so defined. Before the concept of community can be used in social and political theory, these necessary and sufficient conditions have to be interpreted and provided with some 'cash value'. The same is true of similar specifications of the concept of justice by Rawls and of democracy by Skinner. However, once these underlying concepts, whether of community, justice, or democracy *are* operationalised, we seem to end up again with a contestable view, conception or expression of the concept in question. Formal and consensus concepts have to be transformed into debatable and contestable conceptions before they can be used in social and political theory, but, once this transformation occurs, it is difficult to see how ideology, in the sense of a basic set of normative preferences, can be avoided. Rawls put this point very clearly in regard to the transformation of the concept of justice into the various substantive conceptions of justice. 'The various conceptions of justice are the outgrowth of different notions of society against the background of opposing views of the natural necessities and opportunities of human life.'[39]

The same is true *mutatis mutandis* of community. The rigour and precision of the concept of community established by Clark is bought at the cost of empirical vacuity; the terms of the definition themselves have to be further specified and once this occurs we are back in the thick of ideological assumptions. Our ideas about the kind of institutional structures that are going to embody a sense of solidarity and significance are going to involve our deepest assumptions about the basis of human nature and its capacities and powers, and about the possibilities inherent in human life.

Whether an institution or social network embodies a sense of solidarity and significance cannot be a straightforwardly empirical question, not only because there are problems as to what exactly these words might mean, but also because it is impor-

---

[39] Rawls, *A Theory of Justice*, pp. 9–10.

tant not to beg questions about false consciousness. It may be that members of a collectivity subjectively have a sense of solidarity and significance, but to the political analyst such a sense of community may obscure other features of the relationships within the group that might count against this perceived sense of fraternity. For example, some business corporations may embody a sense of solidarity and significance as subjectively experienced by the workers, but a Marxist might deny that such an institution could be a community because the sense of community is too engineered and sectional and disguises the fact of exploitation, which, once subjectively realised, would destroy the sense of community.

Of course, I do not wish to deny that subjective experience is of vital importance to a sense of community; indeed, later in the chapter I shall argue against Rawls' claim in *A Theory of Justice* that the difference principle embodies a sense of community. Clearly, before we can speak of community, or of solidarity, significance, fraternity and so on, there has to be an intention among the members of a group to act in certain ways towards one another, to respond to each other in particular ways, and to value each person as a member of the group. However, although this is central and important, the question as to whether these features are present in a particular relationship does not depend entirely on the avowals of those belonging to the group. For example, the Marxist may point out that, although the workers within a business enterprise may avow a sense of identity with others working for the company, there may well be grave difficulties within the corporation involved in *acting* in accordance with these sentiments, just because of competition for rewards within the company, the promotional structure, the salary scales and so on. This is clearly not the place to probe arguments about false consciousness, but the important point to note in the present context is that the question whether X is a community is not directly an empirical one to be settled by ascertaining the perceptions and sentiments of those who belong to X. Although this evidence is important it is not finally decisive.

We have seen that the concept of community as an essentially contested concept is not entirely correct. The relativism implied by the essential contestability thesis can be overdone. It is possible, on the one hand, to establish a definition for the concept of community in which different conceptions are contestable as well as being politically committed interpretations. To this extent, theorists such as Oppenheim are correct in thinking that it is possible to give a core definition of a social concept that will be acceptable to all parties across the ideological spectrum, and that this core definition will be descriptive and free from ideological and normative taint. On the other hand, this approach, while it may help in terms of clarity about the structure of a concept, is going to be useless so far as social-science explanations are concerned. These core, descriptive definitions are too formal to be used as tools in substantive analyses of social structures and processes, but, once the terms in the formal definition are interpreted or given a 'cash value', then we are back with normative and ideological assumptions once again. What is needed in this kind of context is some recognition of the ways in which social and political concepts are, like Hegel's concrete universals, embodying universal, formal, definitional elements that at the same time have to be interpreted and specified further, a process that will be conducted against a background of assumptions about human nature, moral values and the nature of social life. A full grasp of the concept of community requires that we should hold together these aspects; as Hegel argues, 'the shapes which the concept assumes in the course of its actualisation are indispensable to the knowledge of the concept itself'.[40] In what follows, I shall try to show very schematically how all of this works in practice by looking at the shapes that community has assumed both in history and in the present time. Taking Clark's definition of the concept of community, I shall try to show how, when interpreted, it yields various irreconcilable views of community, and how these have been both embodied in different forms of social life and are closely related to some of the varieties of political thought – conservative, Marxist, liberal and social democratic.

[40] G. W. F. Hegel, *The Philosophy of Right*, trans. T. M. Knox, Clarendon Press, Oxford, 1977, p. 14.

Clearly, the Marxist will want to cast his conception of community into a form that will accommodate a sense of solidarity and significance, but he will differ fundamentally from both the conservative and the liberal–social democrat in his vision of what these features in fact entail, both in terms of institutional and less formal relationships between persons, and in terms of a critique of existing bourgeois institutions. Marx himself did not write extensively on the shape that community would assume within socialist society, but it is possible to piece together the general lines of Marx's understanding of community if one looks at *The German Ideology* and the material in *The British Rule in India.*[41]

Within existing capitalist societies, Marx argues, community is illusory in that men do not meet as primary social beings whose needs demand mutual co-operation and solidarity; rather, they meet as isolated individuals in the market, each seeking to maximise his own utilities: 'separated from the community, withdrawn into himself, wholly preoccupied with his private interest and acting in accordance with his private caprice . . . The only bond between men is natural necessity, need and private interest, the preservation of their property and their egotistic persons.'[42] Capitalism is a system of competition and mutual antagonism; any sense of solidarity can exist only on the basis of changing constellations of economic interests. In addition, because production is geared to satisfying wants rather than needs, there is a progressive division of labour and the consequent attenuation of human powers characteristic of the alienation of man in capitalist society. Within such a system of production, man loses any sense of his own significance and worth: he is treated as an object in the productive process or, in the more usual imagery, as a cog in the mechanism of production.

Feudal society, in Marx's view, with all its degradation and

---

[41] K. Marx, *The German Ideology* trans. R. Pascal, Lawrence and Wishart, London, 1942; Karl Marx and Friedrich Engels, *Selected Works*, vol. 1, Foreign Language Publishing House, Moscow, 1967.

[42] 'On the Jewish Question' in *Karl Marx Early Writings* ed. T. B. Bottomore, Penguin, Harmondsworth, 1963, p. 26.

superstition, embodied far more of a sense of community than capitalist society is able to do. Within the manorial system, men were related to one another in complex ways, with mutual rights and duties attached to the various hierarchically arranged functions, and were secure in a sense of mutual relationship: 'The estate is individualised with its lord; it has his rank . . . his privileges, his jurisdictions, his political position . . . for those belonging to the estate it is more like their fatherland. It is a constricted sort of nationality.'[43] These social ties that were intimately interwoven with each person's sense of identity and significance were pared down by capitalism: 'Free industry and trade abolished privileged exclusivities. In its place they set men free from privileges, which isolate him from the social whole, but at the same time joins him to a narrower exclusivity. Man is no longer bound by the semblance of communities. Thus they produce the universal struggle of man against man, individual against individual.'[44] Within capitalist society, the state is often portrayed as the community, that which stands above the self-seeking of the market and the general exploitative relationships between men in the market. This was, clearly, the vision of Hegel and Lasalle, and Marx decisively rejects it. The state, for Marx, is one more illusory community within capitalist society. Far from being the universal that reconciles the fractures in civil society and the mutual antagonisms of the market, it embodies a particular sectional interest, namely, that of the capitalist class.

However, it would be a great mistake to imply that Marx's own conception of community was greatly influenced by the feudal, pre-industrial model. Although he clearly saw the *Gemeinschaflich* pre-capitalist social order as mediating important social bonds, he also saw it as hierarchical in ways that were thought to express the natural necessities of the human condition. Within the European tradition, these natural necessities were linked to the purposes of God, whereas, in oriental societies, they were thought to express the ineradicable conse-

[43] *Economic and Philosophical Manuscripts of 1844* trans. M. Milligan, Foreign Languages Publishing House, Moscow, 1959, pp. 61–2.
[44] Ibid. p. 62.

quences of karma. Marx particularly emphasises this point in his account of British rule in India:

We must not forget that these idyllic village communities, inoffensive as they may appear, had always been the solid foundation of oriental despotism, that they restrained the mind within the smallest compass, making it the unresisting tool of superstition, enslaving it beneath traditional rules . . . We must not forget that these little communities were contaminated by caste and slavery, that they subjugated man to external circumstance instead of elevating man to be the sovereign of circumstance, that they changed a self-developing social state into a never changing destiny.'[45]

Precapitalist communities were, as Colletti argues, cohesive but confining;[46] the growth of capitalism brought with it mobility and human autonomy but a corresponding loss of communal ties. A truly human community is for the future, when the claims of both community and autonomy will be reconciled in a socialist society. To achieve such a society, a revolution is necessary in order to break the structure of domination over individuals and in order to change the basis of economic activity to a much less competitive and dehumanising form.

It is at this point that Marxist political commitments relate to current preoccupations on the left about the nature of community. If a truly human community can only be achieved after the revolutionary transformation of a society, then a necessary condition of this is the development of *class* consciousness on the part of the proletariat; yet it is just this requirement that often comes into conflict with the admiration many socialists feel for traditional working-class communities, communities that are being broken up by urban renewal. Many socialists have been in the forefront of protests about the breakup of these neighbourhood communities; but other Marxists, perhaps being more consistent, have found this attitude very difficult to understand. John Westergaard has pointed out very clearly the difficulties facing the Marxist in this position: on one hand, he admires the strong sense of community within working-class areas. On the other hand, he feels that the development of class

[45] Marx and Engels, *Selected Works* I, p. 154.
[46] L. Colletti, *Marxism and Hegel* p. 259.

consciousness may actually be inhibited by the attachment working people feel towards persons from their own area and by the consequent exclusivity involved:

Not only has it bcome fashionable to deplore the dilution of tradi-tional working class culture *per se*, a reaction which reflects an odd, conservative nostalgia for a way of life moulded by insecurity, seclu-sion and crude deprivation both material and mental, but this cultural dilution has not infrequently come to be equated with a decline in class consciousness and its replacement by narrow preoccupations of status and respectability or sheer apathy. No substantial evidence has been offered for this equation: it has been asserted, not proven. Underlying it there is commonly a premise which deserves explicit examination. This is the assumption that the kind of working class unity which finds expression in industrial or more particularly poli-tical action draws its nourishment from the simpler and more intimate loyalties of neighbourhood and kind. Consequently it is postulated that as the latter are weakened so the former declines. This assump-tion is highly questionable, for it implies that the solidarity of class which is social in its sweep and draws no nice distinctions between men of this place and that, this name and that, this dialect and that, is rooted in the kind of parochial solidarity which is its very antithesis.[47]

In a similar vein, Frank Parkin points out that 'a class outlook is rooted in a perception of the social order that stretches far beyond the frontiers of community. It entails a macro-social view of the reward structure and an understanding of the systematic nature of inequality.'[48] Indeed, within the history of political thought there is a good deal of negative evidence in support of this conclusion. The British Hegelians, particularly T. H. Green, B. Bosanquet and Sir Henry Jones, all rejected a class analysis of politics and counterposed to this a commu-nitarian view claiming that within modern society there is a common good, the existence of which can be demonstrated by philosophical argument and which all men, whatever their social class, may aspire to play a part in attaining.[49]

The dilemma for the Marxist here depends crucially upon his

---

[47] J. Westergaard, 'The Withering Away of Class' in *Towards Socialism* eds. P. Anderson and R. Blackburn, Fontana, Glasgow, 1965, pp. 107–8.

[48] F. Parkin, *Class, Inequality and Political Order*, Paladin, St Albans, 1972, p. 90.

[49] For a good discussion of this aspect of Green's work see A. MacIntyre, *Secularisation and Moral Change*. See also Vincent and Plant, *Philosophy, Politics and Citizenship*.

conception of community and of the necessary conditions for furthering that community. On the one hand, he assumes ultimately that a really humane community is of the future, in a society devoid of class and exploitation, and that a conditon for achieving this is the development of class consciousness. He understands that neighbourhood communities may well hinder the development of class consciousness and thus of the ultimate form of human community. On the other hand, he understands existing working-class communities can be valuable sources of strength and support within existing capitalist society. The tensions involved in this position are tied up with assumptions made by Marxists both about the possible character of human nature in different social circumstances and about the range of possibilities that can be brought about by change in human society. Eugene Kamenka has put both the goals and the problems involved in the Marxist view of community in the following way:

Here lies the fundamental problem of Marxist humanism. Classical Marxism welded together in one tremendous act of fact and faith the affirmation of industrial development and the longing for the brother-hood and community of the feudal agrarian village. The machines that robbed man of his individuality had a historic mission: while they seemed to support and extend the market divisiveness of commercial society, they would be overthrowing it and lead into the Kingdom of Ends.[50]

Whatever is left to the future in the Marxist conception of community, and whatever tensions this conception produces for Marxists *vis-à-vis* existing working-class communities, two things stand out that mark off this vision of human solidarity from both the conservative and liberal–social democratic stand-points. The conservative vision of community as a functional hierarchical order is regarded by Marxists as embodying some genuine elements of community, but at the same time these elements play an important ideological role in making other, equally important, features of hierarchical systems: the lack of autonomy for those in a subordinate position in the hierarchy,

---

[50] E. Kamenka, 'Marxism and the Crisis in Social Ethics' in *Socialist Humanism*, ed. Erich Fromm, Allen Lane, London, 1967.

and the economic exploitation of the same by those better placed. Indeed, some commentators have seen the lack of hierarchy as the only thing that marks off the Marxian view of community from the conservative approach. Kamenka, for example, says explicitly: 'The socialist vision of the non-commercial society is distinguished from the Romantic conservative view by the rejection of hierarchy and by that alone.' Within liberal capitalist society, the Marxist sees genuine community to be at a vanishing point. There are only transient constellations of individuals around perceived material interests. As we have seen, the sense of community that exists within the working class is in conflict with the claims of class to the extent that these loyalties can become so exclusive as to cover up the ultimate reality of being working class.

While the Marxist view of community has been based ultimately on a Promethean view of man – a vision of man in 'community with others having the means to cultivate his talents in all directions'[51] – traditional conservative thought is based on far less optimistic assumptions about man and his perfectibility. The conservative conception of community is usually backward looking, its appeal connoting a return to a *Gemeinschaflich* type of order, and thus may support attempts to resist change and to buttress the existing power and authority structure. Community, then, is characterised by hierarchy, place and mutual obligation between groups in different positions within the hierarchy. Its vision is one of organism, and its ethic one of mutual service: the social order is an organic unity within which each individual has an allotted place and a part to play. The parts of the hierarchy are ordered functionally and are interdependent. These social arrangements are to be regarded not as constraints and inhibitions on the potentially Promethean nature of man, but, rather, as giving a balanced institutional structure within which men can thrive: they are not chains that bind, but are an inherited social framework that constrains man's propensity for brutishness and his disposition for anarchy. It is, in Burkean terms, a harmonious union that

---

[51] Marx, *The German Ideology* p. 75.

'holds all physical and moral natures each in its appointed place'.

Usually this organically related hierarchical order has been held to be a matter of necessity, expressing either the will of God, the empirically discernible order in nature, and congenital and ineradicable differences between men, or some mixture of the three. A good example of this kind of thinking is found in Edmund Dudley's *The Tree of Commonwealth:* 'God hath set an order by grace between himself and Angel and between Angel and Angel; and by reason between Angel and man and between man and man and man and beast . . . which order from the highest point to the lowest God willeth us to keep without any enterprise to the contrary.'[52] Probably the most developed form of the argument that human society must be seen in an hierarchical way and as corresponding to a natural cosmic order ordained by God is in Hooker's *Of the Laws of Ecclesiastical Polity.* In this work there are, of course, many fine evocations of this theme, but among the most direct is the following: 'God's purpose is to amiably order all things and suitably with the kinds and qualities of their nature . . . The whole world consisting in parts so many, so different is by this only thing upheld; he which hath formed them in order.'[53]

This conception of human community was more than just an intellectual construction found in works of political reflection, it was a view that entered very deeply into people's lived experiences in the precapitalist era in Western Europe. Not only did such conceptions tie in very closely with the perceived social structure, but the social structure itself received symbolic reinforcement through religious, particularly Anglican, teachings, as both Laslett and Schochet have shown. This kind of teaching, which was very difficult to avoid, expressed in less subtle language precisely the vision of society encapsulated in works like *Ecclesiastical Polity.* Indeed, the religious reinforcement for such a conception of community may well have lasted much

---

[52] E. Dudley, *The Tree of Commonwealth* ed. D. M. Brodie, Cambridge University Press, 1948.
[53] R. Hooker, *Of the Laws of Ecclesiastical Policy* ed. Revd John Keble, Rivingtons, London, 1836, Book 5, p. 28.

longer than might have been expected. Flora Thompson writes about an Anglican sermon in the village church of Candleford in the closing years of the nineteenth century: 'Another subject was the social order as it then existed. God in his infinite wisdom had appointed a place for every man, woman and child on this earth and it was their bounded duty to remain content-edly in their niches. A gentleman might seem to some of his listeners to have a pleasant easy life compared with theirs as field labourers; but he had duties and responsibilities which would be far beyond their capabilities. He had to pay taxes, sit on the bench of magistrates, oversee his estate and keep up his position by entertaining. Could they do these things? No of course they could not; and he did not suppose that a gentleman could cut as straight a furrow or thatch a rick as expertly as they could.'[54] The author does not indicate the kind of text on which this kind of sermon may have been preached, but the same parson may well have had in mind Ecclesiasticus 38.24–34, which is quoted by Burke to make much the same point.[55]

The idea that ineradicable differences in human capacities and powers is going to be reflected in an interdependent hierarchical structure is central to the traditional conservative vision of human community. The exercise of capacities and powers, however humble they may be, is morally worthy, and the accompanying ethic is one of 'my station and its duties'. Although this conception of community may now be thought to have lost its legitimating bases – the will of God, the unalterable order of the cosmos, ineradicable differences between persons' capacities and powers – empirical studies in political sociology have shown that it does retain some kind of hold in the most unlikely places, for example among working-class conservative voters. As described by Parkin:

deferential interpretations of the reward and status hierarchy stem from an acceptance of the dominant value system by the members of the subordinate class. It should be emphasized here that deference as a general mode of understanding and responding to the fact of low status does not necessarily entail a sense of self-abnegation. Rather it

---

[54] F. Thompson, *Lark Rise to Candleford* Oxford University Press, 1945, p. 201.
[55] E. Burke, *Reflections on the Revolution in France* Dent, London, 1910, p. 46.

tends to be bound up with a view of the social order as an organic entity in which each individual has a proper part to play however humble. Inequality is seen as inevitable as well as just.[56]

A conservative conception of community will then be one of a stratified but organic and interdependent social order, reflecting the necessary but complementary and functional inequalities in human endowment, and the whole being bound together by an ethic of mutual service between the ranks in the hierarchy. The idea that inequalities are necessary and ineradicable, either because they reflect the will of God or the natural order of the cosmos, or because they are genetically transmitted, is important to the survival of such a hierarchical society. This point has been brought out particularly well by Bernard Williams: 'What keeps stable hierarchies together is the idea of necessity, that it is somehow foreordained and inevitable that there should be those orders.'[57] Trying to mirror in community the order that inheres in nature, rather than trying actively to impose order upon it, is a central hallmark of conservative social thought, and its role has to be understood in the light of Williams' remarks.

For the Marxist and the conservative, community is something of an embarrassment. The Marxist sees community in capitalist society as being used primarily to describe specific localities marked by neighbourliness and kinship. Its particularity and exclusivity standing in stark contrast to the universality of class consciousness, without which there can be no transformation of society and no community of humankind. The conservative sees that the social structure and the attendant modes of consciousness and ethical conviction intrinsic of his vision of community have fallen away, and that the various natural necessities that appeared to make his vision both viable and compelling are losing their force.[58] Both, however, are agreed in seeing modern Western liberal–social democratic

---

[56] Parkin, *Class Inequality and Political Order* p. 85.

[57] B. Williams, 'The Idea of Equality' in *Philosophy, Politics and Society* series 2, ed. P. Laslett and W. G. Runciman, Blackwell, Oxford, 1962, p. 119.

[58] Ibid.: 'Once one accepts . . . that the degree of man's consciousness about such things as his role in society is itself in some part the product of social arrangements, and that it can be increased, the idea of stable hierarchy must disappear.'

society as becoming more and more bereft of a sense of community, and the various forms of community work and development financed by the welfare branches of liberal–social democratic societies as being a somewhat frenetic and misplaced realisation of this. As Robert Paul Wolff says: 'the conservative locates community in a cherished past and the radical in the longed for future'.[59]

However, though the conservative and the Marxist do feel community as something of an embarrassment when confronting existing social relationships, they cannot feel it as much as the liberal–social democrat. The liberal tradition had its very origins in a *critique* of communitarian conceptions and institutions. Many theorists, particularly of the seventeenth and eighteenth centuries, tried to come to terms with the new social developments, such as the development of a market society, industrialization, increasing division of labour and urbanisation, and attempted to provide an understanding of man and society that would help to explain and justify the loss of old communities. This type of social theory sought the basis of human association not in tradition and habit, but in the contract and consent of naturally free persons. The individual was taken to be the basic reality, and all forms of social interaction were taken to be constructions out of the motives and desires of these palpable, free, self-conscious individuals, who derived their freedom and conception of themselves precisely from the decline and loss of closer, more communal forms of social relationships. Thinkers in this tradition, particularly Hobbes and Bentham, have profoundly influenced modern conceptions of man and of the possibilities of modern community. Bentham was so beset with the decline of community that he regarded the question 'who are you and with whom do I deal?' as the central question of modern society, a question that would not have made sense in a small village community, pervaded by shared values and experiences. Eric Hobsbawm has pointed out the extent to which the liberal tradition of political thought is deeply ambivalent on the whole subject of community: 'The

[59] R. P. Wolff, *Poverty of Liberalism* p. 184.

tradition of middle class liberal political thought has not quite known what to do with it. The essence of that tradition was individualist, and the shadow of individualism lies over it still. Fraternity, in this tradition, can only be the by-product of individual impulses, of such qualities as Bentham's benevolence or of those social sympathies with which schools like the positivists operated.'[60]

However, within this tradition of individualistic liberalism, there was very soon a recognition that an uninhibited individualism could lead to baneful effects. What was frequently seen to be left after the decline of traditional community is a mass society of atomised deracinated individuals who could no longer draw upon the support of primary social groups. Such is the diagnosis of the malaise of contemporary society offered by many social critics who are neither traditional conservatives nor believers in some future vision of a total Marxist community. Thinkers as diverse as Hegel and Durkheim have sought to formulate some conception of community relevant to modern industrial society that would preserve the gains in individuality and autonomy realised by the decline of traditional communities, but that would be sufficiently supportive to overcome the drawbacks of anomic existence within modern industrial society. They wanted some conception of community that would allow their commitment to the priority of personal freedom to be maintained while at the same time providing an institutional framework within which men may experience a sense of solidarity and significance to a greater degree than is regarded as possible by both conservative and Marxist critics of modern liberal industrial society. But is there such a conception of community?

The liberal–social democrat will argue that there is. They point to partial communities, occupational communities and communities of interest, and they point to the possibility of strengthening communal bonds within existing organisations by opening them up to greater participation by those who work within them. For the liberal–social democrat, the values of

---

[60] E. Hobsbawm, 'The Idea of Fraternity', *New Society*, 34, (Nov. 1975).

solidarity and significance have to take into account the development of individuality, and this means that the idea of *total*
community, at least as it is usually understood, has to go. There
can be no really substantive sense of community embracing the
whole of society simply because personal freedom in the
liberal–social democratic sense presupposes moral diversity,
disagreement on ends, and social and political pluralism. In
both the conservative and Marxist conceptions of community,
there is an implicit assumption about the existence of a substantive moral agreement and a shared authority, and about the
lack of basically divergent interests. However, the consistent
liberal will at least have to recognise the prospect of moral
diversity and of different centres of authority within society.

This perspective is usually held together by a conception of
human nature that rejects both the rather pessimistic view of
the conservative and the Promethean view of the Marxists. The
liberal–social democrat will argue that no one person can do
everything that another person can do nor everything that he
himself might do. Each person's potentialities are greater than
he can hope to realise, and they fall short of the powers of men
generally. The consequence of this is that each person has to
select which of his interests, capacities and powers he wishes to
pursue and develop; and in doing so he will come into contact
with others with whom he will co-operate in realising a
common venture. Social solidarity does not arise out of organic
unity reflecting natural inequalities, but rather is based upon
co-operation with discrete spheres of interest. Rawls has a
particularly fine description of this sort of ideal: 'We are led to
the notion of a community of mankind, the members of which
enjoy each other's assets and individuality elicited by free
institutions and they recognize the good of each as an element
in the complete activity, the whole scheme of which is consented
to and gives pleasure to all.'[61]

The liberal–social democrat will therefore see solidarity and
significance emerging out of particular interest groups within
modern industrial society, and a view of human nature such as

---

[61] Rawls, *A Theory of Justice* p. 523.

that articulated by Rawls would enable such a viewpoint to be stated in its full philosophical generality. This conception of community within urban industrial society and within liberal assumptions about moral, cultural, political and economic pluralism has been the subject of a good deal of sociological investigation and also of prescriptive social theory. While this conception may, perhaps, have some of its roots in Hegel's work, it has come to be especially identified with Durkheim. He recognises the values of personal autonomy and self-direction achieved through the decline of traditional communities; he is also very sensitive to the dangers of mass society and to the baneful consequences on individuals of the loss of supportive primary groups; he sees occupational groups as a possible source of support for deracinated individuals; he adopts a theory of human nature comparable to that of Rawls; and he makes specific recommendations about how occupational groups could be organised in order to strengthen their supportive role *vis-à-vis* individuals. Durkheim explores these themes in various ways.[62] In *Division of Labour* he explores the role of occupational groups or guilds in other historical societies, in particular ancient Rome and medieval Europe. He sees in them a very important way of promoting a sense of mutual solidarity, significance and shared norms, and thus a degree of mutually shared authority. Only since the time of the French Revolution have these groups or guilds disappeared; Durkheim argues that their persistence in history and over a wide range of culture implies that such small-scale regulative groupings meet some permanent and profound need. He looks forward, however, not to the resurrection of the old guilds – these in fact declined just because they failed to adjust to the development of commercial–industrial society – but rather to guilds in a new form, based upon the modern occupational groups thrown up by the contemporary division of labour. In this kind of vision, Durkheim shared a great deal with R. H. Tawney, who, of course,

---

[62] E. Durkheim, *Socialism* trans. Charlotte Sattler, Routledge and Kegan Paul, London, 1959; E. Durkheim, *Division of Labour in Society* trans. G. Simpson, The Free Press, Glencoe, 1933; E. Durkheim, *Professional Ethics and Civic Morals* trans. Cornelia Brookfield, Routledge and Kegan Paul, London, 1957.

played a major role in shaping the christian socialist tradition in Britain. In *The Acquisitive Society*, Tawney argued that industry should be organised on the basis of professional standards rather than just on a basis of profit and loss, in the hope that within the occupational role individuals might achieve some sense of fellowship and mutual solidarity.

Certainly, many sociologists have followed Durkheim in seeing occupational groups as a source of mutual solidarity, even when they may not have shared Durkheim's preoccupations with the cohesion of modern industrial society and the anomic nature of man within it. Richard Brown and Paul Brennen in 'Social Relations and Social Perspectives among Shipbuilding Workers', Michael Banton in *The Policeman in the Community*, Michael Cain in 'On the Beat: Interactions and Relations in Rural and Urban Policeforces', Jeremy Tunstall in *The Fisherman*, William Goode in 'Community within a Community: The Professions', and I. C. Cannon in 'Ideology and Occupational Community', are just a few recent examples of sociologists who have concluded, with reference to specific occupational groups, that such groups can be regarded as communities generating some sense of solidarity and significance.[63] At the same time, other theorists have turned their attention to corporations, to explore the extent to which they can be seen to be a source of communal values. This is not the place to try to trace this development in any detail; it has in any case been well described by Sheldon Wolin.[64] At the same time, such partial communities need not necessarily be linked to working environments. Community workers in liberal welfare societies often devote themselves to developing what could be seen as analogous communities of interest, for example among the tenants of housing estates or among claimants of social security benefits.

[63] R. Brennan and P. Brown, 'Social Relations and Social Perspectives among Shipbuilding Workers' *Sociology*, 4 (1970); M. Banton, *Policeman in the Community* Tavistock Publications, London, 1964; M. Cain, 'On the Beat' in *Images of Deviance* ed. S. Cohen, Penguin, Harmondsworth, 1971, pp. 62–97; J. Tunstall, *Fishermen* Macgibbon and Kee, London, 1969; W. Goode, 'Community within a Community' *American Sociological Review*, 22 (1957) pp. 194–200; I. C. Cannon, 'Ideology and Occupational Community' *Sociology*, 1 (1967).

[64] Wolin, *Politics and Vision* p. 393ff.

The critic, whether conservative or Marxist, may well reply that, however far the idea of occupational and interest group community might be carried, the conception of community in question is still an exiguous one. Within this framework, we shall always be compelled to talk about qualified, partial or functional communities, not about community in some overall sense. The consistent liberal–social democrat, committed as he is to a pluralist view of culture, politics and the economy, cannot provide a conception of overall community. Criticism may be coupled with the assumption that only an overall community is legitimate as a conception of community, and that the liberal–social democrat, in appropriating the term to describe other types of groups within industrial society, is performing a kind of semantic sleight of hand. Thus Robert Paul Wolff argues that pluralism 'by portraying society as an aggregate of human communities rather than as itself a human community rules out any viable conception of the common good'.[65] A liberal–social democratic perspective provides at best a conception of particular communities based upon common but sectional interests, and cannot provide an account of community overall (granting that most contemporary liberals and social democrats would not want to take Lasalle's or Hegel's way out and argue that the institutions of the modern state provide for a sense of overall community).

However, it is not immediately clear that the liberal–social democrat does not offer a solution to this difficulty. In *A Theory of Justice*, Rawls has argued, using the impeccable liberal device of contract theory, that a basic principle of justice is the difference principle: 'social and economic inequalities are to be arranged so that they are both (a) to the greatest benefit to the least advantaged and (b) attached to offices and positions open to all'. According to Rawls, a society whose basic structure conformed to his principles would at the same time embody a sense of overall community. He is very explicit in his writing on this point:

A further merit of the difference principle is that it provides an

---

[65] Wolff, *Poverty of Liberalism* p. 159.

interpretation of the principle of fraternity. In comparison with liberty and equality, the idea of fraternity has had a lesser place in democratic theory . . . The difference principle does seem to correspond to a natural meaning of fraternity: namely the idea of not wanting to have greater advantages unless this is to the advantage and the benefit of others who are not so well off. The family, in its ideal conception, and often in practice is the one place where the principle of calculating the sum of advantages is rejected. Members of a family commonly do not wish to gain unless they can do so in ways that further the interests of the rest. Now wanting to act on the difference principle has precisely this consequence. Those better circumstanced are willing to have their greater advantages only under a scheme in which this works out for the benefit of the least fortunate.[66]

This view of community is two-tiered; at the first level are sectional interest groups with interests and values that are possibly antipathetic to the interests of other members of the society; the second level is the position in which the relationship between these first-level groups is regulated by the difference principle.

Of course, the conservative will reject the difference principle as a community-yielding regulating principle for sectional interest because, as a principle of redress, it seeks to correct the social consequences of natural endowment rather than to reflect them. The Marxist, on the other hand, will criticise Rawls' view as expressing far too pure an attitude about the way in which moral conviction can change the ordering of society. However, even on its own terms, the difference principle simply does not yield an adequate understanding of community. Behind Rawls' difference principle is his contractual theory and, in particular, the way in which basically self-interested contractors make rational choices about principles of justice in ignorance of how these principles will, in fact, apply to them. The difference principle is chosen not out of altruistic concern for the worse-off members of society, but because it appears to the contracting parties to be the best worse outcome they can estimate. At any point subsequently, the difference principle is justified not because it manifests a sense of altruistic concern, but because it is a consequence of self-interested rational choice

[66] Rawls, *A Theory of Justice* p. 105.

made in conditions of radical uncertainty. It may be that acting on the difference principle will be to the advantage of the worse-off members of society, but, as Rawls himself says in the passage cited earlier, this is a *consequence* of acting on the difference principle, it is not part of the intention behind acting on the principle or, for that matter, even part of the rationale for it.

However, it has already been argued that community can only exist when people have certain intentions towards one another, have certain perceptions of each other, and value one another in certain ways. A sense of community cannot be yielded as a consequence of a strategy undertaken for self-interest rather than fraternal reasons. In fact, this criticism of Rawls mirrors the usual criticism of the claim that market economies are consistent with community because the pursuit of private benefits yields public goods. It may be so, but, because community is in part a matter of certain perceived relations between persons, the intentions that yield these relations are of crucial importance. The benefits to the worse-off members of society that would flow from the difference principle are not the result of altruism on the part of those who act upon the principle, but are, as Rawls sees it, a consequence of rational decision-making in uncertainty. If this is granted, it would seem to follow that the liberal–social democrat has either to concede to the critic that he has no coherent conception of overall community, or argue, as Robert Nozick does that this should not be seen as a defect in liberal theory so long as there is an adequate account of partial communities. Overall, communities in this view may well pose threats to the inviolability and moral autonomy of free persons. However, this kind of liberalism has been on the defensive for over a century, and most liberals have felt the pressure to combine a sense of the inviolability of the individual, which is central to Nozick's argument, with a sense of the moral value of community.[67] The roots of this struggle within the liberal tradition are, perhaps, to

---

[67] C. B. MacPherson, *The Political Theory of Possessive Individualism* Clarendon Press, Oxford, 1962, p. 2.

be found in the work of T. H. Green, and this difficulty within liberal political thought has no more been solved today than it was in the nineteenth century.

The use of the concept of community in current social and political discourse is, therefore, very far from reflecting a consensual meaning. Rather, there are a range of views of community from within various ideological positions, many of which have been ignored in this chapter. We can have a determinate and specific concept of community only from within one of these frameworks. As we have seen, it is possible to produce formal definitions that might be agreed upon by thinkers all the way across the ideological spectrum, but such definitions are virtually useless. Of course, it would follow from all this that, when the term is used in substantive debates about social and public policy, it is never being used in a neutral fashion. There is always going to be some normative and ideological engagement.

It might, of course, be argued with some plausibility that we could produce an adequate and non-ideological account of human community if we had an adequate account of human nature or philosophical anthropology, and, indeed, such a view has had its place in the history of political thought. It is a beguiling view that human institutions could be derived from a correct understanding of human nature. Two of the most influential community theorists of the post-war period, Robert Paul Wolff in *The Poverty of Liberalism* and Erich Fromm in *The Sane Society*, have grounded their arguments about the nature of community in a philosophical anthropology. However, it can be argued that such a hoped-for objective grounding of political theory in 'the facts of human nature' is illusory. Our understanding of human nature and the natural necessities within which we see human life, is itself part and parcel of one or another outlook on human life and not some kind of empirical bedrock theory that would enable us to underpin one point of view and dispose of others. As Stuart Hampshire argues: 'the nature of the human mind has to be investigated in the history of the successive forms of its social expression; the greater the concrete detail and the greater the historical sense of its variety, the more adequate the philosophy will seem.'[68] However, it is just this very richness and variety in the expression of human nature, some aspects of which have been touched upon in this chapter, that lead one to question whether a rich account of the detail of human community is ever going to be founded upon 'facts' about human nature.

So, it is, I believe, difficult to accept that the appeal to community is as unproblematic as communitarians believe it to be. It surely cannot by itself be seen as a given normative framework because it is itself a highly controversial normative concept, the controversies surrounding which cannot be re-solved without considering more systematic forms of social and political theory. The idea that these can just be side-stepped by an appeal to an unanalysed notion of community is deeply unsatisfactory. Of course, a religious group such as a church can regard itself as a community, but in doing so it would be dangerous to generalise from this to a view about the general relationship between the self and the community and about the relationship between the Christian community and the wider society. In addition, we have to be sensitive to the fact that there are traditions in Christian thinking which are themselves very suspicious of the idea of community, as we saw at the start of this chapter.

We have now looked in some detail at these moral issues thrown up by both the practices and institutions of a liberal society as well as the issues of social and political theory posed by the attempt to give liberal society, and its fundamental concepts, justice, freedom, rights and community, a normative basis. In all cases, we can see very clearly that there are complex moral issues to which these religious beliefs might direct their attention. There is, clearly, no final or authoritative conceptual solution to these issues. As the concept/conception argument shows, consensus and authoritative agreement depend crucially

---

[68] S. N. Hampshire, *Thought and Action* Chatto and Windus, London, 1959, p. 234. Cf. MacIntyre in *A Short History of Ethics* p. 268: 'Nor can I look to human nature as a neutral standard asking which form of social and moral life will give it the most adequate expression. For each form of life carries with it its own picture of human nature. The choice of a form of life and the choice of a view of human nature go together.'

on the thinness and vacuity of what is agreed. Once we go beyond this and look at specific conceptions of justice or at the particular forms of ability which a developed conception of human freedom engages with, then we shall be well into the area of moral or ideological contestation. We now need to consider what right, if any, ought citizens *qua* religious believers to have to bring their religious beliefs to bear in the political processes of dialogue and debate which alone can develop agreed answers to such political questions if that is possible at all. What is clear is that these issues are not going to be settled by either authoritative conceptual analysis or some kind of overarching authoritative moral system. So, attention from here on will concentrate on how those who are members of religious communities might think about their political relation to a liberal society, since it is through this relation, if anything, that these issues can be addressed and potentially resolved.

PART III

Liberalism, religion and social unity

Let every soul be subject unto the higher powers. For there is no power but of God: the powers that be are ordained of God.   (Epistle to the Romans)

Introduction

In this part I want to draw the threads of the book together and reach a conclusion however tentative and personal. The message of Part I of the book was that it was difficult to see how there could be a wholly definite and authoritative social and political ethic emerging from the various traditions and schools of Western theology. The relationship between universal and particular, between the claimed truths of the Christian faith and the particularistic circumstances of specific societies, is too contested and controversial to yield an authoritative view. Equally, as we saw in Part II, there can be no authoritative rendering of crucial political and social concepts such as justice, freedom and community. While there may be a core definition of a concept, such core definitions are too thin and unspecific to be useful. Such concepts have to be further specified into richer and more specific conceptions. These conceptions will be elaborated against the background of particular moral traditions, narratives and communities. As such, they may well involve a range of metaphysical or religious assumptions or what John Rawls, in *Political Liberalism*, calls comprehensive doctrines.

Putting these two general points together: the lack of an authoritative Christian political ethic and the lack of an authoritative rendering of crucial political concepts might, of course, lead to a sense of despair. But this need not be so. While there may be no authoritative Christian political ethic, this does not mean that Christianity lacks any kind of social and political implications. Far from it, but they do have to be argued for, and these arguments will have to be pursued in detail if they are to command respect. Appeals to social justice and community, for example, will carry little weight if we are not clear what is meant by invoking these ideals. The arguments, however, will be more fragmentary, as Professor Forrester has argued, rather than arising inferentially from a corpus of systematic theology of whatever sort, just because such theological doctrines lack the capacity as a whole and on their own to produce rich enough *conceptions* of justice or community to carry one further in political dialogue.

Nevertheless, as I hope Part II has shown, there are large normative questions to be raised about the nature of a liberal market society and the assumptions it may make about justice, freedom, individual and community. There are no authoritative renderings of such concepts, as I have sought to show. This is, however, part of what makes political debate in this context possible: if there were such renderings, there would be no politics. It is because people and the moral traditions of which they are a part disagree about particular conceptions of justice, for example, that this is a *political* issue. The issues are there and are unavoidable, and citizens, whether religious believers or not, are inevitably enmeshed in these sorts of disputes or debates at the level of practical policy.

So, if there is no final moral authority or tradition available to us, how do we cope with this diversity, and in what can the unity of society consist if moral opinion in that society is so diverse and the basic terms of political discourse such as justice, community, common good, freedom and democracy are themselves contested?

The point at stake here can also be put another way. If the possibility of securing agreement about basic political issues has to arise, if it is to arise at all, from democratic debate about particular conceptions of, for example, justice and community, what might be regarded as the basic terms of that debate? That is to say, is it, in fact, possible to provide a normative basis for this kind of democratic deliberation about values which will seem legitimate and authoritative to religious believers who hold their beliefs to be true and may well reject pluralism, either as an alleged fact about modern society or as a normative position itself, in the sense that there are many goods which cannot ultimately be reconciled? Two theological examples will make clear the issue here. The first is the classic statement of the liberal view of the relationship between religious belief and the wider political culture set out by Karl Barth, who argues as follows:

The civil community embraces everyone living in its area. Its members share no common awareness of their relationship to God and such awareness cannot be an element of the legal system established by the civil community. No appeal can be made to the Word or Spirit of God in the running of its affairs. The civil community as such is spiritually blind and ignorant. It has neither faith, nor love nor hope. It has no creed and no gospel. Prayer is not part of its life and its members are not brothers and sisters.[1]

On this view, the state should not be seen as the embodiment of Christian values nor should it pursue goals and policies which are justified solely on Christian grounds. Of course, churches and church members can, should and will contribute to debates about public policy, but the form of political deliberation in such a society cannot give any privilege or priority to religious beliefs, values or the alleged grounds for these beliefs. There remains, however, the question of how to justify this conception of politics to those who do not see their beliefs as being one set amongst others that reasonable people can hold.

In contrast, there is the Christendom approach, which is, as we have seen, associated with T. S. Eliot and Canon Demant. For example, compare Barth with Professor E. Mascall, also a protagonist of the Christendom view:

The Christian answer to a state of affairs in which man finds himself under domination of the being that ought to be subject to him is that he can only recover his true lordship if he places himself deliberately under the Lordship of God. This does not mean just the practice of private religion, though that is quite indispensable; it means the deliberate ordering of society in the light of the truths of the Christian faith . . . It means that theology must govern politics.[2]

So the justification of a liberal order to a particular set of

---

[1] Barth, 'The Christian Community and the Civil Community', p. 267.
[2] E. L. Mascall, *Man: His Origins and Destiny* The Dacre Press, Westminster 1940 page 75.

believers as a framework for deliberation about contested ideas of freedom, justice and community, given that there is no authoritative rendering of such ideas, will prove to be a tricky business. If religious beliefs are identity-creating in much the same way as gender and race, these beliefs and their content will be likely to dominate over all other considerations, and, therefore, in a way which will be at least compatible with such beliefs, the process of justification for a politics of pluralism will be a subtle matter. In the next two chapters which conclude the book, these themes will be taken up, but, broadly speaking, there are three approaches. The first, which is discussed in the context of utilitarianism and Rawlsian contractualism, looks at two very different ways in which liberalism can be seen as a minimal moral conception but which within its rather abstract categories nevertheless, it is claimed, an appropriate place can be found for religious belief.

In the subsequent chapter, we shall look at Rawls' idea of overlapping consensus and the nature of public reason in a liberal society. As we shall see in each of these cases, the claim that these approaches adopt a minimal and neutral basis for liberalism does not hold up. If this is so, and if liberalism does have to have a thick moral basis of its own, how do the values characteristic of this moral basis then relate to the equally thick and rich moral and political beliefs of religious believers who are invited to endorse the moral basis of a liberal society?

Policy and pluralism

> If ethical perception is dependent upon particular com-
> munities, practices and narratives, what is it that gives
> moral cohesion to a society comprising many overlapping
> subcultures?
>
> (D. Fergusson, *Community, Liberalism and Christian Ethics*)

> The community is a fictitious body . . . the interest of the
> community is what? The sum of the interests of the several
> members who compose it.
>
> (Bentham, *An Introduction to the Principles of Morals and Legislation*)

This book has had two intertwined themes: the first is the
question of how far a liberal democratic society has to be seen
to have positive and substantive moral grounding; the second
has been the contribution, if any, that the Christian tradition,
which has been a major force within that liberal democratic
tradition and still has significance within liberal societies, could
or should make to the development and defence of these
fundamental norms. In this part I want to draw some of these
threads more tightly together and to make some kind of assessment of the different strands of thought, both secular and
theological, we have encountered in the process of this argument and discussion. However, before going on to that, I want
to consider two other possibilities for explaining the nature of
the normative basis of a liberal order. These are: utilitarianism
and contractualism. The aim is to say something about each of
these approaches and to consider how they do or do not fit
some of the preoccupations of Christian social and political
thought we have been considering so far.

I shall begin, therefore, with utilitarianism and draw attention again to the words of Stanley Hauerwas about the project of liberal political thought of which utilitarianism can be regarded as an important contributor. It will be remembered that he argued that, whatever its defects, the liberal project in political theory must be seen as an extraordinary moral project that seeks to secure 'social co-operation between moral strangers short of reliance on violence'.

The emphasis on the idea of moral strangers is rather important in this context, because Jeremy Bentham, one of the founding fathers of utilitarianism and the author of one of its major texts *An Introduction to the Principles of Morals and Legislation*, was very concerned with precisely this issue and almost exactly in these terms. At the end of the eighteenth century, he saw utilitarian ethics as providing a basis for public decision-making in a society in which people had become strangers to one another.[1] The social and economic changes of the eighteenth century had uprooted people from local communities in which traditions, roles and duties were clearly known and morality was a matter of custom and habit. Now men and women flocked to towns to work in manufacturing industry. Corporate existence and tradition becomes upturned and men meet no longer in clearly defined social relationships but as strangers. According to one commentator,[2] Bentham thought that the question 'Who are you and with whom do I deal?' was the central question taxing modern society. In the light of this fundamental change in human circumstance, Bentham argued that it was necessary to produce a new, rational, objective and impersonal public ethic which could be used as the basis for decision-making. No doubt moral traditions such as Christianity did persist, but the important thing for Bentham was that they no longer existed as a shared moral tradition and inheritance which could form a coherent basis for public life.

For Bentham, utilitarianism – or seeking the greatest happiness of the greatest number – was the only way to cope with the problems posed by the fragmentation of moral traditions and of

---

[1] See Plant, *Modern Political Thought* p. 139.
[2] Manning, D. *The Mind of Jeremy Bentham* Longmans, London, 1968.

moral authority. He is quite clear about what will be the consequences for society of not agreeing on some kind of impersonal decision procedure in respect of decisions that affect society as a whole: either people will seek to impose on others their own specific moral views, even though these are no longer shared and this would be 'despotical' in his terminology; alternatively, individuals or groups would be free to pursue their own moral views, and this would mean that there would be 'as many different standards of right and wrong as there are men'.[3] While the first alternative is, for Bentham, 'despotical', the second is 'anarchical'. The important thing is to develop a second-order decision-making procedure which can account for and accept first-order moral diversity while providing an agreed principle for dealing with conflicts and problems at the public level in such a society.

The principle professed by Bentham is that of utilitarianism, that is maximising the greatest happiness of the greatest number, with happiness being judged in terms of the consequences of actions. Bentham's own formulation of the appropriate principle was rooted in his moral psychology under the terms of which he believed that the fundamental desire of man was to seek pleasure and to avoid pain. Whatever is done is done for the sake of pleasure and to avoid pain. When this does not happen, it does not mean that a different motive has supervened, rather it means that the individual has made a mistake in believing that a course of action would bring pleasure when, in fact, it does not.

For Bentham, utilitarianism was both a private and a public decision procedure. Given the nature of human motivation, individuals faced with alternative courses of action should seek that course of action which is likely to maximise that person's happiness, pleasure or utility. The same was true in the public sphere. However, as Goodin has cogently argued recently, it is perfectly possible to detach utilitarianism from this all-embracing approach of Bentham's and to regard it purely as a

---

[3] J. Bentham, *An Introduction to the Principles of Morals and Legislation* ed. W. Harrison, Blackwell, Oxford, 1967, p. 130.

principle of public decision-making.[4] However, for our purposes, the details of Bentham's psychological theory about
pleasure and pain do not matter, since it is perfectly possible to
formulate a defensible form of utilitarianism just by construing
utility as meaning 'want satisfaction', so maximising the greatest
happiness of the greatest number would come down to the
same thing as 'giving as many people as possible as much as
possible of whatever it is they happen to want'.[5] This would
then become the principle of public decision-making. The
important thing to notice at this stage in the argument
(although more complexity will occur later) is that the utilitarian
regards wants as given and incorrigible. It is not up to public
authority to criticise the wants that people have. Their wants
are what they are, and as such they are taken into the utilitarian
calculation. The principle, therefore, is to do with the aggregation of given wants, not with a moral critique of these wants.[6]

Before getting further into the complexities and controversial
features of utilitarianism, it is worth making two points. One
has to do with its impact on a Christian perspective. The
Christian has private wants and desires in relation to his/her
faith – namely, to be able to sustain it and to follow it; but, for
the utilitarian, all that is required, for example, of a Christian is
an affirmation of a public morality beyond this, namely, a
willingness to accept the legitimacy of other peoples' wants and
the willingness to put them into the aggregative mechanism of
utilitarian decision-making. As we shall see, though, this is not
as simple as it looks. In this sense, the public requirements of
utilitarianism in terms of endorsing a public morality and
framework for decision looks as though it would be much more
minimal than, for example, in relation to a theory of rights. In
this sense, it can well portray itself as the most obvious decision-
making framework and the one that makes fewest demands
upon first-order moral views, whether these be Christianity or
anything else. It embodies a minimal moral conception of
public morality.

---

[4] R. E. Goodin, 'Utilitarianism as a Public Philosophy' in *Political Theory: Tradition and Diversity* ed. A. Vincent, Cambridge University Press, 1997.
[5] See Plant *Modern Political Thought* p. 169.   [6] Ibid.

This is really the second point and it is one which, on the face of it, might be thought to secure a continuing salience for utilitarian theories. Since utilitarianism is about maximising utility, it is about the assessment of the likely consequences of different courses of action in terms of want satisfaction. Consequences seem to be clear and palpable, and thus to avoid many of the philosophical and moral complexities of a rights- or justice-based approach to these issues. This leads MacIntyre to argue:

> No matter how ultimate our disagreements on absolute principle, the very continued existence of a coherent form of social life presupposes an agreement in practice. So the need to continually secure such agreement leads to a continual growth in the influence of utilitarianism.[7]

This is so deep a reason it will turn out to be the major problem with utilitarianism. Since the whole aim of utilitarianism is to provide a mechanism for agreement in a situation of first-order moral diversity, it has to be a *one principle morality* – namely, the maximisation of utility. If it were to be more complex than this, two things would happen. First of all, it would require those holding first-order moral views to affirm a more morally complex second-order decision-making procedure, and this would diminish its effectiveness as such a procedure, since it would become more morally controversial for those holding first-order moral views – such as Christians for example.

Secondly, the existence of other principles – for example a principle of justice within utilitarianism – would run the risk that the requirements of justice within a utilitarian framework might not, in fact, then be construed according to the assumptions and requirements of utilitarianism so much as to one or other of the first-order moral theories, the diverse consequences of which utilitarianisation was supposed to be arbitrating. This would, for example, parallel the problem with natural law and rights where it has been argued that even if we concede that there is a thin, universal moral code, this will still be susceptible

---

[7] A. MacIntyre, 'Against Utilitarianism' in *Aims in Education* ed. T. B. Hollins, Manchester University Press, Manchester, 1964.

to radically different local interpretations, so that the claim that these are interpretations of the same theory becomes quite difficult to sustain. Similarly, if utilitarianism contained principles which went beyond the assessment of consequences in terms of individual want satisfaction, then these other principles would become interpreted in terms of different first-order moral conceptions and, as such, would drag utilitarianism, which is supposed to be a solution to problems of moral diversity, into precisely those selfsame problems. So the strength of utilitarianism as a source of public criteria for judgement in a morally divided society lies in its alleged simplicity.

This simplicity is, however, deceptive, and I shall take just a few examples of how utilitarianism has to be made more complex if it is to be true to moral realities while, at the same time, this increased complexity considerably weakens its force.

First of all, there is the question of wants and preferences, about which there are quite a number of complexities. Bentham took a straightforward and uncomplicated view of these things. I desire X because it is pleasant. X itself is neither right nor wrong. Right and wrong, good and bad, are defined in terms of the pleasure/pain-producing properties of actions and things. So wants have to be taken as given, as do pleasures/pains or utilities/disutilities, because there is no moral standpoint beyond desire and its satisfaction in terms of which to mount a moral critique of want/desire or their objects. John Stuart Mill, of the next generation of utilitarian thinkers, sought rather unsuccessfully to draw a distinction between higher and lower pleasures, because he disputed the hard-headed consequences of Bentham's own views that 'the quantity of pleasure being equal pushpin is as good as poetry'. However, it proved difficult to produce qualitative discriminations between pleasures/pains and their associated wants in ways that were compatible with fundamental utilitarian assumptions.

More recent utilitarians have experienced similar problems. Harsanyi, for example, has argued that utilitarianism must abandon the idea of the incorrigibility of wants and preferences, since wants and preferences may be developed as the result of erroneous factual beliefs, or careless logical analysis, or strong emotions that hinder rational choice. It may be that we have to identify (for public decision-making purposes) wants and preferences in a counter-factual way, namely, the wants and preferences someone would have if preference and want formation were to be purged of all their defects. So Harsanyi argues we have to distinguish between a person's 'true' preferences which should enter utilitarian calculation and their 'manifest' preferences which fail to meet this standard.[8] Such an approach would depend upon a conception of what the basic interests of an agent are, not defining those interests purely in terms of existing wants or preferences or what the agent is currently interested in. Similarly, Goodin argues for what he calls welfare utilitarianism, because we have to recognise that 'people sometimes would derive satisfaction in a way that they do not presently recognise'.[9] It is part of Goodin's argument that welfare utilitarianism is consistent with want-based utilitarianism because promoting peoples' welfare interests (which *ex hypothesi* they may not presently recognise) ordinarily gives rise to 'higher levels of preference satisfaction in the future'. Nevertheless, however plausible the case is for a move away from preference utilitarianism, it causes problems as a form of public decision-making, since both Harsanyi's and Goodin's proposals do require those with first-order moral conceptions to affirm a considerably more complex form of public morality, namely, one which contains an account of basic human interests or needs, which may not be recognised by the agents to whom they are ascribed. Those with strong first-order beliefs may well not be prepared to conscribe to a form of public morality which contains 'thicker' and morally more controversial notions than just want or preference satisfaction. In this sense, while it may, in some respects, be plausible to move away from straightforward want satisfaction, nevertheless this weakens the utilitarian claim to be a relatively uncontroversial way of avoiding a criterionless society.

---

[8] J. C. Harsanyi, *Morality and the Theory of Rational Behaviour* in *Utilitarianism and Beyond* ed. A. K. Sen and B. Williams, Cambridge University Press, 1982.
[9] Goodin, 'Utilitarianism as a Public Philosophy' p. 74, see also pp. 56 and 10.

The same point applies to a further issue about preferences. Take, for example, this passage from Harsanyi:

Some preferences which may well be their true preferences under my definition, must be altogether excluded from our social utility function. In particular we must exclude all anti-social preferences, such as sadism, envy, resentment and malice. Utilitarian ethics make us all members of the same moral community . . . that part of our personality which harbours these anti-social feelings must be excluded from membership.[10]

In a footnote to the article, Harsanyi argues that 'a really satisfactory theory of legitimate and illegitimate interests would be a major step forward in utilitarian moral philosophy'. This is precisely the point, but, in making the theory more complex, it will make it more difficult to legitimate to groups with first-order moral conceptions (such as Christians), particularly if utilitarianism is treated as a method of social and political decision-making rather than as an account of the whole of morality. It seems, as Amartya Sen says in his comment on Harsanyi's argument, that Harsanyi is relying upon some conception of the social good to act as a basis for a critique of some sorts of preferences, but in the simple utilitarianism which, as MacIntyre argues, made it salient for a morally divided society, such a conception of the good was given by preferences, not from a standpoint independent of the aggregation of preferences.[11] Indeed, the point could be put even more sharply in relation to Harsanyi's argument in that, while he says that utilitarianism makes us members of the same moral community – and this is its whole point in a morally divided society – at the same time he seems to be trading illegitimately on not just a conception of the good, but some antecedent sense of the moral community to rule out certain kinds of preferences. If this is so, how can utilitarianism be a precondition of moral community if it has to draw from such a notion to make itself coherent? All of which suggests that thicker moral conceptions are needed to make utilitarianism coherent, while at the very same time the thickness of these conceptions will make it progressively less

---

[10] Harsanyi, 'Morality and the Theory of Rational Behaviour'.
[11] MacIntyre, 'Against Utilitarianism'.

acceptable to these specific moral communities within society which have their own thick form of morality.

A final point could be made about utilitarianism and justice. It has been a constant feature of criticism of utilitarianism as a public philosophy that it lacks a conception of justice. That is to say, it is concerned solely with the aggregative consequences of courses of action. Will policy X procure more utility (want satisfaction) than policy Y? If aggregation is all that matters, then issues of justice are ignored – for example, policy X will maximise satisfaction for the majority, while it may cause a good deal of poverty for a small minority. For the aggregative utilitarianism of Bentham, the choice would be clear. As a single principle morality, you have to choose policy X because it maximises the greatest happiness of the greatest number and the suffering of the minority does not outweigh that. That is to say, considerations of social justice have no part to play. Justice is not an independent value. This has been found to be unsatisfactory by utilitarians who have sought, as John Stuart Mill did, to develop a utilitarian theory of justice in chapter 5 of his essay 'Utilitarianism'. This is a complex issue and I do not wish to make more of it in this context. The important point, though, is much the same as the arguments in relation to preference, namely that, while the incorporation of some conception of justice seems to many of its critics to be central to restoring moral plausibility to utilitarianism, from the point of view of utilitarianism any conception of justice has to be interpreted in terms of want regarding utility maximising considerations. Justice is not an independent ideal regarding principle. Let me make it clear what this actually means in practice. Take, for instance, two possible 'thick' principles of social justice: distribution according to need and distribution according to desert. Readers will recall from chapter 8 that, while there may be an uncontroversial *concept* of justice: to each his/ her due, nevertheless, to be meaningful, this concept has to be further specified into a thicker (and more disputable) conception such as need or desert. From a utilitarian view, if the principles of need or desert cannot be brought into a commensurable framework, then we are left with Bentham's anarchical moral diversity. Hence, for the utilitarian, it is absolutely vital that justice should not be seen as independent of want regarding utilitarianism, and it has to be interpreted in terms of utility or want satisfaction. So need, for example, should be understood in terms of a set of wants of a particular urgency or primacy – as conditions of having other wants satisfied. Desert would also become a want regarding conception in the sense that, if I am deprived of something which I believe that I deserve, then my utility function will decline. Desert and need are not separate principles, but, rather, each is interpretable in a want-regarding way and, as such, the question of moral diversity and agonistic politics does not arise because both conceptions can be made commensurable in terms of want satisfaction and public-policy decisions made on that basis.

Nevertheless, from within specific moral communities, and this would be particularly true of Christianity, there will be embedded quite substantial notions of justice which draw upon the narratives and traditions of those belief communities, and a second-order theory of justice within utilitarianism of the sort which I have outlined, even if one could be developed, might well be incompatible at very many points with the *thick* moralities of first-order moral communities. That is to say that, within these moralities, there may be resistance to the idea that principles of justice can be reduced to want satisfaction. One possible conclusion to draw from all of this would be a claim that it is just not possible to create some kind of neutral or procedural second-order morality which can then provide the basis of a public culture and public criteria for resolving disputes at the first-order level.[12] To be developed enough to deal with the moral complexities, such a second-order morality will find its moral conceptions embodying, as they do, minimal moral conceptions running up against thick and rich but disputed conceptions in first-order moral communities. A possible Christian response here would be to argue that utilitarianism needs a theory of justice to be plausible, but that there is no such account of justice which can transcend the meaning

---

[12] This is precisely Hauerwas' critique in *The Peaceable Kingdom* and *A Community of Character*.

that justice has within particular moral communities and the narratives that sustain them.

I want now to turn to another issue to do with the want-regarding nature of utilitarianism which will be of particular concern to the religious believer invited, as it were, to endorse utilitarianism as a reasonable basis for public policy in a society marked by moral pluralism. As I have said, utilitarianism is based upon the idea of preferences or want satisfaction where wants are treated as a basic doctrine – as given and incorrigible. So there is an obvious issue about the scope of wants or preferences. As a particular type of religious believer, I may, for example, have preferences about how I should live my life, let us say, in regard to sexual relations. I may believe not only that only heterosexual relations are morally legitimate and that is my preference for my life; but also I may believe that homo-sexual relationships are, in fact, morally wrong and that, as such, I do not want others to be able to indulge in such relation-ships and that they should be criminalised. That is to say, I have *internal* preferences about how I should live my own life, but I also have *external* preferences about how other people should live theirs. Given that, for the utilitarian, there is no moral reality beyond preferences and their aggregation, does this mean that, if the majority of people have the religious prefer-ences that I have in respect of other peoples' sexuality, then it is legitimate to legislate based on the external preferences of the majority about how others should live? On a utilitarian view, there could be no case for resisting such a majoritarian want-regarding approach in terms of some external moral vantage-point. If external preferences are to be discounted at all, then it has to be in terms of some kind of morally neutral procedural principle.

The issues at stake here have been brought into sharp focus by Professor Dworkin, one of the leading liberal thinkers of the past thirty years.[13]

Recall that an internal preference refers to my own enjoy-ment of some goods or opportunities; an external preference is

---

[13] Dworkin, *Taking Rights Seriously.*

a preference for the assignment or the denial of goods or opportunities to others. In Dworkin's view, it is illegitimate to count external preferences in political decision-making, and this is so, as it seems, for two reasons. The first is that to count external preferences is to indulge in a form of *double counting* in the sense that my own personal preferences and my external preferences are counted. The second is that to count my external preferences, given that they relate to you and your goods and opportunities, is not to treat you as an object of equal concern and respect because *my* judgement about *your* goods is being weighed along with yours – this is inherently paternalist.

It is very important to appreciate exactly why Dworkin resorts to this device of distinguishing between internal and external preferences. If he is to be consistent in his liberalism, he cannot discount one set of preferences in terms of their *objects*: for example, if I wanted to live in an all-white society because this would presuppose some substantive view of the good. If preferences are to be discounted, it must be in terms of either a formal procedure – as in the idea of double counting – or of a foundational value such as equal concern and respect, which he sees as antecedent to other conceptions of the good.

The issues at stake here for the coherence of liberal theory are very deep. If we adopt what might be called a subjective view of the good, which may be based on a philosophical critique of moral realism and objectivity, or which may just embody sociological reflection on the diversity of values in a modern developed society, then in politics it would seem that government should only value what individuals themselves value if it is to be neutral over conceptions of the good. To rule out one set of preferences or certain aspects of preferences a priori either has to depend upon a theory about what good or appropriate preferences are, and this is inconsistent with liberalism, or, alternatively, has to rule out some preferences on procedural rather than substantive moral grounds.

Some liberal theorists, notably Albert Weale,[14] have seemed

---

[14] A. Weale, *Political Theory and Social Policy* Macmillan, London, 1983.

to suggest that the issue can be solved within a morally subjectivist position without recourse to Dworkin' procedural response in terms of double counting. This argument proceeds as follows. We can imagine two sorts of external preferences. There can be altruistic preferences – supportive preferences where A, in addition to preferences about his own life, also has preferences in regard to B's life *which B also has* and which make a claim to be counted politically. At the opposite extreme, there can be negative or hostile external preferences, where A has preferences about his own life but also a hostile preference in relation to B and his preferences.

Both of these positions can be illustrated with reference to proposals to reform the law on issues of personal morality. Let us assume in the case of both altruistic and hostile preferences that B is a homosexual and that there is at the moment a repressive homosexual law which prohibits sexual acts between homosexuals. In the case of altruistic preferences, A (who is heterosexual) has an altruistic external preference for B: that is, he would like homosexuals to be able to indulge in the sexual practices of their taste, and this is also B's preference for himself. In the case of a hostile external preference, A wants to maintain the legal sanction against private homosexual acts.

If we were to adopt the double-counting reason proposed by Dworkin for ruling out external preferences of any sort both altruistic or hostile, then, if homosexuals, i.e. all the B's in society, were in a small minority, and government could only count internal preferences, and since the reform of the law would only be an internal preference for the B group, it is difficult to see how the law in a liberal society which discounted external preferences on procedural grounds would ever be reformed. At the same time, this would be rather paradoxical because the liberal state is supposed to be as neutral as possible between conceptions of the good. Of course, Dworkin's obvious counter-argument here would be that the initial existence of the law is illegitimate because it involved antecedently counted external preferences on the part of those who wished to prohibit homosexuality. However, is there any other way of dealing with the issue without recourse to the idea of double counting which, at the same time, does not involve taking a particular stand on the conception of the good?

This issue has an importance outside Dworkin's own particular concerns and has exercised other liberal theorists of a more utilitarian persuasion, the basis of whose views will be discussed in the next chapter. For example, Samuel Brittan argues[15] that government should disregard what he calls 'negative interdependence effects'; that is, in his view, those external preferences which have a negative impact on liberty. If these are not discounted, then, Brittan argues, they will yield results which are incompatible with liberal theory. However, in saying this, Brittan seems to come very close to saying that it is not the *externality* of the preference which is objectionable, but its *content*, and this, it might be thought, involves taking a stand on a particular conception of the good. This may seem cogent on its own terms, but, if it is accepted, it would seem to undermine at least an element in the liberal assumption that, if preferences are to be discounted, it should be in terms of a formal procedure rather than a judgement about the moral content of the preference.

The same point comes out very clearly in Harsanyi's contribution cited earlier, in which he argues in favour of excluding what he calls antisocial or, in the terminology above, hostile preferences, such as sadism, envy, resentment and malice. Again, the argument seems to be in terms of the *content* of the preferences rather than the form. Weale, however, develops an interesting argument which is rather different from Dworkin's double-counting one. Whereas Dworkin seems to be in favour of discounting *all* external preferences, both supportive and hostile because to count them would be double counting, Weale argues that supportive preferences can be counted and hostile ones discounted in a way which does still embody a formal rather than a substantive moral principle and can thus be consistent in the liberal assumptions. If we combine the principles of equality of respect with a subjective theory of the good, it would seem that supportive preferences can be counted

---

[15] S. Brittan, *The Role and Limits of Government* Temple Smith, London, 1983, pp. 38ff.

politically if A's supportive preference for B's interests accurately reflect B's own views of his interests. If all A is doing is helping to further B's projects and conception of the good, A is *not* claiming the superiority of his view of the good over B's, which would be inconsistent with liberal assumptions. Of course, if A's preferences for B are not, in fact, in B's view in his interests, then this would be a claim on the part of A to have a superior view of B's good than B has. This would be an exercise of unjustified moral paternalism (at least if B is an adult), which is inconsistent with liberal views. However, in Weale's view, hostile preferences can be discounted when they are held one sidedly by A against B, because this would simply mean that A's view of the good is superior to B's and this would be incompatible with liberal assumptions about the factors which can count in public policy.

This approach seems to me more consistent with a liberal approach than the radical discounting of external preferences on the basis of double counting endorsed by Dworkin. It should be noted, however, that Dworkin argues that the best way to deal with external preferences is, in fact, to secure a set of rights embodying a principle of equal concern and respect which will act as trumps against any attempt to maximise welfare, counting external preferences. Certainly, the counting of the external preferences of, say, a religious majority against the interests of a minority has been a powerful driver in respect of the development of theories of rights, as we saw earlier.

There is, however, also a problem about the idea of rights within utilitarianism from the standpoint of religious belief. Some religious believers might, for example, want to argue that, because their beliefs are part of their identity in the same way as race or religion, then they have a basic interest in having these beliefs recognised and respected. Thus it might be argued there ought to be special protection for religious freedom, and also possibly legal protection for religious belief from ridicule and blasphemy, in the same way as we might recognise race in a liberal society as being a similar basic interest giving rise to rights to protection from discrimination and expression of hatred. Bentham was a clear critic of the idea of rights believing that they were 'nonsense on stilts', and one can see at least one good reason from what has gone before why utilitarians might be wary of rights, and this is because part of the appeal of utilitarianism is its simplicity as a single-principle morality. If it comes to recognise other values such as rights, then these are either independent of utility and hence an additional principle that adds to complexity, or rights are reinterpreted into the language of utility as being to do with the publication of basic interests without which other utilities could not be effectively pursued. This was J. S. Mill's view in chapter 5 of *Utilitarianism*. For Mill, there are basic interests of human beings: physical nutriment and security of persons and possessions. These are rights because they are basic interests. They are, however, justified on utilitarian grounds: protecting these interests as rights will maximise utility. However, while we all share these basic interests, such an argument does *not* give any special recognition to religious interests. If one could claim that ridicule of religion either did infringe security of person and possession or was likely to develop into this, as could have been argued, for example, in Weimar Germany in the context of the Jews, then there could be grounds for protection in law. It is however very important to recognise that the justification for such protection is *not* because special status is given to religious belief, but, rather, religious protection is justified only when it is via a more basic and shared human interest in security.

So there are difficulties in a religious believer endorsing utilitarianism as a principled approach to public policy in a situation of moral diversity. Issues of the nature of justice, the motive of utility maximisation, the non-ideal regarding nature of utilitarianism and its rather radical moral subjectivism and individualism all pose deep concerns for the religious believer who wants to be able to find good reasons within his/her religious morality for supporting a procedure of public and civil policy choice in a situation of acknowledged diversity in conceptions of the good. At the heart of the issue, from which a good deal of the rest flows, is the idea that all human goods are to be seen wholly and solely as objects of desire and preference. In this conception, there is the same kind of distancing between the self and its ends as we have already seen and, as we shall see again, the narrative theologian and communitarian political thinker reject a liberal way of conceiving these problems. At the same time, the utilitarian rejects any idea of natural law as yielding a rich account of human flourishing. Human flourishing consists in want satisfaction with the context of the wants being incorrigible and as subjective.

I now want to discuss briefly an alternative approach, namely, the idea of a social contract as a device capable of generating rules and principles to guide society in a situation of first-order moral diversity. Although the contract tradition is long, salient and subtle, I shall concentrate on John Rawls' *A Theory of Justice*, partly because it raises in a very clear way the issue of the unity of society and partly because problems in the argument of the book, at least as it was perceived, led Rawls to set out his views in a rather different manner in *Political Liberalism*, which will form the starting-point for the final chapter based on how the problem of social unity in the context of moral diversity is brought into focus by modern political philosophers.

There is no doubt that the contract model in Rawls' book addresses the central issue about how it is possible to secure agreement about the principles which should govern the basic structure of society against a background of moral diversity. No doubt members of particular moral communities, from their own point of view, might like to see a society which embodies institutional arrangements which reflect their own specific conception of the good. So, for example, Christians might like to live in a society in which Christian values shaped the way of life in that society. Nevertheless, this would not create a coherent or just society in which the fact of conscientious disagreement has to be respected. Rawls' strategy, so far as the basic principles which should govern the basic structure of society is concerned, is to put the *right* before the *good*. He believes that it is possible to secure agreement on principles to regulate society which could be agreed to by persons whatever their conception of the good. The mechanism for securing this agreement is the contractual model of rational deliberation about principles behind a veil of ignorance. Rawls argues that two principles should determine the basic structure of society – that is to say, the sort of rights that it should recognise and the type of institutions it should have. These two prerequisites are:

1 that each person should have the most extensive basic liberties consistent with equal liberties for others.
2 that social and economic inequalities should be arranged so that they are (i) to the advantage of the worse off and (ii) attached to positions open to fair equality of opportunity.

The legitimacy of the principles is shown by Rawls from the fact that they would be arrived at in a hypothetical contract by rational individuals who were behind a veil of ignorance about themselves and their situation. So, why is the contractual model necessary as a basis for legitimising basic principles of social and political organisation? The answer to this is given by reflecting on the facts of moral diversity (without which there would be no need for such prerequisites). We do differ in our view of what gives value to life; we differ in our attitudes and in our interests. We also differ in our power and our capacity to articulate and argue for a point of view. Hence, if social and political principles were to be the subject of negotiation against the background of all this diversity and existing inequality, the resulting agreement would reflect the impact of these forms of diversity and inequality. To put it bluntly, the interests of the rich and powerful would be likely to prevail. It is necessary, in Rawls' view, to make sure that the basic principles of society create the basis for rational and democratic consent. If we are to have free and uncoerced consent to the basic principles of social and political order, they cannot arise out of a negotiation of this sort. We have to find a way of neutralising personal interests and antecedent inequalities of power. This is done by the contract model and the veil of ignorance. On the model, we are to assume that individuals have to deliberate in the light of only general knowledge about the principles which should govern society. They are to know nothing about their own personal circumstances: their gender, the nature of their genetic endowments, their position in society or even to which generation they belong. They have to reason in a wholly general way about the nature of rules without being able to judge in advance whether they, as individuals, are likely to be beneficiaries of, or, for that matter, disadvantaged by, the choices they make. Thus this model of a general hypothetical contract behind a veil of ignorance is an attempt to spell out in some detail what would have to be the case for us to claim that a set of rules for the basic structure of society was fair and impartial. It is Rawls' contention that it is perfectly possible to construct a determinate line of reasoning which would be followed in such circumstances, and that the line of reasoning would lead to the two principles I have stated. Since these could be assented to perfectly rationally without knowing whether an individual would be a beneficiary or not, so the contract/veil of ignorance device is an attempt to neutralise particular interests, to neutralise attempts to make one conception of the good dominate over others while at the same time producing rich and determinate principles to cover the basic structure of society. In this sense, therefore, it puts the right before the good, and underlying its strategy is the idea that it is possible in a situation of moral diversity still to produce determinate principles of social and political order to which all, whatever their conception of the good may turn out to be, could give rational and uncoerced consent.

Rawls regards his theory as significantly better in this regard than utilitarianism. Utilitarianism had the same overall aim, but, as I have argued, from the standpoint of first-order morality it can be regarded as being defective, and, indeed, if it presents itself as an account of the nature of first-order morality as well as a system of public choice, then it is very clearly defective. For Rawls, utilitarianism does not embody, as his own theory does, a principle of respect for persons, because utilitarianism can countenance the sacrifice of the welfare of some for others. As we saw, utilitarians have tried to overcome this problem by invoking their own theory of justice, but in Rawls' view this does not work.

So, Rawls wishes to avoid a situation in which politics is reduced to bargaining against a background of inequality and moral diversity and the theory of the contract and the veil of ignorance in his model for achieving this. It is not my intention to spend time discussing whether Rawls' account of his two principles can be defended in the way that he believes it can from his contract model. Rather, I want to explain some of the issues at stake in the model and the strategy which lies behind it. The model has been severely criticised by broadly communitarian thinkers such as Michael Sandel, Alasdair MacIntyre and Michael Walzer and, as I said very early in the book, there is a clear parallel between some of the views of communitarian thinkers and narrative theologians. So if we wanted to work out what we thought would be the response of this group of theologians to a political project such as Rawls, then it would be as well to attend to the arguments of the communitarian thinkers. This is also important because Rawls has responded to the communitarian critique of his work by publishing a series of subsequent articles, culminating in a more recent book, *Political Liberalism*, in which he has tried to make his position more consonant with the position of communitarian thinkers.

I want to concentrate on two features of the communitarian critique which are important in themselves, but are also salient to narrative theology. The first has to do with the concept of the person utilised in the theory; the second has to do with the whole strategy of identifying and justifying general principles of the sort Rawls defends, that is to say, the principles of equal liberty and the difference principle in relation to justified inequality, or, more generally, asserting the priority of the right over the good.

As I have said, Rawls accepted the fact that people have radically different conceptions of the good and what gives value to life, but beyond this Rawls also has an account to give about how the individual self relates to the conception of the good so entertained. Conceptions of the good, for Rawls, are *chosen*. The individual always has the capacity to stand back from a commitment to a moral conception, criticise it and reject it. For Rawls:

We should not attempt to give form to our life by first looking to the good independently defined. It is not our aims that primarily reveal our nature but rather the principles that we would acknowledge to govern the background conditions under which these aims are to be found and the manner in which they are to be pursued . . . the self is prior to the ends which are affirmed by it; even a dominant end must be chosen from among numerous possibilities.[16]

The essence of the self is not to be found in the attachment of a person to his or her substantive goals, but rather in the autonomy which allows the person to choose one set of ends or one conception of the good over another. This is closely related to Rawls' concern with the right having priority over the good. Because we are autonomous agents who hold different conceptions of the good, this means that justice, the conditions which have to obtain to enable people to pursue their conceptions of the good, weighs with us as something more important than any other good we might entertain: 'The main idea is that given this priority of right, the choice of our conception of the good is framed within definite limits. The essential unity of the self is provided by the conception of right.'[17] So the idea of a self which is prior to its ends, which stands in an autonomous relationship with these ends, not only seems to be central to Rawls' concern with the nature of right, but also is the basis for the priority of the right over the good to the extent to which the right cannot be traded off against any good however compelling the good in question might be thought to be.[18] So Rawls' notion of the person has a clear link with his overall strategy in regard to justice, as Michael Sandel,[19] one of Rawls' most vigorous communitarian critics, makes clear. He argues that in the same way as Rawls' theory will not accept that basic rules can be arrived at by bargaining and accommodating between existing interests, so too, it cannot accept as an account of the self one which is situated in relation to interests and goals. An autonomous self is crucial to determining the nature of justice independently of a particular conception of the good, as is the contract model and the veil of ignorance. This point could hardly be more critical in relation to basic communitarian and narrative critiques of the liberal project. Whereas, for both the communitarian and the narrative theologians such as Hauerwas and Lindbeck, the self is formed and constituted by being embedded in practice, tradition and narrative, in contrast, for

---

[16] Rawls, *A Theory of Justice* p. 560.   [17] Ibid. p. 563.
[18] Ibid. p. 31.   [19] Sandel, *Liberalism and the Limits of Justice*.

Rawls, 'the essential unity of the self is already provided by the conception of right' – so, in a sense, the Rawlsian strategy reverses the narrative perspective and in Sandel's words, 'conceives the unity of the self as something antecedently established'.[20] Rawls is very forthright about this point, and the issue at stake in asserting the priority of the right over the good could hardly be put more starkly than in the following passage:

> The desire to express our nature as a free and rational being can be fulfilled only by acting on the principles of right and justice as having first priority; therefore in order to realise our nature we have no alternative but to plan to preserve our sense of justice as governing our other aims. This sentiment cannot be fulfilled if it is compromised and balanced against other ends as but one desire above the rest. What we cannot do is express our nature by following a plan that views the sense of justice as but one desire to be weighed against others.[21]

The issues at stake here between Rawls' emphasis upon autonomy and an adherence to the priority of the right above the good compared with communitarian and narrative assumptions of the good and virtue could hardly be more pronounced. For the communitarian/narrative thinker, the self is situated and attached to moral conceptions rooted in narrative, practices, community and types of relationship which flow from them.

Given this contrast with the narrative and communitarian tradition, it is not surprising that Hauerwas refers to Rawls' book as 'an a-historical approach to political theory, as the self is alienated from its history' and, furthermore, in a comment which hardly fits with the passages quoted from Rawls about the link between the self and the priority of the right over the good, he argues that what is missing is 'any suggestion that a theory of justice is ultimately dependent as a view of the good; *or that justice is as much a category for individuals as for societies*'.[22] He argues further that:

> such a view can no longer provide a place for the classical perspectives' insistence on the development of a virtuous people. From the

---

[20] Ibid. p. 21. [21] Rawls, *A Theory of Justice* pp. 574–5.
[22] Hauerwas, *A Community of Character* p. 83.

classical perspective judgements about virtues and goods are inter-dependent, since the good is known only by observing how a virtuous man embodies it.[23]

So, given this characterisation of the Christian ethical tradition Hauerwas would argue that Rawls' whole strategy is wrong, and that the idea that one could develop a conception of justice to govern the basic structure of society by, in some ways abstracting from what on the narrative view gives people a sense of identity and moral virtue and, indeed, a sense of self, is a mistake.[24]

The problem with this position though, is that, given that we live in societies marked by different narratives and different moral traditions, how are we to resolve conflicts between different traditions and points of view? Not in Rawls' way in the narrative thinkers' view, because he requires us to see ourselves in ways that the narrative thinker believes are untrue to our moral experience. But what is the alternative? One is to adopt the Hauerwasian view that the Christian should live 'out of control' and not worry unduly about whether or not there is a public moral framework to resolve differences. The Christian has to follow his/her own lights and the church has to 'be the Church' living its own social ethic. It is not called upon to contribute to the creation of a public ethic since, as we have seen, most of these ethics could only be constructed in ways that are incompatible with the basic assumptions of narrative thought. However, this prospect could equally be seen as being rather bleak with no overall moral resources to bind society together, and this would leave us, as Yoder describes it, with 'No non-provincial general community'.

So much for issues about the nature of the self posed by Rawls' argument. I want, however, to pay some attention to Walzer's critique of Rawls' *A Theory of Justice*, partly because Walzer is a kind of communitarian and partly because we looked at his work on prophecy and political theory earlier in this book and, to some extent, his own commitments to plural-ism and particularism might be a way of addressing some of the

[23] Ibid. p. 217.
[24] Hauerwas, *The Peaceable Kingdom* chs. 1 and 2.

issues raised but not resolved (or perhaps not even confronted) by Hauerwas. Walzer is as concerned as Hauerwas by a Rawlsian strategy in political theory. He sees such an approach as putting too much distance between the theorist and the society or context the theory is addressing. Rather than developing some kind of general theory which in any case will always need differentiated and local interpretation, Walzer wants us to focus on the values and the social meanings which goods have in particular societies. Rawls' theory, at least in *A Theory of Justice*, seems overly universalist, and Rawls certainly refers to 'Archimedean points' and a perspective *sub specie aeternitatis*. Walzer, however, wishes to displace universalist political philosophy by social criticism which is much more like prophecy, as his essay on prophecy[25] makes clear. The prospect starts from within a society, with its traditions, values and social practices and, in the case of ancient Israel, with a sense of covenant and what this implies. These are the resources for political thinking: meanings and values given within a particular culture, not general or universalist considerations. Thus far, Walzer's critique of a Rawlsian position would parallel that of the narrative theologian, but Walzer is interested in justice, as Rawls is, so within his perspective, which as I have said could even be shared by a narrative thinker, how does he conceive the issue of justice? His answer is given in his book *Spheres of Justice*, which is a defence of pluralism against what he sees as the over-restrictive and sociologically insensitive approach adopted by thinkers like Rawls. Rawls derives two principles to govern the distribution of resources and opportunities, benefits and burdens in society. Walzer argues that this is too one-dimensional. Goods have social meanings which are specific to particular societies with their differing narratives and traditions. This has two implications for a theory of justice and for public morality. The first is that we should not expect any sort of universal theory which is supposed to determine the nature of public rules for societies irrespective of their narratives and traditions. Principles have to relate to how people in different societies under-

---

[25] Walzer, *Interpretation and Social Criticism*.

stand the nature of the goods relating to the operation of such principles. So, political thinking has to be particularistic, like, as we saw, Walzer's account of prophecy was. The same point, however, applies within society. It is not just that the social meanings of goods differ between societies, but that they differ within societies. Goods are not all the same; they are embedded in different contexts of meaning formed by different narratives and histories. In the same way as we should not expect trans-social, universalist accounts of justice, so we should not expect one set of principles to apply to the distribution of goods within society, since these goods carry different social meanings and we need to devise principles, rules and conventions about distribution which are relevant to the particular social meanings that goods have. This leads Walzer to the idea of spheres of justice within which spheres of goods with similar social meanings exist. Principles of distribution apply differently between spheres. We would not expect political office to be distributed on the same basis as health care. Equally, these principles, conventions or rules are not philosophically grounded; rather they are regarded as being appropriate against the background of the meaning which goods have within the different spheres. Different narrative traditions and the communities that embody these will conceive of goods in different ways and the social meanings of goods will be very dispersed.

Walzer rejects the Rawlsian conception of the self as set out in *A Theory of Justice* for much the same reasons as Hauerwas. Our identities are not constructed philosophically through some notion of autonomy; they are discovered in the contexts, traditions and narratives of which we are a part. Equally, principles regulating the distribution of benefits and burdens are not generated philosophically, but arise out of, and are intelligible only within, the modes of social life which give those benefits and burdens their particular meaning. So, against what he would see as Rawls' one-dimensional egalitarianism – equal basic liberty plus justified inequalities – Walzer proposes a theory of complex equality. The aim of complex equality is to challenge the growing domination of goods from one particular sphere over others – money, for example, and the way it colonises and takes over other spheres undermining the social meanings of other goods like service and care. Equality, in this sense, is about constantly challenging this tendency for one sphere to take a dominant position over other spheres. This challenge, though, is not rooted in some external philosophical argument, but in internal criticism of the sort that prophecy, in Walzer's understanding of it, is. (Recall that he rejects the idea defended by other biblical scholars that prophets such as Amos and Isaiah held to universalist natural-law views.)

If there is a political theory that might be thought to be consistent with narrative theology, this might be thought to be it except, of course, that Christian political thought itself, whether narratively rooted or not, may not be pluralist in this sense. It may not want to see itself as one narrative tradition among others with no position of dominance being allowed. Even in a narrative view of theology, there can be a commitment to universalism, namely, that the narrative of the Christian faith is the correct one and that, if it can achieve a position of dominance by conversion, it should do so.[26] In one sense, then, Walzer's account of the nature of the self and the relationship between goods and narratives/traditions are all consistent with a narrative view of the Christian faith; his complex egalitarianism, however, may not be so consistent, because Walzer has not explained why adherents of different narratives, traditions and this different sense of social goods in a society should accept a position in which they would not seek a dominant position for their narratively formed view of the good. Here we are straight back to the Rawlsian dilemma. It looks as though we do need certain kinds of principles to govern the relationships between different spheres/narratives/traditions. The narrative/particularist cannot allow that there could be a philosophical strategy for arriving at such a set of principles. Either they exist implicitly in the culture of the society, or they do not. If they do not, they cannot be invented or constructed. From a Rawlsian liberal perspective on Walzer, it looks as if, to quote Paul Kelly: 'A just constitutional settlement on the basis

---

[26] See Hauerwas, *The Peaceable Kingdom* p. 6. Also Lindbeck, *The Nature of Doctrine* p. 118.

of second order impartiality provides the best security against any distribution of advantage transforming its monopoly of wealth or political power into a permanent system of domination.'[27] For the narrative/pluralist, such a settlement is impossible to achieve on abstract or political theory grounds; if it exists, it must already be implicit in the culture of the society.

It would appear, then, that neither utilitarianism nor contractarian ethics could provide a form of justification for liberal institutions or for the kinds of reasons which might underpin policy deliberation within these institutions. Although they are radically different from one another, they pose a similar dilemma for the religious believer. In the context of utilitarianism, the religious believer is obliged to conceive of his or her beliefs as preferences or the objects of desire, and to recast any views that might follow from these beliefs about, for example, justice and rights into the language and conceptions of utility and its maximisation. It also requires the believer to accept that his or her beliefs may be made commensurable with those of others for public decision-making through the medium of utility. Rawlsian contractarianism is likely to be regarded with suspicion by religious believers because it requires that they do not see religious beliefs as constitutive of identity while, at the same time, construing identity in terms of rational autonomy which may not rank high or even be recognised at all within the religions community. The veil of ignorance is an abstraction from the thick identities, communities and moral traditions which actually give people particular reasons for action. So, can these be a form of justification of liberal politics which does not, however indirectly, invoke metaphysical claims and which could provide a justification both for the framework of liberal politics and for the scope of public reason within it, while preserving the integrity of the different moral communities and their diverse conceptions of the good within liberal society?

[27] P. Kelly, 'Contractarian Social Justice' in *Social Justice: from Hume to Walzer* ed. D. Boucher and P. Kelly, Routledge, London, 1998, p. 191.

CHAPTER 12

The civil community, the religious community and the unity of society

Can two walk together, except they are agreed?   (Amos)

Concering the problem of arriving at a global ethic, the theologian Hans Küng argues: 'For today's pluralistic society, ethical consensus means the necessary agreement in fundamental ethical standards which despite all differences of political, social or religious direction can serve as the smallest possible basis for human living and acting together.'[1]

Küng's focus is a global ethics which, in a sense, embodies the issues of this book writ large, but, nevertheless, this point is applicable within societies as well as between them. So, too, is his differentiation between a consensus on a thin morality that limits itself to some fundamental demands and a consensus which, he argues, is not necessary in respect of culturally differentiated thick morality that 'necessarily contains numerous specific cultural elements'.[2] However, this way of bisecting the moral universe is a very tricky business, as we have seen, but is another reaffirmation of the vexed issue of the relationship between the universal and particular. It is, however, in the context of consensus rather than truth, or a political conception of political morality rather than a metaphysical one, at which Rawls' later thought in *Political Liberalism* becomes important together with the defence of this later perspective by Richard Rorty. In this later work, Rawls does want to argue that the kind of political order he suggested in *A*

---

[1] H. Küng, *A Global Ethic for a Global Politics and Economics* trans. J. Bowden, SCM Press, London, 1997, p. 95.
[2] Ibid. p. 94.

Theory of Justice was, in fact, to be understood against the background of the political culture of Western democratic societies, and that it is misconceived if it is understood to have a universalist or metaphysical message to impart. In so far as the critique of communitarians such as Sandel can be described, as it has by Rorty, as being centred on the claim that 'one cannot escape history in this way', the direction of Rawls' later work is to stress that the reasons he wishes to give in social and political philosophy are not addressed on metaphysical grounds to humanity in general (despite the clear tenor of parts of *A Theory of Justice*) but to members of a particular historical community, namely, a liberal democratic society of the sort that the USA is.[3] In *Political Liberalism* Rawls identifies the central issue in a way that mirrors that of *A Theory of Justice*:

How is it possible that there may exist over time a stable and just society of free and equal citizens profoundly divided by reasonable though incommensurable religious, philosophical and moral doctrines . . . How is it possible that deeply opposed though reasonable comprehensive doctrines may live together and all affirm the political conception of a constitutional regime? What is the structure and content of a political conception that can gain the support of such an overlapping consensus? These are among the questions that political liberalism tries to answer.[4]

So the challenge in relation to Christian belief, which is in some forms a reasonable doctrine in Rawls' conception of it, is how far is it possible to construct a set of arrangements which would be acceptable to people from within such different and incommensurable but comprehensive doctrines? What is clear from *Political Liberalism* in a way that was not clear in *A Theory of Justice* is that Rawls does not himself see these institutional arrangements as being rooted in some additional moral and metaphysical theory of the self and its ends to which adherents of comprehensive doctrines would have to assent. Indeed, as we

---

[3.] See J. Rawls in 'Kantian Constructivism in Moral Theory' *Journal of Philosophy*, 77 (1980): 'What justifies a conception of justice is not its being true to an order antecedent to us, but its congruence with our deeper understanding of ourselves and our aspirations, and our realisation that, given our history and the traditions embedded in our public life, it is the most reasonable doctrine for us,' p. 579.

[4.] Rawls, *Political Liberalism* p. xviii.

have seen, narrative and communitarian critics have argued vigorously that such a meta-theory would not command assent from within narratively formed comprehensive communities – such as the Christian churches – because it is argued that the conceptions of the self and its ends which appeared to be and claimed to be postulated in *A Theory of Justice* seem false to the experience of members of such narratively formed communities. So the argument of *Political Liberalism* presents itself in a different way, as a political doctrine and not a metaphysical one. It does not, on the face of it, claim that the fundamental moral identity of persons is to be found in their capacity for autonomy, for example. In this sense, the justification of liberal political institutions would not depend upon ideals which would be controversial within different moral communities within liberal society.

It is worth just dwelling on this point for a moment because, as we have seen, it is very important. Sandel's account of Rawls' earlier argument about political liberalism, which hinged on the idea of putting the right before the good as the way of dealing with moral and political pluralism, depended upon a metaphysical theory of the self from which, as we have seen, the narrative and communitarian theories dissent. So Sandel argues that: 'for Rawls teleology to the contrary, what is most essential to our personhood is not the ends we choose, but our capacity to chose them. And this capacity is located in the self which must be prior to the ends that it chooses.'[5]

However, even if it was ever Rawls' intention to turn this point into a metaphysical theory (which would provoke the narrative dissent that we have seen), this perspective has explicitly disappeared in *Political Liberalism*. In Rorty's view, for example, Rawls is not any longer claiming, if he ever was, that choice is the essence of the self, that our common moral identity is found in the capacity for choice, but rather that *we* – we modern inheritors of the traditions of religious tolerance and constitutional government – put liberty ahead of perfection. This seems to be a correct characterisation of Rawls' position,

---

[5] Sandel, *Liberalism and the Limits of Justice* p. 19.

but, as we shall see, it is a point that will return to haunt the later discussion.

For the moment though, let us explain a little more the conception of political liberalism. It is clear from the passage cited earlier that the idea of an overlapping consensus is crucially important to this conception. So what does Rawls mean by an overlapping consensus as a way of securing the consent of those who, like many Christians, inhabit reasonable comprehensive doctrines?

One crucial building block of the idea of an overlapping consensus is to distinguish between two sorts of comprehensive doctrines whether these are religious, metaphysical or moral. There are comprehensive doctrines which hold that there is only one 'reasonable and rational good'[6] and that from within that sort of comprehensive doctrine the conception of the role of political institutions is to promote that good. Rawls argues that the Christian tradition as represented by Aquinas and Augustine would represent this view of the role and nature of comprehensive doctrine. Such a view would underpin a Christendom approach. In contrast to this view, that there is only one conception of the good for humanity that can reasonably be entertained, Rawls argues that: 'political liberalism supposes that there are many conflicting reasonable comprehensive doctrines with the conceptions of the good, each compatible with the full rationality of human persons'.[7]

The emergence of the idea that persons can reasonably disagree over the conceptions of the good and the comprehensive doctrines with which they are associated is itself partly the product of the Wars of Religion in the sixteenth century (the impact of which seems to have made a big impression on Rawls) and of the operation of liberal institutions themselves:[8] 'this reasonable plurality of conflicting and incommensurable doctrines is seen as the characteristic work of practical reason over time under enduring free institutions.'

So, for Rawls, there are two sorts of comprehensive doctrine: one fully comprehensive, which sees the role of politics as

---

[6] Rawls, *Political Liberalism* p. 134.
[7] Ibid. p. 135.   [8] Ibid.

serving this comprehensive doctrine and, in so far as that comprehensive doctrine makes political demands, exemplifying these and no others in the institutions and values of the political community; the other – reasonable comprehensive doctrines – are doctrines which accept that there are other conceptions of the good set within other comprehensive doctrines which it would make sense to pursue. In this case, proponents of reasonable comprehensive doctrines are prepared to accept a consensus on constitutional rules so long as those rules are based upon reasons which can be accepted by proponents of reasonable comprehensive doctrines each from their own point of view.

The constitutional arrangements so arrived at to perform the function Rawls requires of them will have to be compatible with the points of view of adherents to different reasonable comprehensive doctrines, but they will not embody the standpoint of one particular comprehensive doctrine. If the defence of Rawlsian liberalism has to involve a particular comprehensive doctrine to legitimate it, then its rationale has failed. This is a crucial point to which we shall return, since it is argued that Rawls does have to invoke such a comprehensive doctrine to underpin his theory.

It also follows from Rawls' theory that Christianity can be characterised by some of its adherents as a comprehensive doctrine *simpliciter*. Rawls, as I have said, takes the view that Aquinas and Augustine would be comprehensive theorists – as, for example, would Calvin who was discussed earlier. On the other hand, those with more liberal theological opinions would see Christianity as a reasonable comprehensive doctrine, that is one which can recognise that there are other reasonable alternatives to Christianity. So, at the beginning of Rawls' argument there is a problem about how to characterise Christianity within Rawls' criteria of reasonableness and comprehensiveness.

Rawls is anxious to differentiate a constitutional structure legitimated by an overlapping consensus between reasonable comprehensive doctrines from a *modus vivendi* which might look unprincipled, pragmatic and unstable. In Rawls' view, an overlapping consensus is deeply rooted in the views of those who hold reasonable comprehensive doctrines because it is based upon reasons which are acceptable from the point of view of each of these strong doctrines. A *modus vivendi* is not. An example that Rawls uses to illustrate his point is drawn from the Wars of Religion of the sixteenth century. At that time, both Catholics and Protestants held to their faith in a comprehensive, not a reasonable comprehensive way and each faith therefore saw it as the duty of the rulers to uphold the true religion. In so far as there was a settlement which embodied toleration at that time, this became a *modus vivendi* because it was the result of the balance of power. Toleration was not based upon the view that it was reasonable to hold the alternative position. It was achieved not upon reasonable conviction about the nature of belief or how beliefs are to be held, but upon convenience and *realpolitik*. This point is well made by Charles Larmore:

> The approach is basically a Hobbesian one, since it aims to ground a moral principle (neutrality) on non-moral, purely prudential grounds . . . since it is hostage to the shifting distribution of power: individuals will lose their reason to uphold the agreement if their relative power or bargaining strength increases significantly.[9]

However, as the result of more tolerant and liberal politics to which such inherently unstable forms of *modus vivendi* may have contributed, many doctrines which used to be held in an unqualified way are now held as reasonable comprehensive doctrines and can endorse constitutional principles such as right and the freedom of religion, not because it is more *convenient* to do so, but because it is *right* to do so. This reflects a new perspective in terms of which comprehensive doctrines are now held, and a new perspective on how such doctrines can act in support of liberal political institutions.

How plausible is this strategy?

In some sense, as a general conception, it does address a real need in the dialectic between a liberal political order and the strong identity-enhancing moral communities, including religious communities which are part of such societies. Again, the

---

[9] Larmore, *The Morals of Modernity* p. 133.

point of the strategy of overlapping consensus is well put by Charles Larmore:

> We must look to a core morality that is, as much as possible common ground . . . It must be neutral enough to accommodate people who value belonging and custom . . . Although the moral basis of liberalism must be minimal, it cannot be trivial. But this conviction, by itself, will not answer the question concerning the foundation of liberalism. It will not show that liberal thought can keep its promise of offering a political conception acceptable to people having very different views of the human good, and in particular about the merits of individualism and community.[10]

This is the crux of the issue. Can a political ethic based upon the idea of an overlapping consensus actually be rich enough to draw upon to solve deep political dilemmas while, at the same time, respecting the integrity of the belief systems that contribute to the overlapping consensus?

An overlapping consensus is an agreement on values and norms regulating the public world, the justification of which is independent of any specific comprehensive doctrine, but, nevertheless, compatible with all or almost all of the reasonable comprehensive doctrines in the society in question. An overlapping consensus as opposed to a *modus vivendi* does embody a real sense of social unity, for Rawls, because it is principled. It can be affirmed by those who hold reasonable comprehensive doctrines as being compatible with those doctrines. At the same time, it is neutral: it does not draw its justification from a particular comprehensive doctrine. It also acts for Rawls as the liberal version of the idea of the common good, although he uses the term public good on the whole rather than common good, but he does, at one point, link the idea of justice to the common good.[11] The common/public good is not rich, substantive or first order, since that is the field of reasonable disagreement and the fact of pluralism. Rather, the public/common good is the framework of neutrality itself. It is a common good understood as a minimal moral conception compatible with the range of reasonable comprehensive moral doctrines.

---

[10] Ibid.   [11] Rawls, *Political Liberalism* p. 109.

Nevertheless, a great deal will turn upon Rawls' distinction between comprehensive doctrines and reasonable comprehensive doctrines in assessing this solution to the problem of social unity. In particular we shall have to be concerned with the question of what is involved in: holding one's convictions and comprehensive doctrine in a reasonable way; the relationship between the reasonable comprehensive doctrines and the reasons which secure the overlapping consensus; and, finally, the nature of the claim of the priority of the right over the good.

Rawls takes the view that a reasonable comprehensive doctrine – which is what some sorts of religious beliefs are – it characterised by the following features: it covers the major religious, philosophical and moral aspects of human life in a more-or-less consistent and coherent manner; it organises values so that they are coherent with one another and express an intelligible view of the world; it normally rests upon a tradition of thought and doctrine, and change in a comprehensive doctrine occurs slowly and in the light of what, from its point of view, are seen to be good and sufficient reasons.[12] A reasonable comprehensive doctrine is held on the following grounds:

The doctrine any reasonable person affirms is but one reasonable doctrine among others. In affirming it, a person, of course, believes it to be true, or else reasonable as the case may be. Thus it is not in general unreasonable to affirm any one of a number of reasonable comprehensive doctrines . . . Beyond this, reasonable persons will think it unreasonable to use political power, should they possess it, to repress comprehensive views that are not unreasonable though different from their own.[13]

From a Christian point of view, this raises the question of how to characterise the relationship between oneself and one's beliefs if these beliefs are held on the basis of what Rawls characterises as a reasonable comprehensive view. There are two crucial and interrelated issues here. First of all, is it possible to distinguish clearly between holding one's own religious beliefs in a reasonable way, and scepticism about their beliefs?

---

[12] Ibid. p. 59.   [13] Ibid. p. 60.

Secondly, is there a coherent basis for the view that reasonable comprehensive doctrines should be treated as private rather than public doctrines? That is to say, a basis for accepting that, while one's religious beliefs imply political principles and imperative, nevertheless they should not be pursued in the public realm in this way: that is, as founded solely upon the imperatives of one's comprehensive doctrine. This issue is not very fully considered by Rawls, although it is quite crucial. Some light can, however, be shed upon the issue by considering Thomas Nagel's argument about epistemological restraint.[14] Nagel argues that it is perfectly consistent for an individual to accept the truth of some religious doctrine while still accepting that it would be wrong to make it the basis of public policy in a society in which some reject it. However, things are not quite so clear cut as this, as Nagel recognises, because let us say that I regard my religious beliefs as being true, in that case why should I deny myself the opportunity of using political power to achieve the social and political imperatives of my religion? Why should I put the need to arrive at some kind of shared principles of social and political order over and above my belief in the truth? This is an absolutely crucial issue because, recall, the narrative/communitarian thinker believed that the priority of the right over the good (of which Nagel's dilemma is an example) depended upon an emphasis upon a liberal theory of the moral identity of the self at the core of which was the capacity for choice – a conception which, as we have seen, was vigorously rejected by such thinkers. So, what justification for putting the right before the good can be given in terms of political liberalism of the later Rawlsian sort, which purports not to appeal to a metaphysical theory of the self? The critic might still be inclined to argue that Rawls' distinction between reasonable comprehensive doctrine and comprehensive doctrines, which leads to the willingness of those who hold the former to put the right before the good, still, in fact, presupposes a liberal theory of the self, that is, one which is prepared to hold

---

[14] T. Nagel, 'Moral Conflict and Political Legitimacy' in *Philosophy and Public Affairs*, 16 (1987) p. 227.

convictions in a way that distinguishes the self from those convictions. If this is so, then later Rawlsian political liberalism will be as objectionable to the narrative/communitarian thinker as the earlier version. This is the point which is focussed, rather tendentiously perhaps, by Rorty when he says: '*We* – we modern inheritors of the tradition of toleration and constitutional government – put liberty above perfection.' How can this be justified to someone who holds that his/her reasonable comprehensive doctrine is true?

Nagel believed that he had an answer to this question which could satisfy the conscience of someone who takes his beliefs to be true. His doctrine of epistemological restraint trades upon a distinction between public and private. He argues, and this is very important, that epistemological restraint is *not* scepticism. This is very important because, if the notion of a reasonable comprehensive doctrine rested on the idea that holders of such doctrines have to hold their views sceptically, then it seems clear that most believers in such kinds of doctrines would not be prepared to enter the circle of political liberalism if political liberalism required that they should be sceptical about their own beliefs. However, this is clearly not the case for Nagel who reasons as follows:

We accept a kind of epistemological division between the private and public domain: in certain contexts I am constrained to consider my beliefs merely as beliefs rather than as truths, however convinced I may be that they are true, and that I know it. This is not the same thing as scepticism.[15]

According to Nagel, this distinction between the public and private assessment of beliefs and their implications is partly a matter of the nature of the evidence, and partly a matter of morality. He argues that: 'the distinction between what is needed to justify belief and what is needed to justify the employment of political power depends upon a higher standard of objectivity which is ethically based'.[16] The ethical dimension is linked to the idea that, in the public realm, political deliberation depends upon the idea of arriving at a judgement on a public or

---

[15] Ibid. p. 230.   [16] Ibid. p. 229.

communal basis: 'it must be possible to present to others the basis of your own beliefs so that once you have done so, *they have what you have* and can arrive at a judgement on the same basis'.[17] This is close to Rawls' idea of public reason as a central feature of political liberalism, but the question we are trying to face is how far the achievement of an overlapping consensus between reasonable comprehensive doctrines requires the believer to revise his/her understanding of his/her own stance towards these beliefs. If Nagel's argument goes through, and it is possible to distinguish between epistemological restraint and scepticism, then it may be that, from a Christian point of view, and even from a narrative interpretation of that point of view, it would be possible to see mainstream Christianity as being part of that overlapping consensus because the condition of its being a reasonable comprehensive doctrine is *not* that the adherent of this doctrine has to approach it in a sceptical light.

What is crucial here is the distinction that Nagel draws between two attitudes to my own religious beliefs: internal and personal attitudes, on one side, and external and impersonal ones, on the other:

The idea is that when we look at certain of our convictions from outside, however justified they may be from within, the appeal to that truth must be seen merely as an appeal to our beliefs and should be treated as such unless these beliefs can be shown to be justifiable from a more impersonal standpoint.[18]

Does this combination work from a personal point of view?

There are critics, Brian Barry and Joseph Raz amongst them, who take the view that the principle of epistemological restraint cannot work, and, although Nagel has in fact dropped the principle largely because of Raz's criticism,[19] it is nevertheless Barry's critique that is more important in our context because he argues that Nagel's distinction, when applied at a personal level, is incoherent and, in fact, collapses into scepticism.

Barry focusses on whether a belief which from the inside is

[17] Ibid. p. 232.
[18] Nagel, 'Moral Conflict and Political Legitimacy' p. 230.
[19] J. Raz, 'Facing Diversity: The Case of Epistemic Abstinence' *Philosophy and Public Affairs*, 19 (1990) pp. 3–46.

held by the believer to be certain can be coherently combined, with the view that the same believer can distance himself/ herself and take an external view so that from the outside it can be regarded as dubitable. Unless this difference in perspective is defensible, it is difficult to see how the project of political liberalism can work. Barry argues that the internal/external perspective is incoherent: 'I question, however, whether certainty from the inside about some view can coherently be combined with the line that it is reasonable for others to reject the same view.'[20] He continues:

A partisan of epistemological restraint would suggest that I might be absolutely convinced of the veridical nature of this revelation while nevertheless admitting that others could reasonably reject my evidence. But is this really plausible? If I concede that I have no way of convincing others, should that not also dent my own certainty?[21]

If this is so, then it is difficult to see that the idea of a reasonable comprehensive doctrine, as Rawls calls it, which does seem to depend upon a doctrine rather like Nagel's epistemological restraint, can do the work that Rawls wants it to. He does not want to require as a condition of a liberal constitution that believers in reasonable comprehensive doctrines should hold these doctrines *sceptically*. Indeed, it would be very anti-liberal to require people to hold beliefs in one way rather than another. If, however, the idea of belief in a reasonable comprehensive doctrine collapses into scepticism, then, far from reasonable comprehensive doctrines contributing *via* public reason and the overlapping consensus to the development of political liberalism, it rather follows that Rawls is implicitly requiring that adherents of reasonably comprehensive doctrines should take a sceptical and detached attitude to the nature of their beliefs.[22] This brings us back to a point which rather parallels Sandel's critique of Rawls on the self in that it is a condition of political liberalism that religious beliefs should be held in a way that Sandel criticised in *Liberalism and*

---

[20] B. Barry, *Justice as Impartiality* Clarendon Press, Oxford, 1995, p. 179.

[21] Ibid.

[22] This is essentially Hauerwas' critique in *A Community of Character.*

the Limits of Justice, that is to say, in an external way. One way of putting the point of view of Rawls in the light of this, and a way which its anti-foundationalist supporters approve, would be to say that only those with liberal attitudes to their belief systems can contribute via comprehensive doctrines to public reason and the overlapping consensus. So, for example, it might be argued that, from a Christian perspective, it is only if one holds one's beliefs in a liberal way and, indeed, endorses a liberal theology that one can, in fact, see an overlapping consensus as being compatible with one's comprehensive doctrine. So, for example, Rorty argues that, in the light of these considerations, Rawls 'no longer seems committed to a philosophical account of the human self, but only to a historico-sociological description of the way we live now'. But, since to join the way we live now on Rawls' and Rorty's account entails that we have to put the right before the good or liberty before perfection, this description will be inert to those whose community and narrative take them in a different direction. Indeed, if Barry's argument that Rawls' position depends on scepticism is accepted, then we are nearly back with the view outlined in the first chapter, namely, that liberalism depends upon *doubt* and constitutional ways of coping with that, rather than being compatible with a set of robust first-order beliefs. If the argument about the character of reasonable comprehensive doctrines fails for the reasons given, then it is difficult to see quite how a liberal political order can be justified on these sorts of grounds to those with comprehensive beliefs.

This is, however, not the only problem with Rawls' strategy. Recall that the aim is to produce a justification for liberal institutions via an overlapping consensus and not by an appeal to the idea that liberalism is itself a comprehensive doctrine with its own specific values and ideals. If liberalism is itself a comprehensive doctrine, then, of course, it becomes much more difficult to justify to those who belong to particular moral communities sustained by their own comprehensive doctrines. It is, however, arguable that Rawls' own theory actually has to make use of ideas which imply that liberalism is a comprehensive doctrine. The first of two arguments relevant here has been effectively deployed by Simon Caney.[23] He argues that Rawls' political liberalism embodies two principles:

1 Principles of justice may draw upon moral considerations which cannot reasonably be rejected.
2 Reasonable persons do not concur in the assessments of the worth of different conceptions of the good.

These two principles lead to the conclusion that principles of justice should not be predicated upon the worth of different conceptions of the good. In this sense, *Political Liberalism*, which derives principles of justice from the 'overlapping consensus', is neutral between conceptions of the good and, indeed, again puts the right before the good.

One explanation which Rawls offers to explain pluralism, against the background of which the above principles appear plausible, is what he calls the burdens of judgement. The burdens of judgement are about the nature of reasonable disagreement between people and include the following factors for Rawls:

(a) The evidence bearing on the conflict is difficult to assess.
(b) Even when we disagree about the kinds of considerations that are relevant we may disagree about the weight of these factors.
(c) Our concepts are vague and subject therefore to interpretation and there may be different judgements about these interpretations.
(d) We assess ideas in the light of our own experience and this may differ.
(e) There are different kinds of normative considerations with different force on both sides of the issue – which makes it difficult to make a considered overall assessment.
(f) Not all human ends are coherent and mutually achievable. A view which Rawls associates with Isaiah Berlin and which was noted in chapter 1.[24]

It is because of pluralism rooted in these sorts of considera-

---

[23] S. Caney, 'Liberal Legitimacy, Reasonable Disagreement and Justice' in *Pluralism and Liberal Neutrality* ed. R. Bellamy and M. Hollis, Frank Cass, Ilford, 1999, p. 21.

[24] Rawls, *Political Liberalism* pp. 56–7.

tions that we have to put the right before the good and not seek
the achievement of the ends postulated by a particular comprehensive doctrine by political means. The difficulty with the
argument is that it may be too powerful for Rawls' project.
According to Caney, if the burdens of judgement explain why it
is not possible to achieve a 'consensus about the good . . . they
equally raise doubt about the consensus regarding the right'. If
the burdens of judgement are as they are, will it in fact be
possible to legitimise a conception of right independent of the
good to characterise the public framework for a liberal society?
Most of what Rawls calls the burdens of judgement we have
already met in discussion in Part II about justice, freedom,
rights, community etc., and it is not at all clear that they would
not also apply to arguments about the right. If we really believe
that political liberalism in Rawls' conception can only justify
principles of justice which cannot reasonably be rejected by
anyone (including those holding reasonably comprehensive
doctrines) and if the burdens of judgement are as Rawls says
they are, then this seems to undermine the idea of the justification of justice at all, since justice would be subject to the
same burdens. So this undermines the idea that it is possible to
adopt in a coherent way the strategy of putting the right before
the good and justifying liberal institutions without drawing
upon a substantive idea of the good which, in turn, would
then almost certainly be disputed between different moral
communities.

I want now to turn to an additional argument that makes the
point in a rather different way. The argument is from J. Haldane's paper 'The Individual, the State and the Common Good'[25]
and focusses upon an important qualification Rawls makes to
his theory and whether this qualification is, in fact, coherent
with his overall project. He argues that, while political liberalism's aim is to be compatible with most if not all reasonably
comprehensive doctrines, the only comprehensive doctrines
that run foul of public reason are those 'that cannot support a

[25] J. Haldane, 'The Individual, the State and the Common Good', in *The Communitarian Challenge to Liberalism* ed. E. F. Paul, F. D. Miller Jr and J. Paul. Cambridge University Press, 1996, pp. 59–79.

reasonable balance of political values.' But what does this mean in practice? If we take Rawls' own example of abortion, his claims are really circular. He argues that when we are considering the question we need to consider it in terms of three political values: 'due respect for human life, the ordered reproduction of political society over time . . . and the equality of women as equal citizens'. So, if these are the factors we have to balance, what is a reasonable balance? Rawls argues as follows:

Now I believe that any reasonable balance of these three values will give a woman a duly qualified right to end her pregnancy during the first trimester. The reason for this is that at this early stage of pregnancy the political value of the equality of women is overriding . . . Any comprehensive doctrine that leads to a balance of political values excluding that duly qualified right in the first trimester is to that extent unreasonable.[26]

This is difficult to accept on Rawlsian grounds as an argument. The conception of justice in Rawls' elaboration of it seeks to bypass religion and philosophy's profoundest problems. This cannot be done in this case without invoking a comprehensive doctrine (in this case treating liberalism as a comprehensive doctrine) to criticise the opposite view as unreasonable. The basic questions about political liberalism, therefore, still seem to be unanswered. It seems impossible to defend a liberalism that puts the right before the good just because a conception of the good was to be used to justify the right, and which also involves defending liberal values in hard cases by treating it as being itself a comprehensive doctrine.

These sorts of problems have led a number of thinkers to defend what has come to be called perfectionist liberalism. This is a view of liberalism that is not neutral between conceptions of the good, but, rather, one which embodies a substantive conception of the good as its own. The difficulty with such an approach, however, is not that it is, in principle, implausible, far from it, but rather that, from the point of view of the moral communities within a liberal society, they may be expected to affirm a set of positive liberal values which cut across their own moral conceptions. However, there are elements of perfectionist

[26] Rawls, *Political Liberalism* pp. 243–4.

liberalism which are important for thinking about the relationship between liberal societies and their constituent communities. By perfectionist liberalism I mean a form of liberalism which does not seek to be directly neutral in respect of the good, but elaborates a moral ideal of its own and, in particular, an ideal of autonomy. To put this value at the centre of liberalism differentiates it from all the earlier forms that we have discussed: utilitarianism, contractualism, Rawlsian political liberalism etc. These sought either to be neutral about the good or, in the case of utilitarianism, to reduce goodness to the wide and subjective differentiation in the objects of desire. On the view we are now considering, individual autonomy is the basic good and the central aspect of human flourishing.

On one view of the relationship between this form of liberalism and the belief system of different moral and religious communities within a liberal society, that relationship must be one of tension if not contradiction. After all, there are such belief systems, usually of a fundamentalist sort, that seem incompatible with the idea of human autonomy. If autonomy is the foundational value for liberalism and, in a liberal society, is a persuasive value in the curriculum of public education, for example, then one could imagine that particular religious communities would be hostile to it. These communities might be Christian, Jewish or Islamic and, in so far as they were being required as part of citizenship to assent to an autonomist form of liberalism, then it is not at all clear why they should do so because they might believe that such a value was deeply incompatible with their beliefs.

This would, however, be to move far too quickly because two of the major thinkers in this area of liberalism, W. Kymlicka and J. Raz, have argued strongly, although in rather different ways, for the recognition of cultural and religious groups within a liberal society. The contrast with other forms of liberalism is clear. As we saw with utilitarianism, any recognition of a right that one's religious beliefs should not be ridiculed, could not be justified as a specifically religious or cultural right, but was dependent upon inferences from a right to security. Within a Rawlsian contractual account of justice and liberalism, religious communities had no specific rights *qua* religious communities. Within the later Rawlsian conception of political liberalism, either religious beliefs were to be held reasonably (or even sceptically, according to Barry's critique of Rawls), or they were comprehensive doctrines *simpliciter* which should play no part in the political deliberation of a liberal society. There is a potential paradox here. All of these theories are, in their different ways, minimal liberal moralities and, as such, deny any specific political and social representation for religious belief, whereas, within the two forms of more positive or perfectionist liberalism we are about to consider, both of which place the controversial value of autonomy at the heart of liberalism, there is in fact much greater scope for the social and political recognition of religious belief and the importance of religious communities. Why should this be so?

In order to answer this question, we need to look at Will Kymlicka's *Liberalism, Community and Culture* in which he argues that a positive form of liberalism which affirms the value of autonomy shows, in fact, that cultural membership, which might involve membership of religious communities, should be given a degree of recognition in liberal theory as one of the primary goods necessary for autonomy. The argument forges a link between the development of autonomy and access to and formation by a culture. He argues as follows:

We decide how to lead our lives by situating ourselves in these cultural narratives, by adopting the roles that have struck us as worthwhile ones, as ones worth living . . . Our language and our history are the media through which we come to an awareness of the options available to us and their significance; and this is a precondition of making intelligent judgements about how to lead our lives . . . we make these judgements precisely by examining the cultural structure, by coming to an awareness of the possibilities it has, the different activities it identifies as significant . . . It is of sovereign importance to this argument that the cultural structure is being recognised as a context of choice.[27]

This argument is rather different from Michael Sandel's argument about the encumbered self in the context of Rawls' *Theory*

[27] W. Kymlicka, *Liberalism, Community and Culture* Clarendon Press, Oxford, 1989, p. 166.

of Justice. Sandel used the idea that an individual is situated in a constellation of attachments, loyalties, cultural identities and narratives to undermine the value of autonomy in the sense that moral autonomy could constitute the common moral identity of persons. Kymlicka, on the other hand, is using his conception of the role of community and culture *in the service* of autonomy. Culture is a primary good in Rawls' sense – that is, a pre-condition for acquiring other goods. The exercise of autonomy requires access to culture and meaning. Firstly, it provides the intellectual resources in terms of which alternatives are appraised and understood. Secondly it provides the context of choice: 'it is a good in its capacity of providing meaningful options for us, and for ordering our ability to judge for ourselves the value of our life plans'.[28]

These exercises of judgement and autonomy require resources that are not just material, but also cultural and perspectival. Cultural identity thus serves autonomy. In contrast, in Sandel's view, it is constitutive of our identity and undermines the liberal endorsement of autonomy. Similar views to Kymlicka's are to be found in Margalit and Raz's 'National Self Determination'.[29]

In some ways, this argument could be cast in terms of distinctive or basic human needs. On a natural-law view, as we saw earlier, Aquinas, for example, had an ordered list of human goods which are essential to human nature, and natural law was, in part, about the basis on which such goods could be secured. On the view under consideration here, autonomy is taken as the basic good or ideal, and other sorts of goods are related to that ideal: they are, one might say, the needs which have to be fulfilled in order for us to acquire and exercise the good of autonomy, and this includes a sense of cultural belonging. Needs cannot be identified without reference to a goal; a need is always needed *for* something – for some good or purpose. A basic need is a need for something to achieve a basic good or goal. On the liberal view, physical survival and autonomy are basic goods without which, as moral agents, we could not pursue any other sort of

---

[28] Ibid.
[29] J. Raz, *Ethics in the Public Domain* Clarendon Press, Oxford, 1994, ch. 5.

good. One could, therefore, begin to enumerate a list of basic goods which would include the goods secured by negative rights, including not being killed, not being coerced, threatened, assaulted etc., together with rights of access to positive goods: security, property, health, education and cultural resources. Such an approach would constitute a kind of thin version of natural law. There is no clear reason why religious believers within a liberal society should not be able to endorse a common set of basic goods which would satisfy the basic ends of survival and autonomy, including some recognition within liberalism of the specific rights of religious and other cultural groups as being central to the achievement of autonomy.

Of course, there are difficulties with this approach. Indeed, they will be obvious from what has gone before. Basic needs, including cultural identity, are in the service of the positive value of autonomy, and thus the form of liberalism represented by this may well involve a Rawlsian comprehensive doctrine and incorporate a theory of the self and its nature. Indeed, it would be difficult to see how it could avoid this, since such a view would have to practise a positive defence of autonomy against critics such as Sandel and MacIntyre. Equally, a liberal order based upon a positive defence of autonomy might have to impose its own conception of autonomy on reluctant cultural groups. So, for example, it might be argued that, given the argument about culture as a basic good serving autonomy, then there would be nothing intrinsically wrong with the state supporting Christian, Jewish or Islamic schools with taxpayers' money, particularly if it were to be believed that only this would secure the continuation of these religious and cultural traditions into the future. However, given that the culture provides a 'context for choice' – it provides us with resources both intel-lectual and emotional with which to examine opinions – then it would probably be a condition of state support that the religious ethos of such schools should not be fundamentalist and should expose the students to other religious and non-religious ways of life, while, no doubt, exploring how the original moral com-munity could provide appropriate resources with which to assess these choices. This does mean, however, that such religious communities have to accept the priority of autonomy over the ways in which they might want to sustain the faith of their community via education. This just mirrors the point made earlier that, on this view of liberalism and culture, there has to be a very strong case for autonomy such that it will be a comprehensive doctrine in terms of which other comprehensive doctrines will have their practices shaped and, indeed, constrained. Given that autonomy may not be the way in which religious believers conceive of their relationship to their own beliefs, this does imply still quite a significant tension between a more perfectionist liberalism and the ways in which faith communities conceive of their own life. So, for example, Kymlicka says: 'Finding a way to liberalise a cultural community without destroying it is a task that liberals face in every country once we recognise the importance of a secure cultural context of choice.'[30] This is precisely the point. The religious community has to be shaped by a positive kind of liberalism founded upon a value, namely, autonomy, which may not be central or even recognised at all within the faith community.

It is not clear, however, that there is a real alternative to pursuing this kind of liberalised natural-law approach in trying to figure out the legitimate relationship between faith communities and liberal politics, because the other alternative seems to be one in which we are faced with different narrative/faith communities without a set of public criteria to provide even the framework for dialogue. On the one hand, we have a thin kind of liberalism based upon an assured common moral identity as an autonomous agent and shaping how first-order moral beliefs are to be understood and, more importantly for our purposes, institutionalised in the light of that foundational value. On the other, we have a seemingly criterionless range of moral communities with no narrative common world between them. We may be forced to recognise the dilemma of endorsing a universalism which does not perhaps engage with the particularities of how people live in narrative communities and develop a sense of identity; or a particularism which is thick and rich but seems to

---

[30] Kymlicka, *Liberalism, Community and Culture* p. 170.

accept with equanimity the need to be true to the identity-creating narrative of belief and being prepared to live out of control so far as the public world is concerned.

Of course, it would be natural and, indeed, very tempting in the light of this impasse to adopt the line taken by Joseph Boyle to which I drew attention in the chapter on 'Natural Law and Natural Order', namely, the idea that different moral traditions may, indeed, yield ultimately a set of core and common values: 'Why should it be impossible that the same proposition or prescription can be expressed in different languages or arrived at with very different starting points and presuppositions?'[31] On this view, different moral communities, despite their different narratives, may be referring to the same moral reality and the same religious truths. On this view, thick moralities rooted in ways of life might provide agreed thin prescriptions which could form the basis of a normative social and political order. This is certainly an idea worth exploring if we are concerned about social unity in the absence of a metaphysical theory which can both transcend and secure the endorsement of particular thick moralities. It is, however, a view which involves very considerable philosophical difficulties. Its political importance, however, if coherent, can hardly be overstated.

The idea that behind all religious belief lies a common experience which can become the basis of a common world is described by Hauerwas:

The liberal theologian, according to Lindbeck, assumes that there is some universal experience that all people have that can be characterised as religious. The particular religions and their doctrines are but manifestations of that experience giving it expression in more or less adequate ways. The experience, however, always transcends particular religions so it can be called on as a basis for critique of other expressions. In terms of ethics, liberalism provides the justification for the assumption that there is a strong continuity between Christian and non-Christian morality, especially in a liberal society.[32]

Nevertheless, the narrative theologian is prepared to reject this, and Hauerwas makes no bones about its implications:

---

[31] Boyle, 'Natural law and the Ethics of Traditions' p. 7.
[32] Hauerwas, *Against the Nations* p. 2.

'theology does not describe some universally available experience . . . post-liberal theology is not just a theological programme characteristic of Christianity; rather, Lindbeck
suggests, it corresponds to a particular theory of religion which
he characterises as cultural linguistic.'[33]

This view of religion which denies a common set of religious
experiences whether in religion or politics, is rooted in a
Wittgensteinian theory of meaning, and the loss of a common
world is a clear consequence for Lindbeck. Take the following
representative quotation:

it is the religion instantiated in Scripture which defines being, truth,
goodness and beauty and the non-scriptural exemplifications of these
need to be transformed into figures (or types and antitypes) of the
scriptural ones. Intra-textural theology redescribes reality within
the scriptural framework rather than translating Scripture into extra-
scriptural categories. It is the text so to speak, which absorbs the
world, rather than the world the text.[34]

Earlier in this book, when exploring this vein, I quoted from
Peter Winch when he argued that 'Reality is not what gives
language sense, but what is real and unreal shows itself in the
sense which language has',[35] but the sense which language has
for the post-liberal, post-modernist, narrative thinker means
that reality is given in the character of different narratives and,
since there is no overarching or meta-narrative any longer in
modern society, we lose the sense of a common world. Lindbeck
is clear about this:

the experiences that religions evoke and mould are as varied as the
interpretative schemes they embody. Adherents of different religions
do not diversely thematise the same experience; rather they have
different experiences. Buddhist compassion, Christian love and – if I
may cite a quasi religious phenomenon – French revolutionary
fraternity are not diverse modifications of a single fundamental
human awareness, emotional attitude or sentient, but are radically
different (from the root) distinct ways of experiencing and being
oriented towards self, neighbour and cosmos.[36]

---

[33] Ibid.
[34] Lindbeck, *The Nature of Doctrine* p. 118.
[35] Winch, 'Understanding a Primitive Society'.
[36] Lindbeck, *The Nature of Doctrine* p. 40.

Similar views are to be found in Hauerwas, and in D. Z. Phillips' essay 'Philosophy, Theology and the Reality of God', and Yoder, particularly in the latter's discussion of various forms of 'wider wisdom' in *The Royal Priesthood*. Yoder and Hauerwas concentrate more on the characterisation of Christianity in narrative terms. The philosophical tools for exploring this approach are produced in Lindbeck and by his reading of Wittgenstein. Nevertheless, the conclusion is the same for, in Yoder's words: 'There is no non-sectarian "scratch" to start from, beneath or beyond particular identities, no neutral common ground which some sort of search for foundation could lay bare.'[37]

So, there seems to be a clear impasse here between the particular and the universal, whether in theology or political theory. All experience is adjectival for the narrative particularist, for the universalist it seems that what is universal is lost in the particularity of interpretation. This impasse lies at the heart of modern philosophy, theology and political theory, and I do not have the intellectual resources to suggest in any detail how such an impasse can be resolved. I will, however, make one more attempt at a resolution by looking at the debate which Michael Walzer has held with himself over this between *Interpretation and Social Theory* and his more recent *Thick and Thin*.

In *Interpretation and Social Criticism*, he wrote about moral universalism (and, necessarily in his view, universalism's attendant moral minimalism) in such a way that implied that it was possible to envisage a set of universal moral principles – typically prohibitions – as the basis for subsequent exemplification in thicker more local moral codes. These thicker interpretations would depend on the social meanings of goods in different societies. Quite a good practical example of this would be his discussion of needs in *Spheres of Justice*. There are common human needs – like a need for security – and recognising the awareness or the universality of such needs in an important

---

[37] Yoder, *The Royal Priesthood* p. 129.

thing, but he argues that the interpretation of these needs and what they imply for their satisfaction will differ quite fundamentally between different societies and different historical periods. Nevertheless, the point here is the assertion, which seems consistent with *Interpretation and Social Criticism*, that there can, indeed, be universals that are seen as basic and from which local interpretations are derivative. This is certainly the interpretation of the argument in *Interpretation and Social Criticism* which Walzer himself gives in *Thick and Thin*, and he goes on to criticise it. I shall quote this important passage in full:

> This dualism is, I think, an internal feature of every morality. Philosophers most often describe it in terms of a (thin) set of universal principles adapted (thickly) to these or those historical circumstances. I have in the past suggested the image of a core morality differently elaborated in different cultures. The idea of elaboration is better than adaptation, it seems to me because it suggests a process less circumstantial and constrained and more freely creative: governed as much by ideal as by practical considerations . . . but both of these descriptions suggest mistakenly that the starting place for the development of morality is the same in every case . . . but our intuition is wrong here. Morality is thick from the beginning, culturally integrated, freely resonant, and it reveals itself thinly only on special occasions, when moral language is turned to specific purposes.[38]

He goes on to make a point following from this that is important for Christian critics, particularly to those who wish to appeal to a biblical basis of other faith. He quotes from Deuteronomy 16.20: 'That which is altogether just shalt thou follow, that thou mayest live, and inherit the land which the Lord thy God giveth thee.'

His comment on this is that we may well agree with this while the concept of justice invoked remains thin, universal and minimal, but once it is given a much thicker description, as it is in Deuteronomy, then the situation changes: 'we would not find it so easy to agree . . . or the description might seem so distant and alien as to leave us entirely unresponsive (but we still recognise it as a description of justice)'. In some ways, it is

---

[38] M. Walzer, *Thick and Thin: Moral Argument at Home and Abroad* University of Notre Dame Press, p. 4.

worth remembering, this is not too far removed from Hayek's critique of social justice which we met earlier. In his view, the ideas about social justice which the churches entertain are those relevant to a tribal society. Now what we might understand by social justice is so fragmented by different and incommensurable 'thick' interpretations that we can have no confidence that we are talking about the same thing. It is interesting perhaps to speculate on what grounds Walzer might still believe, as he does, that we would recognise that what the Deuteronomist was talking about was justice if, indeed, it did seem to us so distant and alien.

This is quite a central problem because, if Walzer says, as he does in *Thick and Thin*, that we do share in some minimal sense the same concepts, even though these arise out of and are intelligible only in the terms of the thick moralities of particular societies, then it is not clear what his grounds are for saying that we are, in our different moral localities, interpreting or propounding thick descriptions of the *same* concept, or whether we are really talking about *different* concepts. This mirrors the points made by Lindbeck in his critique of theological liberalism. He argued on Wittgensteinian grounds that we cannot assume that radically different forms of religious language, for example the Hindu and Buddhist, refer to the same thing, or that they worship the same God or Gods. It would only be possible for us to say that we did have the same experience and worship the same God if there was some standpoint beyond these different uses of religious langugage on which we could all argue. However, for Lindbeck there is not. On this basis, the argument of *Thick and Thin* is not clear as to why we now would so clearly recognise the Deuternomist as talking about justice if it does seem so alien and if our own local descriptions of justice are so different from those provided in Deuteronomy. Phillips is instructive on this point when he says:

What enabled Paul to say that he worshipped the God of Abraham was the fact that although many changes had taken place in the concept of God, there was, nevertheless, a common religious tradition in which both he and Abraham stood. To say that a God is not the same as one's own God involves saying that those who believe in him are in a radically different religious tradition from one's own. The criteria of what can sensibly be said of God are found *within* the religious tradition.[39]

One way in which philosophers have tried to deal with this issue of conceptual identity against a background of radically different interpretations is through the idea of essential contestability introduced by Professor Gallie, which was discussed in chapter 10.[40] This provides a scheme for determining whether disputes and differences in the interpretation of a concept allowed us still to claim that it was, in fact, a dispute about the same concept or different concepts. Crucial to securing this sense of interpreting the same thing is the idea of an *original exemplar* of the concept such that all parties to the interpretive dispute would, in fact, recognise that X was an examplar of the concept under dispute and that their own uses of the concept would still make sense in the context of such an examplar. This seems to be very close to what Walzer had in mind in his residual universalism in *Interpretation and Social Criticism* and in *Spheres of Justice*. In *Thick and Thin*, however, his interpretation is radicalised a good deal without his really confronting the issue of conceptual identity.

All of this may seem arcane, but it is not really because post-modernist and radical pluralists have, to a great extent, denied the existence of a common world of human meaning and value. While Walzer explicitly claims the contrary in his recent book, it is not clear that his own conceptual practice does not commit him to this in effect. It does seem to me that, despite all that can be said on the narrative and particularist side of the arguments, we are still a long way from the moment when we should give up the idea of a common nature and common value. Contrary to what is claimed frequently, as Norman Geras has clearly shown, people in situations of moral crisis, often brought on by defects in the moral particularism of their own societies (Nazism would be an example), invoke a sense of common humanity to justify what they do in standing against the impact

---

[39] D. Z. Phillips, 'Philosophy, Theology and the Reality of God' in D. Z. Phillips, *Wittgenstein and Religion* Macmillan, Basingstoke, 1996.

[40] Gallie, 'Essentially Contested Concepts'.

of that particularism. The sustaining of these ideas, it seems to me, are critical for both theology and politics because ideas such as these provide some kind of counterbalance to sectarianism and particularism.[41]

There are also philosophical arguments with which we can seek to resist some of the more fragmenting tendencies of particularism and post-modernism. Two of the arguments are, I believe, particularly salient in the conclusion to the study.

As we have seen, Wittgenstein's later work has had a big impact on the radical particularists. His later writings on the philosophy of language, the emphasis upon context and practice as criteria for the use of language, and the denial of the claim that reason and objectivity are external to linguistic practices, have all had a major contribution to make to particularism. Clearly, the import of Wittgenstein's work is very compelling, but, nevertheless, we should not assume that, because we learn the meaning of words within a particular context, and association with behaviour and practices within these contexts, rather than from some absurd context-free idea of 'naming reality', the consequence is that the meaning of such contextually acquired words is forever tied to the circumstances under which they are learned. It is possible, once words have been learned in this way, to free them more and more from their original contexts. This point was made very cogently by A. J. Ayer in *The Concept of A Person and Other Essays*.[42] Words and networks of words are undoubtedly learned in specific contexts and, indeed, within particular narratives, but this does not, of itself, entail that the subsequent use of such words has to be tied in an internal way to these contexts and those narratives. This sort of point could lend weight to the idea in Walzer's *Thick and Thin* that it is perfectly possible to envisage that out of different narrative contexts there can, nevertheless, emerge a common set of values. These will no doubt be rather minimal, but it would constitute the basic lineaments of a common word. Such commonalities could be built upon as a way of constructing a moral framework which could expand outside the boundaries

[41] N. Geras, *Solidarity in the Conversation of Humankind* Verso Books, London, 1995.
[42] A. J. Ayer, *The Concept of a Person and other Essays* Macmillan, London, 1962.

of particular narratives while, at the same time, respecting the narratives as the cultural contexts in which the language is learned and taught. A common moral word would not appear by a priori moral meaning but would be built up out of different narratives. We cannot, of course, have any metaphysical assurance that this will happen, but, equally, there is no metaphysical reason why it should not. We should certainly not give up on the possibility of securing such a common word which could then, in turn, create a space for the idea of common projects and common interests. The creation of such arguments is not, of course, directly a philosophical or theological task. It can only be achieved practically by dialogue and involvement. It also requires those who belong to strong narrative communities to be open to such dialogue and have a willingness not to see boundaries as impermeable. A common world of value can only be achieved, if indeed it can at all, by dialogue and deliberation. It is not a matter of establishing a priori metaphysical principles and making deductions from them. But it does need those who take the narrative and radical partcularist position to accept, as Geras has cogently argued and provided much evidence for, that there is a vital salience of the idea of humanity and the common interests of humanity which can still arise out of our loyalty and location within narrative communities. It also needs such particularists not to take a position which would be inconsistent for them given their rejection of metaphysics, namely, that there are metaphysical reasons for believing that loyalty to and location in particularistic communities prevents the possibility of entering through dialogue into a wider witness to the nature of humanity.

This could then lead us into the more promising direction sketched out by Habermas . In the essay 'The Unity of Reason and the Diversity of Its Voices' he quotes from Hilary Putnam's article 'Why Reason can't be Naturalised' and adds his own gloss to it:

From the possibility of reaching understanding linguistically, we can read off a concept of situated reason that is given voice in validity claims that are both context dependent and transcendent. 'Reason is, in this sense, both immanent (not to be found outside of concrete language games and institutions) and transcendent (a regulative idea that we use to criticise the conduct of all activities and institutions).' To put the point in my own words: the validity claimed for propositions and norms transcends spaces and times, but in each actual case the claim is raised here and now, in a specific context and accepted or rejected with real implications for social interactions.[43]

The possibility of dialogue between persons situated in moral and religious traditions is not ruled out by the kinds of philosophical positions on which radical particularists wish to rest. Given this, a common world of meaning and dialogue seems perfectly possible and, indeed, a central human imperative.

[43] J. Habermas, *Post Metaphysical Thinking*, Polity Press, Cambridge, 1992, p. 139.

Select bibliography

Allen, J. *Law and Conflict: A Covenantal Model of Christian Ethics*, Abingdon Press, Nashville, 1984.

Aquinas, St Thomas. *Commentary on the Nicomachean Ethics*, trans. C. I. Litzinger, Chicago University Press, 1964.

Summa Theologiae, Blackfriars, Eyre and Spottiswoode, London, 1963.

Atwell, J. E. 'The Accordian Effect Thesis', *Philosophical Quarterly*, 19 (1969).

Augustine, St *De Civitate Dei* trans. as *The City of God* by D. Knowles, Penguin, Harmondsworth, 1972.

Austin, J. L. 'A Plea for Excuses' in *Philosophical Papers*, Press, Oxford, 1969.

Ayer, A. J. *The Concept of a Person and Other Essays*, Macmillan, London, 1962.

Banton, M. *Policeman in the Community*, Tavistock Publications, London, 1964.

Barr, J. *Biblical Faith and Natural Theology*, Clarendon Press, Oxford, 1993.

Barry, B. *Justice as Impartiality*, Clarendon Press, Oxford, 1995.

Barth, K. *Church Dogmatics*, vol. 3/3, trans. G. W. Bromiley and R. J. Ehrlich, T. and T. Clark, Edinburgh, 1961.

Der Römerbrief, 1919 edn, TVZ, Zurich, 1985.

Der Römerbrief, 1922 edn, TVZ, Zurich, 1940.

'The Christian Community and the Civil Community' in *Selected Writings*, ed. C. Green, Collins, Glasgow, 1989.

Barton, J. *Amos's Oracles Against the Nations*, Cambridge University Press, 1980.

'Ethics in Isaiah of Jerusalem', *Journal of Theological Studies*, 32/1 (1981).

Ethics and the Old Testament, SCM Press, London, 1998.

Bell, C. and Newby, H. *Community Studies*, George Allen and Unwin, London, 1972.

Bentham, J. *An Introduction to the Principles of Morals and Legislation*, ed. W. Harrison, Blackwell, Oxford, 1967.

Berlin, I. *Four Essays on Liberty*, Oxford University Press, 1969.

'Does Political Theory Still Exist?' in *Philosophy, Politics and Society Series II*, ed. P. Laslett and W. G. Runciman, Blackwell, Oxford, 1962.

'The Pursuit of the Ideal' in *The Proper Study of Mankind*, ed. H. Hardy and R. Hausheer, Chatto and Windus, London, 1997.

Bittner, R. 'Augustine's Philosophy of History' in *The Augustian Tradition*, ed. G. Matheus, University of California Press, Berkeley, Calif., 1999.

Boyle, J. 'Natural Law and the Ethics of Traditions' in *Natural Law Theory*, ed. R. P. George, Clarendon Press, Oxford, 1992.

Brennan, R. and Brown, P. 'Social Relations and Social Perspectives among Shipbuilding Workers', *Sociology*, 4 (1970).

British Catholic Bishops, *The Common Good and the Catholic Church's Social Teaching*, The Catholic Bishops' Conference, England and Wales, London, 1996.

Brittan, S. 'Hayek, Freedman and Interest Groups' in *The Role and Limits of Government*, Temple Smith, London, 1983.

Brown, P. *Augustine of Hippo: A Biography*, Faber and Faber, London, 1967.

Buchanan, J. M. *The Limits of Liberty*, University of Chicago Press, 1975.

Burke, E. *Reflections on the Revolution in France*, Dent, London, 1910.

Cain, M. 'On the Beat' in *Images of Deviance*, ed. S. Cohen, Penguin, Harmondsworth, 1971.

Calvin, J. *Institutes of the Christian Religion*, 1536 edition, trans. F. L. Battles, Collins, London, 1986.

Cannon, I. C. 'Ideology and Occupational Community', *Sociology*, 1 (1967).

Caney, S. 'Liberal Legitimacy, Reasonable Disagreement and Justice' in *Pluralism and Liberal Neutrality*, ed. R. Bellamy and M. Hollis, Frank Cass, Ilford, 1999.

Chadwick, O. *Hensley Henson: A Study of the Friction Between Church and State*, The Canterbury Press, Norwich, 1994.

Cicero, M. T. *De Finibus*, Loeb Classical Library.

De Republica, ed. C. W. Keyes, Harvard University Press, Cambridge Mass., 1928.

Tusculanarum Disputationum, ed. J. E. Keynes, Harvard University Press, Cambridge Mass., 1927.

Clark, D. B. 'The Concept of Community: A Re-examination', *The Sociological Review*, 21 (1973).

Cobb, J. *Process Theology as Political Theology*, Manchester University Press, 1982.

Colletti, L. *Marxism and Hegel*, trans. L. Garner, New Left Books, London, 1973.

Connolly, W. E. *The Terms of Political Discourse*, D. C. Heath, Lexington and Toronto, 1974.

Cox, H. *The Secular City*, Penguin, Harmondsworth, 1968.

Cronin, K. *Rights and Christian Ethics*, Cambridge University Press, 1992.

D'Entrèves, A. P. *Natural Law: An Introduction to Legal Philosophy*, Hutchinson University Library, London, 1951.

Dahl, R. *Dilemmas of Pluralist Democracies*, Yale University Press, New Haven, Conn., 1982.

Danto, A. *Analytical Philosophy of History*, Cambridge University Press, 1965.

Davidson, D. 'A Coherence Theory of Truth and Knowledge' in *Truth and Interpretation: Perspectives on the Philosophy of Donald Davison*, ed. E. de Pore, Blackwell, Oxford, 1986.

'Agency' in *Actions and Events*, Oxford University Press, 1980.

Davis, C. *Religion and the Making of Society: Essays in Social Theology*, Cambridge University Press, 1994.

Demant, V. A. *A Christian Polity*, Faber and Faber, London, 1936.

God, Man and Society, SCM Press, London, 1933.

Theology of Society: More Essays in Christian Polity, Faber and Faber, London, 1947.

Derrida, J. *Writing and Difference*, trans. A. Boss, Routledge, London, 1978.

Dudley, E. *The Tree of Commonwealth*, ed. D. M. Brodie, Cambridge University Press, 1948.

Durkheim, E. *Division of Labour in Society*, trans. George Simpson, The Free Press, Glencoe, 1933.

Professional Ethics and Civic Morals, trans. C. Brookfield, Routledge and Kegan Paul, London, 1957.

Socialism, trans. C. Sattler, Routledge and Kegan Paul, London, 1959.

Dworkin, R. *A Matter of Principle*, Harvard University Press, Cambridge, Mass., 1985.

Taking Rights Seriously, Duckworth, London, 1977.

'What Liberalism Isn't', *New York Review of Books*, 20 Jan. 1983.

Eichrodt, W. 'Faith in Providence and Theodicy in the Old Testament' in *Theodicy in the Old Testament* ed. J. L. Crenshaw, SPCK, London, 1983.

Eliot, T. S. *The Idea of a Christian Society and Other Writings*, Faber and Faber, London, 1939.

Collected Poems 1909–1962, Faber and Faber, London, 1963.

Eusebius, *Triakontaeterikos (Tricennelia)*, ed. I. A. Heikel, *Eusebius Werke*, J. C. Hinrichs trans. as *In Praise of Constantine* by H. A. Drake, University of California Press, Los Angeles, 1967.

Faith in the City, Church House Publishing, London, 1985.

Feinberg, J. 'Action and Responsibility' in *Philosophy in America*, ed. M. Black, Cornell University Press, Ithaca, 1965.

Fergusson, D. *Community, Liberalism and Christian Ethics*, Cambridge University Press, 1998.

Figgis, N. *Churches and the Modern State*, Longmans, London, 1913.

Finnis, J. *Natural Law and Natural Rights*, Clarendon Press, Oxford, 1980.

Forrester, D. *Theology and Politics*, Blackwell, Oxford, 1988.

Foucault, M. *Nietzsche: Cahiers du Royaumont No. 6*, Editions de Minuit, 1967.

    Power and Knowledge, ed. C. Gordon, trans. G. Gordon, L. Marshall and R. Soper, Pantheon, New York, 1980.

    'Nietzsche, la généalogie, l'histoire' in *Dits et Ecrits* vol. 2, ed. D. Defert and F. Ewold, Gallimard, Paris, 1985.

    The Archaeology of Knowledge, trans. A. M. Sheridan Smith, Harper, New York, 1972.

Fraser, E. *The Problems of Communitarian Politics*, Oxford University Press, 1999.

Frei, H. *The Eclipse of the Biblical Narrative*, Yale University Press, New Haven, Conn., 1974.

    Theology and Narrative: Selected Essays, ed. G. Hunsinger and W. Placher, Oxford University Press, 1993.

    Types of Christian Theology, ed. G. Hunsinger and W. Placher, Yale University Press, New Haven, Conn., 1992.

Fried, C. *Right and Wrong*, Harvard University Press, Cambridge, Mass., 1978.

Fromm, E. *The Fear of Freedom*, Routledge and Kegan Paul, London, 1962.

Fukuyama, F. *The End of History and the Last Man*, Penguin, Harmondsworth, 1992.

    Trust: The Social Virtues and the Creation of Prosperity, Hamish Hamilton, London, 1995.

Gallie, W. B. 'Essentially Contested Concepts' in *Proceedings of the Aristotelian Society*, 56 (1956).

Geras, N. *Solidarity in the Conversation of Humankind*, Verso Books, London, 1995.

Gewirth, A. *The Community of Rights*, University of Chicago Press, 1996.

    Human Rights, University of Chicago Press, 1982.

    Reason and Morality, University of Chicago Press, 1978.

'Rights and Virtues' *Review of Metaphysics*, 30 (Nov. 1985).

Gilkey, L. *Reaping the Whirlwind: A Christian Interpretation of History*, Seabury Press, New York, 1976.

Gillespie, M. *Hegel, Heidegger and the Ground of History*, University of Chicago Press, 1984.

Goode, W. 'Community within a Community', *American Sociological Review*, 22, (1957).

Goodin, R. E. 'Utilitarianism as a Public Philosophy' in *Political Theory: Tradition and Diversity*, ed. A. Vincent, Cambridge University Press, 1997.

Gore, C. *The Moral Witness of the Church on Economic Subjects*, a report presented to the Convocation of Canterbury April 1907, SPCK, London, 1907.

Grässer, E. 'Jesus und das Heil Gottes' in *Jesus Christus in Historie und Theologie: Festschrift für Hans Conzelmann*, ed. G. Strecker, J. C. B. Mohr, Tübingen, 1975.

Gray, J. 'Classical Liberalism, Positional Goods and the Politicisation of Poverty' in *Dilemmas of Liberal Democracies*, ed. A. Ellis and K. Kumar, Tavistock, London, 1983.

Isaiah Berlin, HarperCollins, London, 1995.

Green, T. H. 'Essay on Christian Dogma', *The Works of T. H. Green*, ed. R. L. Nettleship, Longman Green and Co. London, 1911.

Greenberg, M. *Biblical Prose Prayer as a Window to the Popular Religion of Ancient Israel*, University of California Press, Berkeley, Calif., 1983.

Greer, S. and Minar, D. W. eds., *The Concept of Community*, Aldine Press, Chicago, 1969.

Habermas, J. *Post Metaphysical Thinking*, Polity Press, Cambridge, 1992.

'The Entwinement of Myth and Enlightenment: Max Horkheimer and Theodor Adorno' in *The Philosophical Discourse of Modernity*, Polity Press, Cambridge, 1985.

Haldane, J. 'The Individual, the State and the Common Good', in *The Communitarian Challenge to Liberalism*, ed. E. F. Paul, F. D. Miller Jr. and J. Paul, Cambridge University Press, 1996.

Hampshire, S. N. *Thought and Action*, Chatto and Windus, London, 1959.

Hardimon, M. *Hegel's Social Philosophy; The Project of Reconciliation*, Cambridge University Press, 1994.

Harnack, A. von. *Das Wesen den Christentums*, Siebenstern, Gütersloh, 1977.

Hauerwas, S. *A Community of Character*, University of Notre Dame Press, 1986.

Against the Nations: War and Survival in a Liberal Society, University of Notre Dame Press, 1992.

The Peaceable Kingdom, SCM Press, London, 1984.

Hayek, F. A. *Law, Legislation and Liberty*, vols. 1, 2, and 3 Routledge, London, 1972–9.

The Constitution of Liberty, Routledge, London, 1960.

The Mirage of Social Justice, Routledge and Kegan Paul, London, 1976.

Hegel, G. W. F. *Lectures on the Philosophy of Religion*, vol. 1, ed. P. Hodgson, University of California Press, Los Angeles, 1988.

Philosophy of Nature, vol. 1, trans. M. J. Petry, George Allen and Unwin, 1970.

The Phenomenology of Spirit, trans. A. V. Miller, Clarendon Press, Oxford, 1977.

The Philosophy of Right, trans. T. M. Knox, Clarendon Press, Oxford, 1952.

Heron, A. 'The Person of Christ' in *Keeping the Faith: Essays to Mark the Centenary of Lux Mundi*, ed. G. Wainwright, SPCK, London, 1989.

Hirsch, F. *The Social Limits to Growth*, Routledge and Kegan Paul, London, 1977.

Hittinger, R. *A Critique of the New Natural Law Theory*, Notre Dame University Press, 1987.

'Natural Law and Virtue: Theories at Cross Purposes' in *Natural Law Theory: Contemporary Essays*, ed. R. P. George, Clarendon Press, Oxford, 1992.

Hobsbawm, E. 'The Idea of Fraternity', *New Society*, 34 (Nov. 1975).

Hodgson, P. *God in History: Shapes of Freedom*, Abingdon Press, Nashville, Tenn., 1986.

Hollis, M. *Trust Within Reason*, Cambridge University Press, 1998.

Holmes, S. 'The Permanent Structure of Antiliberal Thought' in *Liberalism and the Moral Life*, ed. N. Rosenblum, Harvard University Press, Cambridge, Mass., 1991.

Hooker, R. *Of the Laws of Ecclesiastical Policy*, ed. Revd J. Keble, Rivingtons, London, 1836, Book 5.

Höpfl, H. *Christian Polity of John Calvin*, Cambridge University Press, 1985.

Indicopleustes, C. *Christian Topography* published as *Topographie Chrétienne*, ed. Wolska Canus, Editions du Cerf, Paris, 1968–73.

Joseph, K. and Sumption, J. *Equality*, J. Murray, London, 1979.

Kamenka, E. 'Marxism and the Crisis in Social Ethics' in *Socialist Humanism*, ed. Erich Fromm, Allen Lane, London, 1967.

Kant, I. *Lectures on Ethics*, ed. P. Heath and J. B. Schneewind, Cambridge University Press, 1997.

Kautz, S. *Liberalism and Community,* Cornell University Press, Ithaca, 1995.

Kelly, P. 'Contractarian Social Justice' in *Social Justice: from Hume to Walzer,* ed. D. Boucher and P. Kelly, Routledge, London, 1998.

Kerr, F. *Theology After Wittgenstein,* Blackwell, Oxford, 1986.

Kripke, S. *Wittgenstein on Rules and Private Language,* Blackwell, Oxford, 1986.

Kristol, I. 'When Virtue Loses All Her Loveliness' in *The Public Interest,* vol. 21.

Küng, H. *A Global Ethic for a Global Politics and Economics,* trans. J. Bowden, SCM Press, London, 1997.

Kymlicka, W. *Liberalism, Community and Culture,* Clarendon Press, Oxford, 1989.

Larmore, C. *The Morals of Modernity,* Cambridge University Press, 1996.

Laslett, P. *The World We Have Lost,* Methuen, London, 1965.

Lawson, N. *The New Conservatism,* Centre for Policy Studies, London, 1980.

Lindbeck, G. *The Nature of Doctrine: Religion and Theology in a Post-Liberal Age,* Westminster Press, Philadelphia, 1984.

Lindblom, J. *Prophecy in Ancient Israel,* Fortress Press, Philadelphia, 1962.

Lisska, A. J. *Aquinas' Theory of Natural Law: An Analytic Reconstruction,* Clarendon Press, Oxford, 1996.

Lukes, S. *Power: A Radical View,* Macmillan, London, 1975.

Lyotard, F. *The Postmodern Condition,* trans. G. Bennington and B. Massumi, Manchester University Press, 1984.

MacDonald, M. 'Natural Rights' in *Philosophy, Politics and Society,* Series I, ed. P. Laslett, Blackwell, Oxford, 1956.

MacIntyre, A. *A Short History of Ethics,* Routledge, London, 1967.
  After Virtue, 2nd edition, Duckworth, London, 1985.
  Secularisation and Moral Change, Oxford University Press, 1967.
  Whose Justice? Which Rationality?, Duckworth, London, 1988.
  'Against Utilitarianism' in *Aims in Education,* ed. T. B. Hollins, Manchester University Press, 1964.
  'The Essential Contestability of Some Social Concepts', *Ethics,* 84 (1973).

MacKenzie, W. J. M. *Politics and Social Science,* Penguin, Harmondsworth, 1967.

MacNamara, V. *Faith and Ethics,* Gill and Macmillan, Dublin, 1985.

MacPherson, C. B. *The Political Theory of Possessive Individualism,* Clarendon Press, Oxford, 1962.

Maritain, J. *The Rights of Man and Natural Law,* trans. D. C. Anson, Ignatius Press, San Francisco, 1986.

Markus, R. *Saeculum; History and Society in the Theology St Augustine*, Cambridge University Press, 1970.

'The Latin Fathers' in *The Cambridge History of Medieval Political Thought 350–1450*, ed. J. H. Burns, Cambridge University Press, 1988.

Marx, K. *Economic and Philosophical Manuscripts of 1844*, trans. M. Milligan, Foreign Languages Publishing House, Moscow, 1959.

The German Ideology, trans. R. Pascal, Lawrence and Wishart, London, 1942.

Marx, K. 'On the Jewish Question' in *Karl Marx Early Writings*, ed. T. B. Bottomore, Penguin, Harmondsworth, 1963.

Marx, K. and Engels, F. *Selected Works*, vol. 1, Foreign Language Publishing House, Moscow, 1967.

Mascall, E. L. *Man: His Origins and Destiny*, The Dacre Press, Westminster, 1940.

McClosky, H. J. 'Respect for Human Moral Rights' in *Utility and Rights*, ed. R. G. Frey, Blackwells, Oxford, 1985.

McCormack, B. *Karl Barth's Critically Realistic Dialectical Theology: Its Genesis and Development 1909–36*, Clarendon Press, Oxford, 1995.

McGrath, A. *Reformation Thought*, Blackwell, Oxford, 1988.

Metz, J. P. *Faith in History and Society*, trans. D. Smith, Burns and Oates, London, 1980.

Moltmann, J. *On Human Dignity: Political Theology and Ethics*, SCM Press, London, 1986.

Theology of Hope, SCM Press, London, 1967.

Muilenberg, J. 'The Office of the Prophet in Ancient Israel' in *The Bible and Modern Scholarship*, ed. J. Hyatt, Abingdon Press, Nashville, 1967.

Mussolini, B. 'The Doctrine of Fascism' in *Social and Political Doctrines of Contemporary Europe*, ed. M. Oakeshott, Cambridge University Press, 1939.

Nagel, T. 'Moral Conflict and Political Legitimacy', *Philosophy and Public Affairs*, 16 (1987).

Nicholls, D. *Deity and Domination*, Routledge, London, 1989.

'Christianity and Politics' in *The Religion of the Incarnation*, ed. L. Morgan, Bristol Classical Press, Bristol, 1989.

Nielson, K. 'The Myth of Natural Law' in *Law and Philosophy*, ed. S. Hook, New York, 1964.

Nietzsche, F. *On Certainty*, Blackwell, Oxford, 1967.

The Gay Science, trans. W. Kaufmann, Random House, New York, 1974.

Will to Power, trans. W. Kaufmann and R. J. Hollingdale, Random House, New York, 1968.

'Vom Nutzen und Nachteil der Historie fur des Leben' in *Werke*, ed. G. Colli and M. Montinori, Walter de Gruyter, Berlin, 1967.

Nisbet, R. *The Quest for Community*, Oxford University Press, New York, 1970.

The Sociological Tradition, Heinemann, London, 1967.

'Moral Values and Community', in *Tradition and Revolt*, Oxford University Press, New York, 1970.

Niskanen, W. *Bureaucracy – Servant or Master?*, Hobart Publications, London, 1973.

Norman, E. R. *Church and Society in England 1770–1970*, Clarendon Press, Oxford, 1976.

Novak, M. *Free Persons and the Common Good*, Madison Books, New York, 1989.

The Spirit of Democratic Capitalism, Institute of Economic Affairs, London, 1991.

Nowak, K. 'Die antihistorische Revolution: Symptome und Folgen der Krise historische Weltorientierung nach dem Ersten Welt-krieg in Deutschland' in *Umstrittene Moderne: Die Zukunft der Neuzeit in Urteil der Epoche Ernst Troeltschs*, ed. H. Renz and F. W. Graf, Gerd Mohn, Gutersloh, 1987.

O'Donovan, J. L. 'Historical Prolegomenon to a Theological Review of Human Rights', *Studies in Christian Ethics*, 4/2 (1996).

'Subsidiarity and Political Authority in Theological Perspective', *Studies in Christian Ethics*, 6/1, 1998.

O'Donovan, O. *Resurrection and Moral Order: An Outline of Evangelical Ethics*, Apollo, Leicester, 1994.

Oliver, J. *The Church and Social Order*, Mowbray, London, 1968.

Oppenheim, F. E. 'Facts and Values in Politics', *Political Theory* 1 (1973).

Pailin, D. *The Anthropological Character of Theology: Conditioning Theological Understanding*, Cambridge University Press, 1990.

Pannenberg, W. *Faith and Reality*, Search Press, London, 1975.

What is Man? Contemporary Anthropology in Theological Perspective, trans. D. A. Priebe, Fortress Press, Philadelphia, 1970.

'Hermeneutic and Universal History' in *Basic Questions in Theology*, vol. 1, SCM Press, London, 1972.

'Kerygma and History' in *Basic Questions in Theology*, vol. 1, SCM Press, London, 1967.

Parkin, F. *Class Inequality and Political Order*, Paladin, St Albans, 1972.

Phillips, D. *Looking Backward: A Critical Appraisal of Communitarian Thought*, Princeton University Press, 1993.

Phillips, D. Z. 'Philosophy, Theology and the Reality of God' in *Wittgenstein and Religion*, ed. D. Z. Phillips, Macmillan, Basing-stoke, 1996.

Plant, R. *Hegel*, 2nd edition, Blackwell, Oxford, 1983.
　Hegel on Religion, Orion Books, London, 1997.
　Modern Political Thought, Blackwell, Oxford, 1991.
Porter, J. R. 'Wealth and Poverty in the Bible' in *Christianity and Conservatism*, ed. M. Alison and D. C. Edwards, Hodder and Stoughton, London, 1990.
Prudentius 'Contra Orationem Symmachi' in *Prudentius*, vol. 2, Harvard University Press, Cambridge, Mass., 1995.
Putnam, H. *Reason, Truth and History*, Cambridge University Press, 1981.
Rad, von G. *The Message of the Prophets*, SCM Press, London, 1968.
　Old Testament Theology, Oliver and Boyd, Edinburgh, 1962.
Rawls, J. *A Theory of Justice*, Clarendon Press, Oxford, 1972.
　Political Liberalism, Columbia University Press, New York, 1993.
　'Kantian Constructivism in Moral Theory', *Journal of Philosophy*, 77 (1980).
　'The Idea of An Overlapping Consensus' in *Philosophical Papers*, ed. J. Freeman, Harvard University Press, Cambridge, Mass., 1999.
Raz, J. *Ethics in the Public Domain*, Clarendon Press, Oxford, 1994.
　The Morality of Freedom, Clarendon Press, Oxford, 1986.
　'Facing Diversity: The Case of Epistemic Abstinence', *Philosophy and Public Affairs*, 19 (1990).
Regis, E. *Gewirth's Ethical Rationalism*, University of Chicago Press, 1984.
Rist, J. M. *Augustine: Ancient Thought Baptised*, Cambridge University Press, 1994.
Rorty, R. *Contingency, Irony and Solidarity*, Cambridge University Press, 1989.
　Objectivism, Relativism and Truth, Cambridge University Press, 1991.
Rosenblum, N. *Another Liberalism*, Harvard University Press, Cambridge, Mass., 1987.
Rottenberg, S. 'The Production and Exchange of used Body Parts' in *Festschrift fur Ludwig von Mises*, vol. 2, ed. F. A. Harper, The Institute for Humane Studies, Meveo Park, Calif., 1971.
Rousseau, J. J. *T he Social Contract*, ed. and trans. by F. Watkins, Nelson, London, 1953.
Rushdie, S. *The Satanic Verses*, Viking, London, 1988.
Ryan, W. and Tyrrell, B. J. eds. *A Second Collection of Papers by Bernard J. F. Lonergan*, Darton, Longman and Todd, London, 1974.
Sandel, M. *Liberalism and the Limits of Justice*, Cambridge University Press, 1982.
　'Introduction' to *Liberalism and Its Critics*, New York University Press, 1984.

Sartre, J. P. *L'Existentialisme est un humanisme*, Les Editions Nagel, Paris, 1963.

Schneewind, J. B. 'Moral Knowledge and Moral Principles' in *Revisions: Changing Perspectives in Moral Philosophy*, ed. S. Hauerwas and A. MacIntyre, Notre Dame University Press, 1983.

Searle, J. 'Meaning and Speech Acts', *Philosophical Review*, 51 (1962).

Sen, A. K. *Reason before Identity*, The Romanes Lecture 1998, Oxford University Press, 1999.

Sen, A. K. and Williams B. eds. *Utilitarianism and Beyond*, Cambridge University Press, 1982.

Seneca, *Ad Lucilium: Epistolae Morales*, vol. 2, ed. R. Gummere, Harvard University Press, Cambridge, Mass., 1920.

'De Vita Beata' in *Seneca: Moral Essays*, Harvard University Press, Cambridge, Mass., 1932.

Skinner, Q. *The Foundations of Modern Political Thought*, vol. 2, Cambridge University Press, 1978.

'The Empirical Theorists of Democracy and Their Critics', *Political Theory*, 1 (1973).

Spohn, W. C. *What are They Saying about Scripture and Ethics?*, Paulist Press, New York, 1984.

Steiner, G. *Language and Silence*, Faber, London, 1967.

Steiner, H. 'Individual Liberty', *Proceedings of the Aristotelian Society* (1974).

Stephens, W. P. *The Holy Spirit in the Theology of Martin Bucer*, Cambridge University Press, 1970.

Stern, J. P. *Hitler: the Führer and the People*, Fontana, London, 1975.

Strauss, D. F. *The Life of Jesus Critically Examined*, trans. G. Eliot, SCM Press, London, 1973.

Suggate, A. *William Temple and Christian Social Ethics Today*, T. and T. Clark, Edinburgh, 1987.

Taylor, C. *Hegel and Modern Society*, Cambridge University Press, 1979.

'Atomism' in *Philosophical Papers*, vol. 2, Cambridge University Press, 1985.

'Foucault on Freedom and Truth' in *Philosophical Papers*, vol. 2, Cambridge University Press, 1985.

'What's Wrong with Negative Liberty? Philosophy and the Human Sciences' in *Philosophical Papers*, vol. 2, Cambridge University Press, 1985.

Temple, W. *Personal Religion and the Life of Fellowship*, Longmans, Green and Co., London, 1926.

Thompson, E. P. *William Morris: From Romantic to Revolutionary*, Gollancz, London, 1956.

Thompson, F. *Lark Rise to Candleford*, Oxford University Press, 1945.

Titmuss, R. *The Gift Relationship*, Penguin, Harmondsworth, 1970.

Torrance, T. F. *Kingdom and Church: A Study in the Theology of the Reformation*, T. and T. Clark, Edinburgh, 1956.

Trammel, R. 'Saving Life and Taking Life' in *Killing and Letting Die*, ed. B. Steinbeck, Prentice Hall, New York, 1980.

Troeltsch, E. *The Social Teachings of the Christian Churches*, trans. O. Wyon, 2 vols. George Allen and Unwin, London, 1931.

Tucker, G. M. 'The Role of the Prophets and the Role of the Church' in *Prophecy in Israel*, ed. D. L. Petersen, SPCK, London, 1987.

Tunstall, J. *Fishermen*, Macgibbon and Kee, London, 1969.

Veatch, H. 'Natural Law and the Is – Ought Question' in *Catholic Lawyer*, 26 (1981).

Vincent, A. and Plant, R. *Philosophy, Politics and Citizenship*, Blackwell, Oxford, 1984.

Walzer, M. *Interpretation and Social Criticism*, Harvard University Press, Cambridge, Mass., 1987.

    Spheres of Justice, Martin Robinson, Oxford, 1983.

    Thick and Thin: Moral Argument at Home and Abroad, University of Notre Dame Press, 1994.

Warnock, G. J. 'Hare on Meaning and Speech Acts', *Philosophical Review*, 80 (1971).

Weale, A. *Political Theory and Social Policy*, Macmillan, London, 1983.

Weber, M. *The Theory of Social and Economic Organisation*, trans. A. M. Hervert and T. Parsons, Free Press, Glencoe, 1964.

West, C. C. 'The Common Good and the Participation of the Poor in *The Common Good and US Capitalism*, ed. F. Williams and J. Hauck, University Press of America, Maryland, 1987.

Westergaard, J. 'The Withering Away of Class', in *Towards Socialism*, eds. P. Anderson and R. Blackburn, Fontana, Glasgow, 1965.

White, H. *Metahistory: The Historical Imagination in Nineteenth Century Europe*, Johns Hopkins University Press, Baltimore, 1973.

Wiles, M. 'The Incarnation and Development' in *The Religion of The Incarnation. Anglican Essays in Commemoration of Lux Mundi*, ed. R. Morgan, Bristol Classical Press, Bristol, 1989.

Williams, B. 'The Idea of Equality' in *Philosophy, Politics and Society*, series 2, ed. P. Laslett and W. G. Runciman, Blackwell, Oxford, 1962.

Williams, R. *Key Words*, Fontana, Glasgow, 1976.

Winch, P. *The Idea of a Social Science*, Routledge, London, 1958.

    'Understanding a Primitive Society' in *Ethics and Action*, Routledge, London, 1972.

    'Authority' in *Political Philosophy*, ed. A. Quinton, Oxford University Press, 1967.

Wittgenstein, L. *Philosophical Investigations*, Blackwell, Oxford, 1958.
   Remarks on the Foundations of Mathematics, 2nd edition, Blackwell, Oxford, 1967.
   Tractatus Logico-Philosophicus, Routledge, London, 1961.
Wolff, R. P. *The Poverty of Liberalism*, Beacon Press, Boston, 1968.
Wolin, S. *Politics and Vision*, George Allen and Unwin, London, 1961.
Wollheim, R. *The Thread of Life*, Cambridge University Press, 1984.
Yoder, J. H. *The Politics of Jesus*, W. B. Eerdmans, Grand Rapids, Mich., 1972.
   The Priestly Kingdom, Notre Dame University Press, 1984.
   The Royal Priesthood, W. B. Eerdmans, Grand Rapids, Mich., 1994.

Index of names

Index of subjects

CAMBRIDGE STUDIES IN IDEOLOGY AND RELIGION

Books in the series